AF608004

POLICY WORK IN CANADA

Professional Practices and Analytical Capacities

Policy Work in Canada

Professional Practices and Analytical Capacities

EDITED BY MICHAEL HOWLETT, ADAM WELLSTEAD, AND JONATHAN CRAFT

UNIVERSITY OF TORONTO PRESS
Toronto Buffalo London

Toronto Buffalo London
www.utppublishing.com

ISBN 978-1-4426-4737-4

Library and Archives Canada Cataloguing in Publication

Policy work in Canada : professional practices and analytical capacities / edited by Michael Howlett, Adam Wellstead, and Jonathan Craft.

Includes bibliographical references.
ISBN 978-1-4426-4737-4 (cloth)

1. Policy sciences – Canada. 2. Political planning – Canada. 3. Political consultants – Canada. 4. Canada – Politics and government. I. Howlett, Michael, 1955–, author, editor II. Wellstead, A.M. (Adam Matthew), 1967–, author, editor III. Craft, Jonathan, 1980–, author, editor

JL86.P64P635 2017 320.60971 C2016-904320-7

University of Toronto Press acknowledges the financial assistance to its publishing program of the Canada Council for the Arts and the Ontario Arts Council, an agency of the Government of Ontario.

Canada Council for the Arts Conseil des Arts du Canada

Funded by the Government of Canada Financé par le gouvernement du Canada

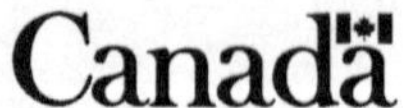

Contents

List of Figures

List of Tables

POLICY WORK IN CANADA

Professional Practices and Analytical Capacities

PART 1

Introduction

1 The Nature of Professional Policy Work in Canada: An Introduction and Overview

MICHAEL HOWLETT, ADAM WELLSTEAD, AND JONATHAN CRAFT

Overview: Policy Analysis as a Field of Practice and Study

Policy analysis is a relatively recent movement, dating back to American experience in the 1960s with large-scale planning in areas such as defence, urban redevelopment, and budgeting (Lindblom 1958a; Wildavsky 1979; MacRae and Wilde 1985; Garson 1986). Seen as a social movement, albeit with a technical discipline, it represents the efforts of actors inside and outside formal political decision-making processes to improve policy outcomes by applying systematic evaluative rationality (Meltsner 1976; Webber 1986; Fox 1990).

Policy analysis texts usually describe a range of qualitative and quantitative techniques that analysts are expected to learn and apply in specific circumstances, providing advice to decision-makers about optimal strategies and outcomes to pursue in the resolution of public problems (Elmore 1991; Weimer and Vining 1999; Patton and Sawicki 1993). However, the extent to which this is done, and variations in practices within governments and between governmental and non-governmental analysts is largely unknown.

Analysts working in different organizations tend to have different interests and to utilize different techniques in pursuing policy analysis. Governments have always analysed their own and other countries' public policies. Much public policy analysis has, however, also been generated by analysts working for non-governmental organizations. Some of these analysts work directly for groups affected by public policies, while others work for corporations, churches, trade unions, or whoever else employs them. Policy analysts also work for private think tanks or research institutes, some of which have close ties with government agencies and pressure groups. Finally, some analysts work independently, many of them associated with the university system.

Analysts working for governments and for groups and corporations affected by public policies tend to focus their research on policy outcomes. They often have a direct interest in condemning or condoning specific policies on the basis of projected or actual impacts on their client organizations. Private think tanks and research institutes usually enjoy substantial autonomy from governments, though some are influenced by their funding organizations' preferences. Nevertheless, they remain interested in the "practical" side of policy issues and tend to concentrate either on policy outcomes or on the instruments and techniques that generate those outcomes. Academics, on the other hand, have considerable independence and seldom have direct personal stake in the outcome of specific policies. They can therefore examine public policies much more abstractly than can members of the other two groups and, as such, tend to grapple with the theoretical, conceptual, and methodological issues surrounding public policymaking.

Exactly who does policy analysis, then, and how they do it, are important questions for understanding the analysis generated and its impact on government decision-making. Until recently the study of professional public policy analysis in Canada lagged behind that in Europe, New Zealand, Australia, and the United States where large-*N* empirical works or detailed anthropological studies had been undertaken (see Colebatch, Hoppe, and Noordegraaf 2011; Durning and Osuna 1994; Page and Jenkins 2005; and more recently Blum and Schubert 2013; and Van Nispen and Scholten 2014). The few studies in Canada tended to be descriptive and focus almost exclusively at the federal level (Prince 1979; Prince and Chenier 1980; Hollander and Prince 1993). Studies in these other countries, however, moved quite some distance towards assessment of the needs of good policy analysis (Thissen and Twaalfhoven 2001) and the integration of those results into the design of educational and training programs for professional policy analysts (Weimer and Vining 1999) and Canadian surveys and interview research based upon these models have now moved this country into the forefront of research in this field.

From Policy Analysis to Policy Work

This research has led contemporary public policy scholars in Canada and elsewhere to increasingly recognized policy analysis as only one aspect of a broader set of practices, or policy work, undertaken by different actors throughout the policy process. For example, Radin (2006, 2013) has documented the evolving and diverse field of American "policy work" with analysts located through and outside of government engaging in a variety of policy practices. Others have documented that policy professionals, even within the same government organization or policy unit, can engage in different types of policy practices (Colebatch, Hoppe, Noordegraaf 2011; Hoppe and Jeliazkova 2006).

Policy work is a term that captures both the applied practice of policy – what it is that policy professionals actually do – and the field of research for its study. Like policymaking itself, *policy work* is a term that escapes parsimonious definition. This is in part because the concept encompasses a large set of activities in policymaking that extend beyond policy analysis – for instance, including not only the provision of "expert" policy analysis to decision-makers but the construction and maintenance of relations among stakeholders, policy diplomacy, and the creation and use of "policy knowledge" (Colebatch 2006).

Policy work is also fluid in that it is in part contingent upon the policy situations and context within which it is undertaken, those who are engaged in it, and a broader set assumptions and preferences about how the policymaking process itself should be understood (Colebatch 2006, 309). As a group of leading policy work scholars concisely put it, "There will never be one, definitive account of policy work because policy is too ambiguous and contested to be defined in neutral ways, and because policy is an ongoing process, that evolves over time and eschews fixed and static demarcations" (Colebatch, Hoppe, and Noordegraaf 2011, 243).

Policy work thus, on the one hand, is a means to better empirically study what Canadian policy workers are actually doing, and on the other it is a theoretical lens to help understand the implications of such practices for policymaking itself. This volume uses the term in both senses, and the concepts of policy work and policy analytical capacity underpin and orient the studies of professional policy analysis in Canada found in the following chapters. Together, they extend the conceptual and empirical study of policy analysis beyond its historical range and traditional orientation.

The Significance of Policy Capacity

Policy analytical capacity (PAC) is a second and related concept, used extensively in this volume. It has emerged from a focus on the ability of public policy organizations to produce sound analysis to inform their policymaking (Dobuzinskis, Howlett, and Laycock 2007, 4–5). There are, however, many types and sizes of organizations that conduct public policy analysis, on a wide range of issues, using various techniques. Techniques of analysis range from more formal ones such as cost/benefit analysis (Pal 2001, 291) to less formal ones such as public consultations (ibid., 256–7). PAC has been developed within this literature to describe the ability of an organization to produce valuable policy-relevant research and analysis on topics of their choosing (Howlett 2009a).

Observers of policy research organizations have suggested that an organization's PAC is strengthened by its ability to "articulate its medium and long term priorities, test the robustness of its policy options by building alternative scenarios, attach both qualitative and quantitative assessments to different policy options ... communicate and defend policy thrusts to its operational arms as well as to its major stakeholders and to the public, [and] formulate policies that can withstand rigorous professional challenge" (Fellegi 1996, 14–15). Attaining a high level of PAC thus requires "a recognized requirement or demand for research (a market), a supply of qualified researchers, ready availability of quality data, policies and procedures to facilitate productive interactions with other researchers, and a culture in which openness is encouraged and risk taking is acceptable" (Riddell 1998, 5).

Chapter-by-Chapter Summary

This volume addresses all of these subjects, providing new empirical research that reveals the types and levels of PAC within federal and provincial governments, as well as policy work and policy analysis in the seldom-studied non-governmental policy sector. It presents the results of a broader and deeper examination of policy work and policy analytical capacity within Canada. The questions that contributors will address include: What are the defining characteristics of sophisticated yet useful policy analysis? What are the institutional constraints that influence the outcome or style of analysis? How does policy analysis contribute to democratic debate? Are there lessons to be learned from the way in which policy analysis is conducted in different jurisdictions, both within and outside of Canada?

The following chapters form a useful extension of these initial lines of inquiry in four ways. First, new data presented here systematically for the first time offer empirical evidence of what policy workers are actually doing that moves the study of Canadian policy work beyond expository accounts. The survey and case studies facilitate critical appraisal of trends in policy work in these areas as well as comparative assessments of the analytical capacity of Canada's broader advisory system.

Second, and relatedly, the research undertaken here moves the study of policy work and policy capacity beyond the confines of the federal government to include that of policy workers within provincial governments and the non-governmental policy sector. The quality and quantity of policy work in provincial governments is significantly different from McArthur's (2007) original thesis about the limitations found at this level. In terms of NGOs, the level of interaction with government officials rather than policy capacity was a far more important consideration in policy work.

Third, the findings also detail the richer diversity of policy practices in which these actors engage and provide a more comprehensive account of the dimensions of policy capacity at the individual, organizational, and subsystemic levels. A new schematic of policy capacity contending that policy capacity includes analytical, managerial, and political skills as well as resource endowments at the individual, organizational, and policy subsystem levels is used to address this concern and is an important aspect and prerequisite of high-quality policy work (Howlett 2009a). This framework helps to draw clearer linkages between notions of policy capacity operating at multiple levels and locations, that involve various types of policy work.

Fourth, the chapters generate a new policy work framework and a reconceptualized policy capacity schematic to provide for its improved depiction. The findings from each chapter can be integrated into a "systematic" policy work framework to bring the policy work discipline out of its "black box" through improved linkages of policy actors, contexts, functions, and outputs.

In chapter 2 Howlett and Wellstead set out the duties and nature of contemporary professional policy analysis in government, using new survey data to re-examine in Canada a classic in the field of policy analysis, Arnold Meltsner's early 1970s work on policy analysis in the bureaucracy. This work serves as a baseline study, setting out the basic elements and contours of professional policy analysis as practised by policy workers in government.

Thirty five years ago, Arnold Meltsner observed that professional policy analysts in the U.S. government undertook several roles in policymaking, the most common of which involved "technical" information processing, while others were more "political." Although he was still prescient, the authors note that more recent empirical studies of professional policy work have found little evidence of the predominance of technicians in the ranks of analysts employed in public policy bureaucracies. However, they also note that there is only very weak and partial information on the situation in most countries, and descriptions of the nature of policy work often remain primarily normative and lacking in empirical referents. This chapter reveals that contemporary policy work in Canada and elsewhere is constituted by more complex and multi-sided practices than Meltsner and his followers described. These findings are significant for those wishing to understand and improve the nature of policy work in contemporary government.

Part 2 of the volume then examines the current status of policy work in Canadian governments. In chapter 3 Wellstead, Stedman, and Lindquist examine the capacity of the Canadian federal government to conduct high-quality policy work. Canada is typical of most countries where much policy-related work tends to be centralized within its national government in its capital city. This has led to continual criticisms that regional and other perspectives are not included in policy reports, recommendations, and decisions.

The authors argue that governments, worldwide, are preoccupied with avoiding policy failure, and having a high level of policy capacity is one indicator of their ability to address this issue. The chapter sets out eight hypotheses about how Canadian regionally based federal policy work can contribute to higher policy capacity for better policy work. Given the vast size and the decentralization of power, very little research has been dedicated to policy work conducted in its regions and whether it contributes to strengthening policy capacity, and this chapter is path-breaking in this regard.

Based upon data derived from a national survey, a structural equation model (LISREL) is used to present results of the analysis. The authors find that, unfortunately, region-based policy work does little to enhance policy capacity. They find policy work at the federal level to be divided along two distinct functional lines: traditional policy "strategic" analysis carried out in Ottawa, and "street-level" implementation-related analysis carried out in the regions. They suggest that if more efforts were made to activate policy work in the regions and incorporate these analysts better into national policymaking, better results would accrue.

In chapter 4, Howlett and Newman continue this analysis, reporting on the findings of original surveys that examine the background and training of provincial policy analysts in Canada. Despite the existence of a large body of literature on policy analysis, large-scale empirical studies of the work of policy analysts are rare, and in the case of analysts working at the sub-national level, virtually non-existent. There has been very little research on this level of policy workers, despite the significant powers they exercise in prominent federal systems such as the United States, Germany, Australia, Mexico, Russia, Brazil, Malaysia, and Canada.

This chapter reports on the first comprehensive survey of the work of policy analysts at the provincial and territorial levels conducted in Canada. It examines the background and training of provincial and territorial policy analysts, the types of techniques they employ in their jobs, and what they do in their work, day by day. The resulting profile of sub-national policy analysts is presented and reveals substantial differences between analysts working for national governments and their sub-national counterparts, with important implications for training and for the ability of nations to accomplish their long-term policy goals.

In most cases, policy scholars interested in the role of policy analysts in promoting and practising evidence-based policymaking rely on very partial survey results, or on anecdotal case studies and interview research. The research presented here is path-breaking in its examination and analysis of this little-studied area of professional policy work in government.

Luc Bernier and Michael Howlett, in chapter 5, look at the situation specifically in Quebec. Using new survey research, they argue the new public management wave in that province in the 1990s was driven by the notion of a need for improved service delivery to the population and tended to undermine future-oriented policy work. After decades spent seeking greater efficiency, they argue the province went too far in a management direction and lacked the capacity to develop public policies on current issues and crises. Particular emphasis is placed on the education and the training of the public servants who develop and formulate public policy and the need to augment their quality and supply.

In chapter 6 Howlett and Wellstead use both the new federal and provincial surveys to systematically compare the commonalities and differences in national and sub-national level policy work in this country. While there are many similarities in governance trends, such as consultation and participation overtaking more technical policy evaluations in policy advice and policy work in government, the authors also find significant differences in the nature of policy work and attitudes at each level, linked to decreased autonomy from political masters experienced by sub-national analysts. The results suggest that sub-national policy work must be studied carefully in its own right rather than simply assumed to reflect better-known national or central patterns of work and that specific prescriptions for improvement be tailored to each level rather than applied from the same cloth.

In chapter 7, Patricia O'Reilly, Greg Inwood, and Carolyn Johns look at another area that has received very little treatment internationally, which is the capacity and nature of policy work at the intergovernmental level. This is very important in federal systems of government, where extensive powers over social and economic life often rest with the sub-national governments, as in the Canadian intergovernmental relations system. However, as the authors note, in an increasingly networked world where governments must cope with increasingly complex and interrelated policy problems, many policymakers must work intergovernmentally or at a multi-level governance level in order to effectively develop and implement policies. This chapter provides an overview of policy analytic capacities and practices in the Canadian federation. Intergovernmental policy capacity is examined for its larger patterns, determinants, practices, and trade-offs, with the authors finding that capacity in this area in Canada is not high and has not been improving in recent years, despite greater need for coordination across jurisdictions.

In chapter 8, Michael Howlett begins to drill down to the intra-governmental level, drawing on survey data on Canadian policy analysts to assess several propositions on the role of public managers in policy work. Once again, little is known and much is taken for granted in the role of public managers in policy processes and the direction and control of policy work. The discussion begins with a conceptual discussion of the nature of policy advice systems in modern governments that situates public managers among actors who affect different stages of policymaking. An empirical analysis using a large-*N* Canadian federal, provincial, and territorial data set on managers' background and activities is then used to assess what managers do and how this differs from other policy workers.

This study finds the distinctions between managers and line policy workers to be indistinct, with most managers working in small groups and undertaking many of the same tasks as more "street-level" policy workers. However, it also finds some, but not all managers have a longer-term perspective than line workers, a factor that can augment the quality of policy work conducted in their units. The chapter concludes with a recommendation for more detailed research into this key type of policy worker in Canada and comparatively in order to help develop this insight.

Jonathan Craft, in chapter 9, continues the examination of specific actors within the Canadian policy advice system, exploring the role and activities of political advisers appointed by the minister's office. Though they are often overlooked in studies of policy analysis and policy work, this chapter argues that such actors now represent an increasingly professionalized and institutionalized category of policy workers within the Canadian "core executive." Through a retrospective analysis of their changing numbers and policy activity, the chapter documents their advent, institutionalization, and specialization as policy workers. They are argued to engage in unique forms of policy work as a result of their politically appointed status. The chapter presents new data on the number of such policy workers as well as their policy practices, further improving accounts of the types and nature of current policy work. It concludes that this set of policy workers are active advisory system participants and bring about a significant re-orientation of policy work featuring more attention to partisan-political aspects of policy earlier in the policy process (Craft and Howlett 2013a).

Part 3 continues this discussion of different groups of policy workers, turning now to those analysts and advisers working outside government in academia, political parties, consultants, scientific research institutes, non-governmental organizations, and similar venues. Most of these groups have received very little detailed treatment in the literature, which has focused almost exclusively on governmental analysts and advisers. Non-governmental actors, however, have become more numerous and increasingly involved in policymaking in recent years, and each chapter is path-breaking in its discussion, presentation of data, and analysis of this "externalization" of policy work and advice.

In chapter 10, Howlett and Migone look at external consultants as policy workers. The use of external policy consultants in government has been an increasing focus of concern among governments in the United States, the United Kingdom, Canada, and Australia, among others. Some of this concern has arisen over the costs incurred by governments in this area, while others have suggested the rise of the "consultocracy" has led to diminished democratic practices and public direction of policy and administrative development.

In chapter 11, Ouimet, Bédard, and Léon revisit the major theoretical perspectives on research utilization by public civil servants and propose a new conceptual framework on the absorption of research knowledge by civil servants. Their empirical findings are particularly interesting, as they converge with the well-known "bounded" aspect of rational action. For example, they show a significant association between civil servants' educational level, on the one hand, and, on the other, their propensity to communicate with academic researchers and to acquire research, a phenomenon that results in better, more informed policies, which could be improved and augmented relatively easily through the recruitment process for policy workers.

However, the authors note that understanding the origins and significance of the use of policy consultants in modern government is difficult, and the evidence is mixed on its impact on policy capacity and the quality of analysis; some see this development as part of a shift in the nature of state-societal relations to the "service" or "franchise" state and away from the "positive" or "regulatory" state, while others see it as a less significant activity linked to the normal development of policy advice systems in modern government. This chapter surveys the data on the phenomena, in general, and clarifies the conceptual basis for the analysis of these increasingly significant policy advisory system actors.

This is followed in chapter 12 by Nicole Klenk, who looks at the relationships between the scientific community and policymakers in government, using the example of the Canadian forestry industry. She notes the relationship between forest research, its producers, and forest policy is extremely complex. This chapter describes the characteristics of government science and explores how it informs forest policy, using the Ontario Ministry of Natural Resources (OMNR) as a case study. A close and effective relationship is found between scientists and policy developers/analysts where the OMNR is legally required to engage in scientific research to inform the development of guidelines and associated evaluations. Other factors that contributed to an effective use of research in the development of policy included the active engagement of policy developers/analysts in the design of projects using "policies as hypotheses" within an adaptive forest management framework. This study provides compelling insights into the use of evidence and "evidence-based policymaking" in Canada, and highlights the difficulties encountered in this process and the significance of legal requirements that compel the use of both internal and external scientific advisers.

Looking at the opposite end of the policy advice spectrum, Greg Flynn in chapter 13 explores the impact that political parties and partisan advice from that quarter have on the policy outputs and policy-making of Canadian government. In particular, he traces how parties channel policy in converting policy demands of the public and their party members into government action when they fulfil party policy and election manifesto commitments and citizens in Canada can influence government policy outputs by participating in parties. In pursuing this course, the chapter establishes a general and heuristic means to examine party member participation in party policymaking through stages of policy development, beginning with abstract notions of policy associated with party ideology, through to the final and concrete stage of election campaign promise and manifesto drafting. The chapter then examines how party members can advance their policy demands into considerations by the government by tracing party member policy proposals through the final two stages of party policy development of the three new governing parties in Canada over the last thirty years. The chapter also considers the extent to which new governing parties in Canada have implemented their election campaign policy commitments.

Overall the chapter demonstrates that – through the examination of party policy and election manifesto development, coupled with a consideration of the implementation of election promises – parties influence government policy outcomes and that parties, at least partially, channel policy. Parties and their members can influence both the choices made by government in terms of their preferred policy options as well as the implementation of those commitments and are a force to be reckoned with in policy work and the provision of policy advice in Canada.

In another path-breaking analysis, in chapter 14 Bryan Evans and Adam Wellstead examine policy work and capacity in the NGO system. Although there have been several Canadian-based studies of federal and provincial government policy workers in recent years – many of which are presented in this volume – most have focused on the governmental sector. Here the very large NGO sector is examined, using survey-based research methods. The chapter examines the results of an online survey of government policy counterparts in non-governmental organizations (NGO) across four fields (environment, health, labour, immigration) in three Canadian provinces (British Columbia, Saskatchewan, and Ontario) and examines their interactions with professional policy workers in government.

One key variable identified in all of the governmental studies is the importance of well-established networks outside of government for policy capacity. This finding correlated with the finding in the public management literature that stresses the need for a network-based, horizontal, collaborative arrangement between government and non-government actors in order to ensure policy success. However, the same surveys have demonstrated that policy workers interact very infrequently outside the comfort of their own department cubicles. The analysis in this chapter finds that formal policy work is rarely done by NGOs, or rather is done "from the side of the desk" as a low priority area while much more emphasis is placed on informal links and relationships. This finding has significant implications for understanding the nature of policy advice and policy work in Canada and elsewhere, and the authors again recommend more research into this phenomenon in order to fully understand its ramifications.

Part 4 of the volume then shifts to examine recent efforts to improve Canadian policy work by augmenting policy capacity, improving policy relationships, or enhancing technologies for analysis and policy work.

In chapter 15, Jonathan Craft and Siobhan Harty focus on "traditional" solutions to capacity issues in policy work, namely more targeted and careful recruitment. In particular they examine "elite" policy recruitment practices in the federal government. Through a case study of the government of Canada's Recruitment of Policy Leaders (RPL) program, this chapter provides new insight and evidence on the (in)effectiveness of a targeted supply-side policy analytical capacity measure.

The chapter focuses on targeted supply-side recruitment that addresses many of the conceptual, organizational, and supply and demand considerations considered by others in this volume. The RPL's utility and effectiveness are evaluated against new and existing data provided by the RPL program leadership and the Public Service Commission of Canada (PSC). They find the RPL program has met some of the federal public service's policy capacity needs, and suggests additional gaps it could fill. The program attracts and places high-calibre policy workers in middle to senior policy roles. In addition, it was found that recruits foster policy analytical capacity (PAC) on several dimensions identified in the literature and are a unique measure to mitigate potential "mid-level" PAC supply shortages.

In chapter 16, Karine Levasseur looks at another avenue for improvement, focusing on improving the relationships between different policy workers and advisers, in this case between charities, non-profits, and other new "partners" for much new Canadian government policy work. She notes a shift in governing from a model that was largely led by "government" to one that is collaboratively led by a variety of "partners" such as government, charities, non-profit organizations, private businesses, and so forth (Osborne 2006; Rhodes 1996; Salamon 2002), and argues that assessing and enhancing the policy capacity of these new partners is an important and required task under this new form of collaborative governance.

Finally, in chapter 17, Justin Longo looks at the impact of new technology on policy work. As governments strive for more seamless horizontality among departments in response to increasing policy complexity, organization-wide knowledge sharing and collaboration is promoted as one means for achieving this. Where social networks are inadequate for facilitating pan-organizational knowledge sharing, and where information and communications technologies (ICTs) reinforce organizational boundaries rather than transcend them, the use of Web 2.0-based enterprise social collaboration tools can facilitate cross-organizational knowledge sharing and collaboration. When applied to government policy formulation, "policy analysis 2.0" builds on earlier experience using computer-supported cooperative work systems to facilitate collaboration among policy workers, but does so using the open architecture of Web 2.0 platforms. As such, Longo argues, policy analysis 2.0 potentially represents a significant realignment of the traditional policy analysis approach and a major reorientation of contemporary policy work whose ramifications and consequences require detailed study and analysis.

Chapter 18 then rounds out the collection, drawing together the different threads of the chapter analyses and discussing their relevance to the theory and practice of policy analysis and policy work in this country and elsewhere.

Taken together, the book brings a team of Canadian researchers with specific expertise in policy analysis from theoretical and applied perspectives, to the study of specific areas of government as well as non-governmental organizational policy work. Their contributions address key gaps in the policy literature and provide a significant conceptual and empirical advance as to the state of policy work in Canada.

Concerns in the mid-1990s about a suspected erosion of public sector "policy capacity" in Canada, particularly federally, raised important questions about governments' ability to meet policy challenges, and flagged areas in need of greater study. This concluding chapter reflects on this volume's findings and represents part of a decade-long research agenda that has sought improved accounts of the nature of policy work, and the state of public sector policy capacity.

The book concludes by drawing out the importance of these findings to the actual applied work of policy practitioners and those who teach and study it. Thus, despite its Canadian focus, this volume offers many clear opportunities to further and complement the international research agenda on policy work and "capacity." This is particularly important, given that this volume presents a clear picture of contemporary professional policy work, and its varied and complex nature (Koliba and Gajda 2009; Kothari, MacLean, and Edwards 2009). The new empirical data and theoretical advances presented here build on important initial thinking about the nature of policy work, "policy capacity," and advisory system configuration and operation in Canada.

2 Policy Analysts in the Bureaucracy Revisited: The Nature of Professional Policy Work in Contemporary Government

MICHAEL HOWLETT AND ADAM WELLSTEAD

Studying the Nature of Policy Work

Professional policy work in government is a difficult subject to categorize and define (Colebatch, Hoppe, and Noordegraaf 2011). At its heart, policy analysis is what Gill and Saunders (1992, 6–7) characterized as "a method for structuring information and providing opportunities for the development of alternative choices for the policymaker." This involves providing information or advice to policymakers on the relative advantages and disadvantages of different policy choices (Mushkin 1977; Wildavsky 1969).

Exactly how this is done, and how it should be done, however, is the subject of continuing debate and research in public policy studies (Colebatch 2006a). This is an especially vexing problem, since more recent empirical studies of how policy research and analysis is actually conducted in governments and how its results are generated, interpreted, and used by political decision-makers have consistently shown the nature of policy work to be quite different from the models proposed by many early policy scholars who worked on the subject (ibid.). The merit of continuing to use earlier classification schemes to inform empirical studies and pedagogical practices (Geva-May and Maslove 2006, 2007), of course, depends on the continuing veracity of these categories outside of their original time and place, and on these schemes' ability to continue to accurately capture the key components of professional policy work in contemporary governments – subjects that prominent critics in the United States and elsewhere have called into question (Colebatch 2006c; Colebatch and Radin 2006; Radin 2000).

Many early works, for example, promoted the idea that many professional analysts in government act, or should act, as "technicians" processing specialized information on subjects in which they share some expertise (Meltsner 1975, 1976). While there can be a range of methodologies used in the provision of such policy advice, many proponents of enhanced policy analysis remained firmly centred on the use and promotion of a specific analytical toolkit based on microeconomics, quantitative methods, and organizational analysis, which they argued could be productively applied by astute policy analysts to provide solutions to most substantive policy problems (Mintrom 2007; Weimer and Vining 1999). Under this influence, education and training of policy workers has for many years been largely a matter of familiarization with standard technical tools such as supply-demand, cost-effectiveness, and cost-benefit analysis, along with the study of cases, workshops, simulations, or real-world projects that illustrate the use and application of these tools (Geva-May and Maslove 2007; Gow and Sutherland 2004; Jann 1991; Wildavsky 1979).

But evidence from more recent research suggests that many analysts are less technical experts than "process generalists" with very little training in formal policy analysis techniques such as cost-benefit analysis or risk assessment and rarely deal with policy matters in the substantive areas in which they may have been trained (Feldman 1989; Page and Jenkins 2005). Similarly, while early studies labelled some such process-oriented work as "political" (Banfield 1977; Dror 1967; Macintyre 1977; Meltsner 1976; Tribe 1972), later work suggests these activities are more nuanced and comprise a large set of interrelated practices ranging from enhancing stakeholder participation in policy deliberations and furthering democratic discourses to mediating inter- and intrajurisdictional turf battles among policy actors and players (Aberbach and Rockman 1989; Adams 2004; Forester 1983; Howlett 2009a; Jenkins-Smith 1982; Mayer, Bots, and van Daalen 2004; Mintrom 2007; Shulock 1999; Weber and Khademian 2008; Workman, Jones, and Jochim 2009).

More and better empirical research is required to better inform both policy pedagogy and practice (Colebatch and Radin 2006). This is essential not only for those who simply wish to better understand the operation and functioning of professional bureaucratic policy analysis but also for those who wish to assess and evaluate activities more accurately to improve training and recruitment, enhance analytical capacity, and ultimately improve analysis and policy outcomes (Anderson

1996; Australian National Audit Office 2001; Di Francesco 1999, 2000; Hollander and Prince 1993; Nicholson 1997; State Services Commission 1999).

This chapter presents the findings of one such recent large-scale empirical investigation into the policy practices of Canadian policy analysts in government. The findings highlight the multidimensional nature of contemporary policy work and its varied and complex nature (Koliba and Gajda 2009; Kothari, MacLean, and Edwards 2009). The findings show that policy analysis and policy work in contemporary governments are considerably more diverse than early studies portrayed. Rather than continue to utilize the results of studies from an earlier age, which, while perhaps prescient, may no longer accurately describe the nature of the actual work carried out by policy analysts in the bureaucracy, policy study, training, and analytical theory and pedagogy, should be amended to better reflect the real-world conditions and realities present-day studies describe.

Overcoming Obstacles to the Better Understanding of the Nature of Policy Work in Government

Current policy studies face two problems in analysing and understanding the nature of policy work in government. First, one way or another, and either directly or indirectly, many students of policy analysis continue to rely on very early studies to provide empirical referents to the kinds of analysis actually practised in government. Numerous studies of policy analysts in the bureaucracy, for example, have relied on Arnold Meltsner's path-breaking early 1970s studies of a small set of Washington, DC, analysts (Meltsner 1975, 1976). In these works Meltsner compressed and highlighted several variables in distinguishing four different kinds of work undertaken by analysts according to their level of competence and skill in dealing with either or both of the technical or political elements he uncovered in the analytical tasks they faced: classifying analysts as "technicians" or "politicians" if they focused on one of these items or as "entrepreneurs," combining both talents, and, finally, "pretenders" (a subtype Meltsner actually found no examples of in his interviews), lacking both sets of skills.

These early insights into the nature of policy work practised in governments heavily influenced many succeeding observers of policy practices who continued to rely on these works in justifying their own categories and conclusions. In the first instance, students of professional policy work in governments like Dluhy (1981) and Mushkin (1977), for example, simply adopted or slightly modified Meltsner's framework, identifying major clusters of analysts as "advocates," "technicians," and "pragmatists," while others put forward more complex modifications yet continued to retain the Meltsner model's basic outlines and shape. Thus, as late as 2006 in the case of the Netherlands, Hoppe and Jeliazkova (2006), like Durning and Osuna (1994) before them in the case of several U.S. states, identified five types of analysts: the process director, the policy philosopher, the policy advocate, the neo-Weberian (or objective technician), and the expert adviser. Like Meltsner, Hoppe and Jeliazkova argued these could be fit into a two-dimensional space in which one dimension involved issue-specific technical expertise, while the second involved distinctions between professional and political loyalties and activities. Although astute, however, Meltsner's findings were developed from observations gleaned from 116 interviews with federal government policy workers in the United States conducted over forty years ago (1970–1), and their continued contemporary relevance is uncertain (Meltsner 1976, 14).

Second, studies of policy work have examined only a very limited range of cases of governments outside the United States. Some policy analytical practices have been studied in the United Kingdom (Page and Jenkins 2005; Prince 1983), Australia (Hawke 1993; Uhr and Mackay 1996; Waller 1992, 1996; Weller and Stevens 1998), New Zealand (Boston et al. 1996; Hunn 1994; State Services Commission 1999), France (Rochet 2004), and Germany (Fleischer 2009; Wagner and Wollman 1986; Wollmann 1989), but the range of cases remains quite limited. Nevertheless, even here the differences found between the United States and these jurisdictions are revealing. On the basis of interviews with mid-level, London-based U.K. policy analysts in 2005, for example, Page and Jenkins (2005, 168) found policy work in the United Kingdom to differ substantially from the technical practices Meltsner found in the United States. As they argued,

> The broad features of our characterization of UK policy bureaucracy are that policy officials at relatively junior levels are given substantial responsibility for developing and maintaining policy and servicing other, formally superior officials or bodies, often by offering technical advice and guidance. These people are not technical specialists in the sense that they develop high levels of technical expertise in one subject or stay in the same job for a long time. They are often left with apparently substantial

discretion to develop policy because they often receive vague instructions about how to do their jobs, are not closely supervised, and work in an environment that is in most cases not overtly hierarchical.

These two sets of problems suggest that additional empirical and comparative studies are needed to bring more light to the nature of professional policy work in modern governments and to move the study of policy work and its pedagogy beyond early ruminations on the subject. This chapter helps to overcome these obstacles by assessing the results of several large-scale surveys of the activities of core government policy analysts in Canada, or what Page and Jenkins (2005) refer to collectively as the "policy bureaucracy," contrasting these findings with those taken from the traditional Meltsner-inspired, U.S.-centred approaches to the subject. The data present a more precise picture of the work world of contemporary professional policy analysts than is typically found in the literature on the subject, and the statistical tests developed here allow the more precise identification of the areas where analysts work, the tasks associated with their jobs, the skills they use in these tasks, the kinds of issues they dealt with, and the nature of their day-to-day interactions. The implications of the differences found between these present-day and older studies for policy pedagogy, management, and theory are set out in the concluding section.

Data and Methods

To probe the key dimensions of policy work in Canada, a survey instrument consisting of a sixty-four-item questionnaire was developed, divided into six main topic areas: demographic characteristics, job experience, education and training, day-to-day duties, techniques, data employed, and attitudes towards policymaking and politics. This followed Radin's (1997) admonition that better empirical assessments of policy work require investigation of at least five elements: (1) the scale and location of policy analysis functions; (2) the political environment surrounding the activity; (3) the analytic methodologies used; (4) the availability and use of information and data; and (5) the dimensions of policy decisions. Batteries of survey questions addressed the nature and frequency of the tasks undertaken by professional policy workers in government, the range and frequency of the techniques they used in their work, the extent and frequency of their interactions with other policy actors, and their attitudes to and views of various aspects of policymaking processes, as well as a range of questions addressing their educational, previous work, and on-the-job training experiences. It also contained standard questions relating to age, gender, and socio-economic status.

The questionnaire was delivered through a web-based survey of 3,856 Canadian provincial and territorial government policy analysts working in every Canadian sub-national jurisdiction carried out by the authors in early 2009 using Zoomerang, an online commercial software service. Mailing lists for the surveys were compiled, wherever possible, from publicly available sources such as online government telephone directories, using keyword searches for terms such as *policy analyst* appearing in job titles or descriptions. In some cases, additional names were added to lists from hard-copy sources, including government organization manuals. In other cases, lists of additional names were provided by provincial or territorial public service commissions who also checked initial lists for completeness and accuracy. The population size was small, so a census rather than a sample was drawn. This method is consistent with other expert-based studies (see, e.g., Laumann and Knoke 1987; Zafonte and Sabatier 1998). A total of 1,357 usable returns were collected for a final response rate of 43.3 per cent (see appendix to this chapter for a breakdown of responses by province and territory).[1]

Combined, the data generated by the surveys provide the basis required to construct an accurate empirical profile of the background and activities of government policy workers that can be compared and contrasted with Meltsner's findings (Howlett 2009b, 2009c). From the sixty-four survey questions, a very large data set containing several hundred variables was analysed using SPSS 16.0. A profile of contemporary policy work was constructed employing exploratory factor analysis, a common statistical method used to describe variability among observed variables in terms of a potentially lower number of unobserved variables known as factors. The internal consistency of the factored variables was estimated using reliability analysis and Cronbach's α (alpha) statistic.

Findings

Analytical Skills Employed and Tasks Performed

First, the study revealed a larger set of analytical tasks and activities undertaken by policy workers than is found in the Meltsner model. Twenty-five survey variables dealt with the nature of the tasks performed by analysts, and a factor analysis of these variables (table 2.1) revealed that analysts undertake a much wider range of activities under the rubric of "analysis" than is usually assumed or asserted in the literature on the subject. Nine distinct sets of job duties were found related to formulation, consultation, implementation, financial analysis, evaluation, data management, communications, environmental assessment, and the use of legal skills and work. The largest number of analysts were found to engage in formulation (28.04 per cent), followed by consultation (21.56 per cent), evaluation (18.92 per cent), and implementation (18.67 per cent), with the smallest number engaging in data management (6.25 per cent).

Types of Analytical Work Performed

Prima facie, this reveals a more complex picture of analytical work duties in government than Meltsner found in the U.S. federal government in the early 1970s. However, analysts' jobs, as both Meltsner's followers (Dluhy 1981; Feldman 1989) and his critics (Hoppe 1999; Mayer, Bots, and van Daalen 2004; Radin 2000) have noted, can combine these tasks in different combinations, and in table 2.2 the results are presented of a second factor analysis of fifteen policy-related jobs performed by Canadian analysts. Table 2.2 shows a more familiar, Meltsner-like, pattern as four distinct types of analytical work emerge. However, unlike Meltsner's technical-political distinction, these four are not variations on these two dimensions of policy jobs but rather relate to tasks linked to policy appraisal, implementation, strategic brokerage, and formal evaluation. The mean scores (where 1 = never and 6 = daily) indicate that policy appraisal, namely intelligence gathering, was the most heavily undertaken task (R = 3.82), followed by strategic brokerage activities (R = 3.37). Evaluation and implementation were less frequently undertaken activities (R = 2.90 and R = 2.56, respectively).

Nature of Analytical Techniques Employed

Taken together, these two tables underscore the existence of considerably more variation in analytical tasks and jobs than is typically asserted by policy scholars or reflected in much policy pedagogy. It is in keeping, however, with other contemporary comparative analyses that have similarly identified a more complex range of duties and activities than those uncovered by Meltsner in his early work

Table 2.1 Tasks Performed by Analysts in Provincial and Territorial Governments

	Components Formulation (Cronbach's α = .831) (*n* = 694)	Consultation (Cronbach's α = .725) (*n* = 549)	Implementation (Cronbach's α = .638) (*n* = 524)
Mean score	$\bar{x}$ = .2804	$\bar{x}$ = .2156	$\bar{x}$ = .1867
Tasks undertaken			
Formal legislative or executive conconsultation			
Legal consultation			
Environmental assessment			
Environmental scans			
Communications and media relations			
Report writing or editing			
Report presentation			
Data collection and entry			
Data management			
Auditing and evaluation			
Formal policy or program evaluation			
Informal policy or program evaluation			
Cost-benefit analysis			
Budget analysis			
Finance			
Program development			.745
Program delivery and implementation			.834
Program administration			.613
Public participation design		.755	
Public consultation		.837	
Stakeholder consultation		.723	
Policy analysis	.749		
Policy development	.767		
Formulating policy options	.809		
Assessing policy options	.792		

Note: 66.34% of the variance explained.

Finance (Cronbach's α = .608) (*n* = 331)	Evaluation (Cronbach's α = .575) (*n* = 548)	Data Management (Cronbach's α = .662) (*n* = 140)	Communication (Cronbach's α = .537 (*n* = 340)	Assessment (Cronbach's α = .561) (*n* = 322)	Legal work (Cronbach's α = .541) (*n* = 354)
$\bar{x}$ = .1082	$\bar{x}$ = .1892	$\bar{x}$ = .0625	$\bar{x}$ = .1571	$\bar{x}$ = .1389	$\bar{x}$ = .1495
					.790
					.815
				.847	
				.773	
			.601		
			.713		
			.717		
		.856			
		.851			
	.579				
	.776				
	.700				
.602					
.800					
.776					

Table 2.2 Jobs Performed by Provincial and Territorial Analysts

	Appraisal (Cronbach's α = .868)	Implementation (Cronbach's α = .614)	Strategic brokerage (Cronbach's α = .731)	Evaluation (Cronbach's α = .856)
Mean score	$\bar{x}$ = 3.82	$\bar{x}$ = 2.56	$\bar{x}$ = 3.37	$\bar{x}$= 2.90
Skill sets				
Collect policy-related data or information	.843			
Conduct policy-related research	.841			
Identify policy issues	.662			
Identify policy options	.691			
Appraise policy options	.606			
Implement or deliver policies or programs		.600		
Negotiate with stakeholders on policy matters		.923		
Consult with the public on policy matters		.542		
Negotiate with stakeholders on policy matters		.923		
Prepare reports, briefs, or presentations for decision-makers on policy matters			.684	
Consult with decision-makers on policy matters			.697	
Brief lower- or mid-level policy managers			.490	
Brief high-level decision-makers, such as Cabinet ministers, ministerial staff, and senior managers			.780	
Evaluate policy results and outcomes				.836
Evaluate policy processes and procedures				.859

Notes: 67.28% of the variance explained.
Mean scores are based on a 6-point scale where 1 = never and 6 = daily.

(Mayer, Bots, and van Daalen 2004; Page and Jenkins 2005; Thissen and Twaalfhoven 2001).

The difference in foundations of these four basic types of analysis from those associated with the Meltsner-inspired literature is underscored by a factor analysis of a third set of variables that examined the frequency of use by respondents of over forty specific analytical techniques in their day-to-day work. Table 2.3 shows clusters of distinct sets of techniques: "classical" policy analytical ones related to evaluation such as cost-benefit analysis, sociological techniques such as social network analysis, and various survey and problem-mapping techniques, consultative techniques, and the use of more sophisticated mathematical modelling tools such as the Markov-chain modelling. This analysis finds some support for Meltsner's two types of "politician" and "technician," since "evaluative" techniques and "consultative" ones are loosely related to Meltsner's "technical" and "political" dimensions. The other tasks practised by analysts, however, such as formal modelling and social network mapping, do not correspond to those normally associated with Meltsner's subtypes.

Whom Do They Interact With?

Similarly, when asked about their networking activities, the core of Meltsner's "political" dimension, a more complex picture than that envisioned by most students of policy analytical work again emerged. A factor analysis of the frequency of respondents' contacts with thirteen different types of contactees (table 2.4) produced two key factors, depending on whether analysts dealt in the main in their work with external actors or internal ones, a distinction lacking in Meltsner's work.

The contacts with internal networks based on a five-point scale were notably stronger ($R = 3.40$) than with those outside of the government ($R = 2.02$), which, as Meltsner (1976, 177–96) indeed argued, suggests that many analysts are largely agency-centred or "desk-bound" and prepare, review, or manipulate financial and other kinds of data, interacting most often with other bureaucratic government actors. Another clearly identifiable set of tasks, however, involves interaction with outside actors such as other governments and non-governmental organizations. Both sets of tasks require analysts with "political skills," such as the ability to bargain, build support, network, negotiate, and compromise, but the content of these actions will be very different, depending on the group with which the interaction takes place.

Table 2.3 Common Analytical Techniques Used

	Evaluative (Cronbach's α = .714) (n = 1,148)	Sociological (Cronbach's α = .565) (n = 681)	Consultative (Cronbach's α = .552) (n = 1,336)	Mathematical (Cronbach's α = .288) (n = 182)
Mean score	$\bar{x}$ = .480	$\bar{x}$ = .150	$\bar{x}$ = .622	$\bar{x}$ = .045
Analytical techniques				
Development of sophisticated modelling tools				.587
Markov-chain modelling				.698
Monte Carlo techniques				.695
Brainstorming			.640	
Consultation exercises			.750	
Focus groups			.712	
Free-form gaming or other policy exercises		.550		
Problem mapping		.664		
Decision/probability trees		.596		
Process influence or social network diagrams		.556		
Preference scaling		.565		
Cost-effectiveness analysis	.713			
Cost-benefit analysis	.780			
Financial impact analysis	.740			
Risk analysis	.574			

Note: 47.2% of the variance explained.

Table 2.4 Nature of Contacts/Networks

	External (Cronbach's α = .878)	Internal (Cronbach's α = .808)
Mean score	$\bar{x} = 2.02$	$\bar{x} = 3.40$
Nature of contacts		
Senior head-office-based management		.873
Other head-office staff		.873
Senior regional management		.637
Central agencies		.721
Municipal government departments	.646	
Federal departments in my region	.675	
Environmental/conservation-based groups	.745	
Industry organizations	.707	
Labour organizations	.728	
Think tanks	.783	
Universities	.715	
Aboriginal groups	.624	
Other non-governmental organizations	.685	

Notes: 56.63% of the variance explained.
Mean scores are based on a 5-point scale where 1 = never and 5 = daily.

The Nature of the Most Common Issue Types

A fourth theme investigated the kinds of issues with which the respondents were involved. This was assessed by asking analysts about the complexity of their day-to-day tasks, as well as the extent to which issues could be dealt with using technical expertise or activities such as consultation. This analysis should reveal whether or not analysts were engaged in largely "technical" or "political" issues, as Meltsner suggested.

The results set out in table 2.5, however, show that three distinct clusters of issues exist, divided along both technical and consultative lines, as Meltsner (1976, 14–48) suggested, but also along a third dimension related to their routine or innovative nature. Again this reveals a dimension to contemporary policy work in government, which most existing studies have not sufficiently taken into account.

Table 2.5 Nature of Policy Issues Most Involved With

	Complex technical (Cronbach's α = .793)	Consultative (Cronbach's α = .717)	Routine
Mean score	$\bar{x}$ = 4.39	$\bar{x}$ = 2.39	$\bar{x}$ = 2.82
Nature of issues			
Issues that have a single, clear, relatively simple solution			.962
Issues that demand input from society-based organizations		.865	
Issues that demand public consultation		.861	
Issues that require coordination with head office	.551		
Issues that require specialist or technical knowledge	.702		
Issues where it is difficult to identify a single, clear, simple solution	.814		
Issues for which data are not immediately available	.809		
Issues that demand the creation or collection of policy-relevant evidence	.758		

Notes: 68.00% of the variance explained.
Mean scores are based on a 6-point scale where 1 = never and 6 = daily.

Conclusion

Professional policy analysts are well-known players in the day-to-day functioning of complex and multidimensional government decision-making systems. Yet, despite their prominence, what little is known concerning the work these actors perform is based primarily on dated empirical studies drawn primarily from the United States.

Much thinking concerning the general nature of professional policy work in government has flowed from these early empirical studies, as have pedagogical notions about what skills analysts should have to improve their practices and contribute to better policy outcomes (Morçöl and Ivanova 2010). However, while the number of texts and articles proposing and reinforcing the use of standard technical analytical tools is legion, the number of empirical studies of the actual day-to-day practices of policy analysts is much smaller and, in many cases and countries, is either non-existent or badly out of date (Colebatch, Hoppe, and Noordegraaf 2011; Colebatch and Radin 2006). As a result, the empirical basis for many prescriptions pertaining to the desirable forms of policy work remains very weak (Colebatch 2006b). More accurate assessments of the actual policy analysis carried out by professional analysis in a range of different governmental contexts are needed, both to inform better understanding of the operation of policy advice systems and to better steer the training and recruitment of policy analysts within them (MacRae 1991; Radaelli 1995).

The results of the study of a large group of Canadian analysts presented here help address some of these problems. They provide the data required for a more accurate assessment of the kinds of analysts found in contemporary governments and of what they do in their work. Using data from an up-to-date large-*N* survey of policy analysts, the study allows meaningful comparisons and contrasts to be drawn with previous, primarily U.S.-based data and findings.

The findings reported here confirm, as Meltsner suggested, that professional policy workers in government should not be treated as a homogeneous group and that there are significant differences among analysts in many important dimensions of their work. However, many aspects of this analytical work were found to differ from the dimensions highlighted in earlier studies of the subject. Analysts, for example, were found to practise as many as nine different policy-related activities and to practise four general types of work that related to policy appraisal, implementation, strategic planning, and evaluation. Moreover, analysts were found to practise four common sets of analytical techniques ranging from consultation to mathematical modelling; to address at least three issue types; and to have different sets of contacts with actors within or external to governments from those typically described in the literature. This all suggests a richer and more nuanced set of analytical practices involved in policy work than many previous studies have postulated.

This kind of more precise information on the day-to-day work of policy analysts is required for studies of policy work and policy workers in government to advance. More accurately assessing the activities, skills, attitudes, and other aspects of the actual policy work carried out by professional policy analysts in government is a pressing need for policy scholars, practitioners, and pedagogues (Brinkerhoff 2010; Brinkerhoff and Morgan 2010; Hawke 1993; Hunn 1994; Nicholson 1996), and large-*N* studies of the kind reported here help to clarify what analysts actually do and, by implication, how they can be managed and trained to do it better.

Appendix

Provincial and Territorial Survey Sample Sizes and Completion Rates

Province	Initial mail list size	Refusals and rejected e-mails	Valid partial completions	Complete	Response rate (%)
BC	513	51	30	194	48.5
Alberta	368	23	8	112	34.8
Saskatchewan	246	27	13	80	42.4
Manitoba	161	20	6	98	73.7
Ontario	1,613	162	52	557	41.9
Quebec*	250	0	44	86	52.0
New Brunswick	162	15	4	62	44.9
Nova Scotia	181	20	15	83	44.1
PEI	27	6	1	4	23.8
Newfoundland	139	24	16	55	61.7
Yukon	75	8	6	58	95.5
NWT	80	2	2	41	55.1
Nunavut	41	8	2	13	45.4
TOTAL (excluding Quebec)	3,856	366	155	1,357	43.3

* Snowball sample methodology – data excluded from totals and from subsequent tables. See note 1.

NOTE

1 Use of a different (snowball) survey methodology in Quebec generated a much smaller sample, so the 130 responses from that province are excluded from the analysis that follows. However, a separate analysis of the results from the Quebec survey identified a pattern of responses similar to those found in the other twelve provinces and territories (Bernier and Howlett 2011).

PART 2

Policy Work in Canadian Government

3 Policy Capacity and Incapacity in Canada's Federal Government

ADAM WELLSTEAD, RICHARD STEDMAN, AND EVERT LINDQUIST

Introduction

Canada's federal public service is a large, complex organization of 370,000 people responsible for delivering a wide variety of policies and programs in many different sectors across a large but relatively sparsely populated landmass (Cote, Baird, and Green 2007). The policy goals of the federal government often overlap, conflict with, or harmonize with the ten provincial and three territorial governments' policy responsibilities. All governments face a formidable challenge of avoiding policy failures. These failures can occur in the agenda-setting stage (overreaching policy agendas), or during policy formulation (an inability to deal with complex problems), decision-making (failure to anticipate adverse consequences or risk), policy implementation (lack of funding or legitimation), or evaluation (lack of monitoring or feedback) (see Howlett 2009c for an extensive overview).

Ensuring strong policy capacity based within a public service is a critical factor in avoiding policy failure. An enduring concern within Canada's federal government is the level of policy capacity. Recent events illustrate the intensity of this debate. In 2007, the Public Policy Forum (PPF), an Ottawa-based think tank, identified declining policy capacity as a critical issue facing the federal civil service. From a series of key informant workshops held across Canada, they found a number of recurring themes, including a hollowing out of expertise and competition from other external organizations such as academia, non-government organizations, and think tanks; the development of policy options too removed from on-the-ground considerations key to the effective implementation of policy; reacting to communications crises and dealing with political sensitivities; and an over-emphasis on internal performance reporting (Cote, Baird, and Green 2007). They concluded with a sobering prognosis that an "unresponsive public service equals an irrelevant public service, and this is more pronounced because the federal public service is less connected to Canadians than provincial and municipal levels of government when it comes to providing services that affect their lives" (8).

In a well-publicized response to the Public Policy Forum's findings, Kevin Lynch, the clerk of the Privy Council (Canada's most senior civil servant), stated that it was a "misconception" to label Canada's federal public service as broken or out of touch with Canadians. He argued that the job of the public service, and more specifically its policy capacity, was "to provide governments with well researched, analytically rigorous, unbiased policy options and recommendations" and not make policy decisions (Lynch 2008b). Such expertise, he argued, is spread unevenly across the civil service and in some cases found outside in non-government agencies, but that is not problematic.

One area where federal policy expertise is unevenly located is in the regions (Wellstead, Stedman, and Lindquist 2009). This chapter examines Canadian policy capacity in the context of a key tension: Canada is a very decentralized country with a highly centralized federal government. We suggest that this disconnect may have contributed to problems in policy capacity and we use survey data to explore the prospects for regional federal policy work to address this crisis in capacity. In Canada's federal government, policy-related work is highly concentrated in the National Capital Region (NCR) (Ottawa-Gatineau), with over 95 per cent of civil servants with policy-related classifications found there (Canadian Public Service Commission 2008). Relatively neglected are the roles of Canada's regionally based policy-oriented employees who are closest to the pressing issues of the day. What do they do, and what is their potential to help address policy capacity problems?

Three key research questions are raised in this chapter. First, to what extent does regional policy work contribute to the policy capacity of the Canadian federal government? However, in order to answer this question, we must first answer two broader questions: can a theoretical framework of policy capacity be developed and, if so, can it be empirically explained? Studies of the perceptions of policy capacity have been conducted, often relying on case studies or interviews with senior government officials (Anderson 1996; Rasmussen 1999). However, Howlett

(2009a) notes that studies that employ quantitative methodologies to examine the specific behavioural characteristics of policy workers are exceedingly rare. The lack of empirical research in the field of policy capacity research is coupled by the underdevelopment of theoretical frameworks. A policy capacity framework (with testable hypotheses) based upon the changing nature of government and the public service, along with the role of street-level bureaucracy literature, is introduced. We hope that the empirical model and theoretical contributions made in this chapter will attract further research and debate in this important public management area. We present data from an online survey of regional federal government employees in a structural equation model to assess their roles, their activities, the drivers of regional policy-related work, and their perceptions of policy effectiveness as an indicator of policy capacity.

The Challenge of Policy Capacity, the Contribution of Policy Analysts, and the Role of Street Bureaucracy

The Changing Nature of Federal Government

Recent literature has detailed the rapidly changing state of government bureaucracies in what has been coined the "new environment" (Pal 2001; Savoie 2003b; Prince 2007). This setting for policy analysis has been characterized by (1) a diverse set of internal and external actors equipped with valuable resources who are keen to provide their policy guidance to government; (2) the public's declining trust in both politicians and the bureaucracies, fuelling their desire to be more involved in policymaking; (3) a general trend towards privatization of operations and program delivery brought on in the spirit of New Public Management (NPM); and finally (4) adapting to new localized governance arrangements that emphasize the role of networks. All of these trends point to the growing complexity in public administration, particularly a growing schism between local and national issues and actors (Klijn 2008).

Policy analysts are now expected to engage in greater consultation, consensus building, and public dialogue as part of their policy work. This inevitably leaves less space for traditional policy analysis. Such an environment is markedly different from classical management where central actors performed a central policymaking role. Moreover, there has been a breakdown of the implicit bargain that was traditionally struck between public servants and their ministers and an opening of public scrutiny: the former would offer professionalism, discretion, and non-partisan loyalty to the latter in exchange for anonymity and security of tenure (Savoie 2003b). Without the anonymity that protects the public service from political influence, public officials are now inclined to promote easy policy options that are certain to be preferred by politicians, and to engage in "firefighting" by focusing on immediate political issues. Relatively neglected is long-term policy planning. The politicization of policy has been fostered by the increasingly decentralized policymaking. As a result, policymakers have increasingly rationalized policy decisions based on political and ideological preferences rather than formal analysis. This politicization of policymaking has fostered the erosion of analytical capacity in government, and a new emphasis on public relations and environmental scans as modes of policy advice (Peters 1996). Officials now use a wider set of policy instruments, particularly procedural ones such as private partnerships, roundtables, and funding to organized societal groups.

The Changing Nature of Public Service: Effects on Policy Capacity

There are many competing definitions of policy capacity. Honadle (1981, 578) defines it as "the ability to: anticipate and influence change; make informed, intelligent decisions about policy; develop programs to implement policy; attract and absorb resources; manage resources; and evaluate current activities to guide future action." Others are more concerned with the ability to respond to change (Weiss 1979a), the intellectual and organizational resources of the state (Cummings and Nørgaard 2004), the management of knowledge and organizational learning (Parsons 2004), or policy formulation (Goetz and Wollmann 2001).

Scholars have asked whether policy capacity has been declining in light of public service reforms, specifically towards NPM approaches. There has been a mixed response. Bakvis (2000) contends that in Canada some federal government departments have improved their capacity. Voyer (2007) notes that some departments such as the Department of Finance, Human Resources Development, and Health Canada responded by increasing their long-term research and analytical capacities through the development of large-scale policy initiatives and investments in policy units. Despite these changes, he found that "the tyranny of the urgent still dominates" policy work across all departments (232). Prince and Chenier (1980) present a comprehensive overview of policy units and their role in the Canadian federal government. They argue that the organizational dynamics of policy work is often overlooked in the literature. Policy units can influence policy capacity in two ways: by the type of work undertaken and the associated degree of "innovation created," and their visibility throughout the organization as a source of expertise.

There is also a large literature examining the changing roles of those engaged in policy work. Typically, policy analysis was portrayed as a rationalistic undertaking consisting of civil servants objectively presenting information to policymakers. Meltsner (1976) was the first to develop a more multifaceted policy-analyst typology. This was later refined by Jenkins-Smith (1982), Durning and Osuna (1994), Mayer, Bots, and van Daalen (2004), and Hoppe and Jeliazkova (2006). Meltsner contended that analysts' particular policy style and an understanding of policy capacity depends on both political and analytical skills, which are shaped by their unique combination of education, professional training, beliefs, and personal motivations. According to Durning and Osuna (1994), the variety and multifaceted nature of policy analysis makes it clear that there is no single, let alone best, way of conducting policy analyses. Their contribution also represents an overlooked aspect of policy capacity scholarship, namely the role that attitudes and beliefs play in influencing policy analysts' day-to-day activities and policy capacity. They demonstrate that only a minority of policy analysts fall into the "objective technician" category. In addition to being guided by their direct work roles and responsibilities, the nature of attitudes towards the policy arena plays a critical role in their work (see Mayer, Bots, and van Daalen 2004). Lindquist and Desveaux (2007) argue that the effectiveness of policy work within current and evolving governance structures (i.e., alternative service delivery and decentralization) will invariably depend on the ability of managers to balance short-term objectives with long-term strategies. Having an optimum mix of roles – as described earlier – may be crucial as well.

A notable shortcoming in the policy capacity literature has been its lack of consideration of the role and contribution of regional policy work to policy capacity. An exception is a relatively dated Treasury Board Secretariat (TBS) 1996 discussion paper, which argued, "Regional sensitization of departmental decision-making must [also] be supported by government-wide policy and decision-making processes" (Treasury Board Secretariat 1996). The paper advocated policy roles beyond program delivery in areas such as issue identification, research, consultation, producing policy option, evaluation, and implementation. Wellstead, Stedman, and Lindquist (2009) described policy work in Canada's federal public service, comparing the demographics, tasks, and attitudes of policy-oriented employees in the regions and in the NCR (Ottawa). They found that these two groups were very different on many fronts. Policy analysis was identified as one of many tasks that the regional respondents simultaneously undertook (coordinator, manager, liaison, program delivery). However, when they undertook policy-related work, it tended to be relatively rudimentary (e.g., collect policy-related information or identify policy issues). The regional respondents were more engaged with the other government agencies, the general public, and stakeholder groups than their NCR counterparts.

A review of the above studies suggests that those working in the regions are on-the-ground personnel. We draw upon Lipsky (1980) to understand their work better. "Street-level bureaucrats" are typically associated with front-line civil servants such as lawyers, social workers, or police officers. They are people from diverse backgrounds who work under conditions of limited resources and uncertainty but work directly with people or implement programs. They often have a degree of autonomy because of the vague goals set out by complex bureaucratic organizations. However, these individuals are difficult to study because of the often informal and intangible nature of their work (Meyers and Vorsanger 2003). We argue that the street-level bureaucrat label can be invoked to understand the work of regionally based policy-oriented employees within Canada's federal government. Page and Jenkins (2005) make a similar claim in their study of U.K. rank-and-file policy workers. Although at the bottom of the policy hierarchy, street-level bureaucrats are also in greater position to influence policy than other civil servants (Riccucci 2005). Street-level bureaucrats assist in reproducing the prevailing relations between individuals and government organizations (Lipsky 1980). Smith (2003) also points to the growing formal structuring of the bureaucrat–citizen relationship, decentralization, and the deliberative processes that involve communities and regions as trends in government that make street-level bureaucrats increasingly the "face of government." In a crowded policymaking environment, the locally based federal government official is often the only link that those who are on the ground have to insights to the national government's stance on issues. This chapter considers the role of policy-based street-level bureaucracy and policy analysis among our respondents and explores the relationship between the activities of regional personnel and perceived policy effectiveness as one important indicator of policy capacity.

Research Hypotheses

From the above literature a conceptual regional policy-capacity theoretical framework along with eight hypotheses is developed (figure 3.1). All of the paths illustrated in figure 3.1 are later replicated in the formal structural equation model.

Hypothesis 1: Regional policy work is defined by two distinct functions: traditional policy analysis and street-level bureaucracy. Traditional policy analysis refers to such tasks as analysis, research, and appraising policy options, whereas street-level bureaucracy tasks include implementing and delivering programs or consulting with stakeholders or the public.

Hypotheses 2 and 3 examine how tasks directly play a role in perceived policy capacity. We expect that those who are frequently involved in the many identified tasks associated with policy work will consider themselves as contributing to policy capacity. We believe this will be true for both traditional policy analysis and street-level bureaucracy.

Hypotheses 2 and 3: Being involved in a high level of traditional policy analysis and a high level of street-level work will contribute to a higher perceived policy capacity.

In addition to the type of tasks undertaken, the nature of policy work will have an impact on perceived policy capacity. Two aspects of this work are examined: the geographic focus of the work and the time period of issues examined. Given their distance from the daily pressures of NCR, those who undertake traditional policy work should undertake longer-term analysis and have a strong national focus in their day-to-day work. In contrast, we expect that street-level activity will be more strongly associated with provincial-level work and with greater attention paid to immediate issues. We expect that a strong engagement in provincial issues will contribute to perceived policy capacity, as these issues are more readily translated to effective action. Also, those dealing with long-term issues consider themselves as contributors to perceived policy capacity. On the contrary, dealing with immediate issues ("fire-fighting") will detract from perceived policy capacity in the regions.

Hypothesis 4: The geographic and temporal scope of regionally based policy work will be determined by the two policy task groups.

Figure 3.1 Theoretical Framework of the Hypotheses Tested

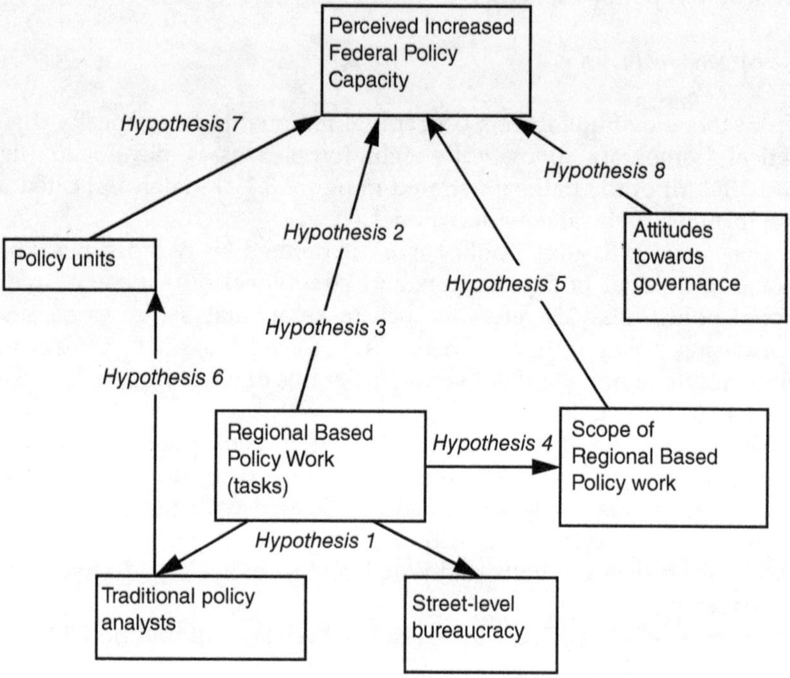

Traditional policy analysis will be more engaged in longer-term and national issues, whereas street-level work will deal with "firefighting" issues and be provincially focused.

Hypothesis 5: The type of policy issues addressed will contribute to a (higher or lower) level of perceived policy capacity: it will be positively related to provincial-level and long-term work.

Hypotheses 6 and 7 examine how formal organized policy units contribute to perceived regional policy capacity. Policy units are indicative of the resources that organizations invest in policy capacity (Prince and Chenier 1980; Voyer 2007). We expect that those who undertake policy capacity work will more likely be part of policy units and that they will contribute to a higher degree of perceived policy capacity.

Hypothesis 6: Those engaged in a high level of traditional policy analysis will be more likely to belong to formal policy work units.

Hypothesis 7: Working in a formal policy unit will contribute to a higher level of perceived policy capacity.

Attitudes about the current state of governance were identified in the literature as an important determinant of an erosion of policy capacity, particularly the "new environment" of policymaking.

Hypothesis 8: A pessimistic attitude towards governance and government will contribute to a decreased sense of perceived policy capacity.

Data and Methods

An online survey, using the Zoomerang® software, of regionally based federal government employees engaged in policy-related work was conducted in early 2007. Approximately 500 Regional Federal Council members (senior regional employees representing their respective department or agency) from all ten provinces and the three territories provided contact information of regionally based employees who met the criterion of undertaking policy-related work as set out by the investigators. A total of 1,442 people were identified. In addition, the Regional Federal Council members themselves were surveyed ($N = 495$) for a total population of 1,937. Because of the small size of the population, a census rather than sample was drawn. The survey garnered 1,125 usable responses for a strong overall response rate of 56.8 per cent. The return rate from the 1,442 identified respondents was 66.1 per cent, whereas the return rate from the 495 Federal Council members was 28.4 per cent.

Structural Equation Model

Structural equation modelling (SEMS) using LISREL software has become a very popular research tool in the social sciences because of its capabilities for understanding and predicting complex phenomena (Kelloway 1995). SEMs are multivariate regression models. Thus, the response variables in one regression equation in any SEM may appear as predictor in another equation, and the SEM variables may influence each other reciprocally, either directly or indirectly or though other variables as intermediaries (Hailu, Boxall, and McFarlane 2005). SEMs contain three basic equations containing four matrices of coefficients and four covariance matrices. Equation 1 reveals all of the direct effects among the endogenous and exogenous concepts (or latent variables). Endogenous concepts are those concepts directly caused or influenced by other concepts, whereas exogenous concepts always act as the cause.

The analysis of the covariance structures procedure assumes that the "true" dependent variables (endogenous), η, are related to the ξ, true independent (exogenous) variables, by a system of structural equations (Equation 1).

Structural equation model: $\eta = B_{\eta} + \Gamma\xi + \zeta$ (Equation 1)

In this equation, B is a coefficient matrix of relationships among the dependent variables, Γ is the matrix of causal effects of the independent on the dependent variables, and ζ is a residual vector for errors in equations. By setting various elements of the β and Γ matrices to zero, the researcher can designate the absence of causal relationships. Similarly, the presence or absence of correlations among elements of ζ can be controlled as indicated by theoretical requirements.

Measurement model for $y = \Lambda_y \xi + \varepsilon$ (Equation 2)

Measurement model for $x = \Lambda_x \xi + \delta$ (Equation 3)

There are two measurement equations. In Equation 2, y is a $p \times 1$ vector of observed indicators of dependent latent variables (η); In Equation 3, x is a $q \times 1$ vector of observed indicators of the independent latent variables (ξ); ε is the $p \times 1$ of measurement errors in y; δ is the $q \times 1$ vector measurement errors in x; Λ_y is a $p \times m$ matrix of coefficients of the regression of y on η and Λ_x is a $q \times n$ matrix of coefficients of the regression of x on ξ In order to identify the model, selected parameters in the equations must be constrained.

Model Variables

In table 3.1, not surprisingly, implementing or delivering policies and programs was the most frequently mentioned item by the respondents (mean = 3.42 and 35.6 per cent, indicating daily involvement). This was followed by identifying policy options and collecting policy-related information. A factor analysis of these twelve items was conducted (with 60.49 per cent of the variance explained), and it produced two distinct broad items consistent with our theoretical stance: "policy work" and "street bureaucracy."

Respondents were asked if they belonged to formal and interdepartmental groups (table 3.2). Just over a third of the respondents indicated

Table 3.1 Self-Identified Roles in the Policymaking Process

	Regional respondents Mean (ranking)	Factor 1: Policy work	Factor 2: Street bureaucracy
Appraise policy options	2.78 (8)	.768	
Collect policy-related data	2.77 (9)	.797	
Collect policy-related information	3.17 (3)	.866	
Conduct policy-related research	2.49 (10)	.808	
Identify policy issues	3.28 (2)	.805	
Identify policy options	2.91 (5)	.802	
Implement or deliver policies or programs	3.42 (1)		.655
Negotiate with stakeholders	2.79 (7)		.830
Negotiate with central agencies	1.99 (12)		.560
Negotiate with program managers	2.96 (4)		.744
Consult with the public	2.12 (11)		.677
Consult with stakeholders	2.85 (6)		.753

Notes: Based on 1–5 scale, where 1 = never and 5 = daily. Extraction method: principal component analysis. Rotation method: Varimax with Kaiser normalization. 60.49 per cent of the variance explained.

they belonged to a formal policy unit. An important aspect of policy work is their temporal (immediate, long-term) and geographic aspects of the respondent's tasks (table 3.3). We also assess respondents' assessments of governmental support for policy capacity. Three items were combined into a scale assessing perceptions that federal governmental support had declined: "There seems to be less governmental capacity to analyse policy options"; "Formal government institutions are becoming less relevant to policymaking"; and "Decisions about government programs and operations are increasingly made by those outside of government." Scores suggest moderate agreement with these items. Finally, overall policy commitment was measured by summing the seven items listed in table 3.4. Here respondents were asked about engagement by management, networks and their headquarters, and resource issues such as funding, level of training, and policy staff. A reliability analysis produced a single summed scale with a very strong alpha of .859.

Table 3.2 Membership in Formal and Interdepartmental Policy Groups

	Regional respondents (%)
Member of a formal policy group	39.0
Member of an interdepartmental policy group	53.8

Table 3.3 Temporal and Geographic Focus of the Regional Respondents

	Regional respondents	
	Number	Mean
Temporal focus of issues examined		
Immediate action items (i.e., "firefighting")	1053	4.07
Short-term files (less than a month)	1046	3.73
Medium-term files (1–6 months)	1042	3.52
Long-term files (6–12 months)	1048	3.47
Ongoing files	1042	4.26
Geographic focus of issues examined		
Local issues	1037	3.98
Provincial issues	1050	3.74
Regional issues	1056	3.98
National issues	1057	3.33
International issues	1024	1.93

Note: Based on 1–5 scale where 1 = never and 5 = daily.

Structural Equation Model Results

The descriptive scores and labels for the exogenous and endogenous variables used in the structural equation model are listed in table 3.5. The model's final likelihood estimates, which were obtained using LISREL 8.8, are presented in both table 3.6 and figure 3.2.

The descriptive models fit the data well in that the observed covariances closely match the model-implied covariances. The fit criteria suggest that the empirical data fit this model ($\chi^2 = 12.73$, $df = 14$, $p = 0.54796$, RMSEA [root mean-square error of approximation] = .000). The modification indices show that no effects, currently excluded from the model, would, if added, significantly improve the model fit. We first examine the impact of the two major functions (POLICY, STREET) on all aspects of respondents' policy work. We then examine the impacts of endogenous variables on each other, beginning with role of policy work units (UNIT), then the issue area (PROVINCIAL, NATIONAL, FIRE, and LONG). There are markedly different results, depending on which of the two major functions were undertaken. Those who frequently undertook traditional policy analysis (POLICY) were far more likely to belong to a formal policy-work unit (UNIT) (y = .507). This group was likely to deal with both national issues (NATIONAL) (y = .351) and provincial issues.

(PROVINCIAL) (y = .229). Regional policy staff (POLICY) were less likely to deal with immediate issues (FIRE y = .138). However, the insignificant path from LONG meant that they were not more likely to deal with long-term issues. Those who were more involved in liaison, networking, or programming activities (STREET) were more engaged in dealing with firefighting issues (y = .355) but also, albeit with a weaker effect, involved in long-term issues (LONG) (y = .167). There was a modest positive effect to provincial issues (PROVINCIAL) (y = .210), suggesting that these forms of activity are not oppositional. This "street-level" (STREET) group was prone not to be part of formal policy units, as indicated by a strong negative estimate (y = -.280) to UNIT.

The effects from the POLICY and STREET variables on perceived policy effectiveness (CAPACITY) were insignificant, meaning doing more frequent activity within these two functional areas did not translate into a greater perceived policy capacity. However, membership in a formal policy unit did translate into a greater sense of perceived policy capacity (β = 0.234).

A number of unexpected results countered our initial hypotheses. First, those who examined provincial issues were more also likely also to examine national issues (NATIONAL) (β = 0.271), suggesting that these forms of work are complementary rather than oppositional. Also, those who dealt with national-level issues in the regions had a greater propensity to examine immediate types of issues (FIRE) (β = 0.207) as well as long-term issues (LONG) β = 0.192). However, as expected, those who were actively engaged in "firefighting" (FIRE) agreed more that the government was playing a declining role in decision-making (DECLINE) (β = 0.192) Finally, those who felt strongly about the government's decline (DECLINE) had a very strong sense that regional policy capacity was decreasingly effective (CAPACITY) (β = -0.360).

Table 3.4 Perceived Policy Capacity of Respondents

	Mean	Number
Engagement by my management	3.46	705
Engagement by networks	3.24	705
Engagement by headquarters	2.81	705
Funding	2.45	705
Staffing full-time equivalents (FTEs)	2.49	705
Training	2.63	705
More direct link to the national policy process	2.40	705
Summed policy capacity variable	2.78	705

Note: alpha = .859.

Table 3.5 Variables Used in the LISREL Model

Variable label	Description	Mean score	Standard deviation
	Exogenous variables		
POLICY	Engaged in traditional policy-related work 1 = never; 5 = daily	2.90	.979
STREET	Engaged in liaison, networking, or program delivery (e.g., street bureaucracy) 1 = never; 5 = daily	2.60	.900
	Endogenous variables		
UNIT	A member of formal policy unit 1 = yes; 0 = no		
PROVINCIAL	Examine provincial issues 1 = never; 5 = daily		
NATIONAL	Examine national issues 1 = never; 5 = daily		
FIRE	Deal with immediate issues (e.g., firefighting) 1 = never; 5 = daily		
LONG	Deal with long-term issues 1 = never; 5 = daily		
DECLINE	The role of government is declining in decision-making 1 = strongly disagree; 5 = strongly agree		
CAPACITY	Support for regional policy work (Perceived policy capacity) 1 = strongly disagree; 5 = strongly agree		

Table 3.6 Structural Equation Model Maximum Likelihood Estimates

Direct effect from	To	Effect	t-value	Standardized effect
POLICY				
	UNIT	.247	15.36	.507
	PROVINCIAL	.284	6.84	.229
	NATIONAL	.390	10.77	.351
	FIRE	-.135	-3.66	-.138
	LONG	.074	1.51	.138
	CAPACITY	.032	1.01	.039
STREET				
	UNIT	-.154	-8.21	-.280
	PROVINCIAL	.292	6.06	.210
	NATIONAL	.028	.66	.022
	FIRE	.392	10.04	.355
	LONG	.214	4.48	.167
	CAPACITY	.064	-1.93	.070
UNIT				
	CAPACITY	.391	6.47	.234
PROVINCIAL				
	NATIONAL	.243	8.58	.271
	DECLINE	.047	2.77	.078
NATIONAL				
	FIRE	.183	5.77	.207
	LONG	.196		.191
FIRE				
	DECLINE	.129	5.90	.192
LONG				
	DECLINE	-.010	-.55	-.018
DECLINE				
	CAPACITY	-.442	-12.04	-.360

Figure 3.2 Structural Equation Model

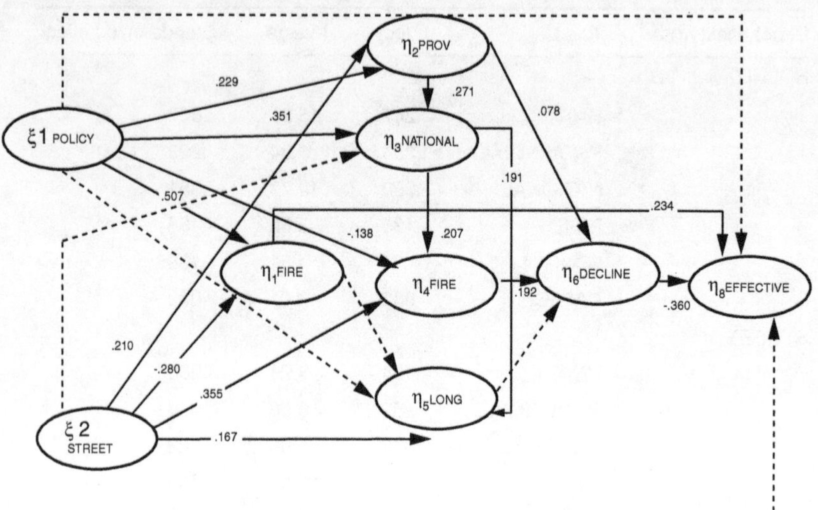

Implications and Conclusion

Governments are preoccupied with averting policy failure. Strong policy capacity is considered to be extremely helpful in this regard. A large body of literature outlining the problems of policy capacity has emerged. However, to help make sense of this relationship, more attention to theoretical frameworks and rigorous quantitative work examining the behavioural characteristics of rank-and-file policy analysts needs to be undertaken. In Canada, to our knowledge, the work of Howlett (2009b) and Wellstead, Stedman, and Lindquist (2009) are the only studies to employ such methods. Given the decentralized nature of policymaking in Canada, we would expect a significant amount of literature dedicated to examining the role of federal government regional policy work. This area of research has gone virtually unnoticed. This chapter employs quantitative methods and a theoretical framework, complete with testable hypotheses, that investigates a virtually unknown phenomenon in Canadian public administration and it asks if regional policy work contributes to federal policy capacity in Canada.

Underlying our specific hypotheses was our suspicion that regional work contributes very little to increasing overall perceived policy capacity within Canada's federal government. Despite well-chronicled trends towards decentralized decision-making, very few regionally based federal government employees are dedicated to policy work (fewer than 1,500) (Wellstead, Stedman, and Lindquist 2009). This number pales compared to what we expect are many thousands who do similar work within the National Capital Region.

This key assumption about the incapacity of regional policy work was supported by a number of hypotheses. We found that the tasks undertaken by the regional respondents fall into two distinct task areas: traditional policy work and street-level bureaucracy-type activities (i.e., undertaking liaison-related activities and program delivery) (Hypothesis 1). Street-level activities represent, in part, the multifaceted nature of policy work uncovered by earlier European studies (Durning and Osuna 1994; Mayer, Bots, and van Daalen 2004). Those regional respondents who did traditional policy-related work undertook fairly rudimentary and the least analytical type of work, most notably collecting information. The descriptive results also indicated that networking with those outside of the federal government, which is an important aspect of "street-level bureaucratic activity," were also underused. However, a high engagement in policy work or street-level bureaucracy did not, as hypothesized, lead to greater levels of perceived policy capacity (Hypotheses 2 and 3).

However, other factors in the respondents' day-to-day activities influenced perceived policy capacity. Hypothesis 4, which compared policy task groups by the geographic and temporal scope, presented mixed results. To our surprise, those involved in policy analysis were not more likely to be engaged in long-term issues. This suggests that these groups – while not focused on long-term analysis – are not sought after for advice when pressing "firefighting" issues emerge. However, a higher level of the street-level activity (program delivery and networking) resulted in a greater involvement in both long-term and immediate ("firefighting") issues. In terms of the geographic focus of policy work, those who frequently engage in traditional policy-related work tended to examine national-level issues but also, albeit to a lesser extent, they examined provincial issues. Thus, they are providing some analysis of localized issues but they remain, as hypothesized, focused on the importance of decisions made in the centre. As expected, those involved in street-level activities remain very locally focused. The geographic and temporal focus of policy work had no direct effect perceived policy

(Hypothesis 5). Along with failed Hypotheses 2 and 3, this means that there are factors beyond what policy-based employees directly do or examine in their work that drive perceived policy capacity.

One factor is the role of formal policy units. These units played a significant role in regional policy work and perceived policy capacity. Highly functioning policy analysts were found in these units (Hypothesis 6). One indicator of perceived strong policy capacity was the presence of these policy units (Hypothesis 7). An important implication from such a finding is that while only a third of the respondents belong to a formal policy unit, the most engaged policy expertise is housed within these units. Although not hypothesized, the model found that highly engaged street-level-based employees were less likely to be part of any policy unit. This suggests the importance and potential benefits of purposeful investments in capacity.

Attitudinal considerations (perceived decline in government activity and policy effectiveness) were the second significant factor. Those who undertake "firefighting" consider the overall decline in the role of government as a whole rather than a specific erosion of policymaking capacity. Also, those undertaking provincial analysis have a greater sense of declining governance. However, the attitude about the larger state of governance in Canada was the most compelling determinant of perceived policy capacity by the respondents (Hypothesis 8). Civil servants who are assumed to be neutral providers of analysis and information are clearly influenced by the growing politicization of policy analysis.

The rapidly changing policy environment described earlier in this chapter suggests that regional policy capacity should receive more serious attention, because it may highlight critical aspects of policy capacity and policy failure in Canada. Future research examining the state of the policy capacity deficit within the federal government should have a regional dimension, with a strong emphasis on the role of the differentiation of traditional and street-level roles, the salience of organized policy units, and the overarching influence of policy and politically driven attitudes and beliefs. With the affordability of web-based online survey tools and the accessibility to policy-based government employees, more quantitative policy capacity research in other jurisdictions will be undertaken. The theoretical framework and empirical approaches introduced in this chapter will provide a useful starting point in future policy capacity research.

ACKNOWLEDGMENT

Funding for this project came from the Treasury Board Secretariat of Canada and Natural Resources Canada. We thank the Alberta and Saskatchewan Federal Councils for their in-kind support and enthusiasm for this project. Research assistance was provided by Sima Joshi-Koop and Andrew Robertshaw. The authors would like to thank the two anonymous referees for their constructive comments and suggestions.

4 Policy Analysis and Policy Work at the Provincial and Territorial Level: Demographics and Description

MICHAEL HOWLETT AND JOSHUA NEWMAN

Introduction: The Supply and Demand for Policy Analysis in Government

Policy analysis has not suffered from a dearth of attention. There are many journals and specialized publications on the subject, and specialized graduate schools operate in many countries, states, and provinces (Geva-May and Maslove 2007; Jann 1991). Anecdotal or case study research has examined many hundreds of examples of policymaking in numerous countries, and many texts describe in detail the analytical techniques expected to be used in public policy analysis (Weimer and Vining 2004) and the nuances of the policymaking processes (Howlett, Ramesh, and Perl 2009). However large-scale empirical works examining the actual "supply and demand" for policy analysis in government are much rarer. And where they do exist, they almost always focus on the "demand" side of the policy advice market, examining the strengths, weaknesses, and other characteristics of knowledge utilization in government (Beyer and Trice 1982; Innvaer et al. 2002; Pollard 1987; Rich 1997; Weiss 1992; Weiss and Bucuvalas 1980; Oh 1997). Work on the behaviour and behavioural characteristics of in-house policy analysts in supplying advice to government, let alone those working outside it, are exceedingly rare (Aberbach and Rockman 1989; Binz-Scharf, Lazer, and Mergel 2008; Bushnell 1991; Nelson 1989; Radin 1992; Thompson and Yessian 1992; Wollmann 1989).

The personal and professional components of the policy advice supply system, along with their internal and external sourcing, are combined in different ratios in different countries and jurisdictions.[1] However, as Halligan (1995) has noted, "The conventional wisdom appears to be that a good advice system should consist of at least three basic elements within government: a stable and reliable in-house advisory service provided by professional public servants; political advice for the minister from a specialized political unit (generally the minister's office); and the availability of at least one third-opinion option from a specialized or central policy unit, which might be one of the main central agencies" (162).

As Halligan (1995) also notes, however, "the emphasis on elements such as the role of political operatives ... depends very much on whether [they] are accorded seniority within the system of government," a practice that is a feature of the U.S. system but "less so in other countries" (162). In other words, the primary component of the policy advice supply system in many countries comprises primarily of what Meltsner (1975) first identified as "bureaucratic policy analysts."[2]

Given the significance of these public sector analysts in the policy advice system of most governments, and the important role they play in efforts to promote "evidence-based" policy analysis (Nutley, Walter, and Davies 2007), studies of their work activities, background, behaviour, and impact should be a staple of the study and evaluation of policy analysis and evidence-based policymaking. However, while there is certainly no lack of studies that urge certain techniques or practices on professional bureaucratic policy analysts (see, for example, Dunn 2004; Patton and Sawicki 1993; MacRae and Whittington 1997), in most countries empirical data on just about every aspect of the actual policy analytical practices followed by bureaucratic policy analysts in government are lacking.[3] And where they exist, these studies have tended to employ partial or unsystematic surveys (Page and Jenkins 2005), or to have followed only anecdotal case study and interview research techniques (Hoppe and Jeliazkova 2006; Noordegraaf 2000; Radin 2000; Rhodes, 't Hart, and Noordegraaf 2007).

Comparative and synthetic studies of the supply and suppliers of policy advice are even rarer (Gregory and Lonti 2008; Halligan 1995; Hawke 1993; Malloy 1989; Mayer, Bots, and van Daalen 2004; Thissen and Twaalfhoven 2001; Wagner and Wollman 1986; Weible 2008). The data are so poor that in most cases it is not clear even if the job classifications and titles typically used by public service commissions to categorize professional policy analysts in government for staffing are accurate or reflect a true sense of what policy analysts actually do on a day-to-day basis. As Colebatch and Radin concluded in their 2006 survey of international practices, much of the basic information required to assess the role played by policy workers in policy processes – evidence-based or otherwise – is lacking: "We need more empirical research on the nature of policy work in specific contexts: how policy workers (and which sort) get a place at the table, how the question is framed, what discourse is accepted as valid, and how this work relates to the outcome at any point in time. What sort of activity do practitioners see as policy work, and what sort of policy workers do they recognize?" (371).

The Sub-National Case: Provincial Policy Analysts in Canada

This general situation is true of most countries. However, as we have seen, even where some little work has been done on the subject, serious gaps remain in our knowledge of bureaucratic policy analysts and their work. And, if information on national or central governments is weak, the number of studies that focus on sub-national units in countries with multi-level governance systems can be counted on one hand (Hird 2005b; Larsen 1980).

This latter point is a substantial issue for the study of evidence-based policymaking and the functioning of policy advice systems and professional policy analysis in many federal countries, such as Brazil, Canada, Mexico, Australia, and the United States, where as many as half of traditional bureaucratic policy analysts may work for sub-national state or provincial governments. In these multi-level systems, sub-national governments control many important areas of policymaking, including health, education, social services, local government, and land, resources, and the environment, and exercise controlling interest over policy development and implementation in these areas (Bache and Flinders 2004; Hooghe and Marks 2001, 2003).

Both these situations are true in Canada, where studies of policy analysts have traditionally focused almost exclusively at the federal level, despite the fact that the provinces control many important areas of social, economic, and political life (Hollander and Prince 1993; Prince 1979; Prince and Chenier 1980; Voyer 2007). This situation began to change only in 2006–7 when studies of non-governmental policy analysts (Dobuzinskis, Howlett, and Laycock 2007) and of regional and central policy analysts employed in the federal civil service appeared (Wellstead et al. 2007; Wellstead, Stedman, and Lindquist 2009). These studies have revealed a set of policy supply practices very different from those suggested by studies of the national level in other jurisdictions, highlighting, for example, significant differences in the attitudes and activities of federal analysts in Ottawa vs those in the regions, and the generally poorer policy capacity of regional organizations (Wellstead et al. 2007; Wellstead, Stedman, and Lindquist 2009).

Regionally based policy analysts working for the federal government, for example, were found to be more commonly engaged in "street-level" advice oriented towards day-to-day firefighting, while the analysts in Ottawa engaged in more "high-level" and long-term strategic planning. The kinds of skills and information sources required for evidence-based policymaking (Howlett 2009b; Riddell 1998; Zussman 2003) were thus found to vary substantially between the two levels of analysts. Such findings have refined and called into question many of the assumptions that went into policy-capacity enhancement undertaken in the country since the publication of the Fellegi Report in 1996, which urged the development of improved analytical capacity throughout the federal government (Anderson 1996; Aucoin and Bakvis 2005; Bakvis 2000; Fellegi 1996; Riddell 2007).

However, while these are important insights, given Canada's very decentralized federal system of government, approximately half of the more than ten thousand bureaucratic policy analysts employed in the country work at the sub-national level in the civil services of the ten provinces and three territories and have been left out of such studies. Information on analytical activities and the supply of policy advice at this level remains extremely rudimentary, generated exclusively from personal reflections and anecdotes of former analysts and managers, or from a small number of single-province interviews or surveys (Hicks and Watson 2007; McArthur 2007; Policy Excellence Initiative 2007; Rasmussen 1999; Singleton 2001a).

In order to correct these problems, in 2008–9 a survey similar to Wellstead et al.'s 2007 federal survey was undertaken of policy analysts working at the provincial and territorial level. This survey was designed specifically to examine the background and training of provincial policy analysts, the types of techniques they employed in their jobs, what they did in their work on a day-by-day basis, and how this related to the needs and prerequisites of evidence-based policymaking. It was intended to assess the extent to which, following Wellstead et al., provincial and territorial analysts like regionally based federal analysts, too, fell into the category of troubleshooters vs planners in their day-to-day activities and orientations. The results of the survey are presented below in the form of a profile of provincial policy analysts, following a brief discussion of the methodology employed in the survey work.

Methods

The survey of policy analysts employed by provincial civil services was carried out in November and December of 2008 using an online commercial software service. It involved the completion of a sixty-four-item survey questionnaire sent to over 4,000 provincial and territorial civil servants situated in all thirteen Canadian provincial and territorial jurisdictions. Mailing lists for the ten provinces and three territories surveyed were compiled wherever possible from publicly available sources such as online government telephone directories, using keyword searches for terms such as *policy analyst* appearing in job titles or descriptions. In some cases additional names were added to lists from hard-copy sources such as government organization manuals. In other cases, lists or additional names were provided by provincial public service commissions, who also checked initial lists for completeness and accuracy.[4] Over 1,600 survey completions were gathered from close to 3,500 valid e-mail addresses for a response rate of 43.3 per cent (see table 4.1). A different (snowball) survey methodology was used in Quebec, so the 130 responses from that province are excluded from the analysis that follows. However a separate analysis of the results from the Quebec survey found a responses similar pattern of to those found in the other twelve provinces and territories (Bernier and Howlett 2009).

The Profile of Provincial Policy Analysts

The data collected from the survey allowed a profile of provincial public servants to be constructed for the first time. Data were divided into five topic areas: demographic characteristics and job experience; education and training; day-to-day duties; and techniques and data employed. Combined, these provide the basis for the first large-scale empirical analysis of the background and activities of sub-national government policy analysts and provide important information concerning their capabilities and capacity to undertake evidence-based policymaking.

DEMOGRAPHICS AND JOB EXPERIENCE

Basic demographic data were collected on provincial policy analysts in terms of characteristics such as gender and age. The responses revealed that provincial analysts are predominantly (57.5 per cent) female and

Table 4.1 Provincial Survey Sample Sizes and Completion Rates

Province	Initial mail list size	Refusals and rejected e-mails	Valid partial completions	Complete	Response rate (%)
BC	513	51	30	194	48.5
Alberta	368	23	8	112	34.8
Saskatchewan	246	27	13	80	42.4
Manitoba	161	20	6	98	73.7
Ontario	1613	162	52	557	41.9
Quebec†	250	0	44	86	52.0
New Brunswick	162	15	4	62	44.9
Nova Scotia	181	20	15	83	44.1
PEI	27	6	1	4	23.8
Newfoundland	139	24	16	55	61.7
Yukon	75	8	6	58	95.5
NWT	80	2	2	41	55.1
Nunavut	41	8	2	13	45.4
TOTAL (excluding Quebec)	3856	366	155	1357	43.3

† Snowball sample methodology – data excluded from totals and from subsequent tables.

fairly young, in that more than 70 per cent are under fifty years of age and more than 40 per cent under forty years old. By comparison, only 61.3 per cent federal policy analysts are under the age of fifty and are majority male (51.9 per cent), reflecting the hiring patterns and demographics of an earlier era of recruitment and hiring (Wellstead, Stedman, and Lindquist 2009). Additional questions confirmed that provincial analysts have tended to come to their present career path and positions fairly recently, as over 40 per cent of provincial analysts had been involved in professional policy analytical activities for five years or less (table 4.2).

Almost 60 per cent had also been in their present organizations for less than five years, including 14 per cent for less than one year. This contrasts sharply with the federal situation described by Wellstead, Stedman, and Lindquist (2009), where a sizeable number (28.4 per cent) had been in their positions for over twenty years. Finally, these analysts

Table 4.2 Length of Employment

Years	Employed as a professional policy analyst		Employed in present organization		Expected to remain in present position	
	Frequency	%	Frequency	%	Frequency	%
No response	31	2.1	21	1.4	38	2.5
0–1 years	78	5.2	214	14.2	179	11.8
1–5 years	537	35.5	652	43.1	809	53.5
6–9 years	297	19.6	229	15.1	214	14.2
10–14 years	191	12.6	119	7.9	157	10.4
15–20 years	181	12.0	126	8.3	67	4.4
20 or more	197	13.0	151	10.0	48	3.2
Total	1512	100.0	1512	100.0	1512	100.0

also do not expect to stay long in their current positions, with two-thirds expecting to stay less than five additional years.

This pattern accords closely with Meltsner's (1975, 117) observation that the typical policy analyst believes he or she is upwardly mobile and "believes he [*sic*] is a short-timer, so he does not worry about maintaining the agency or conserving its jurisdiction," and instead is able to be more "problem-focused" in orientation and approach. However, it also suggests that unlike their federal counterparts, provincial and territorial analysts lack job experience and, combined with their high level of mobility, may not be able to develop and bring substantial expertise, derived from the job, to the consideration of policy problems.

EDUCATION AND TRAINING

A second set of questions examined the education and training of provincial analysts to see what kinds of pre-occupationally derived expertise and knowledge they could mobilize in their work. Table 4.3 highlights the generally very high level of formal education attained by this group of civil servants, with 56 per cent having attained at least some graduate or professional education, and fully 90 per cent attaining college or university-level credentials. This bodes well for evidence-based policymaking, except that, despite their often working in policy areas based in natural resources and science, provincial analysts' study

Table 4.3 Education and Degree Subject Area

	Frequency	%
Level of education		
No response	120	7.9
High school	30	2.0
College or technical	69	4.6
University	448	29.6
Graduate or professional	845	55.9
Total	1512	100.0
Degree subject area		
Business management	214	14.2
Education	72	4.8
Engineering	32	2.1
Humanities or fine arts	71	4.7
Law	98	6.5
Natural sciences	106	7.0
Planning	70	4.6
Public administration	150	9.9
Political science	242	16.0
Economics	177	11.7
Sociology	118	7.8
Geography	97	6.4
Other social sciences	155	10.3
History	87	5.8
English	69	4.6
Other arts or humanities	34	2.2
Public policy	100	6.6
Medicine	6	0.4
Other health sciences	45	3.0
Computing science	24	1.6
Languages or linguistics	31	2.1
Communications or journalism	36	2.4
Environmental studies	98	6.5
Natural resource management	51	3.4

areas of expertise are heavily oriented (about 80 per cent) towards the social sciences.

The five leading degree fields were political science with 16.0 per cent, followed by business management with 14.2 per cent, economics with 11.7 per cent, public administration with 9.9 per cent, and sociology with 7.8 per cent. These five fields accounted for about 60 per cent of degrees (allowing for multiple degrees) conferred, while a wide range of other social science, law, and humanities accounted for another 40 per cent of credentials.

Health sciences, computing science, engineering, and natural science degrees made up only 14.1 per cent of credentials held. These findings suggest the predominance of legal and process-related expertise among provincial and territorial policy workers and a shortage of substantive expertise in high-profile policy problem areas. However, this pattern is typical in Canada and resembles the pattern found by Wellstead et al. (2007) at the federal level.

Another source of expertise and knowledge, of course, is previous work experience. As table 4.4 shows, provincial analysts have varied backgrounds but tend to be recruited directly from academic institutions (22 per cent) or to have come up through their own provincial government, with 44 per cent citing previous work experience in this area. Fewer than 13 per cent claim experience in the federal government and 10 per cent in another provincial government. Another 11 per cent cite experience at the municipal level and 5 per cent experience in another country. While more than 60 per cent cite experience outside government, with 26 per cent in the not-for-profit sector, only 17 per cent cite private sector experience. This is a much lower figure for private sector experience than is found at the federal level, where nearly 40 per cent of federal analysts cite previous private sector employment (Wellstead et al., 2007). In general, then, provincial and territorial analysts are likely to have the most knowledge of their own government's policies and processes and are less likely to have substantial knowledge of governmental or non-governmental organizations. As Page and Jenkins (2005) suggested, this fits the pattern of analysts being internal "process-related" experts rather than having a great deal of "substantive" expertise that they can devote to the collection and presentation of significant amounts of "evidence" in policymaking.

It is also telling that, regardless of their work experience and academic background, provincial and territorial analysts tend to have had little formal training in technical policy analysis, either in their

Table 4.4 Previous Work Experience

	Frequency	%
Academia	332	22.0
Municipal government department or agency	167	11.0
Aboriginal government (Yukon)	7	0.5
Not-for-profit sector	394	26.1
Private sector	253	16.7
Other department or agency in your current province	668	44.2
Department or agency in another provincial government	146	9.7
Federal government	195	12.9
Department or agency in another country	82	5.4

post-secondary educational career or in post-employment training. As table 4.5 shows, nearly 40 per cent of analysts never took a single policy-specific course at the post-secondary level, and close to 70 per cent have taken two or fewer policy-related courses. Moreover, close to 55 per cent of analysts never completed any post-secondary courses dealing specifically with formal policy analysis or evaluation. Again, this is unlike the federal situation, where rates of formal policy training are higher. Another possible source of training, of course, is internal, government-provided training; however, roughly the same percentage of provincial analysts have also never completed any formal internal governmental training on these subjects. And, as table 4.6 reveals, by far the most common form of post-employment training is attendance at policy-related conferences, workshops, or forums. Only 10 per cent cited completion of policy courses with government-run or sponsored training institutes, while another 20 per cent cited completion of policy-relevant courses at a university or college. The former figure, in particular, is much lower than at the federal level.

DAY-TO-DAY DUTIES

What do these sub-national analysts do in their day-to-day jobs? First, they tend to work in small groups, as almost 90 per cent work in formal policy units. This is in keeping with the recommendations of many government reports that analysts should be clustered rather than separated or isolated in departments (Fellegi 1996; Hawke 1993; State Services Commission 1999). As for the activities carried out in these

Table 4.5 Policy Courses and Training

	Frequency	%
Policy-specific courses at the post-secondary level		
No response	156	10.32
0	604	39.95
1	141	9.33
2	142	9.39
3 or more	469	31.02
Total	1512	100.00
Policy analysis courses at the post-secondary level		
No response	139	9.19
Yes	545	36.04
No	828	54.76
Total	1512	100.00
Formal internal training courses		
No response	132	8.7
Yes	556	36.8
No	824	54.5
Total	1512	100.5

units, most analysts are still quite isolated, in that policy units are located overwhelmingly in the provincial capital, with 78 per cent of respondents indicating a very high frequency of daily activities in the capital (see table 4.7). Eighty per cent of analysts report no daily interactions on issues related to international government, 60 per cent few or infrequent interactions with local governments, and 50 per cent infrequent interactions with the federal or other provincial or territorial governments. Fifty-six per cent, however, report very frequent, daily, or weekly interactions with other ministries within their own government. Again, these patterns are different from those found at the federal level, where interactions at the international, intergovernmental, and intra-governmental levels are much higher (Wellstead et al. 2007).

These units are also very small at this level of government. As table 4.8 shows, almost 65 per cent of analysts work in units of fewer than ten employees and about 30 per cent in units of fewer than five

Table 4.6 Sources of Post-Employment Training

	Frequency	%
Attended policy-related conferences	941	62.2
Attended policy workshops or forums	1125	74.4
Completed public administration, politic science, economics, or other policy-relevant courses at a university or college	320	21.2
Completed policy courses with the Canada School of Public Service or any other government-run or government-sponsored training institute	149	9.9

Table 4.7 Location of Policy Work

	In provincial capital		Within own government government	
	Frequency	%	Frequency	%
No response	23	1.51	29	1.92
Daily	1186	78.44	338	22.35
Weekly	39	2.58	527	34.85
Monthly	66	4.37	318	21.03
Quarterly	81	5.36	156	10.32
Annually	59	3.90	70	4.63
Never	58	3.84	74	4.89
Total	1512	100.00	1512	100.00

full-time equivalent employees. And, as table 4.8 also shows, almost 55 per cent of these units have fewer than five people actually working on policy issues. As for the nature of the issues upon which they work, about 40 per cent of provincial and territorial analysts report fairly frequently working on issues that are ongoing for more than a year, slightly fewer than the proportion that report frequently working on issues that are ongoing for between six and twelve months and between one and six months. Almost 60 per cent, however, report frequently working on issues that can be resolved in less than a month, while 66 per cent report working on issues and problems that demand immediate attention (i.e., "firefighting") (see table 4.9). Again, this is a higher level than

Table 4.8 Number of Full-Time Equivalent Employees

	In work unit		In work unit and working on policy issues	
	Frequency	%	Frequency	%
FTEs				
No response	32	2.12	33	2.18
1–5	448	29.63	787	52.05
6–10	500	33.07	458	30.29
11–20	341	22.55	172	11.38
21–50	157	10.38	48	3.17
> 50	34	2.25	14	0.93
Total	1512	100.00	1512	100.00

Table 4.9 Frequency of Work on Short-Term Issues

	Frequency	%
No response	169	11.18
Daily	361	23.88
Weekly	535	35.38
Monthly	220	14.55
Quarterly	120	7.94
Annually	56	3.70
Never	51	3.37
Total	1512	100.00

at the national level, although similar to that of federal analysts working in the regions (Wellstead Stedman, and Lindquist 2009).

This finding about the prevalence of short-term work at this level of government is one that is often decried in the literature on the subject (Gregory and Lonti 2008) but can also be considered to be a primary raison d'être of the policy bureaucracy. As Hawke (1993, 64) put it, "Fire-fighting is part of the job of any manager and is especially prominent in the public service because of the pressures on ministers. It is worth remembering that a key reason for having departmental policy advice agencies rather than distinct contracts for each piece of policy development is the desirability of immediate and unplanned access to informed advice."

Nevertheless, when coupled with a lack of substantive knowledge of the subject areas in which they are working, their small numbers, and their lack of formal training in policy analytical techniques, it suggests that provincial and territorial analysts may not have the capacity required to practise a high level of evidence-based policy analysis and policymaking.

Techniques and Data Employed

This view is reinforced by the answers that provincial and territorial analysts provided about what analytical techniques they employed and with what information sources. First it is important to note that provincial policy analysts think of their jobs as involving the development of analytical services in order to provide advice (analysis) to governments. As table 4.10 shows, 82 per cent of analysts describe their role as either "analysis" or "advice provision." Only 46 per cent think of themselves as "researchers," slightly more than the percentage who think of themselves as "coordinators." These findings are very similar to those reported by Radin (1992) in her study of role descriptions found in the U.S. Department of Health and Human Services, and highlight the existence of several general types of analysts working at this level: researcher/analysts, evaluators, coordinators, and managers, with the last three groups each equal to about half the size of the cohort of researcher/analysts. This structure is borne out by the general kinds of tasks conducted at this level, with less-formal duties such as environmental scans and issue-tracking outweighing more technical financial or legal tasks, and with almost all analysts involved in the development of ministerial briefing notes that outline options and provide advice to governments (see table 4.11). The primary analytical techniques used in these activities are more informal than formal. Eighty-three per cent of respondents (table 4.12) claimed to be involved in "brainstorming," followed by about 70 per cent in "consultation" and 60 per cent in using "checklists."

Cost-benefit analysis is the only formal technique to attain use by over 50 per cent of respondents, only slightly higher than other less-formal techniques such as expert elicitation (48 per cent) and scenario analysis (50 per cent). While this pattern goes against the instructions and admonitions of many textbooks, it is in keeping with the findings of many utilization studies that have found a distinct preference for the

Table 4.10 Description of Policy Role(s)

	Frequency	%
Adviser	1031	68.2
Analyst	1134	75.0
Communications officer	189	12.5
Coordinator	544	36.0
Director	164	10.8
Evaluator	352	23.3
Liaison officer	245	16.2
Manager	278	18.4
Planner	426	28.2
Researcher	737	48.7
Public participation expert	123	8.1
Program analyst	401	26.5
Program manager	158	10.4

Table 4.11 General Policy Tasks Undertaken

	Frequency	%
Department or agency planning	704	46.6
Environmental scans/issue tracking	1030	68.1
Legal analysis	388	25.7
Preparing budget/Treasury Board submissions	608	40.2
Ministerial briefing	1077	71.2
Networking	1000	66.1
Preparing briefing notes or position papers	1302	86.1
Providing options on issues	1269	83.9
Undertaking research and analysis	1304	86.2
Providing advice	1289	85.3

Table 4.12 Specific Analytical Technique(s) Used

	Frequency	%
Brainstorming	1248	82.5
Consultation exercises	1021	67.5
Focus groups	571	37.8
Free-form gaming or other policy exercises	93	6.2
Problem-mapping	470	31.1
Check lists	908	60.1
Decision/probability trees	347	22.9
Expert judgments and elicitation	723	47.8
Development of sophisticated modelling tools	169	11.2
Markov chain modelling	12	0.8
Monte Carlo techniques	23	1.5
Process influence or social network diagrams	122	8.1
Scenario analysis	760	50.3
Cost-effectiveness analysis	630	41.7
Cost-benefit analysis	810	53.6
Environmental impact assessment	418	27.6
Financial impact analysis	579	38.3
Preference scaling	106	7.0
Risk analysis	882	58.3
Robustness or sensitivity analysis	241	15.9

use of "simple" tools vs complex ones by both the producers and consumers of policy analysis (Nilsson et al. 2008; Sabatier 1978). It also suggests, again, that analysts fall into several distinct types that favour the use of specific analytical techniques, but that the most commonly used techniques at this level of government are less-formal, "subjective" analytical techniques involved in the development of briefing notes and papers.

Conclusion

Empirical research into the sub-national level in the Canadian case presented here suggests that, like at the regional level in the federal government, many more analysts fall into the category of short-term, project-oriented "troubleshooters" than the long-term strategic "planners" that textbook accounts have thought them to be, as the result of incorrect inferences drawn from studies of national officials in other countries. Provincial and territorial analysts, like their federal counterparts, are highly educated, relatively young, and mobile. But they do not tend to have substantial formal training in policy analysis and work mainly in small units deeply embedded in provincial and territorial ministries in the provincial or territorial capital. They lack substantive knowledge of the areas in which they work and of formal policy analytical techniques and tend to bring only process-related knowledge to the table. They also tend to work on a relatively small number of issue areas, often on a "firefighting" basis, and, like their federal counterparts in the regions, a large percentage of analysts can be thought of as a kind of cadre of internal experts who can be brought into problem areas as a free-floating "brain trust" of internal "consultants" available to work on a wide range of pressing and troubling policy issues (Weiss 1991).

In terms of the six styles of policy analysis identified by Mayer, Bots, and van Daalen (2004) in their comparative study of policy analytical styles, the predominant sets of analysts identified in the sub-national analysis reported above can be thought of as working in an interactive "client-advice" style somewhat removed from both the traditional "rational" style promoted by textbook and policy schools (Adams 2004; Baehr 1981; Banfield 1977; Lindblom and Cohen 1979; Shulock 1999). Their short-term orientation, relative inexperience, higher levels of job mobility, lack of private-sector experience, and lack of training in formal policy analytical techniques sets them apart from their national counterparts and has significant implications for their ability to influence policy deliberations in the direction of enhanced evidence-based policymaking.

Additional new sets of comparative studies based on large-scale surveys at both the national and sub-national levels, such as the Canadian ones reported here, are needed to bring more light to this topic. More accurate assessments of policy analytical activities in government, especially those governments operating within multi-level governance frameworks, are needed to inform any moves expected to enhance the operation of this important component of policy advice systems through the promotion of evidence-based policymaking (Colebatch 2005).

However, even as they stand, these findings from the Canadian case are important not only to critics and theorists outside of government institutions who wish to better understand the operation and functioning of evidence-based and other kinds of policy advice systems, and especially these systems' professional bureaucratic component (e.g., Koliba and Gajda 2009; Kothari, MacLean, and Edwards 2009), but also to those inside the system who wish to better assess and evaluate such activities in order to improve training and recruitment practices, enhance analytical capacity (Howlett 2009b; O'Connor, Roos, and Vickers-Willis 2007; Preskill and Boyle 2008) and, ultimately, improve analysis and policy outcomes (ANAO 2001; Di Francesco 1999, 2000; Mintrom 2003; Nicholson 1997; Policy Excellence Initiative 2007; State Services Commission 1999).

NOTES

1 The policy advice system that supplies information to governments is, of course, very complex and includes many sources of information, from friends to spouses and close advisers (Meltsner 1990). However, alongside personal opinion and experience there is a more formal policy advice system that purports to deliver knowledge and expertise to governments. This supply network is composed of sources within government – such as professional policy analysts employed in departments and agencies and political advisers attached to ministers' offices and central agencies – and external to government, ranging from private sector consultants to experts in think tanks, universities, political parties, and elsewhere (Boston et al. 1996).

2 Very little is known about the nature of non-governmental policy analysis supplied through think tanks, political parties, and especially the growing legion of consultants who work for governments in the "invisible public service" (Speers 2007). On think tanks, business associations, political parties, and the press in Canada, see Abelson (2007), Stritch (2007), Cross (2007), Murray (2007).

3 This situation has led many observers both inside and outside government to decry the lack of even such basic data as how many policy analysts there are in government, working on what subjects, and with what techniques (Bakvis 1997; Behm, Bennington, and Cummane 2000; Hunn 1994; State Services Commission 1999, 2001; Uhr and Mackay 1996; Waller 1992, 1996; Weller and Stevens 1998). In many cases observers have continued to rely on only one or two quite dated works in justifying their observations and conclusions, especially the early work of Meltsner (1975,

1976) and Durning and Osuna (1994). In Meltsner's case, his observations remain astute over thirty years later, but were based on 116 interviews he conducted in the United States in 1970–1 (Meltsner 1975, 14). While there are some data in these older studies, they covered only a relatively small number of countries, mainly the United States (Meltsner 1976; Durning and Osuna 1994; Radin 2000). More recent studies on "policy supply" have looked at the United Kingdom (Page and Jenkins 2005), Australia (Weller and Stevens 1998); New Zealand (Boston et al. 1996); the Netherlands (Hoppe and Jeliazkova 2006), France (Rochet 2004), and Germany (Fleischer 2009), but in most jurisdictions the answers to basic questions, including how many people are in these positions or what they do, remain unknown.

4 Provincial public service lists often included political appointees who had been left off public lists. However, in most cases public lists and internal lists were very close in size and coverage, with about an overlap rate of 80 per cent or higher. The lists revealed a roughly proportional per-capita pattern of the size of the policy analytical community in Canadian provincial governments, with 1,800–2,000 individuals in Ontario, 400–500 in British Columbia, and about 100 in the smallest jurisdictions. The total number of policy analysts at the provincial and territorial level therefore is probably about 5,200 (3,000 in Quebec and Ontario; 1,000 in BC and Alberta; 500 in Saskatchewan and Manitoba; 400 in the Atlantic provinces, and 300 in the territories). It is expected that this number would be matched by the federal government (Wellstead having identified about 1,300 operating outside Ottawa, the remaining 4,000 being located in the National Capital Region), bringing the total number of policy analysts actually employed in Canada to around 11,000. This is roughly the same per capita ratio as reported by Boston et al. (1996) in New Zealand, where of 35,000 core civil servants in a country of 3.6 million people at the time, 1,450 person-years were devoted to the provision of advice to departments and ministries in 1993 (124).

5 The Policy Analytical Capacity of the Government of Quebec: Results from a Survey of Officials

LUC BERNIER AND MICHAEL HOWLETT

In the 1980s and 1990s, New Public Management reforms took their spirit from the idea that improved service delivery to the population was necessary. Certain authors like Metcalfe underlined the fact that, at the time, the state often neglected management and favoured the provision of "strategic" policy advice. The state was often seen to be interested in policy and not management. After decades of research on efficiency, however, have we pushed too far in the other direction? Do public administrations have the capacity to formulate effective public policies? Do those charged with developing policy have adequate training to do so? This chapter presents the Quebec portion of a set of pan-Canadian surveys on policy capacity in governments. It completes the analysis by presenting the results obtained by a poll of Quebec officials. We are interested, more precisely, in understanding the university education and later training received by officials who participate in the creation and formulation of public policies. In an epoch where financial pressures on governments limit their ability to develop new policies and where policies often must be adapted to cover new challenges, whether officials have the training, time, and resources necessary to develop policy is a key question.

Unfortunately, it is not possible to know exactly how many Quebec officials work on the development of public policy or to identify policy workers in Quebec government from publicly available sources, as the method used to classify jobs does not allow this. To overcome these problems, we first sent our survey to the Secrétariat du Conseil du Trésor, who responded that they too did not have a list allowing the identification of officials who worked in this area. We then worked with members of research and intelligence units with relative success.

Depending on the minister, members of such units could be responsible for policy, but they could also work in communications. We also wrote to all deputy ministers, who relayed our request to their subordinates. In the end we had eighty-six persons completing the survey and forty-four partial completions. Three hundred and twenty-six people visited the survey website. This can't be described as a scientific survey sample in the classical sense, but the results are very interesting. They permit the comparison of the situation in Quebec with results already published on the other Canadian governments.

The presentation of results below follows the order of the questions in the survey itself. As is shown in table 5.1 the respondents to the survey were unequally divided across ministries. It is interesting in a qualitative sense to determine how our request was treated, and that allows for the contextualization of the responses. One official of the Treasury Board Secretariat told us by e-mail that it was impossible to respond to the questionnaire. In another e-mail, another at the Ministry of Revenue told us that he did not make public policy. These varied interpretations of what constitutes public policy are interesting in themselves. The classic definition of public policy given by Thomas Dye is that it is what a government decides to do or not to do about a problem brought to its attention. In this sense all the ministers and organizations that generated responses make public policy, even the Treasury Board Secretariat where public service human resources policy is decided, such as, for example, how to develop exams in which applicants from ethnic communities can become officials.

As is shown in table 5.1, no one in the Executive Council responded to the poll, but a respondent who worked on the aboriginal policy file and eleven on intergovernmental relations can be thought of as operating at the centre, rather than, for example, in ministries like agriculture. We present our findings below and then comment on them in the conclusion.

Who Is Involved with Public Policymaking and Where?

The officials and functionaries who responded are classified in table 5.2. Certain officials in what is referred to as "class 4" can be described as senior officials. Many experts said they were at the "eighteenth level." The second column in table 5.2 sets out the original responses obtained and the third our reclassification. Among those who answered this question, there were forty-nine professionals and eighteen officials.

Table 5.1 In Which Ministry Do You Work?

Ministry	Number
Municipal Affairs, Regions, and Land Occupancy	1
Employment and Social Solidarity	8
Family and Seniors Affairs	5
Finance	1
Justice	1
Agriculture and Fisheries	15
Economic Development, Innovation, and Export Trade	1
Immigration and Cultural Communities	1
Quebec Health Insurance Board	1
International Relations	3
Natural Resources	1
Revenue	1
Health and Social Services	2
Treasury Board Secretariat	5
Public Security	1
Quebec Housing Corporation	1
Tourism	3
Transport	33
Total	84

Seventy-two men and thirty-six women responded to the survey, or, respectively, 67 and 33 per cent of respondents.

These officials all worked in Quebec, except one who was based in Manitoba. Seventy-five per cent had never worked outside the country, 54 per cent never outside the province. Eighty-five per cent worked daily in the capital and 13 per cent in Montreal. Between 80 and 90 per cent never went to a region other than Montreal.

Contrary to the situation with service delivery, then, public policy work is done at the centre. However, 65 per cent of respondents dealt with the federal government at least once a year and 24 per cent monthly. As for the other provincial governments, 49 per cent dealt with them annually and 11 per cent monthly. Two hundred and thirty-five

Table 5.2 Job Classifications

Classification levels	Respondents' choice	Reclassified
Socio-economic planning officer/researcher	9	49
Professional	9	
Senior professional	5	
Distinguished professional	3	18
Expert adviser or professional expert	22	
Engineer	1	
Director	5	
Manager class 4	7	
Manager class 3	3	
Director-general	1	
Manager level 2	1	
Executive	1	
Total	67	

respondents had contacts with foreign governments. And 51 per cent took part in interministerial or intergovernmental committees.

Not all of these respondents were young: 43 per cent were over fifty-one years of age. Only 29 per cent were younger than forty. Eighty-four per cent worked in a unit charged with developing public policy. They also had experience: 64 per cent had worked on policy issues for at least five years and 42 per cent for more than ten years. They worked in all sectors in which the Quebec government was involved. Ninety-two per cent were employed full-time.

They were quite stable in their organizational locations: 60 per cent having worked six years or more in their existing agency while 43 per cent anticipated still working there in six years or more. They did not think the retirement situation would much affect their units in future years. These units were small: 78 per cent counting ten employees or fewer.

The Nature of Policy Formulation Work

The terms *adviser* or *analyst* best describe most policy formulation work. In third place are tasks of *co-ordinator*, then *planner* and *director*. Many tasks are undertaken: planning, preparing ministerial documents, conducting research and analysis, preparing budgets, and proposing policy options. In short, formulation is a varied task. These tasks also vary in frequency. It is relatively rare for activities to be undertaken daily or weekly. Twelve per cent collect data every week, but none negotiates every week with central organizations. It is more surprising to find that 35 per cent never interact with program managers, and 41 per cent never deal with policy implementation. Formulation and policy management thus appear to be quite different activities. Only 30 per cent of program managers undertake these two activities. About 20 per cent undertake a range of tasks linked to policy formulation at least once per year. More conceptual tasks like research, information collection, and evaluation are undertaken by close to 30 per cent at least once a month and, for an equal number, weekly.

Fifty-five per cent never take part in consultations with the public and 32 per cent only once per year. This percentage falls to 18 per cent for those who interact with interest groups. Analysts also spend more time with subordinates or superiors: 64 per cent create briefs with their subordinates at least monthly, and 52 per cent with their superiors. They also inform decision-makers at least once a month in 64 per cent of cases. Analysts also work less on evaluation: 29 per cent indicated they had never undertaken an outcome evaluation, while 33 per cent never evaluated a policy process. Forty-one per cent and 43 per cent, respectively, do so only once per year.

Among the available techniques, brainstorming (76 per cent of respondents), expert consultations (70 per cent), and scenario analysis (73 per cent) are the most popular, followed by consultation exercises (61 per cent) and stakeholder consultations (55 per cent). Forty-seven per cent undertake cost-benefit analysis and 30 per cent risk analyses. Markov chain and Monte Carlo techniques were not used.

The tasks that most concerned respondents were policy analyses (69 per cent), elaboration of policy (67 per cent), decision-making (52 per cent), interest group consultations (56 per cent), formulation of options (49 per cent), editing reports (43 per cent), presenting them (37 per cent), and environmental assessments (34 per cent). Questions linked to human resources were the least cited.

The obstacles that analysts faced in policy formulation were principally a short-term work orientation (50 per cent), inadequate resources (35 per cent), and inadequate time (32 per cent). After that were listed insufficient delegation from the centre (20 per cent), lack of support from the minister (19 per cent), and the fact that the centre ignored their expertise (18 per cent).

Recruitment and Training

Among Quebec officials who had experience in formulating policies, only 7 per cent had worked for the federal government, 7 per cent for another provincial government, and 5 per cent for another country. Twenty-seven per cent had worked for a non-profit and 19 per cent in the university sector. Fifty-eight per cent had worked in another government ministry, indicating a high level of mobility.

These individuals were trained in universities: 57 per cent completed a bachelor's degree and 41 per cent a graduate degree. For those who would like to know in what field, it was quite varied: 15 per cent in management, 11 per cent in public administration, 16 per cent in political science, 18 per cent in economics, 14 per cent in geography, and 8 per cent in law. Seventy one per cent had never taken a university course in policy formulation and 73 per cent never one in policy analysis. Forty-seven per cent had taken some in-house training, 50 per cent took part in workshops, and 71 per cent participated in conferences. Sixty-eight per cent of officials judged that additional professional training in policy would be useful. The subjects they felt would be most useful were an introduction to policymaking, using evidence-based policymaking, and internal and external policy formulation. They were clearly less interested in learning about report-writing and financial management.

The Nature of Work

Daily tasks that most occupied analysts were at the provincial level, as the international level remained a lower priority. Pan-Canadian issues also occupied little of their time. Government priorities structured more of their time than public concerns. If daily and weekly responses are combined in order to best understand the core concerns of analysts' work, government priorities were cited as most important by 43 per cent of responses, versus only 11 per cent for public pressures and 1 per cent for the results of public consultations. Moreover, 34 per cent of issues required coordination with headquarters against 18 per cent with other government organizations. Policy-relevant information was not immediately available for 45 per cent of the issues dealt with at least weekly. Fifty-eight per cent of issues dealt with weekly or daily did not have a simple solution.

Fifty-seven per cent of respondents said they had to respond to emergencies every day or every week. Fifty-four per cent said they were occupied at least weekly with tasks that could be resolved in less than a month. Tasks that took longer to resolve were rare.

Respondents were asked by whom they were consulted. The response was, above all, by the minister's office, rarely by central agencies, and only a few by other ministries. The promotion of policy analysis was diffused through the ministry; most felt that analytical quality had changed little over the years and possibly in the direction of a slight improvement, despite available resources having diminished over the past five years for the majority of respondents.

When we asked what they thought of the engagement of their minister in policy formulation, they were very positive, but weaker in terms of financial support and, above all, the number of employees available was found to be hardly acceptable. They also estimated that training was insufficient in the processes of policy formulation. Overall they judged the analytical capacity of their ministry as "weakly favourable."

Perspectives on the Formulation Process

Quebec officials agreed with the idea that the short term trumps the long term in priority. They estimated that they rarely consulted the public in their formulation work, but took more account of political aspects. They also stated that policy analytical capacity had not improved and that it required more interaction with other governments. The work required greater technical expertise. They considered policy analytical capacity an internal governmental matter and not an external one, even taking into account the increased influence of interest groups. They also felt central agencies should play a greater role in coordination. In response to one question on the subject, a strong majority felt that evidence was required to support policy formulation.

On the other hand, respondents were also of the opinion that greater involvement of the public would make policies more effective – such as by integrating interest groups and/or working in networks with other government ministries and non-governmental organizations. They felt that a reduction in the size of government would have little impact on policy effectiveness but that more control from the minister's office would help. This was also true of access to more information and relevant facts – through the creation of policy units or the support for more personnel.

According to 25 per cent of the sample, the greatest challenge to be overcome by managers to improve analytical activities concerned the lack of time and resources needed to develop quality analyses. The second challenge mentioned by 9 per cent was the focus on the short term, and the third – mentioned by 7 per cent – was the lack of effective multi-sectoral policymaking and insufficient information sharing. Inadequate training was mentioned by 6 per cent.

Evidence-Based Policymaking

Seventy-four per cent of officials who responded to the survey said that the use of evidence-based policymaking was not an idea with which they were familiar. Further analysis of responses in this area about how evidence is used is thus difficult to interpret. While evidence-based methods were little known, officials were favourable to using quality information to guide their work. When necessary, they also frequently accessed government experts, non-governmental experts less frequently, and independent experts the least. Officials often used diverse information sources, principally personal experience, but also university research and scientific research or that provided by industry or by other governments. The proof they preferred for policy formulation was research on best practices and consultations with interested parties. In decision-making, consultations with interested parties was key, rather than consultations with ministries or headquarters. In policy implementation, again it was consultations with interested parties, research results, and best practices research that were central. As for policy evaluations, information on policy outcomes counted above all, and again consultations with interested parties as well as national and international studies.

Conclusion

The first conclusion to note relates to the difficulties encountered simply in identifying who deals with public policy in the Quebec government. This is a matter of how the management of public service personnel is conducted. The portrait of who does what in government is often information collected by unions in preparation for collective bargaining. Why doesn't the state do this? It seems to us that this kind of management information is very useful. Future staffing needs in this area could be better defined as a result.

Another more methodological element to consider is the possibility of excluding the Ministry of Transport from the survey results. It is surprising that so many people who completed the survey came from that one department. Another element to take into account is the translation of the survey instrument. The translation was faithful to the spirit of the English-language survey in order to preserve comparability, but some words in French were too open to interpretation by respondents, such as use of the word *national*.

Because the number of respondents was limited, we also did not examine several issues that could have been addressed with a larger response rate. It would be interesting to know if, for example, the younger officials have experience in the non-profit sector because employment opportunities were more limited upon their arrival on the labour market. Always a function of age, are training levels higher among younger people? These data, and others, could then also be linked to other research using the same survey in order to extract more meaning. At first glance, there are no contradictions in the survey. The answers are consistent.

The weak links between government officials responsible for policymaking and the public, however, is a surprise. Should we view Quebec policymaking as occurring in a vacuum? This represents an intriguing finding from this survey – considering the weak interaction that seems to exist between the centre and the direction of public policy – with the centre defined as central agencies or branches of ministries. Policies are developed in specialized units concentrated in Quebec City by officials relatively advanced in their career, whether managers or professionals. They have rarely been trained specifically in policy analysis at the university. The survey provides a portrait of a government weakly organized to articulate public policy, but it operates within the context of numerous other policy organizations. The survey would have to be repeated within government and non-governmental organizations, and thus require substantial resources, in order to generate a clearer picture of policy work and policy workers in Quebec and in general. It is clear from this survey, though, that the resources devoted to public policy in government are limited, the ability to think long term is rare, and therefore the ability to develop public policy is often deficient.

In summarizing the views collected, it should be possible for the government of Quebec to do better in public policy. Beyond the fact that resources are scarce, it should be possible to develop a longer-term perspective. We can also infer from these data that the time available to deal with public policy is often too limited. The survey results also indicate that the government of Quebec, like other provincial governments, is better organized to provide services than to develop policy. The data collected in the Quebec case confirms the situation that exists elsewhere in Canada on the sporadic nature of the attention given to public policies and their often more reactive than planned nature (Howlett 2009, 11). In this sense, the New Public Management has done its work.

6 Differences in Federal and Provincial Policy Analysis

MICHAEL HOWLETT AND ADAM WELLSTEAD

Introduction: Gaps in Knowledge of Policy Work in Multi-Level States

Despite having been a matter of academic attention for over half a century, the working world of policy analysts is largely unknown, as Colebatch and Radin argued in their 2006 survey of comparative policy analysis. Many studies rely on anecdotal case studies and interview research (Radin 2000; Hoppe and Jeliazkova 2006; Colebatch, Hoppe, and Noordegraaf 2011; Noordegraaf 2010), which, while informative and useful for theory building, raise questions about the robustness of findings.[1]

Large-scale, comprehensive, empirical studies of policy work are not only very rare but are also dated and cover few jurisdictions, most commonly the United States. Some analyses of these studies employ only partial survey evidence (see, for example, Page and Jenkins's 2005 study of the U.K. "policy bureaucracy") and in many cases observers seeking large-*N* empirical data rely on one or two dated American studies, such as Meltsner's (1976) work from four decades ago or Durning and Osuna's 1994 study, to support their conclusions about the tasks, duties, and roles played by policy analysts in contemporary policy processes. These gaps in knowledge about the characteristics and activities of policy workers have led many observers to decry the lack in many countries of such basic data as how many policy analysts there are in government, what subjects they work on, and with what effect (New Zealand, State Services Commission 1991, 1999; Uhr and Mackay 1996; Bakvis 1997, 2000; Weller and Stevens 1998) and to suggest that the conduct of newer, large-*N* surveys of professional policy workers in government is required to advance thinking on this topic.[2] Understanding what sub-national policy workers do and with what effect, however, is a prerequisite to understanding how policy processes and policy advice work in federal states and, more generally, in many states where policy processes involve complex, multi-level governance arrangements.

This situation is especially acute in multi-level countries, since what little work exists focuses almost exclusively on the national or central level (for rare exceptions, see Hollander and Prince 1993; Rieper and Toulemonde 1997; Hird 2005b; Dobuzinskis, Howlett, and Laycock 2007; Liu et al. 2010), despite the fact that sub-national governments have extensive policymaking authority in many important areas of social and economic life, such as health care, social welfare programs, transportation, and urban policy (Howlett 1999). Even high-profile federal states, such as Australia, Germany, the United States, and Canada, whose central government decision-making processes have been studied intensively, have had little attention paid to their sub-national jurisdictions (Wollmann 1989) until recently, and empirical data have been lacking on the policy analytical techniques and practices found in these sub-national governments (Hird 2005b; Voyer 2007; Howlett 2009a, 2009b; Howlett and Newman 2010).

Understanding what sub-national policy workers do and with what effect, however, is a prerequisite to understanding how policy processes and policy advice work in federal states and, more generally, in many states where policy processes involve complex, multi-level governance arrangements. This chapter uses data gleaned from the first large-scale survey of federal, provincial, and territorial policy analysts in Canada to shed some light on these questions.

Policy Work in Multi-Level Systems: The Limited Autonomy Hypothesis

A key question in the study of sub-national policy work is whether, and to what extent, analytical activities differ from those identified at the national or central level. Limited case study and interview-based research examining state- or provincial-level policymaking (see, for example, Halligan 1995; Segsworth and Poel 1997; Rasmussen 1999; Maley 2000; McArthur 2007) is far from conclusive about how sub-national analytical work differs from that conducted by central governments, but it does provide a basic set of working hypotheses that can be tested against larger-scale and more comprehensive empirical survey results.

McArthur's 2007 work on federal and provincial policymaking in Canada is especially useful in this regard. This work highlights the impact upon policy work and workers of organizational differences between sub-national and national levels of government, and, in particular, the consequences for policy work flowing from the smaller size of government and the tighter lines of political control found at the sub-national level. Constricted by these structural characteristics, McArthur argued, provincial government agencies and the analysts they employ suffer from a lack of autonomy from demands placed upon them by political masters and by prominent social actors such as trade unions, business associations, think tanks, and interest groups. As a result, sub-national policy workers are much more constrained and short-term in their activities and orientations than their national counterparts, much more likely to follow political dictates and fashions in government, and much less able to resist pressure-group politics. Liu et al. (2010) found a similar pattern and effect at the local government level.

As a high-profile federal state with significant policymaking responsibilities at the sub-national level, Canada provides a strong case from which to generate insights into the differences and similarities of policy analytical work in multi-level governance systems. This study will evaluate this limited autonomy hypothesis. By comparing policy work and workers at different levels in a multi-level state such as Canada, we would expect to see large similarities across levels of governments, with professional analysts using similar techniques and approaches, but with some major differences between their analytical practices and policy work. This hypothesis will be tested using empirical data gathered from a unique set of surveys of professional policy analysts working in the federal, ten provincial, and three territorial governments of the Canadian federation. As a high-profile federal state with significant policymaking responsibilities at the sub-national level, Canada provides a strong case from which to generate insights into the differences and similarities of policy analytical work in multi-level governance systems (Howlett and Lindquist 2004).

Data

In order to assess this institutional autonomy thesis, data from two sets of surveys of Canadian policy workers conducted in 2007 and 2008 by the authors were combined so that the attitudes, practices, and situations of respondents in Canada's National Capital Region (NCR) (located in the adjoining communities of Ottawa, Ontario, and Gatineau, Quebec) could be compared with those of analysts in the country's thirteen provincial and territorial jurisdictions.[3] Data were divided into five topic areas: demographic characteristics; job experience of analysts; their education and training; the nature of their day-to-day duties; and the techniques and data they employ in their analyses. Overall survey results and demographic profiles for the federal level are available in Wellstead, Stedman, and Lindquist (2009) and for the provincial and territorial level in Howlett (2009a, 2009b). Response rates by provincial and territorial jurisdiction are set out in appendix 1.[4]

The combined data collected from these surveys allowed profiles of federal, provincial, and territorial analysts to be compared and provided the basis for the first large-*N*, comparative, empirical analysis of the background and activities of sub-national and national-level government policy analysts working in a multi-level governance system. The comparison reveals interesting similarities and differences among policy workers and policy work in such systems, and provides the empirical data required to evaluate differences in the practices employed by analysts working in a multi-level state.

Results

Federal, Provincial, and Territorial Commonalities

Table 6.1 illustrates many important similarities in the policy tasks conducted at the federal, provincial, and territorial levels of Canadian government. Regardless of their location or level of operation, policy workers are likely to be engaged in implementation that requires coordination with other levels of government and technical or specialized knowledge, and to exhibit a similar division of short- and long-term tasks. They also share many attitudes towards those in power and have similar views about such topics as their own and non-governmental policy capacity.

Federal Differences versus Provincial-Territorial Similarities

There are also several statistically significant differences between analysts working in national governments and those working at the subnational level. As table 6.2 shows, federal government analysts display

Table 6.1 Similarities across All Three Orders of Government (Mean Scores)

Variable	Federal employees	Provincial employees	Territorial employees
I implement/deliver programs	2.83	2.90	2.87
I deal with issues that emerge as a result of governmental priorities in headquarters	3.73	3.66	3.67
I deal with issues that require coordination with other levels of government	3.04	2.90	3.02
I deal with issues that require specialist or technical knowledge	3.65	3.64	3.50
I appraise policy options	3.43	3.56	3.67
I consult with the public	1.96	1.97	2.17
I deal with regional issues	3.03	3.01	2.71
I identify policy issues	3.85	3.92	4.04
I deal with tasks that demand immediate action (i.e., "firefighting")	3.94	3.81	3.79
I negotiate with central agencies	2.40	2.62	2.62**
I negotiate with program managers	2.85	3.06	3.07**
I deal with short-term tasks that can be resolved in less than a month	3.69	3.69	3.71
I deal with medium-term tasks that are ongoing for 1–6 months	3.60	3.59	3.65
I deal with long-term tasks that are ongoing for 6–12 months	3.61	3.47	3.54
I deal with urgent day-to-day issues that seem to take precedence over long-term thinking	4.18	4.28	4.27
I negotiate with stakeholders	2.68	2.85	2.63**
I consult with stakeholders	2.62	2.76	2.63*
I think policy decisions are increasingly those that are most politically acceptable	3.91†	3.98	3.99
I think there is less governmental capacity to analyse policy options than there used to be	3.37†	3.43	3.52
I think much of the policy capacity is outside the formal structure of government	2.76†	2.91	2.82
I think those who have more authority in decision-making usually have less specialized technical expertise	3.77†	3.80	3.74
I think government is becoming increasingly accountable for its decisions	3.51†	3.66	3.44*
I prefer networking with colleagues	4.04†	4.08	4.06
I prefer more control from central agencies	2.48†	2.69	2.62
I prefer more control from the regions	2.71†	2.80	2.76

Based on a 1 to 5 scale where 1 = never and 5 = daily

† Based on a 1 to 5 scale where 1 = strongly disagree and 5 = strongly agree

* significant at 0.05 level

** significant at 0.01 level

Table 6.2 Differences across Levels of Government

Variable	Federal employees	Provincial employees	Territorial employees
I collect policy-related data or information	3.01	3.98	4.05***
I deal with provincial and territorial issues	2.79	4.55	4.47***
I deal with national issues	4.27	2.61	2.71***
I identify policy options	3.55	3.72	3.87***
I deal with issues that demand input from society-based organizations	2.30	2.64	2.85***
I deal with issues that emerge as a result of public pressure on government	3.08	3.31	3.35***
I deal with issues where it is difficult to identify a single, clear, simple solution	3.96	3.81	3.71***
I deal with issues that are ongoing for more than a year	4.20	3.27	3.33***
I interact frequently with senior regional management	2.47	3.10	2.98***
I interact frequently with other head office staff	3.72	3.83	4.00*
I interact frequently with central agencies	2.50	3.09	3.07***
I interact frequently with municipal government departments	1.40	2.14	2.02***
I interact frequently with federal departments in my region	2.81	2.26	2.13***
I interact frequently with environment/conservation groups	1.57	1.76	1.80**
I am increasingly consulting with the public as I do my policy-related work	2.32†	2.64	2.78***
I think policy problems increasingly require strong technical expertise	3.49†	3.83	3.78***
I think an important role of the provincial government is to foster involvement in the policy process by other non-governmental organizations	3.39†	3.71	3.63***
I think formal government institutions are becoming less relevant to policymaking	2.69†	2.92	3.17***
I think decisions about government programs and operations are increasingly made by those outside of government	2.64†	2.86	3.01***
I network with non-governmental organizations	3.64	4.03	4.09***
I network with other provincial government departments or agencies	3.77	4.36	4.39***
I network with municipal government departments or agencies	3.07	3.80	3.66***
I prefer more control from head office	3.14†	2.83	2.93***
I think policy capacity has increased	3.73†	3.31	3.16***

Based on a 1 to 5 scale where 1 = never and 5 = daily
† Based on a 1 to 5 scale where 1 = strongly disagree and 5 = strongly agree
* significant at 0.05 level
** significant at 0.01 level
*** significant at the 0.001 level

many unique characteristics as compared to their sub-national counterparts. At the same time, there are many similarities between provincial and territorial analysts in these same areas. Some results are unsurprising, such as the likelihood of federal analysts to work on national issues, but others confirm the McArthur expectation that federal analysts tend to deal more often with more complex and longer-term issues. National-level analysts are also more supportive of head-office control and less supportive of the devolution of government programs and services. More significantly for the McArthur hypothesis, federal analysts have many fewer interactions with other governments than do provincial and territorial analysts, and are less likely to be involved with interest groups, NGOs, or other provincial or municipal governments than their provincial and territorial counterparts. Both provincial and territorial analysts, in contrast, share similar attitudes and practices in these and other areas of policy work.

Federal-Provincial Similarities versus Provincial-Territorial Differences

Prima facie, the findings in tables 6.1 and 6.2 support the expectations of the limited autonomy thesis. While there may be basic commonalities in the analytical practices and behaviour of analysts in all three levels of government, they are different, and these differences reflect the institutional characteristics of government at each level, especially the smaller size and operating characteristics of provincial and territorial governments. Further support for this hypothesis can be found by examining similarities and differences between federal-provincial and territorial analysts and between federal-territorial and provincial analysts. The limited autonomy hypothesis suggests that there would be fewer similarities between these sets of analysts than found between federal and provincial-territorial analysts. As tables 6.3 and 6.4 reveal, this is indeed the case. Table 6.3 shows that there are only a few areas of policy work in which the activities of federal and provincial analysts are more similar than provincial-territorial ones. Territorial analysts are less likely to be involved in regional issues, despite their "regional" status in the Canadian north, and are more likely to be involved with head-office management and other head-office staff, while being less involved with think tanks. These latter findings can be linked to the small size and operating characteristics of territorial administrations, again supporting the McArthur hypothesis.

Table 6.4 illustrates the areas in which provincial analysts differ from their federal and territorial colleagues. Like table 6.3, table 6.4

Table 6.3 Federal-Provincial Similarities (Territorial Differences)

Variable	Federal employees	Provincial employees	Territorial employees
I deal with issues that require coordination across regions	3.14	3.12	2.82*
I interact frequently with senior head office–based management	3.67	3.85***	4.14***
I interact frequently with think tanks	1.81	1.82***	1.44***

Based on a 1 to 5 scale where 1 = never and 5 = daily
* significant at 0.05 level
*** significant at 0.001 level

underlines the relatively few areas in which federal and territorial analysts are more similar than are provincial and territorial ones. Significantly, with respect to the limited autonomy hypothesis, provincial analysts are more likely to negotiate and consult with stakeholders, especially industry and labour organizations, and to perceive their work to increasingly involve networks of people both within and outside of government. Territorial analysts do not share these characteristics, given their isolated, sparsely populated landbases in the far Canadian north.

Knowing whether or not it is possible (and accurate) to infer from national studies when describing policy arrangements is essential to the better understanding and improvement of the work carried out by professional analysts in government.

Conclusion

Policy advice systems are complex (Boston 1994; Halligan 1995; Uhr and Mackay 1996; Maley 2000). Given their reliance on institutional configurations, policy advice systems vary by jurisdiction, especially by nation state (Brinkerhoff and Crosby 2002; Brinkerhoff and Morgan 2010) and, somewhat less so, by policy sector (Hawke 1993) and department (Rochet 2004; Voyer 2007). An important and oft-overlooked aspect of these institutional variations, however, is the level of government involved in policy deliberations and policymaking. As Hooghe and Marks (2001, 2003) and others have noted, multi-level governance

Table 6.4 Federal-Territorial Similarities (Provincial Differences)

Variable	Federal employees	Provincial employees	Territorial employees
I deal with issues that require coordination with head office	3.77	3.50	3.79***
I deal with issues where it is difficult to identify a single, clear, simple solution	3.96	3.81	3.71
I interact frequently with industry organizations	2.11	2.36	1.97***
I interact frequently with labour organizations	1.47	1.74	1.56***
My policy-related work increasingly involves networks of people across regions or levels of government or even outside of government	3.56	3.74	3.44**

Based on a 1 to 5 scale where 1 = never and 5 = daily
* significant at 0.01 level
*** significant at 0.001 level

systems place different demands on different levels of government since specific responsibilities for policymaking in major areas like health care, education, and the environment are distributed unequally across levels and jurisdictions (Piattoni 2009). Despite the impact that multi-level governance potentially has on the capacity of analysts to engage in high-level, long-term, sophisticated policy activities, the role and influence of such institutional characteristics on policy analysts and their work have not been systematically evaluated (Riddell 2007; Howlett 2009a, 2009b). Knowing whether or not it is possible (and accurate) to infer from national studies when describing policy arrangements is essential to the better understanding and improvement of the work carried out by policy analysts.

Using a unique, multi-level data set derived from fifteen separate but similar surveys of federal, provincial, and territorial policy analysts in Canada in 2007 and 2008, this chapter tested a hypothesis derived from case study and anecdotal research, which posited that the activities and work of sub-national level analysts would differ in important ways from those undertaken at the national level as the result of differences in the structural configuration of governments and the interactions of analysts with interest group systems. The study examined the behaviour and attitudes of federal, provincial, and territorial analysts in order to discern the similarities and differences between them. It found many similarities in policy work areas related to overall governance trends, such as moves towards increased consultation and participation overtaking more traditional technical policy evaluations, but it also found continuing significant differences between analysts working at each level. Sub-national level analysts have more interactions with societal policy actors and experience more direct control by senior management than analysts employed by central governments. These findings conform to the expectations of the limited autonomy hypothesis, which argues that the level of autonomy from political control and social actors affects policy work and workers. This in turn has important implications for the ability of analysts to undertake long-term independent research and analysis. Where lines of control and social contacts are higher, as in sub-national governments, analysis is expected to be more politically driven and short term.

While it remains up to future research in other countries with multi-level governance systems to reveal how robust these conclusions are, in the Canadian case it was found that policy work among federal, provincial, and territorial analysts, while broadly similar, varied significantly in the direction suggested by the limited autonomy hypothesis. Analysts and policy workers employed in smaller governments were found to have significantly more interactions with central agencies and pressure groups and to differ substantially from federal workers on the issues they dealt with and the nature of the input they received in their work.

The findings suggest, moreover, that scholars cannot simply infer from national studies about trends and activities in policy analysis at sub-national levels of government, but must recognize each level of government as a significant policy actor in its own right. In other words, the policy styles and practices found at different levels of government in multi-level states, while broadly similar, contain different features that affect not only the nature of the processes followed but also the content of decisions reached and policies adopted. This finding helps to illuminate aspects of the behaviour of policy analysts and decision-makers in multi-level systems, and contributes to our understanding of policy work, its institutional components, and its ability or capacity to address important questions involving long-term, data-oriented issues in an objective, technical way (Howlett 2009a). While the specific sectoral nature of these impacts will depend upon the division of jurisdictions between levels found in different countries, in general, subnational policy work can be expected to be more participatory, partisan, pluralist, and short term than at the central level, where policymakers enjoy greater autonomy. As a result, that work will display a corresponding difficulty in marshalling expertise in the pursuit of longer-term solutions to ongoing policy problems.

Appendix 1

Description of Data Set and Response Rates

Federal government analysts were identified through keyword searches in the publicly accessible online Government Electronic Directory Services (GEDS) system. In November 2007, an online survey using Zoomerang® software was conducted from a random sample of 725 policy-based, NCR federal government employees. The survey garnered 395 usable responses for an overall response rate of 56.4 per cent. The provincial and territorial government surveys were carried out in November and December 2008 also using Zoomerang® software and an appropriately amended version of the 2007 federal survey questionnaire. The questionnaire was sent to over 4,000 provincial and territorial civil servants covering each of Canada's thirteen provincial and territorial jurisdictions. Mailing lists for the ten provinces and three territories surveyed were compiled wherever possible from publicly available sources such as online government telephone directories using keyword searches for terms such as *policy analyst* in job titles or descriptions. In some cases, additional names were added to lists from hard-copy sources such as government organization manuals. In other cases, lists or additional names were provided by provincial public service commissions who also checked initial lists for completeness and accuracy. Over 1,600 provincial and territorial policy workers completed the survey, which was gathered from 3,856 valid e-mail addresses for a total response rate of 43.3 per cent (see table 6.5).

Table 6.5 Provincial Survey Sample Sizes and Completion Rates

Province	Initial mail list size	Refusals and rejected e-mails	Valid partial completions	Complete	Response rate (%)
BC	513	51	30	194	48.5
Alberta	368	23	8	112	34.8
Saskatchewan	246	27	13	80	42.4
Manitoba	161	20	6	98	73.7
Ontario	1613	162	52	557	41.9
Quebec†	250	0	44	86	52.0
New Brunswick	162	15	4	62	44.9
Nova Scotia	181	20	15	83	44.1
PEI	27	6	1	4	23.8
Newfoundland	139	24	16	55	61.7
Yukon	75	8	6	58	95.5
NWT	80	2	2	41	55.1
Nunavut	41	8	2	13	45.4
TOTAL (excluding Quebec)	3856	366	155	1357	43.3

† Snowball sample methodology: data were excluded from totals and from subsequent table. See note 4.

NOTES

1 On the merits and demerits of naturalistic and survey research and the need to combine qualitative and quantitative analysis in social research, see Bryman (2004) and Gravetter and Forzano (2010).

2 Even less is known about both the "invisible civil service" (consultants) and those analysts who work outside of government in think tanks, business associations and labour unions, and elsewhere in the NGO sector (Saint-Martin 1998a, 1998b, 2004; Hird 2005a; Abelson 2007; Murray 2007; Speers 2007).

3 The sixty-four-item survey instrument used in these studies asked the respondents a series of questions about the tasks they undertake, the nature of the issues they examine, the kinds of networks with which they are engaged, and their attitudes towards policymaking. The statistical

technique used to analyse the survey results was one-way analysis of variance (ANOVA), which compares the means of more than two samples. In this case the null hypothesis (HO) was

1.1,1 = 112 = ... = iik

where gi is the mean of group i. The *F* statistic was constructed for testing the hypothesis:

F = variation among sample means variation within samples

Homogeneity of variance (the Levine test), ANOVA, and a post hoc pairwise multiple-comparison test using the Dunnett's C method were employed. The Levine test was used to test for equal variance. The ANOVA (*F* statistic) can indicate differences among means but does not identify the means that differ from each other. The Dunnett's C score identifies subsets of groups. Thus, using this technique, it is possible to determine similarities and differences between the three major groups of policy analysts. The survey itself is available from the authors upon request.

4 Because of problems with job classification systems and terminology and privacy laws in Quebec, lists of analysts could not be gathered from publicly available sources. A snowball sampling method was instead used in which the questionnaire was sent to an initial seed of 42 potential respondents, who were asked to pass the survey along to colleagues working as policy analysts. After six weeks, approximately 250 respondents had looked at the survey, with 130 having fully or partially completed it. Given this different data collection technique, the Quebec results have been omitted from the tables presented below. A separate analysis of the results from the Quebec survey, however, found a pattern of responses similar to those found in the other twelve provinces and territories (Bernier and Howlett 2011). Provincial public service lists often included political appointees who had been left off our lists. In most cases, however, our lists and the internal lists were very close, with about an overlap rate of 80 per cent or higher. The lists revealed a roughly proportional per-capita pattern of size of the policy analytical community in Canadian provincial governments, with about 1,800–2,000 individuals in Ontario, 500 in British Columbia, and about 100 in the smallest jurisdictions. The total number of policy analysts at the provincial and territorial level, hence, is about 5,300 (3,000 in Quebec and Ontario, 1,000 in BC and Alberta, 500 in Saskatchewan and Manitoba, 400 in the Atlantic provinces, and 300 in the territories). It is expected that this number would be matched by the federal government (Wellstead having identified about 1,300 operating outside Ottawa, the remaining 4,000 being located in the National Capital Region) bringing the total number of policy analysts actually employed in Canada to about 11,000.

7 Intergovernmental Policy Capacities and Practices in Canada

PATRICIA L. O'REILLY, GREGORY J. INWOOD, AND CAROLYN M. JOHNS

Introduction

All governments require intergovernmental policy capacity (IPC) specifically to produce policy outcomes with an intergovernmental dimension, but federated governments are especially in need of this resource. The Canadian federation consists of fourteen constitutionally sanctioned jurisdictions, which vary in policy capacity. In previous work we have investigated the ways in which that capacity is exercised intergovernmentally, or IPC – that is, the ability of the governments of a federation to work together to make policy (Inwood, Johns, and O'Reilly, 2011). This chapter looks at this capacity in order to better understand the nature of the policy work of the Canadian federation.

We interviewed 139 senior public servants (see table 7.1) and surveyed 300 others to glean their perceptions and understanding of the IPC of our federation. Our research involved a three-level comparative analysis. The first level was a jurisdictional one in which we compared the IPC of the federal, provincial, and territorial governments. The second level was sectoral/policy-based in that our universe of intergovernmental officials came from central intergovernmental agencies and intergovernmental units in finance, environment, trade, and health departments. The third level was structural in that we compared the roles of central agencies to line departments. We situate our analysis in a neo-institutional framework commonly used – although here expanded – in policy studies.

Table 7.1 Distribution of Interviews by Position

Position	Number
Clerk or Cabinet secretary	4
Deputy minister	33
Assistant/associate deputy minister	29
Director general/executive director/director	45
Assistant director, senior policy analyst/adviser	13
Other (manager, scientist, senior coordinator, counsel, chief executive officer, economist)	15
Total	139

Source: Inwood, Johns, and O'Reilly (2011), 28.

Understanding Policy Capacity and Intergovernmental Policy Capacity

While our definition of intergovernmental policy capacity is relatively straightforward – as the capacity of our governments to work together to make and implement policy – the extent to which it exists in the Canadian federation is best understood by distinguishing between IPC and policy capacity (PC) per se. By this we mean that an individual government may display a robust capacity to make policy in a given area as evidenced by policymaking activity and output, but this does not mean that it necessarily has the capacity to engage intergovernmentally where that policy crosses jurisdictional boundaries, or governments agree to work together. For this, other skills and resources are required; and, we would argue, they are required at three different levels of capacity: *internal* IPC, *joint* IPC, and *collective* IPC. We will return to these capacities below, but first we turn to the composition and role of intergovernmental officials in Canada, as well as our findings on the factors that influence overall IPC.

What Intergovernmental Officials Do: Tasks, Backgrounds, Attitudes, and Activities of Front-Line Workers

In general, intergovernmental officials in central agencies and line departments perform key functions in contributing to IPC. These functions are predominantly monitoring, coordinating, and advising (see table 7.2).

It is difficult to ascertain a complete demographic profile of intergovernmental officials in Canada because there is a lack of data. However, during research conducted in the early 2000s, this cohort of officials was a remarkably homogeneous group. Those data showed an overwhelmingly white (81 per cent) and male (71 per cent) group with a median age of forty-six, slightly higher than that of the federal public service as a whole. As for education, 58 per cent held a master's degree, with most trained in the social sciences (over 50 per cent), some (22 per cent) of these with political science and public administration backgrounds, followed by geography and urban planning (14 per cent), business administration and commerce degrees (13 per cent), and a number of other areas of study such as science, engineering, law, economics, and education (all below 10 per cent) (Inwood, Johns, and O'Reilly 2011, 69). These data also note the following about the occupational profile of intergovernmental officials: "Officials' career patterns are dominated by those who have backgrounds in policy analysis. Those who had worked as program management specialists compose the next largest cohort. Overall, they average 17 years' experience in the public service (ranging from six months to thirty-one years) and 13% of those surveyed indicated some prior work experience in the private sector. However, they have an average of only 6.6 years in intergovernmental relations and the majority (56%) have been in intergovernmental relations for less than five years" (70).

Among the factors affecting IPC is career mobility. Some data reveal that the mobility of public service elites in the provinces was increasing in the late 1990s (Carroll, Bierling, and Rosenblatt 2000). Where intergovernmental mobility is concerned, a survey of deputy and assistant deputy ministers conducted in 2006 indicated that 39 per cent of the public service elite had worked for another level of government. This included some 35 per cent of provincial executives, 36 per cent of federal executives, and 62 per cent of territorial executives (Evans, Lum, and Shields 2007).

What does this demographic profile – incomplete as it is – reveal about IPC? Dupré wrote in the mid-1980s that the "workability of executive federalism" was partly a function of "trust ties" between officials, which developed on the basis of educational, training, and professional commonalities (Dupré 1985). However, Dupré's idea of

Table 7.2 Functions and Powers of Intergovernmental Officials

Monitor
- monitor federal, provincial, territorial (FPT), Aboriginal, municipal, international (especially U.S.) developments
- maintain formal contacts with other governments
- exchange information and research with policymakers, academics, stakeholders
- review proposals to Cabinet to provide an intergovernmental perspective

Coordinate
- plan and prepare for intergovernmental meetings
- coordinate horizontal and vertical policy
- develop coordinating policies and courses of action for politicians
- serve as a liaison between governments, central agencies, and line departments, and increasingly between outside actors (Aboriginal, municipal, international)
- negotiate and sign intergovernmental agreements, contracts, and partnerships
- arrange ceremonial functions and protocol duties

Advise
- advise (minister/premier/prime minister) on FPT issues
- develop agendas and positions in preparation for intergovernmental meetings
- provide policy direction and advice to and from line departments

Source: Johns, O'Reilly, and Inwood (2007), 29–32.

workability was more narrowly defined than that implied by our conception of IPC, since it was limited mostly to process matters rather than policy outcomes. Nonetheless, others have observed the importance of a homogeneity of values, attitudes, and beliefs and a shared culture in fostering a certain "*esprit de corps* which both tacitly and explicitly acknowledges the centrality of intergovernmental relations to policy work and which helps provide the basis of the informal network system of intergovernmental relations" (Inwood, Johns, and O'Reilly 2011, 70). At the same time, though, an observable trend in intergovernmental relations and in the broader public service has been increased job mobility (Bourgault 2002; Evans, Lum, and Shields 2007), a factor that may inhibit trust ties and common cultures from incubating. It should be noted as well that a new cadre of younger professionals are now entering the civil service as the previous generation retires. It remains to be seen whether or not they will challenge the established culture of intergovernmental relations in Canada, but if recent data from the federal clerk of the Privy Council on the composition of today's federal civil service are any indication, there seems to be no *major* shift in overall personnel composition yet (Canada, Clerk of the Privy Council, June 2015).

Factors

Neo-institutional policy analysis focuses on the ideas, institutions, and actors (or cultural and political-economic) factors of policymaking. We have used this framework in our analysis of the IPC of the Canadian federation both because it fits with what the officials were telling us and because it includes the key variables on which analysts focus at the nexus of IPC in the fields of public policy, public administration, and federalism (see Inwood, Johns, O'Reilly 2011, Introduction). We have added a fourth factor to the more commonly used neo-institutional framework, that of *relations*, for the same reasons. The work of federalism scholars has long focused on the importance of "intergovernmental *relations*," and the officials we interviewed often referred to them. We also compare the academic literature to officials' thinking about ideas, institutions, actors, and relations, and find some interesting results.

IDEAS

Officials do not think explicitly about ideas as factors very much, even as ideas form a subtext to their comments. Certain key contextual political ideas such as those around debt, deficit, and surplus financing, for instance, are often close to the surface. Ideas related to the degree of centralization and decentralization infuse their comments as well. Certain key contextual administrative ideas such as efficiency, outcomes, horizontality, etc. are also discernible. Interestingly, however, the precepts of New Public Management do not seem to have had much explicit influence in the intergovernmental arena. Officials did express the idea that there is a general need for goal-setting and a more vision-based approach, but offered little themselves on what that vision might entail. Overall, ideas are seldom seen as a factor for change by intergovernmental officials. This stands in some contrast to the academic preoccupation with the role of ideas as an important factor in policymaking.[1] Likewise, the role of knowledge utilization and the role of expertise – particularly related to policy change – are seen as more central by academics than they are by officials.

INSTITUTIONS

Among the most important political institutions for federalism are First Ministers Meetings (FMM) and ministerial and deputy ministerial conferences and meetings. Officials regard these as doing a fairly good job, although there is some expression of the desire for more influence through mechanisms such as co-chairing and agenda-setting by provincial and territorial officials. Among the important administrative institutions are Advisory Councils to FMMs and ministerial and deputy ministerial conferences. These are also thought to function relatively well. Some officials did comment that mechanisms for dispute resolution are needed in intergovernmental relations, but there has been no traction to fulfil this desire, especially where this would entail third party involvement in federal-provincial-territorial relations. The academic viewpoint on political institutions tends to regard FMMs and related conferences as having overall low capacity. They are seen as reactive rather than proactive, and not engaged in long-term policy development. Moreover, academics often decry the closed, executive nature of these political institutions. Academics see administrative apparatus for FMMs and its conferences as knowledgeable but largely advisory, easily politicized, and process focused. For both the political and administrative institutions of federalism, academics argue for more external input and accountability, including that from third party involvement and greater linkages to political institutions such as Parliament.

Perhaps not surprisingly, the constitution is not seen by officials as an important factor in IPC, aside from its being a backdrop to jurisdictional boundaries. Similarly, the courts are not seen as important tools for change, despite the long history of judicial intervention in federalism. However, intergovernmental accords and agreements were regarded as an increasingly important part of the system. Interestingly, though, they were not generally seen as in need of improvement. Officials felt that bilateral and more technical types of accords and agreements were more effective for policy development. Academics reveal a limited interest in constitutional reform as a means to improved federalism and/or policy, and some interest in an improved court system, including a more intra-state federalism approach to the Supreme Court, but wariness about the resort to the judiciary as an umpire of federalism that tends to produce zero-sum outcomes. Academics tend to see accords and agreements as important, but frequently display a more critical approach to their role, particularly with regard to long-term policy development or innovation.

ACTORS

Where political actors are concerned, officials portray a general acceptance of their political "masters," although the variation in interest and ability regarding intergovernmental relations among politicians was cited as a limiting factor. Officials made little note of the role of parliamentarians in federalism per se; Parliament was not on their list of key factors. The same held for political parties. However, politicization of policy issues was seen as problematic. The public are little on the minds of officials, public input being seen mostly as counterproductive to the necessities of diplomacy and negotiation. Academics criticize the lack of parliamentary involvement in intergovernmental relations, with some arguing for a legislative federalism alongside executive federalism. Quite a number of suggestions have been made over the years for linking the two systems. Academics do not see political parties as holding out much hope to improve the policy capacity of the intergovernmental system though, especially given factors such as the diverse interests of the many jurisdictions and electoral turnover. The lack of public participation in intergovernmental relations is seen by many academics as a problem for the capacity of the federation. But some see increased involvement as creating other problems, especially in terms of impeding the efficiency of the system. So the jury is not yet in here.

Officials expressed concerns regarding certain aspects and practices of administrative actors, in particular the power of central agencies to pull policy files from the line Intergovernmental Agencies (IGAs). Officials also cited the problematic aspects of deputy minister leadership being compromised by high turnover rates. Academics cite the ongoing search for improved leadership development and selection of more intergovernmentally savvy ministers. On the administrative front, academics focus somewhat on concerns about central agency power, but more on the lack of a long-term policy-knowledgeable community of professional officials in intergovernmental positions.

RELATIONS

Relations, as we see them in intergovernmental interactions, are both *formal relations* associated with the formal rules and roles typically set up in an institutional setting (especially with regard to that institution's hierarchies), and *informal relationships* found behind the scenes in the panoply of friendships and enmities that invariably infuse any network of human beings. For the officials, formal relations are an important factor, including those delineated in jurisdictional boundaries, which they tend to regard as immutable. The officials also recognize the fact that the formal roles they occupy are conditioned by inequalities of population and economic power in the federation. But it is the informal relations that officials cited as perhaps the most important factor in their capacity to do their jobs. From their point of view, this is a strong determinant of IPC. However, there is little assessment of the nature and impact of informal relations. For instance, few examples of the way in which these relations worked could be conjured by officials, nor were there many recommendations on how they could be systematically fostered. Academics cite formal relations as significant in intergovernmental relations, seeing them in need of reform via institutional change and enhanced accountability, for instance. Informal relations are not disregarded by academics, but there is little ongoing focus or assessment or even knowledge of their interplay.

Disconnection

Talking to 139 senior officials and surveying another 300 revealed to us that there is a disconnection between the focus of academics and that of intergovernmental officials. Officials are more internally focused and show little interest in external factors, or in restructuring the system to improve IPC. The theoretical and academic interests of scholars seem to have relatively little resonance with the officials. The officials indicated mainly that they spend little reflective time pondering the "big ideas" that academics sometimes insist are germane to policy (such as democracy or ideology, or even the role of ideas per se). Interestingly, this difference of perspective may stem from what our editors observe here as a distinction between "policy study" and "policy analysis," or between a more theoretical focus and a more practical focus. It does raise concern about two "solitudes" speaking past each other, as well as the relevance of teaching/training upcoming intergovernmental officials in the post-secondary educational system.

Another disconnection we found was that between the political level and the administrative level in policymaking. It is clear that, in Canada, executive dominance characterizes governance in general and intergovernmental relations in particular. Yet officials feel there is more potential capacity in administrative factors than in political factors. There is, as well, disconnection between intergovernmental central agencies and intergovernmental line departments. When a policy concern becomes "hot," it gets pulled up and away from line officials and into the hands of central agency operatives. For instance, the health policy debates of the late 1990s and early 2000s became the purview mainly of first ministers and finance departments rather than the health department policy specialists. In other words, in the trade-off between process and policy and between short-term finance considerations and long-term restructuring considerations, the centre usually wins.

These disconnections inside and outside the working environment of intergovernmental officials speak to a lack of understanding of the political and administrative trade-offs being made in the federal system. If certain factors are playing key roles in determining policy capacity, they need to be understood and nurtured in order to be used. Lack of recognition means lack of capacity. Likewise, failure to come to terms with the limiting factors that inhibit governments' ability to move ahead on needed policy reform is also a form of lost capacity. Ideas, institutions, and actors are being underutilized in intergovernmental policy work, and both the formal and informal relations of its milieu are setting the stage for a continuation of these limitations.

PC and IPC Trade-offs

Beyond the factors affecting IPC, some limitations of intergovernmental policy output in our Canadian federation, or any federation, for that matter, stem from the nature of policy capacity per se. Here it is important to distinguish, first, an individual government's own policy capacity (How much policy capacity does province x have?). A survey of Canadian deputy ministers and assistant deputy ministers in 2006 indicated there was significant variation when comparing jurisdictions, and that policy capacity was a concern within all jurisdictions (Evans, Baskoy, and Shields 2011). A jurisdiction can have strong PC and weak IPC. For example, it can have a strong policy sector but carry little weight in the federation or have little explicit expertise on the intergovernmental dimensions of the policy issue. Conversely, it is difficult to have strong IPC in a sector if PC is lacking. Many jurisdictions found this, for instance, when they downsized their own policy shops in response to the precepts of New Public Management (NPM) reforms in the 1990s, or austerity initiatives in the early 2000s. They found themselves disadvantaged at the intergovernmental policy meetings.

Second, it is important to distinguish between three different levels of IPC: what we refer to as internal IPC, joint IPC, and collective IPC. Internal IPC is that developed by a single jurisdiction to be taken to an intergovernmental forum or used intergovernmentally. Joint IPC exists between two or more governments working together in an intergovernmental forum or on an intergovernmental policy issue. Collective IPC exists across all of the federation working as a whole on an intergovernmental policy issue. These different levels of IPC can, and often do, trade off against each other. Resources for one may result in reduced resources for another; attention to one may result in reduced attention to others; and strategic trade-offs may be made as governments interact in the competitive environment of the Canadian federation.

Internal IPC, which each government chooses to develop within its own government to be taken to intergovernmental forums or expended on intergovernmental policy issues, can vary widely across jurisdictions and sectors in Canada. Some governments develop strong internal intergovernmental units (although this does not necessarily translate into strong *policy* capacity), while others expend fewer resources on it. In the austerity days mentioned above, although the internal policy shops were often downsized, it is interesting that most of the intergovernmental units within particular governments were not. Intergovernmental forums were fairly well protected from the downsizing.

While one might expect internal IPC would be used to further joint or collective IPC, this is not always the case. The federal government is often accused of using its own strong internal IPC to bypass joint or collective policy decisions with unilateral policy action or overbearing bilateral or multilateral deals. Likewise, joint IPC can be used to bypass collective IPC when bilateral or multilateral deals displace collective agreements. And of course, joint deals between two or more governments can sometimes deliberately exclude important actors such as the federal government or key provinces, thus diminishing potential policy capacity. Policy agendas are often narrowed by a smaller set of governments, although it should also be noted this smaller set can also set an example for emulation by future governments.

We had very little collective policymaking in Canada in the 1990s and early 2000s, and even less during the Harper government years. Our governments rarely all come together to think and act collectively about our greater policy needs. Even when they are all in the same room, they usually act to protect their own interests rather than that of the whole. The 2003 and 2004 Health Accords perhaps provide a good example of the common good being surpassed by a common battle over funding alone.

Last, the factors driving policy capacity in the federation are, of course, at play in all four of these types of capacity. Any attempts by the practitioners of the federal system to strengthen any of these internal or intergovernmental policy capacities would have to take into account the barriers and enhancers that would come into play in doing so. Neither they nor their advisers could, for example, ignore the currency of existing economic ideas, the ad hoc nature of contemporary collective intergovernmental forums, the power relations between the central agencies and the line departments, the hierarchy between the political and the administrative actors, the dominant formal and informal relations of the federation, and so on, in any attempt to enhance the overall IPC of the federation.

Conclusion

The editors of this volume have postulated that (1) different styles of policy analysis can be found in different organizations and jurisdictions, and (2) these styles are not random or completely manipulable by policy actors but are linked to larger patterns of political behaviour and culture and are, in a sense, quasi-permanent features of the policy analysis landscape. Our study would confirm that the world of intergovernmental policy analysis and policymaking is unique, and any change to IPC would have to take that uniqueness into account.

As the world's policy problems continue to develop, our national policy decisions are caught up in an intergovernmental system with limited IPC for dealing with them. All types of IPC are low, with Collective IPC being particularly under-utilized. The system is reactive, short-term oriented, and prone to the quick fix. Multi-level policy decision-making is underdeveloped. It is also ill-understood. We need to understand our IPC first, before we can improve it. Governments choose to maintain and utilize whatever capacity they have, but without understanding it, it will not be there for the taking. As one official said, "You have to know your capacity to grow your capacity."

NOTE

1 For a review of the academic literature regarding the factors discussed here, see Inwood, Johns, and O'Reilly (2011).

8 Public Managers and Policy Analytical Capacity in Canada

MICHAEL HOWLETT

Introduction: Public Managers and the Policy Process – The Need for Empirical Analysis

Public managers have prominent role in the public administrative and advisory systems, with the result that, as a whole, they tend to shoulder a large share of public scrutiny, and blame, for failures resulting from poor policy processes. Managers are often lumped together with the agencies they serve as "the bureaucracy," which in itself is seen in many circles as largely responsible for many failures in public sector governance. As a result of their perceived "bureaucratic incompetence" and "resistance to change," public managers in particular are often blamed for poor policy formulation and weak implementation. Their motivations and commitments are also frequently questioned. Much of the economics-inspired literature on bureaucratic behaviour, for example, is based on the assumption that a typical public manager is a significant policy player and is motivated largely by personal interests and/or narrowly defined institutional interests such as information or budget maximization in dealing with public affairs (Hicklin and Godwin 2009).[1]

The above views contrast sharply with the perceived policy roles of public managers held by managers themselves and those held by many others interested in public administration (Andersen 2010; Rhodes, 't Hart, and Noordegraaf 2007). Many public managers perceive their roles as simply performing necessary functions (such as policing the street and collecting taxes) required to maintain government machinery, and therefore to fall outside the scope of policymaking. Those who direct public programs in public sector organizations also seldom see a connection between their work and the policy world. Many public managers, when they do think about the subject, see their policy roles as limited to policy implementation, since a common perception among both political executives and public managers is that policy and policymaking is the business of policymakers, not managers and administrators.[2]

Several recent developments have led to a renewed questioning of the negative perceptions held by many observers and of the historical "politics-administration dichotomy" view often held within government. They have reinforced the need to more accurately characterize the actual policy roles that are played by public managers, something Meier (2009, 7) termed "the missing variable" in policy studies. First of all, the decentralization and devolution of administrative tasks undertaken in many countries have transferred critical policy roles to public managers situated in lower and middle levels of governments or agencies.

Second, the emergence of network or collaborative government as a new form of participatory and consultative governance structure in many countries has enlarged the scope of influence for public managers, as their exercise of authority is no longer strictly top-down but also influences bottom-up processes. Third, the customer orientation in public sector governance under NPM rubrics, which has affected virtually every country, has also strengthened the voice and leverage of agencies that deliver goods and services to the public and the public managers who direct them (Wu et al. 2010). In theory, public managers are able to exercise great influence in the policy process through three roles they play in it: organizational, political, and technical. The organizational role focuses public managers' attention on issues internal to their organizations, such as human resource management, financial management and budgeting, and administrative procedure, and is the role that has been the most studied, since it is the "default" role found in the limited conception of a politics-administrative dichotomy, which, as discussed above, has formed the core area of managerial activity in Western administrative systems over the past century (May and Geva-May 2005).

The two remaining roles, however, are newer and comprise a good part of an emerging expanded vision of public management activity in policymaking. The technical role requires public managers to think analytically and systematically about the causes and consequences of policy issues, as well as the likely outcomes of the policy options available to tackle them. The political perspective focuses public managers' attention on how the incentive structure of players in the policy process is aligned with their respective behaviour patterns, as well as upon how the interaction of how these players affects policy outcomes (Wu et al. 2010).

While the weights assigned to these three roles might differ considerably for public managers at different levels of government and in different types of public sector organizations, in order to conduct them, public managers need knowledge of the policy process, including knowledge concerning key players and dynamics at each stage of the policy process and concerning the practices prevalent in different countries and/or policy areas. They also require the analytical skills to diagnose a situation and to develop appropriate strategies for dealing with it. For example, analytical tools such as political mapping and stakeholder analysis can enable public managers to assess the support for, and resistance to, existing and proposed policy measures, while cost-benefit analysis helps them to compare the consequences of options available.

Several testable hypotheses can be derived from the literature concerning how public managers actually act in policy deliberations. The long tenure of public managers in the public sector, for example, not only helps them sustain attention to particular policy issues, but also enables them to take a long-term perspective on public policy, which political executives and others often lack. The job security and expertise that public managers, especially career civil servants, enjoy shield them from short-term political pressure, such as winning elections or maintaining parliamentary coalitions, felt by political masters in dealing with policy issues. In addition to providing a longer-term perspective on policymaking, this also means that they can give more weight to technical considerations in devising and implementing policies. Furthermore, the involvement of public managers is more likely to spread across multiple stages in the policy process, while engagement of policymakers at the top may be concentrated on specific stages, such as agenda setting, decision-making, or evaluation, again providing public managers with more opportunities to affect some aspects of policy content more than others.

A typical public manager may be heavily involved in some stages, somewhat involved in other stages, and not at all involved in certain stages (Howlett, Ramesh, and Perl 2009). However, if these individuals, collectively, are the "missing variable" in policy studies, their role(s) in the policy process must be (1) distinct and (2) at least as significant as those of other actors vis-à-vis their impact on policy outcomes. This chapter uses large-*N* survey data to examine the characteristics of policy managers and compare them with those of non-managerial policy analysts in an effort to advance understanding of one piece of this "missing variable" in policy studies. Before doing so, however, it is necessary to first set out the nature of the "policy analytical community" of which both managers and non-managers are a part.

Policy Advice Systems in Modern Governments

Understanding the nature of professional policy analysis, its influence, and its effectiveness in different analytical contexts involves discerning how a policy advice system is structured and operated in the specific sector of policy activity under examination and how professional policy work is conducted within this system. At their most basic, policy advice systems can be thought of as part of the knowledge utilization system of government, itself a kind of marketplace for policy ideas and information, comprising three separate components: a supply of policy advice provided to or by governments, its demand on the part of decision-makers, and a set of brokers whose role it is to match supply and demand in any given conjuncture (Lindquist 1998; Howlett and Lindquist 2004, 2007).

The first set of actors is composed of those "knowledge producers" located in academia, statistical agencies, and research institutes who provide the basic scientific, economic, and social scientific data upon which analyses are often based and decisions made. The second set is composed of the "proximate decision-makers" themselves who act as consumers of policy analysis and advice, that is, those with actual authority to make policy decisions, including cabinets and executives as well as parliaments, legislatures, and congresses, and senior administrators and officials delegated decision-making powers by those other bodies. The third set is composed of those "knowledge brokers" who serve as intermediaries between the knowledge generators and proximate decision-makers, repackaging data and information into usable form. These include, among others, permanent specialized research staff inside government as well as their temporary equivalents in commissions and task forces, and a large group of non-governmental specialists and consultants associated with think tanks and interest groups. Although often thought of as "knowledge suppliers," policy analysts in government almost by definition exist in the brokerage subsystem, repackaging rather than "creating" new knowledge (Feldman 1989; Verschuere 2009).

Different types of "policy advice systems" exist, depending on the nature of knowledge supply and demand in a particular sector or jurisdiction, and what analysts do in brokering information, how they do it, and with what effect depends in large part on the type of advisory system present in the area in which they work (Noordegraaf 2010). This helps to explain why different styles of policy analysis can be found in different policy fields (Howlett and Lindquist 2004; Mayer, Bots, and van Daalen 2004), since these can be linked to larger patterns of behaviour of political actors and knowledge suppliers that condition how policy advice is generated and deployed (Aberbach and Rockman 1989; Bennett and McPhail 1992; Bevir and Rhodes 2001; Bevir, Rhodes, and Weller 2003; Peled 2002).

Some of this variation in advisory systems is temporal and due to the fact that the introduction of elements of formal or professional policy analysis into the brokerage function has a different history in each jurisdiction. In the sense employed in this chapter, in the United States, for example, policy analysis originated in the wartime planning and "scientific management" thinking of the mid-twentieth century but was applied more widely only in the 1960s and 1970s to large-scale social and economic planning in areas such as defence, urban redevelopment, and budgeting – especially as a result of the implementation of the Planning Programming Budgeting System (Garson 1986; Lindblom 1958a; Wildavsky 1969). U.S.-style "policy analysis" has since then spread around the world, with the development of professional associations and dedicated schools and teaching programs in many countries, but only in a very uneven pattern (Geva-May and Maslove 2006, 2007; Mintrom 2007). Many countries were much less influenced by this movement than others. Some countries, including many in Western Europe, for example, had traditions of legal oversight of government or centralized top-down public administration that placed the evaluative and analytical tasks of government within the judicial or financial branches of the civil service and delayed the arrival of problem-analytically-oriented policy brokers (Bekke and van der Meer 2000). Other countries, such as those in Eastern Europe under socialist regimes, featured large-scale planning bureaus that did analyse problems systematically but in a context very different (central planning) from that of the policy analysis movement as it developed in the liberal-capitalist confines of the U.S. government (Verheijen 1999). Many other countries in the developing world until very recently lacked the internal capacity and external autonomy required to conduct the independent analytical tasks required of U.S.-style professional policy analysis (Brinkerhoff 2010; Brinkerhoff and Crosby 2002; Brinkerhoff and Morgan 2010; Burns and Bowornwathana 2001).

Given its reliance on existing institutional arrangements for political decision-making, however, the exact configuration of an advisory system can be expected to vary not only temporally, but also spatially, by jurisdiction, especially by nation-state and, somewhat less so, by policy issue or sector. That is, the personal and professional components of the policy advice supply system, along with their internal and external sourcing, can be expected to be combined in different ratios in different policymaking situations (Hawke 1993; Prince 1983; Rochet 2004; Wollmann 1989). Understanding these variations is critical in understanding the role professional governmental policy analysts play in the policy advisory, and policymaking, processes.

In general, four distinct "communities" of policy advisers can be identified within a policy advice system, depending on their location inside or outside of government, and by how closely they operate to decision-makers: core actors, public sector insiders, private sector insiders, and outsiders (see table 8.1). The actual set of jobs and duties performed by each set of policy advisers in both government and non-governmental organizations must be empirically determined in each instance (Colebatch, Hoppe, and Noordegraaf 2011). Understanding the manner in which the four communities do or do not relate and reinforce each other is a critical, and very much understudied, determinant of the overall capacity and effectiveness of the system. Important aspects of the functioning of policy advice systems include such factors as whether or not or what type of "boundary-spanning" links exist between governmental and non-governmental organizations (Weible 2008), and whether or not opportunities exist for employees to strengthen their skills and expertise (O'Connor, Roos, and Vickers-Willis 2007) or to outsource policy research to personnel in private or semi-public organizations and consultancies. However, generally speaking, managers can potentially play a very significant role as "privileged insiders" similar to that played by executive staff with proximate access to key authoritative insiders (Rhodes, 't Hart, and Noordegraaf 2007).

In what follows, survey evidence from a study of Canadian policy analysts conducted by the author and several colleagues in 2007–9 is

Table 8.1 The Four Communities of Policy Advisers

	Proximate actors	Peripheral actors
Public/governmental sector	Core actors Central agencies Executive staff Professional governmental policy analysts	Public sector insiders Commissions and committees Task forces Research councils/scientists
Non-governmental sector	Private sector insiders Consultants Political party staff Pollsters	Outsiders Public interest groups Business associations Trade unions Academics Think tanks Media

used to examine the make-up, education, and activities of policy managers and to compare and contrast these with those skills, knowledge, and practices performed by non-managerial analysts. This is done in order to assess if managers and non-managers differ significantly in their activities and if managers exhibit any greater knowledge and prowess, or analytical capacity, than non-managers. In this way, this study will help to determine the extent to which policy managers, as a "missing link" in policy studies, deserve more careful study and attention (Boardman, Bozeman, and Ponomariov 2010).

Methods

In what follows, the analytical capacities of different categories of employees of government organizations are assessed through a large-scale survey of the activities of core government analysts, or what Page and Jenkins (2005) refer to collectively as the "policy bureaucracy." The study is based on fifteen large-scale surveys of Canadian policy workers conducted in 2007 and 2008 – two of federal analysts, and thirteen of the provincial and territorial analysts.

The two federal surveys were conducted by Wellstead and Stedman in 2007; both online surveys used Zoomerang® software. They examined approximately 1,500 federal civil servants located outside Ottawa who had been identified as policy analysts by 500 Regional Federal Council members (senior regional employees representing their respective federal department or agency) from all ten provinces and the three territories. A total of 1,442 people were identified. In addition, a random sample of 725 policy-based federal government employees in Canada's National Capital Region (located in the adjoining communities of Ottawa, Ontario; and Hull, Quebec) were identified through the publicly accessible online Government Electronic Directory Services. The survey garnered 395 usable responses for an overall response rate of 56.4 per cent (Wellstead et al. 2007; Wellstead, Stedman, and Lindquist 2009; Wellstead and Stedman 2010).

The provincial and territorial government surveys were carried out by the author in November and December 2008 also using Zoomerang software and an appropriately amended version of the 2007 federal survey questionnaire. The questionnaire was sent to over 4,000 provincial and territorial civil servants situated in all thirteen Canadian provincial and territorial jurisdictions. Mailing lists for the ten provinces and three territories surveyed were compiled wherever possible from publicly available sources such as online government telephone directories using keyword searches for terms such as *policy analyst* appearing in job titles or descriptions. In some cases, additional names were added to lists from hardcopy sources such as government organization manuals. In other cases, lists or additional names were provided by provincial public service commissions, who also checked initial lists for completeness and accuracy. Over 1,600 survey completions were gathered from 3,856 valid e-mail addresses for a total response rate of 43.3 per cent (the actual distribution by jurisdiction is set out in appendix A) (Howlett 2009a; Howlett and Newman 2010). A different (snowball) survey methodology in Quebec generated a smaller sample, so the 130 responses from that province are excluded from the analysis that follows. However, a separate analysis of the results from the Quebec survey found a pattern of responses similar to those found in the other twelve provinces and territories (Bernier and Howlett 2009, 2011).

The data collected from the surveys allowed a profile of federal, provincial, and territorial policy analysts employed in the public service to be constructed for the first time. Combined, these data sets allow accurate empirical analysis of the characteristics, background, and activities of a wide variety of sub-national and national-level government policy analysts. They reveal much of interest concerning the similarities and differences found among policy workers and policy work in such systems (Howlett and Joshi-Koop 2011; Howlett and Oliphant 2010; Oliphant and Howlett 2010).[3]

In what follows, this same data set is used to construct a profile of policy managers, which is then compared and contrasted with that of non-managerial policy analysts. In this way, what is unique and what is common about the duties, background, and activities of policy managers, if anything, will be revealed. If policy managers are a significant "missing link" in policy analysis, we should find some evidence of substantial similarity between the tasks managers perform and those of regular analysts, but also some significant differences that would underline their importance and unique role in policy work.

Data and Findings

From the sixty-four survey questions common to the three studies, a very large data set containing several hundred variables was analysed using SPSS/PASW 18.0. The total sample size in the combined survey was 3,028 analysts. Of these, 735 or 24 per cent indicated that they were "managers" and/or "program managers" (see table 8.2).[4]

These managers were evenly distributed by level of government, with about 50 per cent of the sample located at the national and subnational levels. A profile of the policy work of these managers and non-managers was undertaken using frequency, means, and factor analyses in order to provide a map and comparison of managerial activity vis-à-vis that of other "ordinary" analysts.[5] These statistical tests were used to develop demographic profiles of managers and analysts and identify the areas where the managers worked, the tasks associated with their jobs, the skills they used in these tasks, and their attitudes towards their ability to perform their work. Together these allow a more precise picture of the work world of professional policy analysts and managers to be assembled than has been done (Colebatch 2006a).

As table 8.3 shows, managers tend more to be male and slightly older than non-managers. This suggests that they would be more senior, in conformity with historical hiring patterns (a comparison of the gender means by age grouping in table 8.3 suggests that this is related to historical hiring patterns, as the propensity to be male increases with the age of the analyst).

Managers also (see table 8.4) are more likely to have had experience in other sectors than non-managers, including especially earlier experience in not-for-profits and the private sector (on the significance of previous private sector experience on managers' attitudes and behaviour, see Boardman et al. 2010).

Table 8.2 Sample Sizes and Distribution: Managers and Non-Managers

	Non-managers (%)	Total managers (%)	Managers	Managers and program managers
Total sample = 3,028	2,293 (75.7)	735 (24.3)	661	74
Distribution				
Provincial and territorial	(49.4)	(52.1)		
Federal	(50.6)	(47.9)		

Table 8.3 Gender and Age of Managers and Analysts (%)

Gender	Managers	Non-managers		
Male	51.2	44.8		
Female	48.8	55.2		
Age	**Managers**	**Mean**	**Non-managers**	**Mean**
< 30	5.6	0.41	14.9	0.37
31–40	22.1	0.48	26.5	0.42
41–50	35.9	0.47	28.7	0.44
51–60	32.7	0.60	26.2	0.54
> 61	3.7	0.77	3.8	0.61

Again probably reflecting changes in hiring practices in recent years, managers tend to be slightly less well-educated than non-managers, with a sizeable number having only a high school diploma and about 10 per cent having earned less than a college degree, versus just over 3 per cent for non-managers.

For training in policy matters, these educational and generational differences remain small but distinct, with more managers tending to cite on-the-job training and non-managers formal training in post-secondary institutions or government-run training institutes (see table 8.5). Overall, therefore, policy managers have a profile roughly similar to that for non-managers, outside of slight, and probably declining, differences in gender, work experience, training, and levels of formal education.

Table 8.4 Previous Policy Work Experience and Educational Attainment (%)

Previous work experience	Managers	Non-managers	Educational level	Managers	Non-managers
Academia	22.6	20.7	High school	5.9	0.0
Municipalities	11.0	9.3	Community or technical college	3.9	3.4
Not-for-profit	27.3	23.9	Undergraduate degree	7.6	5.3
Private sector	32.9	26.2	Graduate degree	30.5	32.4
Provincial or territorial	23.0	15.8			
Federal	8.0	5.9			

Table 8.5 Types of Training (%)

Training	Managers	Non-managers
Attended policy-related conferences	67.8	59.2
Attended policy workshops	73.6	65.9
Completed policy-relevant university or college courses	41.9	52.2
Completed government-run or sponsored courses	38.3	48.4

Work Activities

What about their work activities? Earlier work on Canadian policy analysts has shown them to be located primarily in specialized policy units (Howlett and Newman 2010). However, managers are much less likely to be so located (see table 8.6), with most, again not surprisingly, enjoying a wider range of links than non-managerial analysts to more senior administrative levels.

Despite these differences, however, as far as duties are concerned, managers and non-managers are involved in many of the same tasks (see table 8.7). Again, not unexpectedly, managers tend to be slightly more involved in administrative tasks such as department or agency planning and preparing budgets than non-managerial analysts, who tend to be more engaged in research and similar activities.

Table 8.6 Work Location of Managers and Analysts (%)

Membership in formal policy unit	Managers	Non-managers
Yes	41.0	67.0
No	59.0	33.0

Table 8.7 Work Activities of Managers and Analysts (%)

Task	Managers	Non-managers
Department or agency planning	89.2	84
Environmental scans/issue tracking	100	100
Legal analysis	33.5	30.3
Preparing budget/Treasury Board submissions	54.5	47.5
Ministerial briefing	75.4	72.5
Networking	82.0	77.1
Preparing briefing notes or position papers	100	100
Providing options on issues	100	100
Undertaking research and analysis	76.0	79.1
Providing advice	95.0	89.6

Significantly, however, overall, managers undertake most of the same tasks as non-managers, demonstrating a significant hands-on role in basic policy analytical activities.

This is not to say, however, that managers and non-managers are equally involved in all the specific tasks associated with policy analysis and policymaking in government. As table 8.8 shows, both managers and non-managers tend to cluster into two types: one being a set of actors who engage primarily in tasks related to policy research and analysis, and the other to implementation, negotiation, and consultation. While the differences are slight, more non-managers tend to correlate more strongly with on-the-ground activities and more managers with research and analysis, suggesting a larger role for managers in policy formulation and decision-making.

Managers and non-managers also fall into two groups when it comes to the temporal nature of the tasks they are involved with. As table 8.9 shows, both groups divide into two components, depending on their

Table 8.8 Cluster Principal Component Analysis of Activities of Managers and Non-Managerial Analysts

Task	Managers		Non-managers	
	Component 1: Research	Component 2: Negotiate	Component 1: Research	Component 2: Negotiate
Appraise policy options	0.840	0.090	0.794	0.242
Collect policy-related data or information	0.836	0..043	0.838	0.009
Conduct policy-related research	0.825	0.030	0.823	-0.039
Identify policy issues	0.855	0.180	0.813	0.250
Identify policy options	0.871	0.199	0.848	0.266
Implement or deliver policies or programs	-0.119	0.585	-0.047	0.648
Negotiate with stake-holders on policy matters	0.214	0.805	0.166	0.830
Negotiate with central agencies on policy matters	0.416	0.500	0.332	0.567
Negotiate with program mangers on policy matters	0.270	0.681	0.220	0.708
Consult with the public on policy matters	0.042	0.691	0.041	0.665
Consult with stake-holders on policy matters	0.093	0.749	0.140	0.765
	Rotation method	Varimax with Kaiser normalization		

proclivity to work on tasks and issues that are essentially short-term (six months or less) versus longer-term ones (greater than six months). Managers are slightly less likely to work on short-term issues and slightly more likely to work on long-term ones, again emphasizing their role in planning analytical activities. However, once again, this

Table 8.9 Cluster Analysis of Duration of Tasks

Task	Managers		Non-managers	
	Component 1: Long-term	Component 2: Short-term	Component 1: Long-term	Component 2: Short-term
Tasks that demand immediate action (i.e., "firefighting")	-0.015	0.803	-0.007	0.816
Short-term tasks that can be resolved in less than a month	0.125	0.861	0.098	0.870
Medium-term tasks that are ongoing for 1–6 months	0.752	0.430	0.730	0.425
Long-term tasks that are ongoing for 6–12 months	0.902	0.019	0.895	0.027
Tasks that are ongoing for more than a year	0.768	-0.053	0.736	0.074
	Rotation method	Varimax wih Kaiser normalization		

distinction should not be exaggerated, as managers have a profile very similar to that for non-managers, and many managers also play a very significant role in addressing shorter-term issues.

This finding is borne out by table 8.10, which shows the frequency with which each group cites particular types of issues that occupy them at least "weekly."

INTERACTIONS WITH OTHER POLICY ACTORS

Finally, there is the issue of whom managers and non-managers tend to interact with in their activities. As table 8.11 shows, both managers and non-managers tend to cluster into three groups – those who interact mainly with external actors, those who interact mainly with head office officials, and those who interact with regional governments – in the Canadian case, provincial or territorial, federal, and aboriginal.

As table 8.12 shows, managers are slightly more likely to interact with head office and regional governments and non-managers with outside actors, but, again, the differences are not as great as would be

Table 8.10 Duration of Tasks (% Who Say "Weekly")

Level of involvement	Managers	Non-managers
Firefighting	15.7	23.1
Tasks that can be resolved in a month	24.7	31.4
1–6 month tasks	35.9	38.9
6–12 month tasks	34.4	31.4
More than one year	21.1	21.9

expected if there were a sharp management/non-managerial divide between the two groups of policy workers. This is borne out again in table 8.12, which shows how many of each group dealt with these other kinds of actors at least weekly.

Conclusions

Policy managers are players in policy advice systems about whom we require much more precise information than has typically appeared in the literature. Accurately assessing their activities, skills, attitudes, and other aspects of their policy work is required for studies of the subject to advance.

The present study of a large group of policy managers in Canada presents a more nuanced picture of the complexity and multidimensionality of policy work than is usually assumed in the literature on the subject. Policy managers are not simply administrators, and there is no evidence of a strong politics/policy-administration dichotomy in their ongoing policy work. The analysis presented here suggests that the policy roles played by policy managers are significant and in most respects very similar to those played by non-managerial policy analysts. However, it also suggests that managers enjoy some advantages over non-managers in their access to key decision-makers and their ability to deal with longer-term issues, and notes a more significant role played by managers in policy formulation and design.

The study also reveals that this group, like the larger group of non-managers, should not be treated as a homogeneous entity but that there are significant differences among managers in many important dimensions of their activities, differences that transcend the simple "political" versus "technical" dimensions found in early work on policy analysts

Table 8.11 Cluster Analysis of Interactions

Task	Managers			Non-managers		
	Component 1: External Networking	Component 2: Head office	Component 3: Regional	Component 1: External Networking	Component 2: Head Office	Component 3: Regional
Senior head office–based management		0.901			0.878	
Other head office staff		0.873			0.868	
Senior regional management			0.597			0.644
Central agencies		0.787			0.729	
Other provincial government departments		0.510	0.495		0.442	0.440
Municipal government departments			0.565	0.433		0.539
Federal departments in my region			0.632			0.516
Environmental/conservation-based groups	0.544			0.477		0.497
Industry organizations	0.726			0.674		
Labour organizations	0.689			0.669		
Think tanks	0.733			0.769		
Universities	0.694			0.708		
Aboriginal groups			0.693			0.771
	Rotation method	Varimax with Kaiser normalization				

Table 8.12 Network Interactions (% Who Say "Weekly")

Level of involvement	Managers	Non-managers
Senior head office–based management	29.9	28.1
Other head office staff	30.4	28.2
Senior regional management	40.6	37.2
Central agencies	30.1	32.8
Other provincial government departments	37.6	35.8
Municipal government departments	18.3	20.6
Federal departments in my region	35.9	36.5
Environmental/conservation-based groups	15.3	16.0
Industry organizations	27.4	28.1
Labour organizations	14.1	14.3
Think tanks	15.7	18.5
Universities	21.9	20.1
Aboriginal groups	19.9	22.0

in the bureaucracy such as that of Meltsner (1975, 1976) and those who followed in his footsteps. In particular, managers at this level were found to differ in their short- versus longer-term orientations and their typical on-the-job interactions. However, not all managers have a longer-term orientation or deal more with head office and other governments than with external actors, and some differ little from non-managerial policy workers in many respects.

These similarities and differences suggest that policy managers' roles and activities do in fact require further investigation. They highlight the multidimensional nature of professional policy work and its varied and complex nature (Koliba and Gajda 2009; Kothari, MacLean, and Edwards 2009). Policy advice systems, and especially these systems' professional bureaucratic component, are complex and require more careful and systematic empirical analysis than has generally been done. Those who wish to better assess and evaluate such activities in order to improve training and recruitment practices, enhance analytical capacity, and, ultimately, improve analysis and policy outcomes (ANAO 2001; Di Francesco 1999, 2000; Nicholson 1996, 1997; State Services Commission 1999), for example, should devote more effort to investigating these distinctions and their implications.

Appendix A: Provincial Survey Sample Sizes and Completion Rates

Province	Initial mail list size	Refusals and rejected e-mails	Valid partial completions	Complete	Response rate (%)
BC	513	51	30	194	48.5
Alberta	368	23	8	112	34.8
Saskatchewan	246	27	13	80	42.4
Manitoba	161	20	6	98	73.7
Ontario	1613	162	52	557	41.9
Quebec†	250	0	44	86	52.0
New Brunswick	162	15	4	62	44.9
Nova Scotia	181	20	15	83	44.1
PEI	27	6	1	4	23.8
Newfoundland	139	24	16	55	61.7
Yukon	75	8	6	58	95.5
NWT	80	2	2	41	55.1
Nunavut	41	8	2	13	45.4
TOTAL (excluding Quebec)	3865	366	155	1357	43.3

† Snowball sample methodology – data excluded from totals and from subsequent tables.

Appendix B: Specific Duties of Analysts (Provincial and Territorial Governments)

Legal					Data				
	Work (n = 694)	Formulation (n = 549)	Consultation (n = 524)	Implementation (n = 331)	Finance (n = 548)	Evaluation (n = 140)	Management (n = 340)	Communication (n = 322)	Assessment (n = 354)
Formal legislative or executive consultation									0.790
Legal consultation									0.815
Environmental assessment								0.847	
Environmental scans								0.773	
Communications and media relations							0.601		
Report writing or editing							0.713		
Report presentation							0.717		
Data collection and entry						0.856			
Data management						0.851			

Appendix B: Specific Duties of Analysts (Provincial and Territorial Governments) (*cont.*)

Legal					Data				
	Work (*n* = 694)	Formulation (*n* = 549)	Consultation (*n* = 524)	Implementation (*n* = 331)	Finance (*n* = 548)	Evaluation (*n* = 140)	Management (*n* = 340)	Communication (*n* = 322)	Assessment (*n* = 354)
Auditing and evaluation					0.579				
Formal policy or program evaluation					0.776				
Informal policy or program evaluation					0.700				
Cost-benefit analysis				0.602					
Budget analysis				0.800					
Finance				0.776					
Program development			0.745						
Program delivery and implementation			0.834						
Program administration			0.613						

Appendix B: Specific Duties of Analysts (Provincial and Territorial Governments) (*cont.*)

Legal					Data				
	Work (n = 694)	Formulation (n = 549)	Consultation (n = 524)	Implementation (n = 331)	Finance (n = 548)	Evaluation (n = 140)	Management (n = 340)	Communication (n = 322)	Assessment (n = 354)
Public participation design		0.755							
Public consultation		0.837							
Stakeholder consultation		0.723							
Policy analysis	0.749								
Policy development	0.767								
Formulation policy options	0.809								
Assessing policy options	0.792								

NOTES

1 The hostile environment in which they operate in many countries further undermines public managers' policy efforts, giving rise to popular demands to downsize government and transfer many public responsibilities to the private or non-profit sectors, reducing the capacity of the administration precisely at a time when it might need to be improved (Brinkerhoff 2010; Brinkerhoff and Morgan 2010).

2 This narrow self-perception of the policy role of public managers is rooted in traditional public administration theories developed on the basis of the U.S. and European experiences, which have historically advocated a strong separation between administration and politics, with the latter belonging exclusively to the realm of political executives. Although the notion of the empirical and conceptual validity of this separation between administration and politics has been challenged by generations of scholars, its staying power in influencing practices can be seen clearly from many key reform measures introduced in the recent New Public Management (NPM) era in many countries that often aimed to more clearly separate "policymaking" agencies from "implementation" agencies in order to boost administrative efficiency and effectiveness. In the Netherlands, for example, reforms in the 1990s created completely separate agencies for policy and administration (Painter and Pierre 2005a).

3 While policy capacity can be thought of as extending beyond analysis to include the actual administrative capacity of a government to undertake the day-to-day activities involved in policy implementation (Painter and Pierre 2005; Peters 1996), policy analytical capacity is a more focused concept related to knowledge acquisition and utilization in policy processes. It refers to the amount of basic research a government can conduct or access; its ability to apply statistical methods, applied research methods, and advanced modelling techniques to these data; and employ analytical techniques such as environmental scanning, trends analysis, and forecasting methods in order to gauge broad public opinion and attitudes, as well as those of interest groups and other major policy players, and to anticipate future policy impacts (O'Connor, Roos, and Vickers-Willis 2007). It also involves the ability to communicate policy-related messages to interested parties and stakeholders and includes "a department's capacity to articulate its medium and long-term priorities" and to integrate information into the decision-making stage of the policy process.

4 Eighty-four respondents who indicated they were "program managers" but did not also describe themselves as "managers" were eliminated from the sample.

5 Data were divided into five topic areas: demographic characteristics and job experience; education and training; day-to-day duties; and techniques and data employed. Overall survey results and profiles for the federal level are available in Wellstead and others (2007), Wellstead, Stedman, and Lindquist (2009), and at the provincial and territorial level, in Howlett (2009a, 2009b). The general nature of the duties carried out by analysts is set out in appendix B.

9 Policy Work and the Political Arm of Government

JONATHAN CRAFT

The Ministerial Executive Assistant can be anything from an extremely powerful policy-influencing, unelected official to a glorified, overpaid baggage-handler

(Lenoski 1977, 171)

Introduction

This chapter leaves the ranks of the public service to examine another type of policy worker: appointed political staffs. These actors are institutionalized members of contemporary executives and key instruments of the "political arm" of government (Aucoin 2010; Osbaldeston 1987). Despite longstanding recognition that they are a basic component of typical policy advisory systems (Halligan 1995; Prince 2007), they are among the most understudied. Plassé's conclusion some twenty years ago stands: "Little research has been done on ministers' offices or on their staff, even though these ministerial support units occupy a central position in the decision-making process of our governments" (Plassé 1994, iii). By international standards this reality is even more acute, with analysis of the policy work of Canadian political staffs lagging well behind that of their Westminster counterparts (Eichbaum and Shaw 2010; Maley 2011; Gains and Stoker 2011; Craft 2015a). This chapter seeks to close this gap with historical analysis of the evolution of Canadian political staff as policy workers. The principal argument advanced is that partisan advisers,[1] as a subset of appointed political staffs, have emerged through a three-staged process of institutionalization, expansion, and specialization. These actors are now engaging in increasingly specialized and unique forms of policy work that are consequential to the operation of the executive and policymaking (Craft 2015b).

There is widespread agreement that the institutionalization of Canadian political staffs within the executive began in the mid-twentieth century. This is most often explained as a product of elected officials seeking greater capacity to implement the government's policy agenda, to improve public service policy responsiveness, and to avoid ministerial "overload" (Aucoin 2010; Doern 1971; Savoie 1999; White 2005). The second stage of the posited evolution is also generally supported by data confirming an aggregate expansion of federal political staffs during the latter part of twentieth century (Aucoin 2010; Craft 2016). This increase requires specification, however. Disentangling the precise number who undertake policy versus administrative, communications, or clerical work can be difficult. However, as is argued below, by historical standards, there is a clear pattern of growth of political staffs with exclusive policy responsibilities within first ministers' and ministers' offices.

The third and final stage, specialization, is supported by empirical evidence but remains normatively contentious. Almost from the very outset of their deployment, some have argued political staff should be limited to basic administration and partisan-political support functions for ministers (Mallory 1967). Others have, however, advocated for a greater role for such staffs, particularly as actors that may provide much needed support and capacity for ministers to engage in policy development, in addition to supporting political aspects of their work as elected members of parliament, ministers, and partisans (Savoie 1983; Tellier 1968; Zussman 2009). The normative debate now takes place against a backdrop of increasing contemporary evidence and official government of Canada documents recognizing partisan advisers as specialized policy workers (Aucoin 2010; Benoit 2006; Craft 2016; Craft 2015a; Savoie 1999, 2003b; Wilson 2015, 2016). Their specialization flows from an increasingly differentiated division of labour that characterizes their officially recognized policy functions, and their exemptions from certain public service rules and regulations (King 2003), both of which enable them to engage in unique partisan-political policy work that non-partisan public service policy workers cannot.

The chapter begins with a historical review of the emergence of political staff within the Canadian political executive. The narrative is well known but when re-examined from a policy work perspective it provides context for the ensuring examination of their emergence as specialized policy workers. Throughout attention is paid to the evolution and contemporary policy work of partisan advisers in the Prime

Minister's Office as well as those in ministers' offices. The former have received the lion's share of attention, but interesting comparative dynamics can be teased out on the emergence of partisan advisers at both institutional locations, as well as their collective policy work within the executive. The final section provides a review and analysis of the contemporary policy work of political staffs. Studies and official government documents are used to demonstrate the unique forms of partisan-political policy work that confirm advisers' unique policy functions. It has been suggested that political staffs are one of the most significant institutional innovations within the Westminster-style governments (Maley 2011, 1469). This characterization seems appropriate in the Canadian case, given the increasing attention and empirical evidence of their influence in contemporary Canadian policy work (Aucoin 2012; Craft 2016).

Looking Back: The Institutionalization, Expansion, and Specialization of the Political Arm of Government

The historical evolution of the prime minister's and ministers' offices political staffs in this introductory section is not provided for nostalgic purposes, but rather as a means to contextualize and better understand the political arm's policy work. Punnett (1977) has suggested that a Prime Minister's Office (PMO) provides three main functions: secretarial and administrative capacity, a source of political advice to the prime minister, and a "supply of factual information about the affairs of government, to enable him to face his ministers from an informed base. If he is to be free from dependence on departmental civil servants, this factual information can only come from a private bureaucracy" (74–5). This description hints at the specialized nature of partisan advisers, but becomes clearer with the benefit of time that allows for its careful examination.

The contemporary PMO has become a prominent fixture in Canadian politics; it was, however, from Confederation until the 1930s, adeptly managed by prime ministers themselves, assisted by a small coterie of seconded public servants (Punnett 1977). It is difficult to imagine, but prime ministers had no partisan entourages, no "chiefs of staff," no PMO "policy shops." In describing the PMO support structures in place in the early twentieth century, Mitchell Sharp, a long-serving deputy minister, explains that ministers had few staff. He writes that even "Prime Ministers King and St Laurent had only a handful of people in their offices, nearly all of whom (like Pickersgill, who served both King and St Laurent) had originally been selected by the Public Service Commission for departmental jobs" (Sharp 1995, 112). The PMO staff numbers remained relatively constant up until the Diefenbaker (1957–63) government, but precise calculation is difficult for the St Laurent to Diefenbaker period, as significant numbers of staff were seconded to the PMO from the public service (D'Aquino 1974; Lalonde 1971). Subsequent to Diefenbaker, as per table 9.1 below, PMO staffing complements grew steadily in the mid-twentieth century. The majority of this growth was for administrative and clerical staff, a trend that has carried over to modern day PMOs (Axworthy 1988; Goldenberg 2006). There were, however, also discernible increases to the number and type of political staff "doing policy," particularly in the late twentieth century (Aucoin 2010).

Retrospective analysis of the situation at the minister's office level is even more striking. Prior to the 1950s, they included primarily administrative support staffs consisting of a "secretary to the executive" in addition to a couple of stenographers, a messenger, and the minister's private secretary (Mallory 1967). In 1958 a new category of "special assistant" was created for "press officer" duties[2] (ibid.). Other students of the minister's office have noted that a "typical" minister in the St Laurent government (1948–57) "seldom had the services of more than a single political confidant" (Lenoski 1977, 166). Legislative changes in the 1960s paved the way for the expansion and specialization of the political arm. The exclusion of the ministers' "private offices" from the 1963 Civil Service Act negated the previously established limits on political staffs established through Treasury Board Minutes. The Public Service Employment Act (1967) codified the "special assistant" category of exempt staff and the classification of other positions.[3] The institutionalization, expansion, and specialization of ministers' office political staffs was underway. The authorized complement grew from five in the 1940s to twelve in the 1970s (Aucoin 2010), and the subcategorization of the special assistant category (then including parliamentary relations, constituency relations, and legislative assistant categories) ushered in the period of specialization of political staff that has continued with increasingly discrete classifications of political staff activities, including policy (Lenoski 1977, 169–70). On the point of policy specialization within the ministers' office, it is worth quoting Lenoski at length:

The continuing diversification of responsibilities assumed by ministers in large measure has accounted for greater role specialization on the part of their bigger staffs. Whereas the executive assistant at one time could take care of virtually everything single-handedly, the necessity of providing additional assistants for varying reasons has led to a fairly strict differentiation of duties among many minister's staffs. Moreover, together with the executive assistant and several special assistants for designated purposes, the staff complement backing up a representative minister at the present time, will include some research, administrative and/or departmental assistants. Under these latter, and still other, classifications can be subsumed political operatives who concentrate on anything from press relations to speech preparation, policy analysis and a host of other requirements that must be met to help the minister fulfil his various duties.

Responding to requests for greater flexibility and in an attempt to curtail the "personal services contract" by which ministers expanded their staffs, Cabinet approved a new exempt staff position of

Table 9.1 Political Staff and Expenses for the Prime Minister's Office (1962, 1967, and 1970)†

PMO Staff	1962–3‡	1967–8	1970–1
Principal secretary	–	1	1
Executive assistant	1	1	1
Special assistant	4	3	10
Press office	2	4	6
Correspondence	15	22	41
Regional desks	–	–	7
Secretaries	7	8	17
Private secretary	1	1	1
Constituency office	–	–	1
PMO staff total	30	40	85
Budget (salaries, contracts, and travel expenses)	$181,550 (approx.)	$331,585	$900,839

Adapted from Lalonde (1971), 532.

† Figures are for fiscal years 1 April to 31 March.

‡ Lalonde notes that the figures do not include seconded public servants working in the PMO.

"special assistant – policy adviser" in 1978 (Williams 1980, 219). From an examination of available Cabinet conclusions and secondary sources this is the first explicit formal recognition of the partisan adviser role.

The political arm of government owes its structural and operational origins to changes introduced by Prime Ministers Pearson and Trudeau. Pearson brought Tom Kent into the PMO in 1963 as special policy adviser (Aucoin 2010; Doern 1971). Doern (1971, 49) writes of Kent's presence in the PMO, "It represented a policy and a policy presence in a much more visible and direct sense than ever before." Trudeau expanded on the formal institutionalized partisan advisers into the Prime Minister's Office in 1968 regularizing the practice of appointing non-public servants in advisory roles, and with this established the architecture, division of labour, and practices that in many ways remain in contemporary PMOs. The use of appointed political staffs was part of a broader "rationalization" of government. That is, a consciously orchestrated exercise aimed institutional and operational redesign to meet the challenges of modern executive governance, and to support the empowerment of the Cabinet and PMO over departments (French and Van Loon 1984; Doern 1971). The implications of the inclusions of appointed political staffs as part of this process signalled the need for politically oriented policy workers. As Trudeau's former principal secretary at the time has written, "A new category of official was created – the political adviser. Their role was different from that of public servants who had for years served Prime Ministers they would advise on the interaction of policy and politics and not be subject to the formal rules of the public service" (Axworthy 1988, 258). No prime minister has since reversed course. Pierre Trudeau's PMO numbered sixty in 1969, and by his last year in office 1983–4 the Trudeau PMO had grown to twice the size of that of Prime Minister Pearson with a budget of approximately $4.2 million and a staff of eighty-seven (258; Punnett 1977, 77). Again, it is important to be clear in that, though twice the size of the Pearson PMO, most of the new Trudeau PMO staff were clerical, with only twenty or so considered senior advisers (Axworthy 1988, 258).

However, from a policy work perspective, this period was a watershed, not only in the institutionalization and expansion of political staff but also as the genesis of the specialized partisan policy capacity of the executive. As Aucoin has cogently argued, the specialization of partisan advisers was tied to Trudeau's overarching rationalization project. It involved not only the regionalization of policy work in the PMO to meet representational imperatives that animate Canadian politics, but also extended to corporate policy coordination, steering, and content alignment to promote policy coherence. The number of advisers was increased, greater policy specialization was introduced, and regional responsibilities were differentiated by the creation of "regional desks." The PMO was also to coordinate the activities of the senior political staff of ministers in order to promote the political policy objectives of the government. In short, even these political/partisan functions were to conform to the paradigm of rational management (Aucoin 1986, 11). The intended benefits of additional partisan-political policy capacity in the reconfigured PMO are, however, judged to have been slow to accrue. D'Aquino (1974), himself a PMO staffer, later reflected on the need for more capacity. Scholarly assessments have pointed to a range of reasons for the uneven development of PMO's policy capacity, including a limited number of policy-specific PMO staff, strong ministers whose policy advice Trudeau trusted, and Trudeau's preference for multiple sources of advice, including strengthened central administrative agencies staffed by chosen close associates (Aucoin 1986). Campbell (1988, 269) highlights similar limitations and adroitly points out that the first Trudeau PMO (1968–72) lacked a formal policy unit, with only Lalonde and a few others playing a major policy role. Even when one was established in the subsequent majority government, its ability to effectively provide policy capacity was meagre. PMOs have hovered around the 100 staff member level since the late 1970s, but the advisory capacity of the PMO has fluctuated and been deployed in various ways.

The next wave of major reforms to the political arms structure and operation were introduced by the Mulroney (1984–93) administration. It continued the trend of having its own "in-house" PMO policy shop and expanded the PMO staff complement to 117 in 1985–6 (Axworthy 1988, 258). This expansion was a product of an explicit emphasis by Mulroney on beefing up the policy capacity of the PMO, with the policy staff expanding from three during the Trudeau years to over a dozen (Aucoin 1986). The principal secretary position eventually replaced with the first ever PMO "chief of staff" with the appointment of Derek Burney in March 1987. In addition, the creation of a Deputy Prime Minister's Office (DPMO) was another innovation.[4] The prominent influence of this office and its staff in policymaking during the administration was well documented through their activities in chairing key Cabinet committees (Aucoin 1986; Savoie 1994).

Ministers' offices also received a makeover, with the longstanding "executive assistant" classifications replaced by "chiefs of staff." The new title and reclassification at a rank comparable to that of deputy minister (with accompanying increases in remuneration) were a clear signal to the public service that the political arm would be seeking to flex its policy muscle. As Savoie (2003, 124) bluntly puts it, "Mulroney's decision had one purpose – to check permanent officials' influence on policy." Chiefs of staff and political staff more generally were explicitly used as a means to contest or counterbalance the perceived influence of the entrenched bureaucracy. With an expanded Cabinet of forty ministers, the number of ministerial staff increased correspondingly. It was common to find a group of thirty or forty people working in a minister's office under the direction of a "chief of staff" (Larson 1999, 57). By 1990–1 the exempt staff totalled 460 (99 of whom staffed the PMO). This expanded contingent of exempt staff was rolled out in ministers' offices across government to ensure a more muscular overall political management and to provide greater political and policy advisory capacity for ministers (Bakvis 2000, 78).

From a policy work perspective, ministers' offices under the direction of political staffs had clearly articulated policy functions. As O'Connor (1991, 23–5) explains, the chief of staff position was created to "offer policy advice over and above that provided by the department he or she could achieve this in part by soliciting opinions different from those held by the departmental advisers," and chiefs of staff "provided an interesting challenge to the deputy minister and the department in terms of policy development and control." Plassé's (1994) study of federal Mulroney chiefs of staff ($N = 19$) found that chiefs self-reported their most frequent duties to involve providing advice to the minister, managing the office, ensuring liaison with the minister, and review of departmental policies. O'Connor's review of the chief of staff role lists the tasks:[5]

- the monitoring of progress of departmental and ministerial priorities;
- the management of the minister's political profile and communications priorities;
- the management of the minister's paper flow;
- the administration of the minister's departmental, Parliament Hill, and constituency offices;
- the minister's speech-writing agenda;
- Cabinet, parliamentary secretary, caucus and opposition liaison;

- liaison with the party apparatus at the national, regional, and constituency levels;
- overall scheduling and travel industry, association, and special interest group contacts; and
- liaison with the Prime Minister's Office, the Privy Council Office, Treasury Board, and other departments.

The majority of chiefs noted that they participated in decision-making in various forms such as departmental management committees and projects, and advice to the minister on all matters. Plassé's (1994) conclusion is that chiefs were able to carve out a policy function that, in general, complemented that of the department. A subsequent assessment is, however, less laudatory. Savoie's (2003, 124) analysis confirms that political staff had become established policy workers, but importantly he draws attention to the mixed results of their policy work: "The chiefs of staff, however, had a mixed reception, often dependent on the quality of the incumbent. They introduced a new level between ministers and permanent officials, which gave rise to misunderstandings and complications. In some instances, the chief of staff acted as a mediator between the minister and permanent officials, screening advice going up to the minister and issuing policy directives going down to officials, much to the dismay and objections of deputy ministers. Many chiefs of staff took a dim view of the competence of permanent officials, who took an equally jaundiced view of them."

The election of the Chrétien governments (1993–2003) saw another prime minister put his stamp on the structure and operation of the political arm. As a long-time parliamentarian and Cabinet minister in various portfolios, he brought first-hand experience working with PMOs past. Chrétien's PMO has received detailed treatment by students of public administration and journalists on its operation and the continued concentration of power or "court government" style (see Bakvis 2000; Savoie 1999, 2003b; Simpson 2001). As per table 9.2, the size of the PMO was reduced during the early years of the Chrétien government but increased during his final mandate. It reverted to the ministerial executive assistant model, eliminating chiefs of staff, save in the PMO. The PMO had no principal secretary, but long-time senior Chrétien political aide Edward Goldenberg served that function when Chrétien was leader of the opposition and performed the same general function but under the title of senior policy adviser. Goldenberg explained that Chrétien "expected me to focus on his major policy

Table 9.2 Federal Exempt Staff by Department (30 March 2001 to 31 March 2011)

	Year										
	2001	2002	2003	2004	2005	2006	2007	2008	2009	2010	2011
Office of the Prime Minister	83	81	77	64	68	65	79	92	94	112	99
Total ministerial exempt staff	461	461	488	428	461	194	414	442	487	532	520

Source: Adapted from a larger table provided to the author in correspondence with the Office of the Chief Human Resources Officer, Treasury Board of Canada Secretariat, 24 October 2011 in response to request no. 31029. Figures include employees on leave without pay.

priorities, and to work with cabinet ministers and deputy ministers to implement them. In addition, because of our long experience together, he told me that my role would include providing advice on overall political strategy, federal-provincial relations, and much else as circumstances required" (Goldenberg 2006, 96).

In his aptly titled *The Way It Works*, Goldenberg dismisses accounts of a controlling PMO or "court government," preferring to characterize the PMO role as one of "oversight" and "coordination," advice-giving and communication, and "gatekeeping" (Goldenberg 2006, chap. 5). From the perspective of policy work, his account makes clear that his role, as senior partisan adviser, extended to select policy files of interest to the prime minister or himself or to major policy issues as they arose. The PMO also maintained a policy "shop" that continued to engage in policy work in an organized and coherent fashion. They "were responsible for how the PMO managed and coordinated government policy priorities and that the [PMO] policy director and their staff took responsibility for making sure that all the cabinet ministers followed through on election campaign commitments; they also carefully monitored the agendas of all cabinet committees, identified problems between departments and ministers, offered advice, and worked to fix problems" (96).

This description highlights the point that partisan advisers engage in important procedural policy work in addition to substantive considerations (Craft 2016). That is, they serve as coordination agents within the executive on the content dimensions of policy as well as how policy itself develops. It also signals the "firefighting" type of policy work that often accompanies the work of partisan advisers (Benoit 2006; White 2005). The PMO "policy shop" was staffed by approximately seven policy advisers and structured to mirror Cabinet committees and broad policy (social policy, economic policy, etc.). It was hierarchically organized, with "junior" PMO partisan advisers reporting to the director, who then reported to the senior policy adviser and chief or prime minister as needed. Their job involved monitoring, liaising, firefighting, and coordination between the PMO and ministers' offices[6] (Goldenberg 2006; Savoie 1999). This account is consistent with Jeffrey (2010, 249), who found "the role of Hosek's [PMO director of policy] policy group was to staff the two cabinet committees, liaise with the respective PCO and departmental officials, and troubleshoot on upcoming legislation or other policy proposals."

These published accounts confirmed that the policy work of PMO staff was almost exclusively through oral exchanges with officials, ministers, and other partisan advisers.[7] This was either within the PMO up to the prime minister or in consultation with the PCO, who would subsequently draft up "clerk's notes" or other written memoranda for the prime minister. This resonates with the published accounts as presented by Goldenberg (2006, chap. 5) of almost exclusively oral policy work. Those consulted and Goldenberg's published account paint a picture of considerable policy capacity within the PMO but of policy work that remained dependent upon public service processes and practices. That is, policy was most often produced collaboratively with the public service as lead on official documents integrating partisan advisers' input and then issuing them to the PM and Cabinet for review. PMO staff assumed the lead in some files, either given their political implications or the interest of the prime minister, but policymaking was managed primarily by the senior public service through regularized channels and processes (Goldenberg 2006; Savoie 1999). This further supports the notion of specialization for partisan advisers as policy workers, in that it suggests a special, or at least pronounced involvement in policy work associated to key government agenda items, and less focused involvement in "housekeeping" or more run-of-the-mill policy development.

Chrétien reduced Cabinet from forty to twenty-three ministers, with the effect of also reducing the number of aggregate political staff

(Kernaghan and Siegel 1995, 382). This was seen as a response to growing criticisms about powerful and unelected political staff (particularly in the PMO), a signal of renewed trust in the public service, and a commitment to decreased expenditure through reductions to the political arm of government (Aucoin 2010). By 1999–2000 the number of partisan staff across the board began to increase. The largest increases were at the ministerial office level and not in the PMO, which has maintained fairly stable staffing levels. Benoit (2006, 146) found that exempt staff during that era were "well placed to influence both the bounce and bobble of bureaucratic political interface and the pace and progress of public policy in Canada." In addition, others all underscore significant advisory and policy-related activity as well as influence (Zussman 2009; Aucoin 2010; Thomas 2008, 2010; Esselment, Lees-Marshment, and Marland 2014; Wilson 2015). Their findings deal particularly with prime ministerial advisers, but also ministerial political staffs to a more limited degree.

The Paul Martin minority government (2003–6) saw a vastly different organizational and operational style, particularly at the PMO. As per table 9.2, it saw a reduction in PMO staff but an increase in the overall number of political staff, with the exception of the 2006 election year. Recent accounts of the Martin years emphasize the impact of the large group of close Martin advisers known as "The Board." Furthermore, the organizational and management style has been labelled as much more horizontal and "flat" than that of PMOs past. This large group of advisers went from running a decade-long quest for leadership to running the Martin PMO. By all accounts, even those of "board members," it was a much more horizontal and consultative PMO. As noted by Jeffrey (2010, 452), "In a striking departure from the standard hierarchical structure of his predecessors, Martin's PMO was a loose horizontal organization. It contained no fewer than four deputy chiefs of staff." A consultation with Tim Murphy, who served as PMO chief of staff for the duration of the administration, confirmed this flat horizontal structure.[8] Mr Murphy also confirmed that the PMO and ministerial partisan-political policy advisory process continued to be largely informal and oral. While some written notes were produced, they were focused on events or were for media use. In short, the public service still carried the pen on all written advice going to the prime minister, but partisan advice from senior PMO advisers was sought out and integrated into that advice. Martin had close to ten senior advisers who bypassed the chief of staff and reported to him, another departure from the typical Chrétien practice. Accounts describe the policy advice and policy-making process in the Martin PMO as fluid, chaotic, disjointed, and quite simply unorganized (Wells 2006; Jeffrey 2010). As one Martin adviser candidly put it, "For sure, at a minimum we never got the policy function right" (Jeffrey 2010, 454). The Martin PMO was assessed overall to be light on policy capacity. Its policy leads were seen as less capable than those of PMOs past, with principal secretaries playing limited roles. The flat organizational structure saw the large group of PMO and external Martin advisers weighing in on policy items, creating a loss of policy coherence and influence flowing from the policy shop (533).

Two final points also deserve some mention. First, Martin created a political Cabinet committee that included formal partisan advisers as members. Martin's chief of staff, principal secretary, and senior PMO deputy chief of staff (operations) participated, in addition to regional political ministers on the committee chaired by the prime minister. This committee was designed primarily to deal with the political positioning and strategizing rather than policymaking per se, but formal inclusion and reliance on partisan advisers is a striking organizational shift (Jeffrey 2010, 451). Second, while the Martin PMO reverted to the practice of including a principal secretary, it was not considered to be very policy specific; rather, it was designed to deal more with francophone and Quebec related issues. Murphy recounts that as chief of staff he was the point person who would meet with the clerk and the prime minister, as well as chair the "all staff" PMO meetings.[9]

The Harper Years

Upon taking office after the 2006 general election, Prime Minister Stephen Harper immediately scrapped changes introduced by his predecessor. Conservative party executive and political scientist Ian Brodie was appointed PMO chief of staff. Brodie was given the task of organizing the first Conservative PMO in over a decade. Several interviews with Harper PMO staff described the early days as chaotic. The team was finding their footing, and processes were being put in place. It was explained that Stephen Harper's having been Leader of the Official Opposition was helpful, as several positions and processes could simply be transferred or slightly amended at the PMO. Much of Harper's opposition office staff migrated over to PMO jobs or was dispatched to staff ministers' offices.[10]

The PMO was organized under more traditional hierarchical terms, with all staff reporting through the PMO chief of staff. There was no principal secretary during the first minority government. Ray Novak, Harper's long-time executive assistant, was later promoted to principal secretary during Guy Giorno's term as PMO chief of staff. In 2013, after the abrupt resignation of PMO Chief of Staff Nigel Right, Novak was again promoted to PMO chief of staff. The newly elected Conservatives assembled a policy team under the direction of Mark Cameron, a former Liberal ministerial staffer. This study's interviews with Cameron and others from the early Harper PMO revealed that its structure and processes, as well as staffing, were largely left to Cameron.[11] The policy team was assembled along traditional lines, with PMO policy staff assigned to support the four existing Cabinet committees designed along broad policy sectors (i.e., economics, social affairs), as well as the powerful Operations (OPs), and Priorities and Planning (P&P) committees.

A watershed reform involved the deployment of a written formal PMO briefing note system. This is in direct contrast to oral and informal partisan-political policy advisory practices as reported from those of PMOs past (Goldenberg 2006; Jeffrey 2010). This system was implemented over time within the first minister's office and eventually ministerial offices as well. Those interviewed from the Harper government explained that the formal written policy advisory system operated in parallel to the public service policy advice system. Junior partisan advisers would take the lead in developing written partisan-political policy advice that would be provided up the chain of command via the PMO policy shop and be offered at the same time as public service advice. These written, formal, routinized partisan-political briefing notes were reported to accompany *virtually all* policy advice from the public service.[12] This written policy advisory system was supplemented by oral briefings, which occurred formally in a daily morning meeting, or as needed, with multiple PMO chiefs and PMO policy directors providing policy advice *during* Cabinet meetings (Craft 2016). This same system was gradually instituted at the ministerial office level. This type of partisan-political policy work is in addition to regularized interactions with senior public servants during the development and coordination of Cabinet materials, Cabinet committee business, and the substantive and procedural activities tied to other major policy activities such as budgets, speeches from the throne, and the penning of mandate letters (Craft 2016).[13]

The implications for policy work are substantial. Not only does this confirm further specialized policy work undertaken by partisan advisers themselves, but it also reveals that ministers and the prime minister now received two types of written policy advice – one partisan-political and one non-partisan public service source of policy advice.[14] Multiple PMO respondents at various levels of seniority described the partisan policy advisory process as consisting of a mix of oral and written advice. However, there was universal agreement that overall the majority of advice to the prime minister was provided in writing. There were changes in both the organization and operation of the Harper PMO as four chiefs of staff headed up the PMO over the course of two minority governments (2006–8, 2008–11). In addition, several individuals staffed the PMO director of policy position since 2006. Harper and his various chiefs of staff, like those before, left their mark on the organization, process, and policy development and advisory practices of the PMO.

In 2016, Liberal Justin Trudeau became Canada's twenty-third prime minister and, like his predecessors, has organized the PMO to suit his policy and governing needs. It features a chief of staff and principal secretary along with a policy "shop," but how policy advice is provided to the prime minister by PMO staff or how partisan advisers engage in policy work with central agency counterparts or others in the advisory system remains unknown. However, the prime minister's publicly stated preference for "Cabinet" government suggests that ministers' office political advisers may play an important role in the policy process in this government. Further study of that government's organization and use of the political arm of government will help further clarify the nature and politics of policy work in Canada.

Policy Work and the Political Arm: Specialization and Appointed Political Staffs as Policy Workers

The above review contextualizes the evolving nature of the political arm of government. Turning to official government documents is instructive for supplementing the above accounts of the actual policy work political staffs. The government of Canada's top bureaucratic office, the Privy Council Office (PCO), in setting out the raison d'être of ministerial exempt staff, underscores the point that ministers require both professional public service advice as well as political advice. As the PCO guide to ministers and ministers of state explains, "The purpose of establishing a Minister's or Minister of State's office is to provide Ministers and Ministers of State with advisers and assistants who are not departmental public servants, who share their political commitment, and who can complement the professional, expert and non-partisan advice and support of the public service. *Consequently, they contribute a particular expertise or point of view that the public service cannot provide*" (Privy Council Office 2011, 45, emphasis added).

Thus, institutionalized partisan advisers are an officially recognized component of the policy advisory system. The guide implicitly paints their advisory activity as political and not "administrative." That is, it suggests the expertise they provide is distinct from that of a non-partisan public service. While not explicitly defined, this advisory activity can be termed partisan-political. The term *partisan-political policy advice* is introduced here to set out the separate and distinct partisan-political form of policy advice that partisan advisers provide. This type of policy advice involves the application of a political lens to policy analysis (Head 2008) – that is, policy advice activities that differ from the traditionally conceived policy advisory activities involving non-partisan, primarily technical, bureaucratic, rational and/or analytical policy analysis (Head 2008; Radin 2000).[15] This involves the provision of policy advice to elected officials by remunerated actors involving input of new, or commentary upon existing courses of policy (in)action by analysis of such activity based on its feasibility, desirability, and consistency with stated partisan-political objectives, commitments, and/or its anticipated political/operational consequences. This is precisely the type of policy work that partisan advisers were found to undertake in the recent study of the Harper administration. This is in addition to non-partisan or "administrative-technical" types of policy work that would be undertaken with non-partisan public servants (Craft 2016).

The PCO guide also includes a range of policy work that political staffs are likely to undertake, which includes a blend of both "traditional" policy analysis functions as well as politically oriented policy work. It lists a range of activities such as "reviewing briefings and other advice prepared by the department; assisting the Minister in developing policy positions, including those that reflect the Minister's political perspective" (Privy Council Office 2011). Additional details are provided in Treasury Board Secretariat guidelines that detail the expected activities of political staffs and even provide job descriptions. The director of policy "is also responsible for advising and briefing the minister on all relevant policy issues" (Treasury Board Secretariat 2011, 66). It is clear that partisan advisers are thus potential sources of policy advice along partisan-political as well as "administrative-technical" dimensions.

The 2011 Treasury Board Secretariat's classifications include a variety of positions by which ministers can organize their exempt staff, several of which have explicitly stated policy functions, such as policy advisers, senior policy advisers, directors of policy, and the chief of staff.[16] Ministers' offices have thus become much more sophisticated in their internal division of labour and exempt staff specialization. The implications for policy work are clearly articulated by formal documents: ministers' directors of policy are "responsible, in collaboration with the department, for overseeing policy development on behalf of the minister" (Treasury Board Secretariat 2011, 66).

In addition, partisan advisers engage in policy work with a broad constellation of actors both inside and outside of government. Published accounts make clear that significant PMO-PCO policy interactions occur, and political staffs themselves engage in policy tasks related to the coordination of departmental policy as well as PMO-ministers' office interactions for partisan-political and "administrative-technical" matters. The TBS guidelines clearly spell out that chiefs of staff "must liaise, on behalf of the minister, with the Prime Minister's Office and other ministers' chiefs of staff in order to address government-wide issues" (Treasury Board Secretariat 2011, 66). Partisan advisers' policy work also has an exogenous component to it that involves their interactions with a range of policy stakeholders outside the halls of government. This is reflected not only in empirical studies of their policy work (Craft 2013, 2016; Savoie 1999, 2003) but is also now codified in TBS guidelines, which specify, for example, that directors of policy in ministers' offices "should liaise with key stakeholders in order to inform or consult on important policy initiatives within the minister's purview" (Treasury Board Secretariat 2011, 66).

Conclusion

This chapter has broadened the concept of policy work beyond the confines to a "non-partisan" public service or non-governmental actors. It has demonstrated that Canadian partisan advisers have evolved slowly through three stages of institutionalization, expansion, and specialization in their policy work. The final phase of their evolution, specialization, is argued to be particularly germane to the policy work literature, in that partisan advisers are uniquely able to engage in policy work in ways in which other policy actors cannot. As "exempt" political staffs, partisan advisers are able to provide policy advice and undertake policy activities that are partisan-political. They are, however, also potentially active participants, through their interactions with other policy workers (partisan and non-partisan) in other forms of policy work. Their unique location within the executive, at the precipice of power in close proximity to ministers and senior officials, facilitates their own policy work as well as that of other policy actors who seek to gain access, influence, or edify the work of policy (Craft and Howlett 2013a). Beyond their formal recognition in government documents, partisan advisers highlight the fact that policy work is not apolitical and that many of the substantive and procedural activities of executive policy work are partisan-political. Other chapters in this volume have provided a rich empirical and descriptive body of evidence that points to the wide array of techniques and practices of policy work. This chapter reveals that the political arm has itself evolved in its attempts to engage policy work, and that attention to political staffs as policy workers, throughout the executive, improves our understanding of the diversity and the contemporary nature of policy work.

NOTES

1 The term *partisan advisers* will be used to define remunerated political appointees employed by a minister of the Crown at the federal or provincial level with an officially acknowledged policy advisory role. It excludes other types of "exempt" political staff who do not play a primary policy advisory function (i.e., clerical staff, communications staff, etc.). The term also excludes political staff employed in non-ministerial offices such as the Senate (save those who work for a senator appointed to Cabinet), for private members of legislatures, or in the constituency offices of elected officials. The term *partisan* is used to distinguish between policy workers (including the public service) who may engage in "policy-politics" whereas non-partisan public service cannot engage in "partisan-politics." The term *partisan* as it applies to this study is further specified in chapter 2 of this study. Campbell styled Canadian partisan advisers as "amphibians" to capture their combined partisan and policymaking activities.

2 P.C. 30/1188, dated 8 March 1950. The expansion was, however, again for primarily administrative and clerical capacity. Allowing for executive assistant to the minister, head clerk, secretary to the executive, clerk grade 4 or stenographer grade 3, clerk grade 3, stenographer grade 2B, stenographer grade 2A, or clerk grade 2A or messenger, and confidential messenger.

3 Statutes of Canada, 166–7, chap. 71, s. 37.

4 Prime Minister Trudeau appointed the first-ever deputy prime minister in 1977. The position was expanded and formalized with the creation of its own "office" under Mulroney.
5 For an earlier delineation of the activities of exempt staff in two Canadian governments, see Lee (1971). See also Flemming (1997).
6 Consultation with senior Chrétien PMO staff, 15 September 2011.
7 Ibid.
8 Consultation with Tim Murphy, 20 October 2011.
9 Ibid.
10 Interview with former Harper PMO director of policy, 2 September 2011.
11 Interview with former Harper PMO chief of staff, Ian Brodie, 14 October 2011.
12 While written memos have been used (see Mallory 1967, 30), the practice in place in the Harper years involved more than summary of the docket or policy document in question. It was intended to provide written partisan-political analysis as well as a *recommendation* from partisan advisers.
13 Mandate letters are centrally (PMO/PCO) created documents given to new or reassigned ministers and deputy ministers. They outline the general parameters, ministerial (and departmental) priorities, key deliverables, and budgets, and identifies other departments/ministers they will need to work with. These documents figure prominently in chapter 5 on the role of first minister's office staff federally. For a short history of the origins and importance of mandate letters see Savoie (1999, 137–9).
14 Interview with former Harper PMO Chiefs of Staff Ian Brodie and Guy Giorno.
15 The degree to which senior public servants are aware of political context and poses "political acumen" has long been recognized and debated in studies of elites and policymaking (see, for example, Campbell and Szablowski 1979; Heclo and Wildavsky 1974). Even allowing for such political awareness, appointed political staffs are hired to provide policy advice that is explicitly political and partisan (Prasser 2006; Prince 2007; Eichbaum and Shaw 2010).
16 See Treasury Board Secretariat (2007) for a detailed breakdown of the various exempt staff categories.

PART 3

Policy Work outside Government

10 The Role of Policy Consultants: "Consultocracy" or Business as Usual

MICHAEL HOWLETT AND ANDREA MIGONE

Introduction: Policy Consultants and Policy Advice

It is very useful to examine professional policy work as existing within larger "policy advice systems" that transcend the boundaries of internal government expertise and knowledge transmission (Nicholson 1997). Recent studies from New Zealand, Israel, Canada, and Australia argued that government decision-makers sit at the centre of a complex web of policy advisers (Dobuzinskis, Howlett, and Laycock 2007; Maley 2000; Peled 2002; Eichbaum and Shaw 2007), which include both "traditional" political and policy advisers in government, non-governmental actors in NGOs, think tanks, and similar organizations, and less formal or professional forms of advice obtained from colleagues, friends, relatives, and members of the public and political parties, among others.

A key player among these advisers is the "consultocracy" or the range of private sector consultants brought into governments on a more or less temporary basis to augment internal expertise. Understanding the nature of this "external" professional policy analysis, its influence, and its effectiveness in different analytical contexts involves discerning how a policy advice system is structured and operated in the specific sector of policy activity under examination and how professional policy work is conducted within this system. The role that analysts and advisers *outside* of government play in policymaking has been little studied and is little understood, although the common wisdom is that for-hire consultants play a significant role in policymaking, arguably an increasingly significant one (Dent 2002; Guttman and Willner 1976; Kipping and Engwall 2003; Martin 1998; Wagner and Wollman 1986).

European studies noted their explosive, though unevenly distributed, growth in use (FEACO 2002). A 2007 U.K. government survey estimated their cost at $5 billion in 2005–6 (House of Commons Committee of Public Accounts 2007, 1), representing a 30 per cent increase in this estimate over the three-year period 2003–6. Similar figures have been reported in New Zealand and Australia (see State Services Commission 1999; and ANAO 2001). However, generally, information is scarce, and better studies of policy advisory activities originating outside of government are required to provide better analytical frameworks and to better situate policy workers within the context of alternative sources of policy advice to governments (Adams 2004).

Policy Advisory Systems

At their most basic, we can think of policy advice systems as part of the knowledge utilization system of government, itself a kind of marketplace for policy ideas and information, comprising three separate components: a supply of policy advice, and the demand for it by decision-makers and a set of brokers whose role it is to match supply and demand in any given conjuncture (Lindquist 1998). We can see these systems as arrayed into three general "sets" of analytical activities and participants linked to the positions that actors hold in the "market" for policy advice.

The first set of actors is composed of "proximate decision-makers" acting as consumers of policy analysis and advice – actors with actual authority to make policy decisions, including cabinets and executives as well as legislatures, and senior administrators and officials to whom decision-making powers have been delegated by those other bodies. The second set are those "knowledge producers" located in academia, statistical agencies, and research institutes who provide the basic scientific, economic, and social scientific data upon which analyses are often based and decisions made. The third set comprises "knowledge brokers" serving as intermediaries between the knowledge generators and proximate decision-makers, repackaging data and information into usable form. These include, among others, permanent specialized governmental research staff, their temporary equivalents in commissions and task forces, and a large group of non-governmental specialists associated with think tanks and interest groups. Although often seen as "knowledge suppliers," policy advisers almost, by definition, exist in the brokerage sub-system where most professional policy analysts can be found (Verschuere 2009; Abelson 2002; Dluhy 1981).

This model suggests, moreover, that there are different types of "policy advice systems," depending on the nature of the knowledge supply and demand, and what analysts do in brokering information, how they do it, and with what effect is largely dependent on the type of advisory system present in a specific government or area of interest. This helps to explain why we find different policy analysis styles in different policy fields (Mayer, Bots, and van Daalen 2004; Howlett and Lindquist 2004), since these can be linked to larger patterns of behaviour of political actors and knowledge suppliers conditioning how policy advice is generated and deployed (Peled 2002; Howlett and Lindquist 2004; Bevir and Rhodes 2001; Bevir, Rhodes, and Weller 2003; Aberbach and Rockman 1989; Bennett and McPhail 1992).

Some of this variation in advisory systems is temporal, and the introduction of elements of formal or professional policy analysis into the brokerage function has a different history in each jurisdiction (Prince 1979, 1983, 2007).[1] Given its reliance on institutional arrangements for political decision-making, however, an advisory system's exact configuration can be expected to vary temporally, spatially, by jurisdiction, especially by nation state, and, somewhat less so, by policy issue or sector. That is, personal and professional components of the policy advice supply system, along with their internal and external sourcing, can be expected to combine in different ratios in different policymaking situations (Prince 1983; Wollmann 1989; Hawke 1993; Rochet 2004). Understanding these variations is critical in understanding the role that professional governmental policy analysts play in the policy advisory and policymaking processes.

Generally, however, four distinct "communities" of policy advisers can be identified within the policy advice system, depending on their location inside or outside of government, and by how closely they operate to decision-makers: core actors, public sector insiders, private sector insiders, and outsiders (see table 10.1).

The actual jobs and duties performed by each set of policy advisers in either type of organization must be empirically determined in each instance. Understanding how the four communities do or do not relate and reinforce each other is a critical, and very much understudied, determinant of the system's overall capacity and effectiveness.[2] Important aspects of the functioning of policy advice systems include such factors as whether or not or what type of "boundary-spanning" links there are between governmental and non-governmental organizations (Weible 2008) and whether or not employees have opportunities to strengthen their skills and expertise (O'Connor, Roos, and Vickers-Willis 2007) or

Table 10.1 The Four Communities of Policy Advisers

	Proximate actors	Peripheral actors
Public/governmental sector	Core actors Central agencies Executive staff Professional governmental policy analysts	Public sector insiders Commissions and committees Task forces Research councils/ scientists
Non-governmental sector	Private sector insiders Consultants Political party staff Pollsters	Outsiders Public interest groups Business associations Trade unions Academics Think tanks Media

to outsource policy research to personnel in private or semi-public organizations and consultancies.

Generally consultants can play a very significant role as "privileged outsiders," similar to that of political party staff or pollsters with special access to key insiders, linking the external and internal advisory system sub-components together (Clark 1995; Druckman 2000). Like the other members of this quadrant, this makes them potentially very influential in policy debates and outcomes. Unlike the other two, they have been little studied.

A Review of the Literature on Policy Consultants

Little is known regarding non-governmental policy advice in most countries (Hird 2005b) except to note the general weakness of actors like think tanks and research institutes in most jurisdictions (Smith 1977; Stone and Denham 2004; McGann and Johnson 2005; Abelson 2007; Stritch 2007; Cross 2007; Murray 2007). Even less is known about the growing legion of consultants who work for governments in the "invisible public service" (Speers 2007; Boston 1994), and much more research into these areas is needed.

Page's (2010) study of regulatory policymaking identified four types of expertise relevant in government: (1) scientific expertise, (2) policy expertise, (3) process expertise, and (4) instrument expertise. In earlier work Page and Jenkins (2005) stressed how internal government experts are usually process experts, and more recent work confirmed a distinct lack of scientific, policy, and instrument expertise among bureaucrats, opening the door, again, to external experts to exercise influence in these areas (Page 2010).

While the exact dimension of the phenomenon is unclear, the *use* of external policy consultants in government has been an increasingly important focus of concern among governments in the United States, the United Kingdom, Canada, and Australia, among others (ANAO 2001; House of Commons Committee of Public Accounts 2010; Bakvis 1997; Macdonald 2011; Project on Government Oversight 2011). Some of this concern arose over the costs incurred by governments (Craig 2006), while others have suggested the rise of the "consultocracy" led to a diminishment of democratic practices and public direction of policy and administrative development (Saint-Martin 2004, 2005b). As Saint-Martin (2005a, 671) noted, "Some have written about the 'new cult of the management consultant' in government and have described consultants and 'intellectual mercenaries' as 'hired guns' that 'politicians can use to bypass reluctant civil servants, while others have coined the term "consultocracy"' to underline the growing influence of consultants and the public management process."

A third focus emerged with more fine-grained analyses of spending patterns related to the difficulties that governments encountered in precisely assessing how the money has been spent (Macdonald 2011) and in creating structures capable of monitoring this activity (House of Commons Committee of Public Accounts 2010).

Some accounts include policy consulting in a more general shift in overall state-societal relations – away from the "positive" or "regulatory" state (Majone 1997) and towards the "service," "franchise," or "competition" state (Butcher, Freyens, and Wanna 2009; Perl and White 2002; Radcliffe 2010; Bilodeau, Laurin, and Vining 2007). This approach centres on the idea that the contemporary "service state" is based on many more external-internal links in the provisions of services – where contracting is often the norm – than the pre–Second World War "autarkic state," which relied on "in house provision of all kinds of services" aiming to deliver "consistency, reliability and standardization" in service provision (Butcher, Freyens, and Wanna 2009, 22). This old system has been replaced, they argue, by the contemporary service state: "a hybrid mixture of part public part private activities, delivery chains that do not remain in neat boxes or organizational settings, loose combination of actors and providers who are each necessary to see something delivered" (31). Here, the state is the chief contractor, and the extension of contracts to policy and administrative matters should be neither surprising nor unexpected. Some scholars argue that for-hire consultants play a role in policymaking, arguably an increasingly significant one (Dent 2002; Guttman and Willner 1976; Kipping and Engwall 2003; Martin 1998; Wagner and Wollman 1986).

Others see the use of consultants in policymaking as less significant, linked to the normal development of policy advice systems in modern government, as business groups and others require specialized expertise in their efforts to lobby governments, and government agencies in turn require similar expertise in order to deal with business, NGOs, and other active participants in policymaking as interest intermediation grows increasingly professionalized and institutionalized (Halligan 1995; Lahusen 2002, 697).

Czarniawska and Mazza (2003) suggest that consultants are likely to play a limited mandate role, arguing they are poorly organized to exercise any kind of permanent policy influence, relying strongly on a variety of appropriate political and institutional characteristics to exercise influence. This view is supported by the findings of van Houten and Goldman (1981) and Saint-Martin (1998a and 1998b) and provides the main working hypotheses proposed herein. That is, we know that the activities of professional governmental policy analysts in the internal policy advice supply network are very closely tied to available resources in personnel and funding; they face demands from clients and managers for high-quality results, and for high quality data and information on future trends (Howlett 2009a; Riddell 2007). We should expect non-governmental analysts to share these same resource constraints and thus not to automatically influence government deliberations. Their influence on policymaking is therefore likely to vary by issue and circumstance, and the sources and direction of these variations are important information for both policy theorists and practitioners interested in understanding the role of the "hidden" or "invisible public service" (Speers 2007) in Canada.

Different Interpretations of the Role, Nature, and Activities of Consultants in Government

Policy scholars remain divided about the role of consultants in the policy process. Their views vary from estimations of their "strong" influence on policymakers to suggestions that this influence is at best diffuse and weak (Bloomfield and Best 1992). Policy and management consultants are seen as either independent "agents of change" (Lapsley and Oldfield 2001; Tisdall 1982), or as weak, "liminal" subjects dependent for any potential influence on allowances made by their employers (Czarniawska and Mazza 2003; Garsten 1999; Bloomfield and Danieli 1995).

Such dichotomous views require more nuanced analyses (Clark and Fincham 2002) not only to more accurately assess the quantitative questions such as how many consultants there are, and if these numbers have grown, but also to carefully examine the qualitative questions about the nature of their influence on governments, from the provision of direct advice, to the more indirect creation of specific kinds of knowledge and its mobilization/utilization in policy deliberations (Van Helden et al. 2010; Weiss 1977, 1986). However, both empirical and conceptual understandings of the origins and significance of the development of policy consultants are mixed. As Speers (2007) noted in her study of Canada's "invisible private service," management consultants had been involved for the past several decades in every stage of the policy process.

Still, partially because of difficulties in generating empirical data on the subject, few studies assess this question in purely policy terms (for notable exceptions see Saint-Martin 1998, 1998b, 2004, 2005, 2005a, 2006). Rather most draw upon studies of management consultants in government or more generally in making such assessments. Several significant problems stand in the way of clarifying this debate.

First, concerns about the use of consultants in government are not recent, as numerous publications on the subject from the 1970s attest (Wilding 1976; Meredith and Martin 1970; Rosenblum and McGillis 1979; Guttman and Willner 1976; Kline and Buntz 1979). However, more recently concerns emerged not just about the size and number of consultancies, but about their apparent growth as both a percentage of government employees and expenditures (Speers 2007) and concomitantly about their increased influence and impact on the content and directions of government decision-making (Saint-Martin 1998b; Speers 2007).

Second, as noted above, generally the quality of available data is poor (Howard 1996; Perl and White 2002; Lahusen 2002), being very inconsistent and relatively rare while generally stressing the growth of the expenditure involved (FEACO 2002; House of Commons Committee of Public Accounts 2007; State Services Commission 1999; ANAO 2001).

This problem affects questions of accountability and efficiency: whether contracts are competitively priced (Macdonald 2011). At times, governments are hard pressed to assess these situations. The U.K. House of Commons Committee of Public Accounts (2010, 5) argued that it was not "convinced by the Cabinet Office's argument that it is impossible to measure whether government's use of consultants represents value for money."

Third we must clarify the conceptual basis of the analysis before attempting more detailed empirical investigations to evaluate these diverse claims about the size, extent, and influence of policy consultant work in government. We should, for example, separate out "policy consulting" from categories such engineering or technical services consulting or even from "management consulting," the category often used to capture policy consulting in official government reports and documents (Saint-Martin 2006; Jarrett 1998). Many "consulting" activities are difficult to distinguish from those related to more general government goods, and especially service, "contracting" (Davies 2001, 2008; Vincent-Jones 2006). It is also often difficult in official statistics to distinguish "consultants" from "temporary and part-time workers" (Macdonald 2011; Project on Government Oversight 2011). These important distinctions – which are often glossed over in much of the small literature on policy consultants and consultants in government – lead, for example, to the overestimation of the number of consultants when lumping them together with "contractors" and especially "part-time" employees, which include large numbers of temporary office workers (Macdonald 2011; McKeown and Lindorff 2011). Policy consultants' numbers are overestimated also when using the numbers of management consultants, which include figures for consultants in information technology and others not ranked separately in many government databases (Perl and White 2002; Macdonald 2011). In Canada, for example, the new Proactive Disclosure project (which publicizes federal contracts over $10,000 of value) provides information for the departments and agencies of the federal public administration. However, only a very small percentage of these include a more detailed breakdown of the services provided that would allow researchers to assess whether the contracts have a policy dimension at all.[3]

Fourth, while there may be concerns with this growth in terms of the impact on public service unionization, professional standards, accountability for funds, and the like, it is difficult to determine the extent of *policy* influence from such numbers. Even when policy consultants are properly identified – a far from simple task – the question of their influence over policy processes and outcomes remains unclear. Some studies stressed the role played by a few large companies in monopolizing the consultancy market and suggested the record of these firms in providing good advice is shaky at best (O'Shea and Madigan 1998). Others noted the large numbers of smaller firms involved in the industry and the often very weak position they find themselves in when advising large clients such as government departments (Sturdy 1997). Similarly while some studies focus on the reputational aura that some consultants can muster, given their status as experts and professionals (Evetts 2003a, 2003b; Kipping and Engwall 2003), others note the disregard with which their credentials are held by many employers (Czarniawska and Mazza 2003; Brint 1990).

Clarifying the Conceptual Issues

While it is not yet clear in the public sector if their use has reached the levels attained in the private sector, it is clear that the number of consultants in government has grown since the issue was first flagged in the 1970s (South Australia 1993; House of Commons Committee of Public Accounts 2007, 2010; House of Commons Committee on Health 2009; National Audit Office 2006, 2010).

Pattenaude (1979) breaks down a typical "consultant episode," identifying ten phases, from problem recognition to evaluation of the resulting consulting experience, which helps organizing the study of the subject.[4] Two excellent studies undertaken fifteen years apart in South Australia and the United Kingdom illustrate these situations (South Australia 1993; House of Commons Committee of Public Accounts 2007). We address the content of these analyses below.

WHAT DO THEY DO? THE ROLES CONSULTANTS FILL

Tisdall (1982) listed the activities of management consultants (see table 10.2). This work can be done on a contract or fee-for-service basis, as very short-term or multi-annual commitments. Services can be provided by individuals or large multinational firms with thousands of employees and contracts, and they can be delivered on a project or ongoing basis. Often consultants perform tasks or deliver services identical with those provided or delivered by government employees (Macdonald 2011; Project on Government Oversight 2011). However, in many areas they take on important "change management" or other roles, providing

Table 10.2 Activities of Management Consultants

Business administration	Company policy and development
Distribution and transport	Economic and environmental planning
Finance	Marketing
Personnel	Production
Information systems	Data processing

Source: Tisdall (1982, 86).

insights into either or both the nature and modalities of contemporary "best practices" that agencies might wish to adopt (Lapsley and Oldfield 2001).

WHY DO THEY DO IT? TECHNOCRATIC VS BUREAUCRATIC EXPLANATIONS

What are the reasons for the "consulting explosion" (Ernst and Kieser 2002) in these task areas? Brint (1990) identified four somewhat contrasting "principal positions" that experts can have in public policy processes. He focuses on key variables affecting the experts' ability to dominate policymaking, including their capacity to frame issues as technical ones, and whether or not the political environment is organized in to allow them to continually exercise their technocratic powers and potential. His four resulting policy situations are:

1. *Technocracy* – experts are seen as having an increasing influence on policymaking, as the subjects of government action become more complex and technical.
2. *Servants of power* – experts exist as mere "servants" of the powerful, providing "window dressing" or a legitimate gloss on decisions taken for non-technical reasons.
3. *Limited mandates* – an intermediate position, where experts can be expected to overrule or dominate policymaking, but only in specific areas, which require technical knowledge.
4. *Extensive mandates* – another intermediate position but closer to the technocracy one, where professional non-governmental bodies are seen as having a large impact on more than just areas of policymaking within their specific range of expertise, but not upon all topics as suggested by the technocracy thesis.

Consultants can be involved in each situation. However, explanations found in the private sector literature tend to fall into three categories: skills supplementation; symbolic impression management; and legitimization and change management (Ernst and Kieser 2002; Rosenblum and McGillis 1979). Each is discussed below.

Skills Supplementation: The Technocratic Explanation

Sometimes consultants are brought in simply to offset complacency. That is, to "stir things up" without necessarily being attached to a specific agenda for action (Czarniawska-Joerges 1989). The most benign explanation for the increased use of consultants in government centres on skill shortages or the need for temporary augmentation of the skill sets available to organizations, although this is often tied, for the public sector, to concerns about such shortages being made more acute by recent successive rounds of downsizing in which core competencies suffered. Generally, this view sees few problems in employing temporary workers to supplement or enhance in-house talent (see Bloomfield and Danieli 1995 for such a discussion of IT consultancies).

However, others see this as an inherently wasteful practice, as private firms charge high rates for their talent, and public managers often gravitate towards this quick solution to their human resource shortages rather than develop sufficient in-house human capital (Kline and Buntz 1979; Project on Government Oversight 2011). Continual recourse to external expertise can lead to a gradual shift in in-house competences (Page and Jenkins 2005; Page 2010).

Symbolic Impression Management: The Bureaucratic Politics Explanation

Another common thread in the literature regards the use of consultants less benignly and downplays the expertise issue. Clark (1995) suggested that in both the private and the public sectors, consultants can be used as tools in bureaucratic infighting over preferred courses of action, budgetary allocations, and the like, through "impression management." They can be used to heighten the legitimacy of specific proposed courses of action (Clark and Salaman 1996), often leading to "duelling consultants" advocating specific possible activities (van Houten and Goldman 1981).

Formal Restrictions on Internal Hirings: Mandates Roles for External Actors

In both previous cases, consultants were used on an "optional" basis. While the use of external experts or service providers is not compulsory, in some instances these choices may be mandatory (Rosenblum and McGillis 1979). Using outside experts to evaluate ongoing programs, for example, is a common technique to bring more "neutrality" and "objectivity" into the evaluation (Speers 2007).

What Are the Management Issues Associated with the Use of Consultants?

Several issues adhere to the management of consultants, regardless of its cause, growth, and size. Government studies (South Australia 1993; House of Commons Committee of Public Accounts 2007) focused on six areas of interest using survey and interview data:

1. The extent of use of external consultants;
2. The rationale for engaging consultants;
3. The selection process;
4. How external consultants were engaged;
5. How external consultants were recorded and reported; and
6. How the use of consultants was reviewed and evaluated.

Two of these areas are particularly problematic, receiving detailed treatment in the literature: the selection/engagement process and management of consultants once hired. Some work analyses how governments select consultants (Corcoran and McLean 1998) and their impact in bolstering or undermining internal government advisers and capacities (Wilding 1976; Kline and Buntz 1979; Rosenblum and McGillis 1979). In general, however, few authors tested theories of the policy influence of experts against evidence from the role consultants have played in policymaking (McGivern 1983; Mitchell 1994; Lapsley and Oldfield 2001). This is problematic in terms of goals and expectations, performance measurement and review, relations with in-house staff and other consultants, and so on (Rehfuss 1979; Lippitt 1975).

Problems in Clarifying the Empirical Issues: Data Issues in Comparative Government Reporting

While increasingly concerned about the use of consultants, government found it very difficult to ascertain the exact amount of spending, its use, and its impact, and faces several critical data and methodological challenges. Studies were undertaken in many counties in the 1990s and 2000s as concerns with the "hidden" costs of the "corporatization" of the public service led to expanding benchmarking measures for government efficiency to measure external consulting and professional service contracts (Bilodeau, Laurin, and Vining 2007). Mostly these studies argued that the use of consultants increased substantially and often did not represent "value for money," compared with using internal government expertise (House of Commons Committee of Public Accounts 2010).

Accounting for this increased expenditure on consultants, however, faces several critical challenges, given the current state of governmental financial and personnel reporting, and many efforts have foundered on these issues. While parliamentary and government accounting office inquiries often concluded that in many cases more value would be gained by governments reducing the number of external contracts, always the data used to draw these conclusions were very weak, ironically, as the inquiries themselves acknowledge.

Below we summarize recent efforts to investigate these subjects in the United States, Australia, the United Kingdom, and Canada at both the national and sub-national levels and the issues they raise for investigators and future research.

UNITED STATES

Growth in government use of contractors in the United States is high profile and undeniable, with the Bush Administration overseeing "the most significant increase in recent history in the largely hidden workforce of contractors and grantees who work for the federal government" (Light 2006, 1). The study identified $400 billion in contracts and $100 billion in grants in 2005, leading it to conclude that official estimates of the size of the U.S. federal government were much underestimated and its true size to be 14.6 million employees (including civil servants, postal workers, military personnel, contractors, and grantees), up from 12.1 million in 2002, and just 11 million in 1999 (see table 10.3).

The study concluded that in 2005 over half of federal employees (a number estimated at 7.6 million) were contract employees (Light 2006, 1). A Program on Government Oversight (POGO) study analysed the total compensation paid to federal and private sector employees, and annual billing rates for contractor employees across thirty-five occupational classifications covering over 550 service activities. In

Table 10.3 True Size of U.S. Government, 1990–2005

Measure	1990	1993	1999	2002	2005	Change 1999–2002	Change 2002–2005
Civil servants	2,238,000	2,157,000	1,820,000	1,818,000	1,872,000	2000	54,000
Contract jobs	5,058,000	4,884,000	4,441,000	5,168,000	7,634,000	727,000	2,466,000
Grant jobs	2,416,000	2,400,000	2,527,000	2,860,000	2,892,000†	333,000	32,000
Military personnel	2,106,000	2,106,000	1,744,000	1,386,000	1,456,000	1,436,000	–20,000
Postal service jobs	817,000	817,000	820,000	872,000	810,000	767,000	–43,000
True size of government	12,635,000	12,635,000	12,005,000	11,046,000	12,112,000	14,601,000	2,489,000

Source: Light (2006, 11).

† Grant data are from 2004, the last year for which complete data were available at the time of this analysis.

thirty-three of these, federal employees were less expensive, with external rates as much as five times higher than those of government employees. POGO estimated the government pays billions more annually in taxpayer dollars to hire contractors than it would to hire federal employees to perform comparable services. Specifically, it showed the federal government approving service contract billing rates paying contractors 1.83 times more than federal employees in total compensation, and more than twice the total compensation paid in the private sector for comparable services. Furthermore, the federal government failed to determine how much money it saves or wastes by outsourcing, insourcing, or retaining services, and has no system for doing so (Project on Government Oversight 2011, 1). However the study also noted that "all of the increase in contract employees is due to increased spending at the Department of Defense" (Light 2006, 1), a fact that highlights the misleading nature of much data on government's contracting out of services.

AUSTRALIA

Michael Howard (1996) attempted to estimate expenditures on consultants by Australian governments over the period 1974–94 (see table 10.4).

While apparently detailed and precise, however, Howard also concluded that in at least half the departmental cases the annual totals he presented had to be "laboriously constructed from the itemisation of individual consultancies" (65). This was because guidelines passed in 1987 to help monitor expenses "did not specify totals as a requirement" (67), an omission not corrected until 1991. Thus, only four departments presented totals for number and cost of consultancies from the first year of reporting, and did not present totals until 1990–1. Furthermore, at least two agencies "did not comply with the new Requirements until the last two years of the period" (67), and in several other cases where totals were provided, they were not consistent with the itemization they were ostensibly based upon.

There was also a significant problem of "departments diverging from one another in the exact basis on which they reported and altering their own basis of reporting during the period" (Howard 1996, 69). Only in 1991 were departments required to "distinguish between consultants engaged during the year and those paid during the year" (67) (about 10–20 per cent of consultancies occurring over several reporting periods), but only two departments fully complied with this requirement.

Table 10.4 Commonwealth Departments: Expenditure (AUS$ million) on Consultancies, 1987–1994

Department/portfolio	Years							Total 1988/9–93/4	Change 1988/9–93/4 (%)	Average annual change 1989–93/4 (%)
	1987/8	1988/9	1989/90	1990/1	1991/2	1992/3	1993/4			
DFAT-AIDAB		122.078	405.398	575.299	194.581	116.197	182.380	1595.933	49.40	9.88
Administration services	70.300	65.634	58.146	47.016	30.918	33.907	33.230	268.851	-49.37	-9.87
Defence	6.646	18.890	23.061	31.940	20.875	39.953	33.235	167.953	75.94	15.19
Employment, education, and training		9.551	9.352	17.390	19.600	9.551	7.608	73.052	-20.35	-4.07
Health, housing, and community services	3.052	4.013	6.638	10.902	9.578	13.758	14.766	59.655	267.94	53.59
Transport and communication	4.282	3.228	8.047	7.8871	9.051	6.302	6.291	40.789	94.86	18.97
Primary industries and energy	1.804	3.348	4.796	8.316	8.403	8.357	7.262	40.483	116.89	23.38
Arts, sports, environment, tourism, and territories	4.481	4.481	5.778	5.369	5.366	6.244	7.957	35.195	77.58%	15.52%
Finance	0.472	0.802	0.764	1.372	3.578	10.938	17.991	35.446	2142.87	428.57
Industry and technology		4.110	8.622	5.694	3.087	3.103	3.532	28.184	-14.07	-2.81
Immigration and ethnic affairs		2.458	6.834	4.424	5.821	2.672	6.479	28.688	163.58	32.72

Veterans' affairs		1.445	2.699	2.167	2.548	4.240	4.074	17.173	181.85	36.37
Prime minister and Cabinet		1.360	1.732	1.975	3.000	4.655	4.007	16.792	194.64	38.93
Foreign affairs and trade	0.747	1.035	1.659	3.757	1.031	1.795	4.190	13.468	304.73	60.95
Attorney-general		1.397	1.398	1.328	3.041	2.889	2.614	12.666	87.09	17.42
Social security		1.939	1.412	2.089	2.265	2.355	2.514	12.574	29.66	5.93
Industrial relations		0.847	0.847	0.884	1.107	1.385	2.530	7.915	198.68	39.74
Treasury		0.042	0.218	0.566	0.518	1.368	1.780	4.492	4116.31	823.26
All	91.784	246.661	547.716	728.357	324.367	269.669	342.441	2459.211	38.83	7.77
All (bar DFAT-AIDAB)	91.784	124.583	142.318	153.059	129.786	153.471	160.061	863.278	28.48	5.70
All (bar DFAT-AIDAB, DAS)	21.484	58.949	84.172	106.042	98.868	119.565	126.831	594.427	115.15	23.03
All (bar DFAT-AIDAB, DAS, Defence)	14.838	40.059	61.111	74.102	77.994	79.612	93.596	387.414	9259.61	1851.92

Source: Howard (1996, 70).
AIDAB = Australian International Development Assistance Bureau
DAS = Department of Administrative Services
DFAT = Department of Foreign Affairs and Trade

Furthermore, idiosyncratic reporting practices made it difficult to assess the precise nature of consulting. Howard estimated the amount of double counting involved because of these differences to range from 5 to 15 per cent in the particular year concerned.

Howard faced a third problem in compiling consistent data over a multi-year period as the administrative boundaries of departments changed over the twenty-year period in question. In Australia for example, the 1974–94 period he examined dovetailed with the era of the "super-ministries" announced in July 1987.

Fourth, the data collected pertained "only to consultancies commissioned by departments, not by statutory authorities in the same portfolio" (Howard 1996, 69), so that consultancies commissioned by the latter were excluded, even if that agency or commission was nominally within a department's purview and remit. Overall these problems resulted in data tables larded with caveats and explanatory notes and the obscuring of the overall pattern of expenditures observed.

The total reported spending on consultants in the Australian Commonwealth government for the period 1988–9 to 1993–4 was AUS$2.459 billion. However, total reported spending on consultants fluctuated widely over the period. The total rose from AUS$247 million in 1988–9 to AUS$728 million in 1990–1 but then fell away over the next two years, before partially rising again in 1993–4. As he noted, "This pattern, however, gives a quite artificial impression as it results from distortions to an underlying trend produced by two agencies, AIDAB and DAS. Excluding these two cases, spending by all other Commonwealth departments increased steadily over the period – from $58.95m. in 1988–89 to $126.83m. in 1993–94 – with a downturn occurring in only one year (1991–92)" (Howard 1996, 69).

Moreover, Howard concluded that much of this pattern was more apparent than real and depended on data reporting issues rather than changes in government practices in reporting (increasing their number early on) and in designation of services (reducing it later). A state-level investigation in South Australia found very similar results (South Australia 1993). It concluded that during the five year period from July 1987 to June 1992, government departments and statutory authorities in South Australia spent AUS$146 million on consultancies. However, it also noted that often evidence used to support these decisions was incomplete and that some agencies kept few records, if any.

The South Australian committee found that developing expertise within the public sector is a more cost-effective method of operation in areas where there is a recurring need to engage external consultants. The committee said it was "concerned that some agencies consider it necessary to employ external consultants to make important and often controversial decisions. This is an abrogation of responsibility, and in many instances executive officers are paid and empowered to make these decisions and should do just that" (South Australia 1993, ix).

UNITED KINGDOM

Similar data problems were found in the United Kingdom when the National Accounting Office examined the use of consultants over a multi-year period. A survey of 152 departments in October 2000, for example, found that in purchasing professional services in 1999–2000, there had been a 7 per cent increase in real terms, compared to 1993–4. Of this, 38 per cent (£231 million) was spent on management consultancy, 11 per cent (£67 million) on legal services, 5 per cent (£28 million) on financial, and 3 per cent (£21 million) on human resource advice and assistance. They also noted that departments were unable to allocate the remaining 43 per cent (£263 million) to particular categories.

The pattern of contracts roughly paralleled relative budget sizes of departments, and most contracts were quite large, as 55 per cent of all departments' spending on professional services was covered by contracts worth over £149,000, and only 6 per cent less than £10,000. Twenty-five suppliers accounted for 37 per cent of all departments' expenditure. Only half of the contracts were awarded following full competition. By 2005–6 the public sector in England spent approximately £2.8 billion on consultants, with central government accounting for £1.8 billion, or three times the 1999–2000 rate. Between 2003 and 4 and 2005–6, spending on consultants rose by a third, from £2.1 to £2.8 billion, and most of this depended on increased spending by the National Health Service. Only two departments had shown a consistent decrease in their spending on consultants over the period. This changed somewhat over the next several years, as figure 10.1 shows.

In 2009/10 the British Treasury, the Department for Transport, and the Department for Education all spent more than 50 per cent of their total staff cost on consultants. The Departments of Energy and Climate Change and the Home Office spent 40 per cent of their budget on consultants. The NAO concluded that "central government is repeatedly using consultants for core skills, including project and programme management and IT, and is increasingly turning to a select list of suppliers." And although they found central government to have "made

Figure 10.1 Change in U.K. Government Spending on Consultants, 2006–2010, by Department

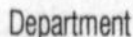

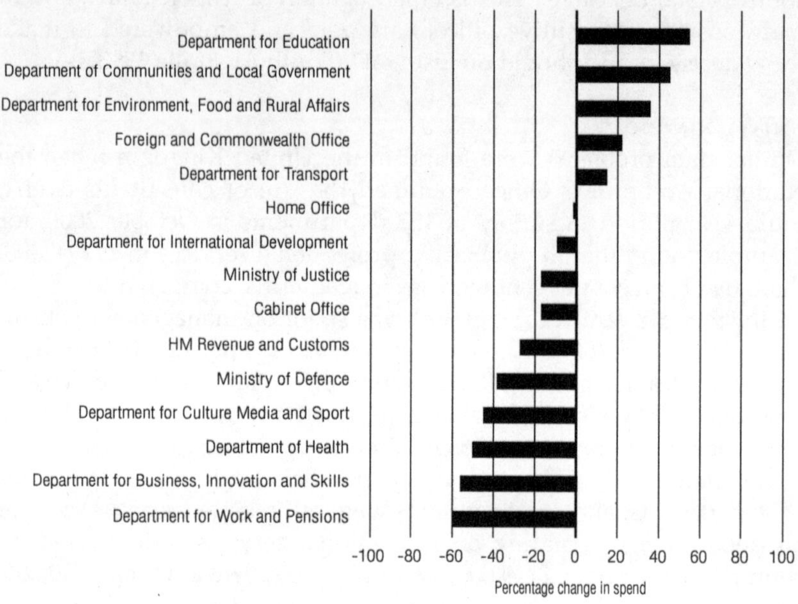

Source: National Audit Office survey

some progress in implementing previous recommendations and good practice in using consultants … much more can be done to improve value for money. In particular, departments are making good use of framework agreements and qualified procurement staff are regularly involved in the buying process. However, areas where departments require significant improvement are: collection and use of management information; the assessment of whether internal resources could be used instead of consultants; controls on awarding contracts by single tender; completing and sharing post-project performance reviews; actively engaging with and managing the relationships with key consultancy suppliers; and planning for and carrying out the transfer of skills from consultants to internal staff" (National Audit Office 2010, 3).

However, once again, data quality was poor; the NAO acknowledged, for example, that "the responses to our survey revealed considerable variation in the quality of departments' information on their expenditure on professional services." Departments lacked detailed data on their expenditures on professional services, including fee rates, quality of services, and suppliers' information – all critical data for the efficient management of these contracts (National Audit Office 2010, 5).

Similarly, another report noted, "Departments do not collect and aggregate adequate management information on their use of consultants (such as types of services purchased and procurement route used) to better understand over time their use of consultants and the benefits they bring" (National Audit Office 2006, 1).

Departments were found not to assess properly whether internal resources could, in the long term, be better suited than external ones and generally to have adequate processes in place to review post-project performance and share this information across departments. They were also found lacking in exercising adequate controls, especially when awarding single-tender contracts and to have little in-depth knowledge of the array of contracts they let or to transfer skills from external consultants to internal agents (National Audit Office 2006, 17). They concluded, "In general, the quality of departments' management information is poor. There is little depth to management information on consultants, and incomplete information on interims. Few departments can provide accurate information on" important subjects. As a result:

- Departments and the Office of Government Commerce do not routinely know how much money is spent on consultants, hampering proper evaluation.
- Consultants are often used when in-house staff have the necessary skills and are less expensive.
- A consultant may not perform well for one department but still be employed by another, charge a significantly higher price for the same service, or redesign a similar process from scratch which they have successfully implemented elsewhere in the public sector (House of Commons Committee of Public Accounts 2007, 32–3).

CANADA

Several secondary studies examined the role of consultants in Canada (Bakvis 1997; Saint-Martin 1998b, 2005b, 2006; Speers 2007). Perl and White (2002) found "evidence for a growing role played by policy consultants at the national government level is compelling in Canada" (52). Annual government-wide expenditure on "other professional services" reported in the Public Accounts of Canada for fiscal years 1981–2 through 2000–1 showed "a continuous increase from C$239 million in 1981–82 to C$1.55 billion in 2000–01," a 647 per cent increase over twenty years. As a share of total government expenditures, it rose steadily from 0.35 to 0.97 per cent over the same period (53).[5]

Perl and White noted the difficulties these data entailed in attempting to enhance their level of specificity to focus on "policy consultants" rather than all kinds of professional services, many of which are, for example, in the information technology area.[6] The Public Service Commission of Canada study highlighted these same issues regarding the use of temporary help services in eleven Canadian public service organizations (Public Service Commission 2010). The study found temporary help services were "improperly used to address long-term resourcing needs" outside of Public Service Employment Act staffing mechanisms. "In our opinion, the study reveals an additional workforce within the public service – one that is not subject to the PSEA, and that is used for long-term and continuous work" (3).

Two practices resulted in the long-term use of temporary help services. The first was the use of full-time "temporary help" service contracts (see table 10.5). The second was the "use of individual temporary help service workers in a continuous working relationship with the contracting organization, either by offering workers a series of temporary help service contracts or by using combinations of contracts and non-permanent appointments that fall under the PSEA, such as a term, casual or student appointments" (Public Service Commission 2010, 4).

The study found that nearly one in five of the contracts reviewed (18.4%) was for a duration exceeding 52 weeks, the longest being 165 weeks (Public Service Commission 2010, 15). Such long-term contracts were more common for professional and technical workers than for administrative workers. Regarding continuous working relationships, 16.3 per cent of temporary help workers in these organizations were appointed to a public service position by the same organization in which they held their contracts (4, 13). Over half of these temporary hirings were justified as stemming from increased workload (24).

David Macdonald (2011, 5) argued this trend intensified as federal government departments initiated measures to "cut expenditures in an age of austerity." The cost of federal personnel outsourcing of temporary help, IT consultants, and management consultants between 2005 and 2010 ballooned by almost 80 per cent, to nearly $5.5 billion. The growth in personnel outsourcing is concentrated in four large

Table 10.5 Top 10 Canadian Government Contract Areas, 2005–2010

Description	Total (April 2005–June 2010) ($)
Other professional services	3,833,835,461
Architectural and engineering services	3,629,932,477
Computer equipment	3,319,088,496
Management consulting	2,422,039,296
IT	2,179,246,399
Business services	1,329,298,953
Telephone and voice services	1,085,863,138
Software	988,382,443
Temporary help	845,899,781
International development goods and services	697,115,212

Source: Macdonald (2011).

departments – Public Works and Government Services Canada, National Defence and Canadian Forces, Human Resources and Skills Development, and Public Safety and Emergency Preparedness – which together make up half of all federal government outsourcing (see tables 10.5 and 10.6)

Macdonald (2011) also found a strong concentration of outsourcing within very few companies (see table 10.6).

Conclusion: The Need for Careful Definitions and Conceptual Clarity to Guide Empirical Research into the Role(s) of Consultants as Policy Advisers

Beside an increased scrutiny of increased costs (ANAO 2001; House of Commons Committee of Public Accounts 2010), what has been the impact beyond use of consultants? This is an ongoing research program. Better models of policy advisory activities both within and outside of government are required, however, in order to provide better frameworks for analysis and to better situate policy workers within the context of alternate sources of policy advice to governments (Adams 2004), understanding its structure and operations. As Halligan (1995, 162) argued, "The conventional wisdom" for many years on policy advice in government was that a good policy advice system should consist of

Figure 10.2 Percentage Change in Expenditures for Temporary Health Services and Salary Costs for Indeterminate, Term, and Casual Employees, 1999–2000 to 2008–2009 (in Unadjusted Dollars, Reference Year 1999–2000)

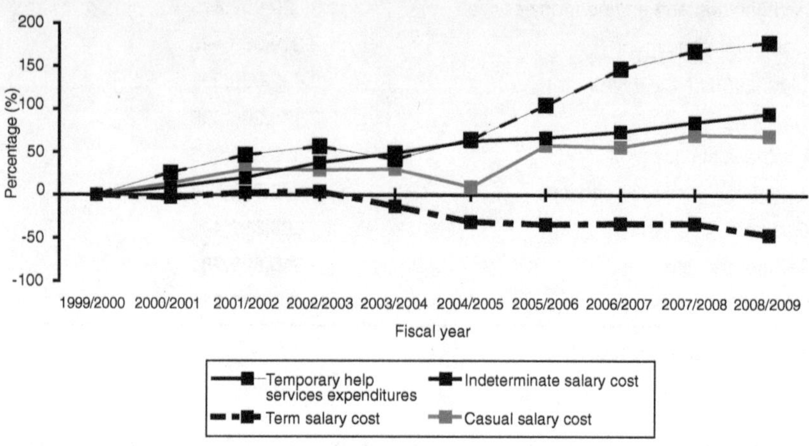

Source: Public Service Commission (2010, 23).

Figure 10.3 Sources of Outsourcing Costs: Canada, 2005–2011

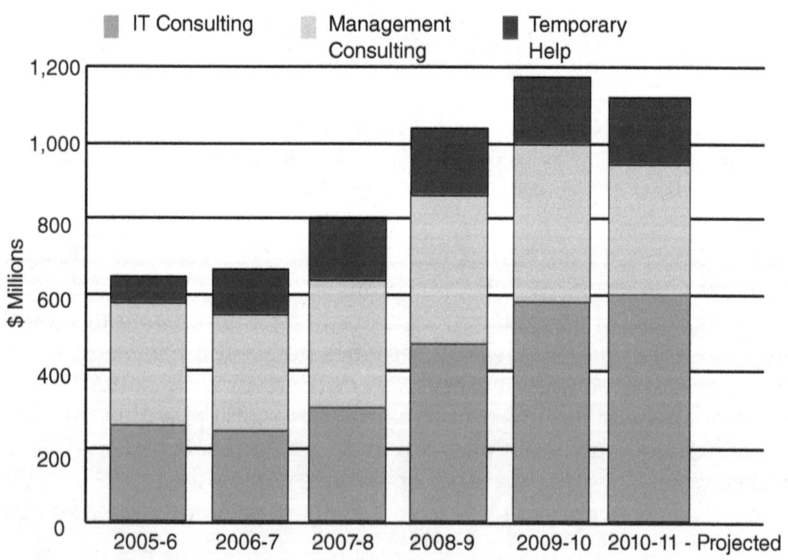

Source: Macdonald (2011, 9).

Table 10.6 Top 10 Canadian Outsourcing Companies, 2005 ($ millions)

Company name	Department focus (% of outsourcing)	Total FY 2005 ($)	IT ($)	Management ($)	Temporary help ($)
CGI Information Systems	CRA (45.2)	549.5	531.3	16.5	1.7
Calian Ltd	DND (95.5)	450.0	11.5	427.8	10.7
Resolve Corporation	HRSDC (100)	270.4	–	270.4	–
IBM Canada	PWGSC (45)	230.7	202.3	27.9	470.5
Altis Human Resources Inc.	Transport Canada (39.5)	120.6	2.0	5.7	112.8
Brainhunter Ottawa	PWGSC (88.9)	116.8	96.2	13.5	7.1
Excel Human Resources		111.4	18.3	7.2	85.9
Coradix Technology Consulting Ltd		86.7	68.9	11.5	6.4
Oracle Corporation Canada		85.0	84.7	200.2	–
Ajilon Canada		83.0	66.4	12.0	4.6

Source: Macdonald (2011, 15).
CRA = Canada Revenue Agency
DND = Department of National Defence
HRSDC = Human Resources and Social Development Canada
PWGSC = Public Works and Government Services Canada

"at least three basic elements within government: a stable and reliable in-house advisory service provided by professional public servants; political advice for the minister from a specialized political unit (generally the minister's office); and the availability of at least a third opinion from a specialized or central policy unit, which might be one of the main central agencies."

Halligan (1995) argued that "externalization" of policy advice was normal and to be expected, with the essential question being not so much whether such advisers should be employed by government, but rather in what proportion vis-à-vis internal analysts and advisers. Yet, as Anderson (1996, 119) noted, "A healthy policy-research community outside government can play a vital role in enriching public understanding and debate of policy issues, and it serves as a natural complement to policy capacity within government." Many conclusions are not well supported by data, which are either not kept at all or kept in a very poor and inconsistent state across years and agencies. The situation cannot be easily changed unless governments modify the way in which data are collected about outsourcing in general and consulting in particular. In the meantime there is need for better empirical research aiming to achieve a careful set of relevant definitions and concepts about the central subject of inquiry.

NOTES

1 In the United States, for example, it originated in the wartime planning activities and "scientific management" thinking of the mid-twentieth century but was applied more widely only in the 1960s and 1970s to large-scale social and economic planning in areas such as defence, urban redevelopment, and budgeting – especially as a result of the implementation of the Planning Programming Budgeting System (PPBS) (Garson 1986; Lindblom 1958a; Wildavsky 1969). U.S.-style "policy analysis" has since then spread around the world, with the development of professional associations and dedicated schools and teaching programs in many countries, but only in a very uneven pattern (Mintrom 2007; and Geva-May and Maslove 2006). Many countries were much less influenced by this movement than others. Some countries, including many in Western Europe, for example, had traditions of legal oversight of government or centralized top-down public administration that placed the evaluative and analytical tasks of government within the judicial or financial branches of the civil service and delayed the arrival of problem-analytical oriented policy brokers (Bekke and van der Meer 2000). Other countries, such as those in Eastern Europe under socialist regimes, featured large-scale planning bureaus that did analyse problems systematically but in a context (central planning) very different from that of the policy analysis movement as it developed in the liberal-capitalist confines of the U.S. government (Verheijen 1999). Many other countries in the developing world until very recently lacked the internal capacity and external autonomy required to conduct the independent analytical tasks required of U.S.-style professional policy analysis (Burns and Bowornwathana

2001; Brinkerhoff and Crosby 2002; Brinkerhoff 2010; Brinkerhoff and Morgan 2010).

2 *Policy capacity* can be defined as a loose concept that covers the gamut of issues associated with the government's arrangements to review, formulate, and implement policies within its jurisdiction (Painter and Pierre 2005c; Peters 1996). *Policy analytical capacity* is a more focused concept related to knowledge acquisition and utilization in policy processes. It refers to the amount of basic research a government can conduct or access, its ability to apply statistical methods, applied research methods, and advanced modelling techniques to these data, and employ analytical techniques such as environmental scanning, trends analysis, and forecasting methods in order to gauge broad public opinion and attitudes, as well as those of interest groups and other major policy players, and to anticipate future policy impacts (O'Connor, Roos, and Vickers-Willis 2007). It also involves the ability to communicate policy-related messages to interested parties and stakeholders.

3 Only the following administrative units provide detailed information about the nature of the contracts that have been let: Canadian Environmental Assessment Agency, Infrastructure Canada, National Parole Board, Office of the Auditor General of Canada, Parks Canada, Privacy Commissioner of Canada, Public Safety Canada, RCMP External Review Committee, and Western Economic Diversification Canada.

4 Pattenaude's Stages of Consultancy
Phase I: Problem recognition
Phase II: Generation of solution strategies
Phase III: Decision to seek a consultant
Phase IV: Problem specification
Phase V: Search for consultant
Phase VI: Consultant selection and contracting
Phase VII: Utilization of consultant
Phase VIII: Evaluation of consultant product
Phase IX: Integration of consultant product to organization
Phase X: Evaluation of experience with consultant
Source: Pattenaude (1979, 203–5).

5 Some limited provincial data does exist, however. In 2001, the Office of the Auditor General of British Columbia tabled a report. The BC government ministries spent about $46 million over the previous three years on advisory services. This suggests that government frequently uses management consultants to assist it in its decision-making. The impact of a consulting project can be many times more significant than the size of the

contract used to engage the consultant. Consultants may, for example, provide advice that affects programs with expenditures in the hundreds of millions of dollars or that have significant social and economic impacts (Office of the Auditor General of British Columbia 2001, 5). The BC audit covered a sample of management consulting engagements across five ministries. It revealed many of the same data problems found in Australia and the United Kingdom: "We initially intended to take a statistical sample of such contracts across government. However, the nature of the information maintained in the ministries made this impracticable. There is no central contract management system for government. In fact, every ministry has its own system and each varies from the next in terms of the type of information collected. For this reason, and because ministry contract management systems do not differentiate between management consulting contracts and other professional service contracts, it was impossible to determine the population size from which to draw a statistically representative sample" (54).

Instead, the study concentrated on the five ministries with the largest expenditures in management advisory services: Ministry for Children and Families; Ministry of Health; Ministry of Forests; Ministry of Advanced Education, Training and Technology; and Ministry of Employment and Investment. On the basis of this limited information, we believe this allowed us to cover about two-thirds of total expenditures on consulting services within ministries and gave us a good cross-section of government activities.

6 In Canada access to the data about government expenditures in this area has become somewhat easier since the implementation of the Federal Accountability Act on 12 December 2006. The act has legislative, procedural, and institutional facets that are designed to increase the transparency and accountability of government spending. From the institutional point of view, the act also introduced important changes, such as creating the Office of the Procurement Ombudsman, which addresses perceived fairness issues in procurement. The office has relatively little information on the topic of policy consulting and policy management as it pertains to external advisers. Its focus appears mostly to be on ensuring a fair and competitive business environment for the companies that bid on government contracts.

11 Inside the Black Box of Academic Researchers–Policy Analysts Interactions

MATHIEU OUIMET, PIERRE-OLIVIER BÉDARD, AND GRÉGORY LÉON

Introduction

Concerns about the knowledge resources of policymakers and the apparent disconnect between, on the one hand, scientific research and evaluation studies, and, on the other, policy work gave rise to the field of inquiry on knowledge utilization, which evolved from the mid-seventies onwards (Havelock 1975; Rein and White 1977; Sabatier 1978; Bozeman and Blankenship 1979a; Weiss and Bucuvalas 1980; Weiss 1979b, 1980). In the hope that scientific research could lead to better policy decisions, and ultimately to better policy outcomes, proponents of *evidence-informed policymaking* (Black 2001; Lavis et al. 2005; Mays, Pope, and Popay 2005) argue that research evidence – as one of the many inputs into the policymaking process, not its sole foundation – should be more seriously considered by policy actors.

Although the policy studies and policy analysis literature appears at times to have a life of its own, it can actually be thought that policy analysis, as an object of inquiry, intersects with the knowledge utilization and mobilization research program and the evidence-informed policymaking perspective. More precisely, policy analysts appear to be instrumental in implementing the principles and practices that underpin evidence-informed policymaking (Howlett 2009b; Williams 2010). As distinct communities, academics and policymakers are, along with other actors, part of what might be called the policy advice system (Howlett 2011). In this context, policy analysts act as a kind of knowledge broker, while often overlooked, operating at the junction of the two communities through their analytical and advice-giving tasks (Cohn 2007). Accordingly, it then becomes relevant to examine the kind of research evidence they mobilize in their policy work and the relations they have with non-governmental actors such as academic researchers.

The literature on policy analysis is replete with conceptual accounts of policy analysis: typologies of the roles, activities, and functions of policy analysts (e.g., Mayer, Bots, and van Daalen 2004), the modes of policy analysis and policy styles (e.g., Howlett and Lindquist 2004), and the overall relation of those conceptualizations to models of the policymaking process (e.g., Enserink, Koppenjan, and Mayer 2013). However, one finds very few *empirical* studies on what policy analysts actually do and what kinds of relations they have with academic researchers. What is more, it appears that there is no systematic research evidence on the types of interactions that are more likely to lead to increased scientific research absorption by policy workers within the public service.

In order to address this gap in knowledge, the overarching goal of this study was to improve the understanding of direct interactions between academic researchers and a specific class of civil servants, namely policy analysts. The specific objectives of this study were:

1. To build a database including dyadic relationships between policy analysts and academic researchers;
2. To collect information on the attributes of these sampled relationships; and
3. To test the assumptions, derived from social network theory, specifically the strength of ties derived from network interactions.

The remainder of this chapter is divided into four sections. In the next section, the study is situated within the research literature on knowledge utilization more specifically. The absorptive capacity framework is briefly described as it guided the entire program of research that our team pursued, within which this specific study occupies a central place. The research hypotheses are presented at the end of this section. All relevant information about the methods is reported in the third section, where we present detailed information about the study design, data collection, and analytical approach. The empirical results, in the form of descriptive and multivariate statistics, are reported in the fourth section. Finally, the chapter ends with a short discussion and a conclusion.

Literature and Research Hypotheses

As can be expected, it appears from empirical studies that policy analysts do interact, to some extent, with academic researchers (e.g., Ouimet et al. 2010, 439; Howlett 2011, 258). While the nature of these interactions remains unspecified, they are generally thought to be of some importance to knowledge acquisition and mobilization. While the most recent systematic review (Oliver et al. 2014) depicts a variety of factors such as timing and timeliness, attitude towards research, skills, and expertise (see also Orton et al. 2011; Mitton et al. 2007; Lavis et al. 2005; Innvaer et al. 2002[1]), they converge on the one aspect: direct interactions that civil servants have with academic researchers are the most frequently cited facilitators of research use. A frequent recommendation is to increase linkages and exchanges between civil servants and researchers by using multiple venues such as developing workshop methodologies to increase this type of interaction (Gagliardi et al. 2008). The review by Mitton et al. (2007) found that most knowledge transfer and exchange strategies examined in the published intervention studies involved social interactions (e.g., face-to-face consultation and meetings between decision-makers and researchers, education sessions for decision-makers, networks, and communication practices).

While these reviews cover some important ground in identifying factors that are thought to hinder effective knowledge mobilization by policymakers, the vast majority of the studies reviewed provides little evidence that would support their practical importance. For instance, in a methodological appreciation of the state of knowledge on knowledge transfer among policymakers and managers, Lavis et al. (2005, S39) conclude, "The research evidence about decision-making by health care managers and policy makers is not that plentiful, rigorous (in the sense of using more than one method of data collection and adequately describing the sampling and measurement methods) or consistent (in the sense of similar factors emerging in a number of contexts)." In other words, suggesting that interactions are an important factor is not sufficient to demonstrate their effectiveness. In fact, in a rare study focusing on the impact of interactions on knowledge utilization, Kothari, Birch and Charles (2005) reveal limited evidence supporting their effectiveness in maximizing knowledge utilization, although their multi-case study suggests some effect on providing a greater understanding to the end user. Nonetheless, direct interactions between researchers and civil servants have been suggested as one of the leading causes of research utilization within the public service.

The main assumption in the empirical literature is that the stronger these direct interactions are, the higher the level of research utilization will be. However, to the best of our knowledge, this assumption has never been tested explicitly and systematically. It is one thing to say that direct interactions are positively associated with research utilization, but it is another to say that *strong* direct interactions are positively associated with the same outcome. Furthermore, according to social network theorists (Granovetter 1983, 2003), weak ties may in fact lead to better informational outcomes than strong ones, as it is through weak ties that non-redundant and new information might travel most effectively. As the leading factor influencing research utilization by civil servants, direct interaction between researchers and civil servants remains a "black box" of unknown content.

Our study has looked inside this black box and examined the nature of the relationships between academic researchers and policy analysts by replacing the traditional unit of analysis (the civil servants) by "researchers–policy analysts" relationships themselves. To the best of our knowledge, this study is the first egocentric network study focusing on network ties between academic researchers and policy analysts.

The study was guided by the absorptive capacity framework, more precisely, the adapted version developed by Todorova and Durisin (2007). The relevance of this framework resides in the fact that it allows integrating the key factors increasing the absorptive capacity of civil servants that are reported in the empirical literature (for a list of these factors, see Oliver et al. 2014; Innvaer et al. 2002; Lavis et al. 2005; Rich and Oh 2000). The concept of absorptive capacity allowed us to make important conceptual clarifications that guided us throughout our investigation.

Each component of the framework is described in Ouimet et al. (2009). In the framework, *social interactions* between researchers and policy analysts are hypothesized as affecting all components of absorptive capacity, as is the case with access to information sources (through an effective research knowledge management system) and policy analysts' prior knowledge (which is moderated by recruitment and skill development policies). As one of the most commonly cited factors influencing the utilization of scientific research by managers and policymakers (Oliver et al. 2014), direct interactions with researchers are a way for policy analysts to develop the different components of absorptive capacity, more precisely, to better appreciate the potential

Figure 11.1 A Theoretical Framework of the Absorption of Research Evidence by Policy Analysts

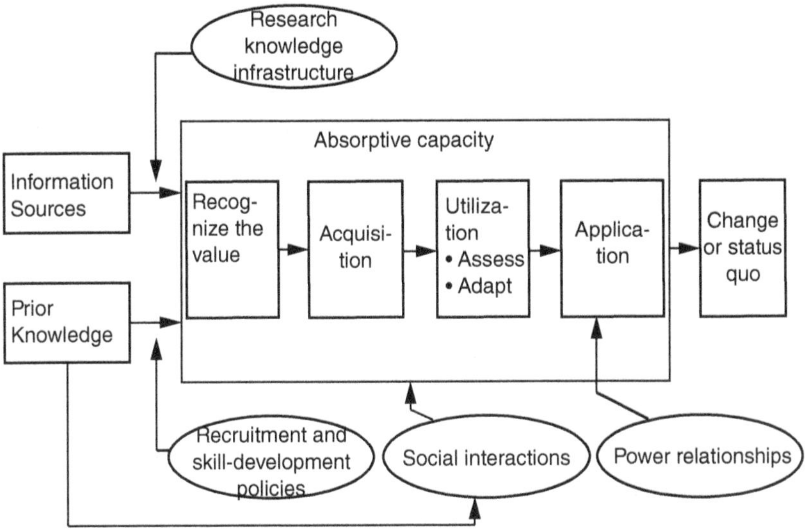

value of scientific research, to acquire scientific research and/or to increase their propensity to use scientific research in their policy analysis and/or to convince policymakers that they should consider the evidence prior to making decisions (Albert, Fretheim, and Maiga 2007). This study focused on a sub-part of the conceptual model presented in figure 11.1 in that it tested hypotheses related to social interactions. More precisely, this study provides an empirical test of two research hypotheses:

H1: The stronger the relationship between an academic researcher and a policy analyst, the higher the impact of the information acquired from the relationship on policy analysis;

H2: The weaker the relationship between an academic researcher and a policy analyst, the higher the impact of the information acquired from the relationship on policy analysis.

These two research hypotheses operationalize an old, but still salient, theoretical debate in social network theory. Since the work of mathematicians Pál Erdős and Alfréd Rényi (1959), networks of any type (biological, social, etc.) were considered as forming randomly (i.e., read, new ties are added randomly to a network). Barabási and Albert (1999) launched a theoretical debate in positing that networks do not develop randomly, but are rather scale-free and operate following two mechanisms: (1) they expand continuously by the addition of new nodes, and (2) new nodes attach preferentially to nodes that are already well connected. The idea that new network relationships do not develop randomly is an old one in sociology, a discipline that for a long time has discovered that humans tend to attach to others who share common characteristics with them (i.e., a phenomenon called homophily – for a review, see McPherson, Smith-Lovin, and Cook 2001). Another stylized fact in sociology is that outcomes of network interactions depend on the strength of the network ties. Originally developed by Mark Granovetter in the context of job market (Granovetter 1983), the strength of weak tie theory has never been tested in the context of research mobilization among policy analysts. To the best of our knowledge, our study is the first to examine the effect of weak vs strong ties between academic researchers and policy analysts on the content of policy analysis.

Methods

Study Design

We used a cross-sectional, egocentric web survey[2] to collect information on policy analysts/academic researchers network interactions. The survey was conducted between November and December 2012 among policy analysts working for the government of Quebec. The targeted population was policy analysts who belonged to a specific governmental professional group (105), namely agent of socio-economic research and planning (i.e., *agent de recherche et de planification socio-économiques*). As described in official external recruitment postings for this professional group, the principal and customary duties of these agents, depending on the nature and requirements of the job, are to perform study and research activities for social and economic issues at the local, regional, and/or provincial levels. These agents analyse factors such as legislation, fundamental research, technological and cultural change, public and private investment, demographic trends, and statistics in general. They can also assess the impact of these factors on public policies and attempt to predict the implications, either at a sectoral or broader level, in dealing with different policy issues.

The policy analysts in the targeted population were located in eight of the twenty-two Quebec ministries, i.e., Ministry of Agriculture, Fisheries and Food; Ministry of Culture and Communication; Ministry of Sustainable Development, Environment, Fauna and Parks; Ministry of Economic Development, Innovation and Exportation (now merged with the Ministry of Finance and the Economy); Ministry of Education, Leisure and Sport; Ministry of Immigration and Cultural Communities; Ministry of Natural Resources; and Ministry of Health and Social Services. These ministries were purposely selected on the basis of the results of the Ouimet et al. (2010) study, which showed that, over a twelve-month period (from September 2007 to September 2008), a higher proportion of policy analysts located in these ministries had contacted a university researcher than policy analysts in other ministries (50 per cent or more in the selected ministries as compared to 46.1 per cent on average for the seventeen surveyed ministries). For each of the selected ministries, we searched the website and analysed the organizational chart for directorates whose main activities include policy research (e.g., support, development, implementation, etc.), policy development and planning (e.g., strategic planning), or program implementation. On the basis of these criteria, 160 directorates were selected, and their managers were officially invited by regular mail for a research collaboration. From these 160 directorates, 45 did not answer our request for collaboration. Twenty-three directorates did not have any policy analyst who belongs to the targeted governmental professional group. This procedure generated a sample of 255 policy analysts who were all invited to participate in the study.

Data Collection

The database of 255 policy analysts including their full name and e-mail address and a survey questionnaire was transmitted to a contracted research firm in Quebec City (Infras International Inc.), which administrated the entire web survey. An explicit consent formula was included in the opening to the questionnaire along with eligibility assessment questions. To be eligible, a participant had to (1) be working as a policy analyst in one of the selected ministries for at least twelve months *and* (2) not have missed more than two months of work within the twelve months prior to the survey, *and* (3) have personally contacted – *or* been contacted by – one or more academic researchers within the twelve months prior to the survey. Three reminders were sent by e-mail until the survey closed.

Of the 255 invited individuals, 54 did not access the survey's website (subtotal = 201 individuals), 9 did not consent to participate (subtotal = 192 individuals), 99 were not eligible on the basis of the three inclusion criteria listed above (i.e., 27, 14, and 58 individuals, respectively), and 10 did not complete the questionnaire (subtotal = 83 individuals). Therefore, 83 individuals out of the 156 (i.e., 255 – 99 non-eligible individuals) completed the questionnaire for a net response rate of 53.2 per cent.

Survey Instrument

The survey instrument including closed-ended questions was elaborated along two lines of inquiry. The first section of the questionnaire focused on the relation attributes between the respondent and up to three academic researchers, and the researchers' profile (i.e., institution, age, and gender). Two questions were used prior to mobilizing the name generator (i.e., the procedure used in ego-centric surveys to generate names of people with whom participants interacted): (1) "As part of your work with the government of Quebec, in the past twelve months have you personally contacted one or more university professors in Quebec or elsewhere in the world?" (yes or no), and (2) "As part of your work with the government of Quebec, in the past twelve months have you been contacted by one or more university professors from Quebec or elsewhere in the world?" (yes or no). Respondents who answered "no" to these two questions were ineligible to participate.

The following name generator was used immediately after asking the two questions: "Please indicate the number and then the name of the university professor(s) with whom you have exchanged (either because they have contacted you or because you have contacted them) during the last twelve months. Please enter the number (1, 2, or 3). Note: If you have had exchanges with more than three professors, please limit your response to the number 3 and, on the next page, enter the name of the three professors of whom you have the best memories of the exchange."

The second section of the questionnaire included a set of questions on each recalled specific relationship (up to three). We chose to set a limit of three relationships to keep the length and duration of the survey reasonable. Finally, the third section of the questionnaire covered the respondent's socio-professional profile and views about academic research.

As each respondent provided information about interactions with up to three academic researchers, the data collected in the survey were used to generate a database of dyads in which the unit of analysis was the policy analyst/academic researcher interaction, independent of the number of interactions between the same two individuals. One hundred and eighty-eight dyads were identified from the survey data. Data collected for 3 dyads were excluded from the analysis if the nature of the conversations was strictly personal (2 dyads) and the identified researcher was not from an academic organization (1 dyad). Therefore, the database includes 185 dyads.

Measures

THE DEPENDENT VARIABLE: PERCEIVED TIE IMPACT ON POLICY ANALYSIS

The dependent variable in this study is the perceived impact of the dyadic tie on policy analysis, defined as the perceived usefulness of the information acquired from exchanges with an academic researcher in the production of a written policy analysis. The respondents were asked, "In the past twelve months, have you written one or several status reports [*états de situation*] (yes or know)?" In Quebec ministries, status reports can vary in length, depth and/or content. However, in all cases, these documents are produced by policy analysts to inform decision-makers and always include a contextual analysis of the issue and of potential options. Then, the respondents who answered "yes" to the above question were asked, "Has the information obtained in contacts with [full name of Professor *i*] during the past twelve months been useful to you in writing a 'status report' (yes or no)?" The dependent variable is thus dichotomous, taking the value 0 or 1 if the information obtained during the exchange with the professor was not perceived as useful or judged useful in writing a status report, respectively.

THE MAIN INDEPENDENT VARIABLE: TIE STRENGTH

Marsden and Campbell (1984) found that a measure of closeness, referring to the emotional intensity of a relationship, is "on balance the best indicator of the concept of tie strength." In our study, tie strength was measured with the following question: "Based on the discussions you've had with Professor [name of *i*] over the past twelve months, would you say that you feel you've been talking with: (a) a friend, (b) a close colleague or collaborator, or (c) an acquaintance?" As very few respondents answered "a friend," it was decided to create a dichotomous variable taking the following values: 0 = an acquaintance, and 1 = a friend or a close colleague or collaborator (i.e., 0 = weak tie; 1 = strong tie).

Analytical Approach

Prior to reporting the results of the test of our research hypotheses, we present the characteristics of the survey participants (i.e., the sample of policy analysts), of the university professors named by the analysts, and of the relationships (i.e., the dyads). These characteristics were all measured through the survey instrument, thus self-reported by the sampled policy analysts.

Resolving a logistic regression equation was the chosen way to test the research hypotheses positing that the stronger the relationship between a researcher and an analyst, the higher the impact of the information acquired from the relationship on the policy analysis; and inversely, the weaker the relationship between a researcher and an analyst, the higher the impact of the information acquired from the relationship on the policy analysis. The dichotomous dependent variable was regressed on tie strength and on a set of adjustment variables.[3]

More precisely, the association between tie strength and the perceived tie impact was adjusted for a dichotomous variable capturing the consultation of the professor's work, measured with the following question: "Have you ever read scientific articles, research reports or scientific work, either whole or in part, published by Professor [name of *i*] (yes or no)?" Controlling for this factor is highly important, as the well-known theoretical argument stressing the importance of direct interactions with researchers implicitly assumes that these social interactions are an effective way for civil servants to acquire research evidence. In other words, the causal mechanism linking direct interactions with researchers with research mobilization is that potential users learn about researchers' own research through these interactions.

The examination of the effects of social relationships using a database of dyads (i.e., ego-centric network data) can be biased if one does not control for social homophily, the tendency of interacting with similar others, based on characteristics such as gender, age, etc. (McPherson, Smith-Lovin, and Cook 2001). In this study, the estimation of the effect of tie strength on perceived tie impact was adjusted for gender homophily. Gender homophily was controlled for by using two dummy variables: one taking the value of 1 if the analyst is a man and the professor a woman (and 0 otherwise), and another one taking the value of

1 if the analyst is a woman and the professor a man (and 0 otherwise), the reference category being "same gender" (i.e., the analyst and the professor are from the same gender).

For policy analysts, interacting with academic researchers is a means to physically access research evidence. However, access to research evidence cannot be solely physical, but should also be conceptualized as cognitive (Ouimet et al. 2009). Prior knowledge is a key antecedent of research absorption (see figure 11.3). In other words, policy analysts with training experience in research should have less difficulty in mobilizing research evidence than analysts without this type of educational background. Having completed a research-oriented master's (i.e., the research track) and/or doctoral (i.e., PhD) graduate program has been shown to be a significant predictor of the consultation of scientific articles in our study population (Ouimet et al. 2010). Therefore, in the regression analysis, the estimation of the effect of tie strength on perceived tie impact was adjusted for a dichotomous variable taking the value of 1 if the analyst holds a research-oriented master's and/or doctoral diploma, and 0 otherwise.

In Quebec ministries, the professional duties of policy analysts are broadly the same, but can vary according to the type of directorate to which they belong. Using the name of the directorates combined with Internet search, we were able to classify the directorates into three mutually exclusive categories: (1) research directorates (i.e., supporting and developing research collaborations and partnerships for the whole ministry), (2) policy and planning directorates (i.e., supporting the formulation and adoption of policy statements, action plans, strategic plans, etc., and to a lesser extent, their monitoring and evaluation), and (3) program directorates (i.e., mostly involved in program implementation). Two dichotomous variables were entered in the regression models, one referring to "research directorates," the other referring to "policy and planning directorates." The category "program directorates" was the reference group. Furthermore, regression estimates were adjusted for the ministry using the Ministry of Health and Social Services as the reference category.

Finally, two dichotomous variables were included in the regression equation to control for the number of relationship(s) generated by survey participants. The 185 dyads were classified into three categories: (1) lonely dyad, (2) two dyads, and (3) three dyads. The reference was lonely dyad. This procedure allowed controlling for potential clustering effects in the model, that is, the possibility that the perceived tie impact is influenced by the number of relationship(s) (i.e., up to three) recalled by survey participants.

Results

Sample Characteristics

SURVEY PARTICIPANTS

The proportion of men (48.2 per cent; $n = 40$) was almost the same as the proportion of women (51.8 per cent; $n = 43$). One-quarter of survey participants were fifty-five years old or more (25.3 per cent; $n = 21$), 13.3 per cent ($n = 11$) were between fifty and fifty-four, 12 per cent ($n = 10$) were between forty and forty-nine, 38.6 per cent ($n = 32$) were between thirty and thirty-nine, and 10.8 per cent ($n = 9$) were twenty-nine or younger. On average, survey participants had 5.6 (± 5.0) years' experience in their current job occupation and 11.7 (± 9.2) years' experience as analysts in the public sector at either the local, provincial, or national level. French is the mother tongue of the vast majority of participants (95.2 per cent, $n = 79$).

Of the eighty-three policy analysts who completed the web survey, 28.9 per cent ($n = 24$) were employed by the Ministry of Health and Social Services, 14.5 per cent ($n = 12$) by the Ministry of Culture and Communication, 13.3 per cent ($n = 11$) by the Ministry of Immigration and Cultural Communities, 12 per cent ($n = 10$) by the Ministry of Agriculture, Fisheries and Food, the same number were from the Ministry of Education, Leisure and Sport, 8.4 per cent ($n = 7$) from the Ministry of Sustainable Development, Environment, Fauna and Parks, 6 per cent ($n = 6$) from the Ministry of Natural Resources, and finally, 4.8 per cent ($n = 4$) were from the Ministry of Economic Development, Innovation and Exportation (now merged within the Ministry of Finance and Economy). About two-thirds of the survey participants (67.1 per cent, $n = 55$) were working in a program directorate, while 16.9 per cent ($n = 14$) and 15.7 per cent ($n = 13$) were from a research directorate (i.e., supporting and developing research collaborations and partnerships for the whole ministry) and in a policy and planning directorate, respectively. One-fifth of the policy analysts (20.5 per cent, $n = 17$) had at least one employee under their supervision. A large proportion of the respondents were permanent employees (81.9 per cent, $n = 68$), 16.9 per cent ($n = 14$) were non-permanent or contract employees, and one participant was hired as an external consultant.

As for the participants' involvement in the non-mutually-exclusive policy activities (that form the policy cycle) within the previous twelve months, 69.9 per cent (*n* = 58) had contributed to the planning or elaboration of new policies, new programs, new measures, new strategies, or new frameworks or action plans, 62.7 per cent (*n* = 52) had contributed to their application, execution or follow-up, 39.8 per cent (*n* = 33) had contributed to the programming and elaboration of policy implementation plans, and 36.1 per cent (*n* = 30) had contributed to policy evaluation.

The majority of the surveyed policy analysts (55.4 per cent; *n* = 46) held a research-oriented graduate diploma, that is, a master's degree in research with master's thesis and/or a research doctorate (PhD). Survey participants did their university studies in different, non-mutually-exclusive, academic disciplines. More specifically, 12 per cent (*n* = 10) of the eighty-three policy analysts studied economics, 16.9 per cent (*n* = 14) studied political science, 15.7 per cent (*n* = 13) studied sociology, 9.6 per cent (*n* = 8) studied social work, 6 per cent (*n* = 5) studied anthropology, 3.6 per cent (n = 3) studied psychology, 6 per cent (*n* = 5) studied history, 7.2 per cent (*n* = 6) studied education sciences, 10.8 per cent (*n* = 9) studied health sciences, nearly one-fifth (18.1 per cent; *n* = 15) studied in natural sciences (e.g., mathematics, life sciences, chemistry, physics, biology, etc.), 10.8 per cent (*n* = 9) studied business administration, except for accounting (e.g., management, finance), one-fifth (20.5 per cent; *n* = 17) studied in humanities (other than history and law – e.g., literature, languages), only two participants studied law, one participant studied industrial relations, and finally, one participant studied philosophy or theology. Of the eighty-three policy analysts, 44.6 per cent (*n* = 37) reported that they had access to bibliographic databases from which they can download or print articles published in scientific journals from their workstation, while 39.8 per cent (*n* = 33) reported having no access and 15.7 per cent (*n* = 13) did not know whether they have access to such databases. Of the thirty-seven policy analysts who reported having access to such databases, 83.8 per cent (*n* = 31) have searched for scientific articles in electronic bibliographic databases from their workstation as part of their work with the Quebec government during the previous twelve months. The most searched databases searched were Google Scholar (32.3 per cent, *n* = 10 of the thirty-one database users) and PubMed (i.e., database of references and abstracts for life sciences and biomedical topics) (22.6 per cent, *n* = 7 of the thirty-one database users).

The vast majority of the surveyed policy analysts (84.3 per cent, n = 70) had written one or several status reports (i.e., routinely produced documents aimed at informing decision-makers through a contextual analysis of a policy issue and an analysis of potential options) in the previous twelve months. On average, they had written 7.9 (± 6.9) status reports during this period. At the end of 2008, we surveyed 1614 policy analysts from Quebec ministries about their consultation of scientific articles and found that 78.4 per cent of the analysts had consulted one or more scientific articles in the previous twelve months (Ouimet et al. 2010). Interestingly, nearly four years later, using a much smaller sample and slightly more restrictive operational definition of policy analyst, we found a very similar result. In effect, 80.7 per cent (n = 67) of the survey participants reported that they had consulted an article published in a university-level specialized scientific journal as part of their work with the government of Quebec in the previous twelve months. On average, the sixty-seven readers of scientific articles have consulted 33.5 (± 69.8) articles (a minimum of 2 and a maximum 500 articles). We asked those sixty-seven readers about the nature of the scientific articles consulted. Of the 67 policy analysts who had consulted one or several scientific articles, 74.6 per cent (n = 50) reported that at least one article was empirical (study comprising data collection) and qualitative (comprising non-quantitative analyses), 68.7 per cent (n = 46) reported the consultation of one or more empirical quantitative studies (comprising descriptive or correlational statistical analyses), 65.7 per cent (n = 44) reported the consultation of empirical mixed-method studies (comprising both qualitative and quantitative data analyses), and finally, 65.7 per cent (n = 44) of analysts reported consulting one or several non-empirical (study comprising no data collection) and conceptual (study that is reflexive, theoretical) studies. Of the 57 policy analysts who have both consulted scientific articles and written one or several status reports, 77.2 per cent (n = 44) reported that information found in one or several scientific articles was useful to them in writing a status report in the previous twelve months.

Finally, 83.1 per cent (n = 69) of the survey participants *have personally contacted* one or several university professors in Quebec or elsewhere in the world as part of their work with the government of Quebec in the previous twelve months, while 79.5 per cent (n = 66) of the survey participants *have been contacted* by one or several university professors. It should be recalled that 100 per cent of the participants have personally contacted and/or have been contacted by one or more university professors, as it was part of the eligibility criteria. Nearly half of the eighty-three policy analysts (48.2 per cent; *n* = 40) recalled relationships with three university professors, 30.1 per cent (*n* = 25) with two university professors, and 21.7 per cent (*n* = 18) recalled a relationship with only one university professor.

NAMED UNIVERSITY PROFESSORS

The eighty-three surveyed policy analysts were asked to name up to three university researchers who had contacted them and/or whom they have personally contacted in the previous twelve months as part of their work in the government of Quebec. They named 163 unique university professors. From these university professors, 60.1 per cent (*n* = 98) were men and 39.9 per cent (*n* = 65) were women. Of the 136 university researchers classified by surveyed participants, 27.2 per cent (*n* = 37) were fifty-five years old or more, 30.1 per cent (*n* = 41) were between fifty and fifty-four, 35.3 per cent (*n* = 48) were between forty and forty-nine, and only 7.4 per cent (*n* = 10) were between thirty and thirty-nine years old. Policy analysts were unable to classify 16.6 per cent (*n* = 27) of university researchers in an age category. Only 4 of the 163 university professors were from outside Canada (i.e., two from France, one from Belgium, and one from Italy), and surprisingly, only 1 of the named professors was from another province of Canada (i.e., University of Ottawa, Ontario) and none were from the United States. The university with the largest number of named university professors in the survey was Université Laval, which is located in Quebec City, the capital of Quebec. More precisely, 38.7 per cent (*n* = 63) of the university professors were from this university. The Université de Montréal (14.1 per cent; *n* = 23), the Université du Québec à Montréal (10.4 per cent; *n* = 17), and the Université de Sherbrooke located in the Eastern Townships (9.2 per cent; *n* = 15) are the second, third, and fourth universities with the larger number of named professors in the survey, respectively. Only 5.5 per cent (*n* = 9) of the 163 university professors were from McGill University, the highest world-ranked English teaching university located in Quebec.

University professors were from twelve different types of faculty/schools, namely (in descending order): Human and Social Sciences (including History, Arts & Letters) (36.2 per cent; *n* = 59), Medicine (14.7 per cent; *n* = 24), Natural Sciences and Engineering (11.7 per cent; *n* = 19), Agricultural Sciences and Food (8.6 per cent; *n* = 14), Education (8 per cent; *n* = 13), Administrative Sciences (including one school of

Public Administration) (7.4 per cent; n = 12), Forestry, Geography, Geomatics, Land Planning, Architecture, and Art and Design (4.9 per cent; n = 8), Law (3.1 per cent; n = 5), Nursing (1.2 per cent; n = 2), Theatre (0.6 per cent; n = 1), and Theology and Religions (0.6 per cent; n = 1). We were unable to classify five university professors (3.1 per cent) as the result of either misspelling of their full name by respondents or homonyms.

THE RELATIONSHIPS

More than half of the 185 sampled university professor–policy analyst relationships (57.3 per cent; n = 106) were between two individuals of the same gender, while in 29.2 per cent (n = 54) of the dyads, the policy analyst was a woman and the professor a man. In only 13.5 per cent (n = 25) of the dyads, the policy analyst was a man while the professor a woman. The age difference between the policy analyst and the university professor was impossible to determine in 34 dyads. More than the half of the remaining 151 dyads (55.6 per cent; n = 84) took place between two individuals of the same age group. In 22.5 per cent (n = 34) of the 151 dyads, the policy analyst was older than the professor, while the reverse was true in 21.9 per cent (n = 33) of the ties.

From the 185 dyads, 78.9 per cent (n = 146) involved strictly professional conversations, while 21.1 per cent (n = 39) involved both professional and personal conversations. On the basis of discussions policy analysts had with the university professors over the previous twelve months, only 2.7 per cent (n = 5) were described as very formal conversations, 38.9 per cent (n = 72) as formal, more than half (51.4 per cent; n = 95) as informal, and 7 per cent (n = 13) as very informal. The survey data showed that none of the policy analysts had familial links with any named university professor. On average, policy analysts had known the named professors for 4.4 (± 5.3) years, and, on average, they had entered into contact with them approximately 6.9 (± 12.7) times as part of their work during the previous twelve months.

The most frequent means by which policy analysts communicated with the professors over a twelve-month period was e-mail (94.1 per cent; n = 174 dyads). In-person communication at a certain event (62.7 per cent; n = 116 dyads) and by telephone (61.6 per cent; n = 114 dyads) were the second and third most frequent means of communication reported by policy analysts. In-person meeting at the analyst's office (22.7 per cent; n = 42 dyads), at the university professor's office (20.5 per cent; n = 38 dyads), at a restaurant (14.6 per cent; n = 27) and through videoconference (13 per cent; $n = 24$) were other, less frequent means of communication with university professors. Policy analysts were also asked how they had met each named professor for the first time. The most frequent context for the first meeting was during a work meeting (36.7 per cent; $n = 68$), followed by a colloquium/conference (23.8 per cent; $n = 44$) and university training (18.4 per cent; $n = 34$). Few (16.2 per cent; $n = 30$) of the first meetings between analysts and professors happened on no particular occasion (e.g., from the analyst's workstation via e-mail or telephone). For 3.7 per cent ($n = 7$) of the dyads, it was impossible to capture the first meeting context.

In 112 of the 185 dyads (60.5 per cent), policy analysts have, from their own initiative, tried to establish a relationship/communication with the professor. From a list of six potential primary motivations in contacting the university professors, obtaining an expert opinion was the most frequent (33.9 per cent; 38 of the 112 dyads), closely followed by enlisting the professor's participation in an activity such as a panel of experts or for a presentation (30.4 per cent; $n = 34$). From the 112 dyads where policy analysts have from their own initiative tried to establish a relationship with the professor, 9.8 per cent ($n = 11$) and 7.1 per cent ($n = 8$) were first motivated by the aim of facilitating the policy analyst's understanding of certain scientific research results and of obtaining a study (report, scientific article, work) authored by the professor, respectively. Obtaining a study (report, scientific article, work) authored by another professor (2.7 per cent; $n = 3$) and trying to reach one of the professor's colleagues or acquaintances (1 dyad) were much less frequent primary motivations in contacting professors. Finally, in 15.2 per cent ($n = 17$) of the 112 relationships for which policy analysts had from their own initiative tried to establish a relationship/communication with the professor, other primary motivations were openly mentioned, for example, offering a training contract, a research contract, obtaining or validating information, etc.

Of the 112 dyads where policy analysts had from their own initiative tried to establish a relationship with the professor, 81.3 per cent ($n = 91$) were initiated because of the professor's expertise in the field concerned. In 41.1 per cent ($n = 46$) of the 112 dyads, the professor's reputation was what convinced the policy analyst to contact him or her. The professor's scientific publications (33 per cent; $n = 37$) was the third most-used clue reported by policy analysts in their decision to establish a relationship with the professor. The professor's past contributions to government or quasi-government organizations (17.9 per cent; $n = 20$),

Figure 11.2 Means of Communication with the University Professors (in % of 185 Dyads)

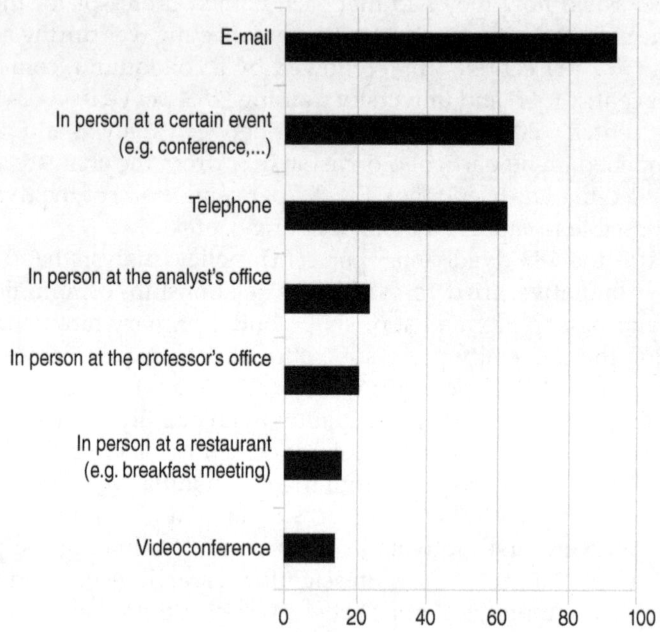

affiliated institution (16.1 per cent; n = 18), title (14.3 per cent; n = 16), and appearances in the media (13.4 per cent; n = 15) were other, less frequent factors that seem to have convinced policy analysts to establish a relationship with a university professor. Finally, other factors were openly reported in 20.5 per cent (n = 23) of the 112 dyads, the most frequent being reference from a colleague or from someone else (8 per cent; n = 9).

In 146 (78.9 per cent) of the 185 dyads, the professor informed the analyst of his or her research results that had a connection with the analyst's work. Apart from his or her own research work, the professor informed the analyst of other research results connected to the analyst's work in 52.4 per cent of the dyads (n = 97). In more than three-quarters of the dyads (77.8 per cent; n = 144), the policy analyst had read scientific articles, research reports, or scientific work, either whole or in part, published by the professor. In a general way, the policy analyst

Figure 11.3 What Convinced Policy Analysts That the Professor Was the Person They Should Contact (in % of 112 Dyads)

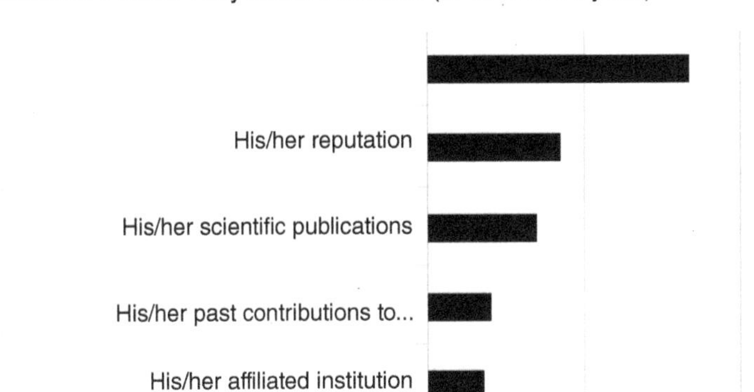

described the relationship with the university professor in the execution of work with the government of Quebec as very useful in 43.2 per cent ($n = 80$) of the dyads, as fairly useful in 46.5 per cent ($n = 86$) of the dyads, and as barely or not at all useful in only 8.1 per cent ($n = 15$), and 2.2 per cent ($n = 4$) of the dyads, respectively. Finally, in more than a third of the dyads (37.8 per cent; $n = 70$), the policy analyst reported that the production of his or her work for the government of Quebec would have been substantially different if he or she had never been in contact with the professor.

Regression Results: Testing the Strength of Weak Tie Theory

Table 11.1 presents the crude perceived tie impact rate, which is the percentage of weak or strong ties through which the information obtained has been perceived as useful by the policy analyst in writing one or several status reports. It also reports the unadjusted and

Table 11.1 Perceived Impact of the Tie on the Production of Written Policy Analysis According to the Strength of the Tie[a]

Tie strength	Sample of dyads	Crude perceived tie impact rate[b]	Unadjusted rate ratio (95% CI)	Adjusted rate ratio (95% CI)[c]
Weak	68	36.8	1.00	1.00
Strong	92	69.6	1.89 (1.47–2.22)	1.79 (1.25–2.13)

a CI denotes confidence interval. Weak ties were the reference group (coded 0).
b The crude perceived tie impact rate is the percentage of weak or strong ties through which the information obtained has been useful to the policy analyst in writing a status report.
c The rate ratio has been adjusted for whether the policy analyst had read scientific articles, research reports, or scientific work, either whole or in part, published by the professor, the gender difference between the policy analyst and the professor, whether the policy analyst holds a research-oriented graduate degree, whether the analyst was working in a research directorate, a policy and planning directorate, or in a program directorate, the ministry, and whether the dyad was part of a cluster of two or three recalled ties or not.

adjusted rate ratios, the latter being controlled for potential confounding variables.

The logistic regression equation was estimated on 160 of the 185 dyads for which the policy analyst had written one or several status reports in the previous twelve months. In 68 (42.5 per cent) of these 160 ties, the policy analyst felt as if he or she had been talking with an acquaintance (i.e., weak ties), while in 92 of these ties (57.5 per cent), the policy analyst rather felt as if he or she had been talking with a close colleague, a close collaborator, or a friend (i.e., strong ties). In 36.8 per cent of the weak ties, the policy analyst reported that the information obtained from exchanges with the professor was useful in writing one or several status reports. The crude perceived impact rate was 89 per cent higher for strong ties (unadjusted rate ratio, 1.89; 95 per cent CI, 1.47–2.22). After adjusting for confounding variables, the perceived impact rate was 79 per cent higher for strong ties as compared to weak ties (adjusted rate ratio, 1.79; 95 per cent CI, 1.25–2.13).

In the logistic regression equation including adjustment variables, only two independent variables were significantly associated with the dependent variable, namely tie strength and whether the policy analyst had read scientific articles, research reports, or scientific work, either

Table 11.2 Perceived Impact of the Ties between Production of Analysis and Reading Scholarly Work

Tie strength	Sample of dyads	Crude perceived tie impact rate†	Unadjusted rate ratio (95% CI)	Adjusted rate ratio (95% CI)
No reading	39	28.2	1.00	1.00
Reading	121	64.5	2.28 (1.60–2.84)	1.90 (1.16–2.26)

Notes: CI denotes confidence interval. Ties where the policy analyst had not read any scientific article, research report, or scientific work, either whole or in part, published by the professor were the reference group (coded 0).
The crude perceived tie impact rate is the percentage of ties where the policy analyst had (or had not) read scientific articles, research reports, or scientific work, either whole or in part, published by the professor for which the information obtained has been useful to the policy analyst in writing a status report.
The rate ratio has been adjusted for tie strength, gender difference between the policy analyst and the professor, whether the policy analyst holds a research-oriented graduate degree, whether the analyst was working in a research directorate, a policy and planning directorate, or in a program directorate, the ministry, and whether the dyad was part of a cluster of two or three recalled ties or not.

whole or in part, published by the professor (table 11.2). As mentioned, the theoretical argument stressing the importance of direct interactions with researchers assumes that these social relationships are effective ways for civil servants to acquire research evidence.

In 121 (75.6 per cent) of the 160 ties, the policy analyst had read scientific articles, research reports, or scientific works, either whole or in part, published by the professor, while in only 39 of these ties (24.4 per cent), the policy analyst had not read any scientific article, research report, or scientific work published by the professor. In 64.5 per cent of the dyads where the policy analyst had read scientific articles, research reports, or scientific works published by the professor, the policy analyst reported that the information obtained from exchanges with the professor was useful in writing one or several status reports. The crude perceived impact rate was 128.7 per cent higher when the policy analyst had read scientific articles, research reports, or scientific works published by the professor as compared with the situation when he or she had not (unadjusted rate ratio, 2.28; 95 per cent CI, 1.60–2.84). After adjusting for confounding variables, the perceived impact rate was 90 per cent higher when the policy analyst had read scientific articles, research reports, or scientific works published by the professor as compared with the situation where he or she had not (adjusted rate ratio, 1.90; 95 per cent CI, 1.16–2.26).

Discussion and Conclusion

Findings from the multivariate analyses suggest that the knowledge mobilization could be biased *when it relies on information acquired from interactions with a researcher*, as the mobilization of the information in policy analysis is thus likely to depend, notably, on the emotional intensity of the tie linking the analyst with the researcher, a phenomenon that is not logically related to the accuracy, validity, or reliability of the information communicated by the researcher. These findings depart from expectations derived from the rational choice theory portraying individuals as being not influenced by emotions. The emotional strength of a social tie could be working as a social heuristic (Gigerenzer and Gaissmaier 2011, 472) used by policy analysts to reduce the costs of assessing the quality of the information conveyed by an academic researcher (Jones and Cullis 1993, 70) prior to the mobilization of this information in the production of a status report. One very important aspect of the process of mobilizing research evidence is to document the level of uncertainty that characterizes specific research studies. Concerning this matter, there are validated critical appraisal tools (CATS) aimed at identifying methodological flaws *in all types* of research studies and providing users of research evidence with the capacity to make informed decisions while taking into account the uncertainty of research claims, whether causal or descriptive. Ideally, informed decisions about the quality of research evidence should be based on the use of CATS rather than on the reputation or the sole opinion of researchers. In this respect, an interesting finding is that in more than 40 per cent of the relationships where policy analysts have from their own initiative tried to establish a relationship with the researcher, the researcher's reputation is what convinced the policy analysts that they should contact him or her. However, the systematic use of CATS in public administration would be a radical cultural change that would not be without cost (i.e., training how to use CATS, costs related to the use of CATS, the social costs of criticizing the work of *renowned experts*, etc.).

Our findings also suggest that the perceived usefulness of the relationship in the production of written policy analyses significantly depends on the fact that the analyst had consulted some of the professor's work. This provides indirect evidence suggesting that social interactions with researchers serve as a means of research acquisition, as posited in the absorptive capacity framework. More direct evidence that interactions were a means to acquire research evidence is that in nearly 80 per cent of the relationships, the professor informed the analyst of his or her research results that had a connection with the analyst's work, and in more than half of the relationships, the professor informed the analyst of research results produced by other researchers. This finding is also partly reassuring in that reading the professor's work might provide additional information on the methodological rigour of the researcher, pending the ability of the analyst to systematically identify methodological strengths and weaknesses in research studies without having to rely solely on social heuristics.

A broader goal of this study was really to open the black box of real interactions between university researchers and policy analysts. To this end, this study provides new evidence in support of the homophily theory, which posits that individuals preferentially interact with similar others. Although our sample of policy analysts includes a nearly equal proportion of men and women (48.2 per cent and 51.8 per cent, respectively), nearly 60 per cent of the relationships were between individuals of the same gender, and surprisingly, only 13 per cent of male policy analysts interacted with female professors while 40 per cent of the named professors were female.

The main weaknesses of this study are the self-reported and cross-sectional nature of the data. Its main strengths include its capacity to generate new knowledge on what is going on inside the black box of interactions between academic researchers and policy analysts as well as on the application of the strength of weak tie theory to the study context. However, the study findings cannot be generalized beyond the study population. An obvious next step would be to replicate the study in other provinces and countries to explore potential differences that might be related to variations in cultural traits. For us, the next step would consist in following up with semi-structured interviews with a random sample of participants with the hope of gaining a better understanding of our study findings.

NOTES

1 Innvaer et al. (2002) focuses on the utilization of scientific research by policymakers, Lavis et al. (2005) on the use of research by both policymakers and managerial decision-makers, Mitton et al. (2007) on "knowledge transfer and exchange" at the health policy level, and Orton et al. (2011) on the use of research evidence by public health decision-makers. The systematic review of Lavis and colleagues (2005) can be considered as an update of (and an improvement on) the systematic review undertaken by Innvaer and colleagues (2002), as it was conducted three years later and as it focused on two types of civil servant rather than one, namely, policymakers and managerial decision-makers. Mitton et al.'s (2007) review led to results very similar to those of the two preceding systematic reviews, except that Mitton et al. found both observational and intervention studies.

2 The Social Sciences and Humanities Research Council has funded this study (file 410-2009-25-5). Study protocol was submitted to the Laval University Research Ethics Board, who granted ethics approval (approbation #2009-087 A1/24-10-2012).

3 ODDSRISK, a Stata module to convert logistic odds ratios to risk ratios, was used to examine the magnitude of the association between tie strength and perceived tie impact (Hilbe 2007). First, we report the crude perceived tie impact rate, which is the percentage of weak or strong ties for which the information obtained has been perceived useful by the policy analyst in writing one status report or several. Second, the unadjusted rate ratio with its corresponding 95 per cent confidence interval is reported. The unadjusted rate ratio is calculated by estimating a logistic regression (using the ODDSRISK module) with tie strength as the only independent variable. Finally, adjusted rate ratio is reported, that is, the rate ratio that has been adjusted for the following set of variables: (1) whether the policy analyst had read scientific articles, research reports, or scientific work, either whole or in part, published by the professor, (2) the gender difference between the policy analyst and the professor, (3) whether the policy analyst holds a research-oriented graduate degree, (4) whether the analyst was working in a research directorate, a policy and planning directorate, or in a program directorate, and (5) whether the participant who recalled the dyad also recalled one or two more dyads (i.e., to control for the clustering of dyads).

12 Government Science and Policy Advice: Evidence-based Policymaking at the Ontario Ministry of Natural Resources and Its Implications for the Practice of Policy Analysis

NICOLE KLENK

Introduction

The idea of evidence-based policymaking (EBPM) has been put into practice in numerous government agencies in Europe and North America as a response to demands for increased efficiency and transparency in public policymaking and for achieving high standards of policy performance (Bogenschneider and Corbett 2010). Proponents argue that EBPM holds the promise of demystifying and systemizing how public policymaking is done by using clear protocols for the mobilization of the most relevant and rigorous knowledge base, ultimately with the hope of reducing the number of policy failures (Greenhalgh and Russell 2006). Within the academic community there is debate on the meaning and the logistical dimensions of EBPM. Notable questions include whether the original model of EBPM developed within the health care sector, using the systematic review of clinical trials as the most rigorous form of evidence, is applicable to other sectors and, to what extent there is analytical capacity within government agencies to perform EBPM (Howlett 2009b; Hodgkinson 2012).

Within the organizational management community, the concept of evidence-based management shares the normative ideals underpinning EBPM in that its proponents believe in its potential to improve decision-making transparency and performance and to facilitate organizational learning (Briner, Denyer, and Rousseau 2009). The idea of evidence-based management has received critical attention by academics concerned with the political dimensions of the social construction of evidence (Morrell 2008; Bartlett 2011; Cassell 2011). There is debate, in particular, over the extent to which facts and values can be kept separate within evidence-based management (Hodgkinson and Rousseau 2009). Critics also point to the politics of adjudicating the relevance and rigour of different sources of knowledge (e.g., quantitative versus qualitative scientific research, expert judgment, practical knowledge) and warn about the implications of excluding certain types of evidence, which could potentially affect some knowledge producers' access to funding (Learmonth and Harding 2006; Learmonth, Lockett, and Dowd 2012).

In this chapter we have chosen to examine the Ontario Ministry of Natural Resources (OMNR) as a *critical* case study of the practice of EBPM (Flyvbjerg 2006). This is a critical case in the sense that the ideals guiding EBPM are most likely to be achieved where knowledge producers and knowledge users are governed by the same policy priorities and are mandated to inform each other's work. Indeed, this government agency houses both forest science researchers and forest policy analysts. The ministry expects its forest scientists to conduct policy-relevant research that informs the work of its forest policy analysts and allocates resources accordingly (Klenk and Hickey 2011).

The research questions guiding our inquiry were as follows:

- How is knowledge mobilization perceived and performed by researchers and policy developers in the OMNR?
- What are the social and political practices involved in how evidence is constructed for EBPM at the OMNR?
- What do policy analysts at the OMNR perceive as relevant science?

In this chapter I begin by describing the theoretical framework for analysing the practice of EBPM. Next, I describe the survey conducted at the OMNR and present the results. In the discussion I distill the implications of our critical case study for the practice of policy analysis.

Theoretical Framework

Models of Evidence-Based Policymaking

Rationalist theories of policy analytical capacity represent policy analysts as "rational actors" who have the capacity to assess all plausible policy alternatives on the basis of complete information and to then prioritize options in an optimal way to reach a stated goal (Lindblom 1980). Models of EBPM tend to share this rationalist ideal. For example, for Bogenschneider and Corbett (2010), EBPM refers to a set of scientific methods that scientists agree constitute a proper way for helping distinguish fact from belief and requires that policy analysis be dispassionate and impartial. Similarly, Briner, Denyer, and Rousseau (2009) propose a model of EBPM that consists in the conscientious, explicit, and judicious use of four distinct sources of evidence: practitioners' expertise and judgment, evidence from local context, critical evaluation of the best available research evidence, and perspectives of those people who might be affected by the decision.

In keeping with this rationalistic model of policy analysis, the Knott and Wildavsky scale was developed to measure the absorption of information in policy development (Webber 1992). In Belkhodja and colleagues' (2007) study of the extent and organizational determinants of research utilization in Canadian Health Services Organizations, for example, they used a Knott and Wildavsky scale that included seven stages: (1) *reception* (e.g., I have received research results concerning the areas for which I am responsible); (2) *cognition* (e.g., I have read and understood the research reports that I have received); (3) *reference* (e.g., I have cited research evidence to colleagues and in my work); (4) *adaptation* (e.g., I have adapted the format of the research results to provide information useful to our decision-makers); (5) *effort* (e.g., I have made efforts to promote the adoption of research evidence in my field); (6) *influence* (e.g., research evidence has led me to make professional choices and decisions that I would not have made otherwise); and (7) *application* (e.g., the utilization of research evidence has led to concrete change in the programs or services provided by my organization). The scale is cumulative in the sense that each supervening stage builds on the prior one (e.g., cognition builds on reception) (Landry, Lamari, and Amara 2003).

However, in reality, policy analysis in EBPM is much more complex than this rationalistic and linear model of "information absorption" suggests because knowledge mobilization is only one part of the process and does not encompass all the practices involved in the construction of evidence. To better understand the difference between these practices I describe them separately, even though I recognize that they are inextricably linked.

Knowledge Mobilization

Four explanations have been proposed for whether/how policy analysts mobilize knowledge: engineering, organizational, cultural, and interactive (Landry, Amara, and Lamari 2001; Landry, Lamari, and Amara 2003; Amara, Ouimet, and Landry 2004). The engineering explanation suggests that knowledge mobilization depends on the compatibility, complexity, observability, validity, and applicability of research contents in addition to its basic-theoretical/applied, general/abstract, quantitative/qualitative characteristics. The organizational explanations posit that the size of agencies, organizational structures and processes, types of policy domains, needs of organizations, and positions (professionals or managers) may affect research mobilization. In this explanation, policy analysts tend to use research that they consider pertinent and credible and that addresses their needs and reaches them at the right time. The cultural explanation refers to the need to adapt research products to a context of application to overcome the prevalent gap observed between science and policy. The interaction explanation refers to the relationship between knowledge producers and knowledge users; previous studies have suggested that a more sustained and intense interaction between them contributes to greater research utilization.

The complexity and social dimensions of knowledge mobilization at the science-policy interface requires that our models of EBPM move beyond the "input-output," "delivery-uptake," and "supply-demand" models, which tend to assume a rationalistic and linear model of policy analysis. EBPM must take into consideration the characteristics of the knowledge producer and her particular objectives and constraints, which will influence how her research is perceived and mobilized. It is also crucial to clarify the role of social and political practices in the determination of what is "relevant," "rigorous," and "useful" evidence, which we do in the next section.

The Construction of Evidence

It is a truism that evidence is not simply somewhere out there waiting to be found by policy analysts. Indeed, "objective facts" do not necessarily become evidence, even if they somehow land on a policy analyst's desk. Furthermore, the expression "information absorption" used to characterize knowledge mobilization does not do justice to the multifaceted practices required to *make* "objective facts" usable for a context of application. The construction of evidence involves interpretation, argument, rhetoric, and exclusion (Putnam 2002). We explain each of these practices in turn.

Interpretation in the context of policy analysis refers to assessing the significance of knowledge claims, research results, or experiential knowledge for achieving a particular objective (Yanow 1996). Evidence is always interpreted in relation to particular means and ends (which may be moving targets), and this iterative process often involves dismissing, disregarding, or rendering invisible some alternatives because they are not part of the interpretive lens of the policy analyst.

In addition, the practice of interpreting research is linked to argumentation, because what constitutes good evidence for a particular set of means and ends is inherently contestable, especially in decision-making amid uncertainty and complexity. The construction of evidence requires making a case for action that reflects and addresses the needs of audiences concerned with more than the technical aspects of policy objectives and constraints, to include the business, political, and other contextual implications of using particular knowledge (Hodgkinson 2012).

Hence constructing evidence in EBPM also involves rhetoric in that scientific arguments are used as a means of persuasion for influencing collective action (Condit, Lynch, and Winderman 2012). As described by Greenhalgh and Russell (2006, 34), such arguments also involve exclusionary practices: "The selection and presentation of evidence for policymaking, including the choice of which questions to ask, which evidence to combine in a synthesis and which synthesis to bring to the policymaking table, should be considered as moves in a rhetorical augmentation game and not as the harvesting of objective facts to be fed into a logical decision-making sequence."

In addition, it is an open question whether critical policy decisions are made on the basis of evidence or intuition and other non-conscious cognitive-affective processes (Hodgkinson 2012). Studies have found that evidence is excluded when it either challenges the legitimacy of extant practices or when it is inconsistent with the decision-maker's views (Munro 2010). In this chapter, I am interested primarily in gaining a better understanding of the practices involved in knowledge mobilization and the construction of evidence in EBPM in the context of OMNR forest policymaking. To address this issue, I used a survey and semi-structured, open-ended interviews to probe the nature of OMNR research and how it set research priorities, and descriptive accounts of how research evidence informs particular policy processes.

Methods

Case Study

As detailed in Klenk and Hickey (2011), the data for this study came from a fall 2009 survey and interviews of forest scientists and policy analysts at the Ontario Ministry of Natural Resources, Canada, including the Ontario Forest Research Institute (OFRI), the Centre for Northern Forest Ecosystem Research (CNFER), and the forests Branch of OMNR Policy Division. We initially invited seven policy analysts and twenty scientists to participate; although all of the policy analysts responded, the interview response rate for scientists was lower (60 per cent, $n = 12$).

Data Collection

Our Internet-based questionnaire combined Belkhodja and colleagues' (2007) survey of the extent and organizational determinants of research utilization in Canadian Health Services Organizations, and Amara, Ouimet, and Landry's (2004) survey of the utilization of university research in government agencies in Canada. The design of the interview was semi-structured and open-ended. Questions addressed three main topics: (1) the characteristics of OMNR forest research; (2) how forest research priorities were set at the OMNR; and (3) a request for an example of how forest research informed a particular forest policy process. Within each topic, questions were asked about several items. The opinion questions used three or four level scales (see tables 12.1–12.7), though respondents were also given the choice of "no opinion" or "neutral," depending on the question. The questionnaire concluded with an open-ended question for respondents to provide additional comments on the science-policy interface at the OMNR. Interviews lasted about one hour and were conducted in person ($n = 17$) or by telephone ($n = 2$).

Analysis

We used the Kruskal-Wallis non-parametric test (Keller 2004) to determine if there was a significant difference between the responses of scientists and policy analysts to the survey questions. There were only two significant differences (within one topic), so for simplicity we sometimes report the average response of scientists and policy analysts.

Table 12.1 Frequency with Which OMNR Scientists Engage in Knowledge Mobilization Strategies

Knowledge mobilization activity	Score	Rank
Publishing results in academic journals	2.9	5
Workshops within your agency	2.6	4
Direct communication with staff in the field	2.6	4
Provincial workshops	2.4	3
Publishing research results in professional journals (such as the Forestry Chronicle)	2.4	3
Disseminating research results through reports to partners	2.4	3
Meeting with policy developers/analysts	2.1	2
Meeting with policymakers at the executive level	1.7	1

1 = never, 2 = occasionally, and 3 = regularly.

We ranked the items within each topic by the average score of respondents (as used in the Spearman rank coefficient method).

Results

Knowledge Mobilization

The most frequently used knowledge mobilization strategy of OMNR scientists was publishing results in academic journals (table 12.1), followed by within-agency workshops and direct communication with staff in the field. Other knowledge mobilization activities, in decreasing order, included participating in provincial workshops, publishing in professional journals, disseminating research results through reports to partners, and meeting with policy analysts. Scientists reported seldom meeting with policymakers at the executive level.

Publications in academic journals were the most important source of evidence used by policy analysts (table 12.2), followed by talking with researchers at professional associations, meetings, and other venues, reading "grey" literature, and active involvement in research projects. The least important source of evidence was perceived to be participation in expert panels or committees involving researchers.

With respect to direct communication with knowledge producers, policy analysts most frequently sought information from the OMNR

Table 12.2 Perceived Importance of Different Sources of Evidence for OMNR Policy Analysts

Information seeking activities	Score	Rank
Reading publications in academic journals	3.5	5
Talking with researchers at professional associations, meetings, and other venues	3.2	4
Reading "grey" literature	3.1	3
Participation in conferences and workshops involving researchers	3.1	3
Active involvement in research projects	3.0	2
Membership on expert panels and committees involving researchers	2.5	1

1 = completely unimportant, 2 = somewhat unimportant, 3 = somewhat important, and 4 = very important.

and other provincial forest researchers (table 12.3), followed by private firms, researchers at the Canadian Forest Service, and the general public. They seldom sought information directly from university researchers or researchers/analysts in non-governmental organizations.

With regards to organizational support for bridging the science-policy gap, scientists and policy analysts strongly agreed that the OMNR seeks to build the capacities of researchers to conduct research that informs policy (table 12.4), that OMNR scientists introduce new concepts to frame debates or stimulate debate with policy analysts, and that the OMNR seeks to build the capacities of policy analysts to use research results in the policy process. Respondents were less likely to agree that the OMNR seeks to build the capacities of researchers to influence policy analysts, that scientists and policy analysts work closely together, or that the organization provides opportunities for networking/learning between scientists and policy analysts.

The Construction of Evidence

The most common way in which policy analysts engage with knowledge utilization (following Knott and Wildavsky's stages) is by making efforts to promote the adoption of evidence related to their field (table 12.5), though in decreasing order they also receive research results concerning the areas for which they are responsible, read the

Table 12.3 Frequency with Which OMNR Policy Analysts Seek Evidence from Knowledge Producers

Knowledge producers	Score	Rank
OMNR scientists	2.4	6
Provincial government forest scientists	2.3	5
Private firms (consultants, researchers, analysts)	1.8	4
CFS scientists	1.7	3
General public	1.7	3
Academic researchers	1.6	2
NGOs (scientists, analysts)	1.4	1

1 = never, 2 = occasionally, and 3 = regularly.

Table 12.4 Extent to Which OMNR Scientists and Policy Analysts Agree with Propositions about the Science Policy-Capacity-Building Processes at the OMNR

Propositions	Score*	Rank
The OMNR seeks to build the capacities of researchers to conduct research that informs policy	3.5	5
OMNR scientists introduce new concepts to frame debates or stimulate debate with policy analysts	3.4	4
The OMNR seeks to build the capacity of policy analysts to use research results in the policy process	3.3	3
The OMNR seeks to build the capacities of researchers to influence policy analysts	3.2	2
OMNR scientists and policy analysts work closely together	3.1	1
The OMNR provides opportunities for networking/learning between scientists and policy analysts	3.1	1

* Includes OMNR scientists' and policy analysts' scores.
1 = strongly disagree, 2 = disagree, 3 = agree, 4 = strongly agree.

research results they have received, use research evidence to make professional choices and decisions that they would not have made otherwise, and cite research evidence produced by agency colleagues as a reference in their work. They reported seldom adapting the format of the research results to provide information useful to the decision-making process.

Table 12.5 Frequency with Which OMNR Policy Analysts Engage in the Knott and Wildavsky's Knowledge Utilization Stages

Knowledge utilization stages	Score	Rank
Made efforts to promote the adoption of evidence related to your field	2.9	4
Received research results concerning the areas for which you are responsible	2.7	3
Read the research results that you have received	2.7	3
Used research evidence to make professional choices and decisions that you would not have made otherwise	2.7	3
Cited research evidence of agency colleagues as a reference in your work	2.6	2
Adapted the format of the research results to provide information useful to our decision-making process	2.4	1

1 = never, 2 = occasionally, and 3 = regularly.

In relation to analytical activities, policy analysts reported, in decreasing order of frequency, that they were engaged in outcomes, evaluation, or quality assurance projects (table 12.6); in-depth reviews of the literature; research studies that combined university and non-university investigators; and external research studies that required data contributed from the OMNR. They were less often involved in research studies as co-investigators, data collectors, or principal investigators.

All respondents tended to agree that OMNR research informed the development of forest regulations and policy analysts' understanding of forest issues (table 12.7). Respondents tended to disagree that OMNR research informed policy implementation or that it helped resolve societal conflicts over forest management issues in Ontario. Scientists and policy analysts differed in their perception of the extent to which OMNR research informs the development and evaluation of Ontario forest policy.

Discussion

In this section we begin by discussing the survey results on knowledge mobilization and the construction of evidence in relation to an

Table 12.6 Frequency with Which OMNR Policy Analysts Engage in Analytical Activities

Research activities	Score	Rank
Been involved in outcomes, evaluation, or quality assurance projects	2.2	5
Carried out in-depth review of the literature	1.9	4
Been involved in a research study that combined university and non-university investigators	1.9	4
Contributed data from your organization for an external research study	1.7	3
Been a co-investigator for a research study	1.6	2
Collected data for a research study	1.6	2
Been a principal investigator for a research study	1.3	1

1 = never, 2 = occasionally, and 3 = regularly.

illustrative example of how OMNR research has been used in forest policy. We then discuss the implications of our results for the practice of policy analysis.

Knowledge Mobilization and the Construction of Evidence

Our results suggest that policy analysts were much more likely to seek information from OMNR researchers than from other knowledge providers and that OMNR research has been used to a much greater extent than research from other knowledge providers in forest policy analysis. The preference for publications as a source of evidence was justified in the interview by the statement that "peer-reviewed papers speak for themselves." This perspective is reflected in the results for the Knott and Wildavsky scale, which indicate that policy analysts mobilized OMNR research evidence to make professional choices and decisions that they would not have made otherwise. However, there was an apparent reticence in adapting research results to provide evidence useful to the decision-making process.

Although the survey results suggest that both researchers and policy analysts preferred publications as a knowledge mobilization strategy and source of evidence, in the interviews respondents often mentioned that the most effective mechanism to ensure research mobilization was through face-to-face conversations. Social mechanisms of knowledge

Table 12.7 Perceptions of the Extent to Which OMNR Forest Research Informs Forest Policy

Proposition	Score*	Scientists	Policy analysts/ developers	Rank
Informed the development of Ontario forestry regulations (including legislation, codes, and guidelines)	3.5	4.0**	3.2**	5
Informed OMNR policy analysts' understanding of forest issues	3.3	3.3	3.4	4
Informed OMNR policy revision	3.3	3.7	3.1	4
Informed OMNR policy evaluation	3.1	3.6**	2.8**	3
Informed OMNR policy implementation	2.8	3.0	2.7	2
Helped resolve societal conflicts over forest management issues in Ontario	2.5	2.1	2.7	1

* Includes OMNR scientists' and policy analysts' scores.
** Significant difference between scientists' and policy analysts' scores (alpha = 0.01).
1 = not at all, 2 = somewhat, 3 = much, 4 = very much.

mobilization at the OMNR were facilitated by within-agency workshops and the personal relationships between scientists and policy analysts. The survey results suggest that scientists and policy analysts do work closely together. It is through these social interactions that scientists and policy analysts interpret, and make a case for the use of, particular information as evidence to inform decision-making.

Of course the context in which such conversations happen is of critical importance in what knowledge comes to be deemed relevant and useful. The development, evaluation, and revision process of the OMNR forest management guides are illustrative of the social construction of evidence in EBPM. According to the interviews, in the revision of the forest management guides, the relationship between researchers and policy analysts was at its closest because of the need to develop and validate guidelines, design effectiveness-monitoring programs, engage in problem-solving, and ensure regulatory compliance.

By the late 1990s, OMNR had produced more than thirty forest management guides and recently decided to reduce the number of guides to five: a landscape guide, a stand and site guide, a silviculture guide, a resource-based tourism guide, and a cultural heritage values guide. To revise their guides, the OMNR used an "adaptive management" form of EBPM, treating policy decisions as hypotheses and mobilizing the four sources of evidence recommended in EBPM: the best available science, practitioner expertise, stakeholder consultations, and local contextual knowledge. Interviewees stressed that peer-review publications were the most rigorous source of evidence, but because of the number of guidelines involved in each guide and the limited resources of the OMNR in funding, research capacity, and time, not all of the standards were able to be treated as hypotheses. When asked what determined which guidelines would become hypotheses, respondents consistently replied that those most risky vis-à-vis litigation were more likely to be the subject of research projects and/or effectiveness-monitoring programs. According to interviewees, in cases where scientific evidence is lacking, but the guidelines involve lower risk of litigation, they are more likely to be supported by expert opinion. Of the four sources of evidence used at the OMNR, interviewees stressed the legitimacy of science and to a lesser extent professional opinion, though the "adaptive management" process also involves stakeholder consultation and interpreting evidence in relation to local contextual factors.

However, the survey results suggest that scientists and policy analysts differed in their perception of the extent to which OMNR research informs policymaking. Scientists tended to agree more with the proposition that OMNR research informs policymaking than policy analysts. One way of understanding this difference in perception is by examining what policy analysts count as policy-relevant research. In the interviews, the most common meaning ascribed to the term *relevance* was the extent to which research was immediately applicable to the design, evaluation, and revision of forest management standards and best practices. Thus, regulatory research conducted at the OMNR was deemed highly useful and policy-relevant. However, some scientists at the OMNR conduct "applied" research on forest management in relation to the structure and function of forest ecosystems and the human impact on forests, without focusing directly on setting and evaluating standards. Such research can be said to be less (immediately) useful and policy-relevant. In addition, interviewees recognized that such research runs the risk of challenging established practices and decision-makers' beliefs, potentially leading to unexpected political, financial, and other costs if it were used to inform policy. Its usefulness and relevance was therefore assessed in relation to its compatibility with current policy directions. The status of such research has been tenuous and is consistently at risk of cutbacks (e.g., witness the cuts in government funding for in-house research in provincial and federal forest service agencies as well as in other natural resource and environmental agencies in the last few years).

The results of the survey and interviews suggest that scientists and policy analysts recognize that knowledge mobilization involves social processes and can have political implications for knowledge producers (whose research is not deemed useful and relevant) and for decision-makers. However, policy analysts are reticent to acknowledge the social and political practices involved in the construction of evidence because doing so would put the process at risk of being characterized as biased. This reticence has important implications, however, for the practice of policy analysis, to which I turn next.

Implications for the Practice of Policy Analysis

Survey results suggest that policy analysts at the OMNR engage in a wide range of research-related activities. Their policy analytical capacity, as it relates to setting forest management standards, establishing monitoring plans, and mobilizing evidence does not appear to be in question. Both scientists and policy analysts agree that the OMNR has put into place structures and processes to build policy analytical capacity. However, with respect to the construction of evidence, there is a need to develop some critical analytical skills. For instance, when asked to what extent OMNR research was used instrumentally (e.g., in operational regulations), conceptually (e.g., shaping policy developers/analysts' ideas about forests), and politically (e.g., shoring up political positions on preferred policy options), the majority of interviewees replied that OMNR research was mostly used instrumentally and conceptually, but it was also sometimes used politically, depending on who was involved in the policy process. These results suggest that politics are not an intrinsic part of policy analysis in EBPM.

But the extent to which and in what ways policy analysts are able and willing to integrate the different sources of evidence is itself the outcome of a political decision, which (re)produces boundaries between evidence that is deemed "relevant," "rigorous," and "useful," and evidence that is dismissed, ignored, and rendered invisible. Hodgkinson (2012, 411) argues, "How the problem is framed, what criteria are to be adopted for inclusion versus exclusion, and the threshold in respect of each inclusion-exclusion criterion are all political issues, in the sense that different stakeholders may well want to contest these micro-decisions, each of which will undoubtedly have a fundamental bearing on the answers eventually 'revealed' in connection with the focal policy and practice."

In the scientific and policy communities, no one disputes the idea that knowledge should inform decision-making; however, how the "usefulness," "rigour," and "relevance" of knowledge are determined in practice and the political dimension of setting such standards is an outstanding issue (Hodgkinson and Starkey 2011; Learmonth, Lockett, and Dowd 2012; Willmott 2012). Controversy surrounds the latter point because of the risk that EBPM will create an "illusion of rationality, a multilayered façade that masks underlying difference of interpretation, purpose and power among the various stakeholders involved and affected by the decision in question" (Hodgkinson 2012, 406).

The implications of these results for the practice of policy analysis at the OMNR are that the reticence to acknowledge the social and political construction of evidence in EBPM does not protect the policy analysis process from contestation by knowledge producers, knowledge users, and stakeholders. Rather, it risks making the "adaptive management" form of EBPM appear as a rationalistic facade concealing in a black box the inevitable political decisions involved in constructing evidence to support particular policy directives.

In order to develop a critical approach to policy analysis, Bartlett (2011, 28) suggests that policy analysts should ask themselves several questions: "Whose interests am I serving in this situation, whose voice is being silenced, what assumptions underlie the rationale for intervention and can they be challenged, and what categories are being used to describe and analyze the situation and are they conceptually sound?" Policy analysis, it should be remembered, is a form of argumentation involving rhetoric and exclusion and is not akin to providing proof that the application of certain evidence will achieve expected results. Rather, as Baughman, Dorsey, and Zarefsky (2011, 64) point out, "The role of evidence is to provide the justification for claims that solutions will be effective or that courses of action should be taken. Accordingly, a critical property of evidence in applied settings is its power to convince, persuade, or influence. What warrants decisions under these conditions … is not only good evidence but good argument. Evidence is part of an argument but clearly not the whole thing."

Rather than view the presence of politics in EBPM as dependent on who is involved in the policy process, a more plausible perspective would take politics as a given in EBPM and develop policy analysis practices that critically assess whose voice, values, and knowledge claims are favoured or dismissed in the policy process. According to critical policy analysis theorists, EBPM should involve disclosing exclusionary practices (e.g., excluding the voice of certain stakeholders and knowledge producers) that result in decisions that reproduce hegemonic power structures within policy systems (Griggs and Howarth 2011).

Conclusion

This study of the science-policy interface at the OMNR suggests that where there is a close relationship between knowledge producers and knowledge users, knowledge mobilization and EBPM is facilitated. Indeed, the results suggest there is no apparent deficiency in policy analytical capacity at the OMNR in relation to knowledge mobilization. There is, however, a reluctance to acknowledge the intrinsic politics of EBPM in setting standards of knowledge relevance and usefulness, which affects the *critical* policy analytical capacity of OMNR policy analysts. For instance, our results suggests that regulatory research is deemed policy-relevant and useful for setting forest policy standards at the OMNR, but that "applied" research that has no immediate application to setting standards is deemed much less policy-relevant and useful. "Applied" OMNR research, moreover, is more likely than regulatory research to challenge the status quo in terms of policy direction and therefore is potentially a politically risky source of evidence for EBPM. The future of "applied" research at the OMNR rests in the balance, and faces more cutbacks if it is not perceived as sufficiently policy relevant and imminently useful or if it is perceived as a political liability.

The implications of our study for policy analysis are that policy analytical capacity should include an ability to critically assess the exclusionary practices involved in the social construction of evidence in EBPM and the ability to treat evidence as part of an argument for justifying a course of action, recognizing that evidence is contingent and inherently contestable. Our critical case study shows that the tension between expertise, politics, and democratic practice cannot be transcended in the practice of policy analysis. The recommended path for policy analysts is therefore to embrace the role of interpretive and deliberative practitioner, rather than uphold the positivist status of expert arbitrator of knowledge relevance and usefulness.

ACKNOWLEDGMENTS

This chapter uses data previously published in an article on the characteristic and utilization of government science (Klenk and Hickey 2011). I would like to thank Dr Brendon Larson for his comments on a previous version of this chapter and acknowledge funding support from Dr Larsen's SSHRC Standard Research Grant and his Early Researcher Award from the Ontario Ministry of Research and Innovation.

13 Mandates, Political Parties, and Policy Capacity

GREG FLYNN

Policy capacity is associated with the ability of governments to decide upon and implement their preferred policy choices that affect the operation of the economy or society at large (Davis 2000; Painter and Pierre 2005b). On this basis, policy capacity is concerned both with the inputs into the policy process by the range of policy options to be considered by government, and the outputs in the final policy choices that are made and implemented. In this context, notions of policy capacity have traditionally involved consideration of the formal apparatuses of the state, and the public service or bureaucracy in particular. For example, the alarm bells that sounded towards the end of the 1990s over the loss of policy capacity in Canada were concerned primarily with the ability of federal and provincial public services to deliver sound policy advice to the governments that they served. These developments are associated with the reductions in the size of government coinciding with periods of government austerity as well as the introduction of public service reforms associated with the move towards New Public Management. At the same time, however, the democratization of governance practices that occurred during this period and through these reforms opened up avenues of participation in the policymaking process for policy actors normally considered to be outside the traditional boundaries of government (Anderson 1996). This has, in turn, provided opportunities for a wide range of policy actors to influence the policy choices that governments make and implement and thereby extend notions of policy capacity beyond the government itself.

This chapter explores the broader impact that one set of external actors, namely political parties, may have on the policy outputs of government in Canada. In particular, it traces the policy channelling role that parties play in converting policy demands of the public and their party members into government action through the fulfilment of party policy and election manifesto commitments and the ability of citizens in Canada to influence government policy outputs through participation in parties. In pursuing this course, the chapter first sets out the theoretical contradictions implicit in the literature associated with the role of parties as policy channelling organizations. Second, it establishes a general and heuristic means to examine party member participation in party policymaking through a series of stages of policy development, beginning with abstract notions of policy associated with party ideology through to the final and concrete stage of election campaign promise and manifesto drafting. The third section examines the extent to which party members are able to advance their policy demands into consideration by the government by tracing party member policy proposals through the final two stages of party policy development of the three new governing parties in Canada over the last thirty years. The fourth section furthers this tracing by considering the output side of the policy equation by examining the extent to which new governing parties in Canada have implemented their election campaign policy commitments. The final section draws some conclusions on the policy capacity of political parties in Canada. In particular, it demonstrates that through the examination of party policy and election manifesto development, coupled with a consideration of the implementation of election promises, that parties play at least some role in influencing government policy outcomes and that parties, at least partially, fulfil their policy channelling function. In short, this chapter reveals that parties and their members possess the capacity to influence both the choices made by government in their preferred policy options as well as the implementation of those commitments.

Parties as Policymaking Organizations

The study of political parties as avenues of policy development in Western democracies presents somewhat of a paradox. Parties have been considered an essential element of democratic governance, variously labelled as necessary, inevitable, and supported by the claim that the practice of democratic politics without them as inconceivable (Bryce 1921; Schumpeter 1942; Sartori 1962). The continued dominance of parties as the primary vehicles of participation in most political systems, be it in relation to organization of government, the conducting of election campaigns, or the representation of multiple views in governance systems, would seem to make these statements as true today, despite the changing nature of party systems and party competition throughout the latter half of the twentieth century. Parties were, are, and continue to be a cornerstone of democracy in most democratic states. This perception of inevitability undoubtedly arises from the number of roles they undertake that are fundamental to the manner in which citizens in democratic countries experience and participate in government, including local and national candidate recruitment and nomination, leadership selection, the conducting of election campaigns, issue agenda setting, and government policymaking (Cross 2004). Parties serve as the theoretical link between citizens and government, particularly in relation to the development of public policy, and ensure the practice of responsible government (King 1969; Katz 1987; Müller 2000). In this sense, parties not only exist as organizations that contest elections, but also serve as sites of interest aggregation and articulation in order to provide citizens with the opportunity to advance their policy demands to government as part of their policymaking functions (Budge, Robertson, and Hearl 1987; Dalton and Wattenberg 2000).

At the same time, however, parties have also been in an ongoing state of decline, of decreased relevance to citizens, and limited in their overall effectiveness, especially in relation to their role as policymaking bodies (Clarke et al. 1996; Clarke and Stewart 1998; Dalton and Wattenberg 2000). Despite their apparent pre-eminence, there are also indications that parties have been usurped as the preferred choice of democratic participation by other avenues of influence, such as interest groups and social movements (Lawson and Merkl 1988; Dalton and Kuechler 1990; Thorburn 2007). Coinciding with this development is the criticism that parties are increasingly elitist and alienated from ordinary citizens, particularly in relation to citizen engagement in policy development (Budge, Robertson, and Hearl 1987; Blondel and Cotta 1996; Clarke et al. 1996). They are viewed as failed institutions of citizen engagement in politics and policymaking. The shift from the mass-membership-based organizations of the 1950s and 1960s to the current elite-driven and more professional associations that represent parties in the 1990s and 2000s has also apparently resulted in changes to the level of citizen and party member involvement in party electioneering functions, and the drafting of election policy platforms in particular (Panebianco 1988; Farrell and Webb 2000). The result is the near-universal conclusion that participation in policy development is negligible for party members and non-existent for almost all other members of the public (Jaensch 1994; Marsh 2005; Carty 2006).

There is, however, another side to the coin, at least in relation to the Canadian voters and the party system. While overall party membership levels have declined from the halcyon mass membership days of the 1960s, and parties have undoubtedly become more professionalized in their operations, people continue to participate in politics through the medium of membership in parties. In this regard, one of the underlying criteria or incentives provided by individuals to join parties is their belief in the policy positions that those organizations advocate (Cross and Young 2002, 2006). And while it is potentially possible to explain this apparent dichotomy on the basis of the naivety and idealism of those party members, much of the party member survey research demonstrates the opposite – that party members are acutely aware of their potential lack of influence in party policymaking, at least in the determination of the content of party election policy manifestos (Carty 2006; Cross and Young 2006). There is a similar paradox on the party organization side of the participation ledger. Canadian parties could operate without extensive extra-parliamentary organizations, yet have chosen not to do so (Clark 2004). Furthermore, parties continue to provide members with opportunities to participate in policy-related activities within their organizations (Carty 1991; Wolinetz 2007). These developments become even more problematic for the "lack of party member impact" thesis, in that the major parties in most democratic states devote considerable time, personnel, and financial resources to these policymaking endeavours – more time, energy, and effort than necessary or available for these activities to be simple facades of legitimation (Mair 1994). To the contrary, all of the major political parties in Canada, possessed with scarce resources and declining party memberships, continue to conduct these costly and time-consuming exercises in an effort to engage the public and their memberships in an open discussion of policy issues.

The potential link of party member policy preferences to government policymaking choices is further strengthened by the electoral and post-electoral behaviour of election campaign teams and party leaders. Party policy platforms feature prominently in election campaigns in democratic states, with Canada being no exception, and serve to tie purported government policy action to the legitimacy provided by elections (Rallings 1987). Over the course of the last three decades in Canada, parties have increasingly relied on comprehensive, coordinated, single document policy manifestos. While generally viewed as electoral support generating devices, these documents also provide wide-ranging, detailed, and publicly legitimized plans for governing from a policy perspective. Furthermore, in the aftermath of election victories, party leaders have consistently claimed a mandate to implement the commitments contained in their election manifestos and have modelled their initial policy actions in government on the basis of the identified priority commitments in these documents. While there is some debate concerning the existence and fulfilment of election policy mandates in Canada and other countries (see Rose 1984; Pétry 1995), parties and politicians continue to assert the right to fulfil their election campaign promises on the basis of voter approval (Grossback, Peterson, and Stimson 2005). Accordingly, the behaviour of parties, both before and after elections, does not conform to the suggestion that they lack the ability to influence the policy outcomes of government.

Party Policy Development Processes

The major political parties in Canada all possess similar policy development processes that involve some level of party member involvement, although the level and timing of such participation may vary over time and from one party leader to the next. In this context, these processes can be, at least heuristically, divided into a series of stages that progress from relatively abstract principles to fully developed plans and policies for governing. The impact of party members can be traced through each individual stage of the process to permit broader assessment of the policy channelling role that parties are expected to play in democratic states as well as their influence on the policy choices that governments make and implement while in office.

The initial policy development stage involves the establishment or incorporation of an ideological disposition into the policy foundation of the party. At the broadest and most general level, almost every party is based on some form of foundational ideology or specific philosophical view of governing (Downs 1957). This adoption of ideology represents a conscious and deliberate attempt by party founders to achieve a "definitional monopoly of the political world" and convince others of the way things are, the way they ought to be, and the way to get from the first point to the second (Nesbitt-Larking 2002). Ideology provides a model for understanding politics as being organized around a system of concepts or a range of activities and thereby supplies the public with a shortcut to understanding the manner in which their political environment operates (Christian and Campbell 1996).

Policy development at the ideological stage is not concerned with specific policies or election commitments, but rather with broader conceptions of the policy direction that the government needs to move towards. While often taken for granted, the underlying belief structure of a party may have as much, if not more, of an impact on final policy positions of a party than any perceived short-term electoral advantage. In this regard, these belief structures also provide a more reliable indicator of expected party responses to unanticipated issues or other crises or disasters that may run counter to specific commitments contained in election manifestos (Mulgan 2000). The main conception of ideology in Western democratic states has usually been rooted in the consideration of economics or religion, pitting "right-of-centre" or liberal and conservative parties versus "left-of-centre" or social democratic parties against one another or sectarian parties competing against one another or non-sectarian parties for the ability to participate in government formation. However, the foundational belief structures of parties have often also encompassed other aspects of ideology, particularly following the postmodern revolution of the latter half of the twentieth century (Inglehart 1997).

While this stage of policy development usually occurs at the outset of the creation of a party, it could also arise out of a transformative event or even as a result of a need to modernize a failing organization in order to keep it reflective of prevailing public attitudes. In this context, a party's foundational ideology could be determined or revised by a select group of elite individuals, such as those persons seeking to alter the operation of a party system through the introduction of a "new" party, or through a broad level of participation of a wide group of persons or party members. Whatever the reason for its adoption, a party's foundational ideology will determine its approach to policy and government and where it will compete with other parties for resources, members, and votes within the party system.

The second stage of party policy development involves consideration of the core policy goals and issues that concern a party. Core goals and issues do not cover the entire spectrum of possible values that a party may hold or consider. Rather, this level of policy development is focused on the few key tenets that will further the implementation of the ideological foundation of the party. They are the specific policy areas or themes that party members consider the most important issues to be dealt with and are the dominant policy area considerations when in government. As with ideology, this stage of policy development is not concerned with specific policy positions or plans for what a party will do if elected to govern. In contrast to more concrete stages of policy development that consider specific policies, the examination of the core goals is concerned with the key values that are constantly held by party members and whose implementation will result in the realization of a party's ideological goals.

The degree of emphasis on particular policy goals, issues, or themes may vary from one election to the next in keeping with the concerns facing the government at any one time and the perceptions of problems by the public and by party members. However, parties overall become synonymous with particular issue areas or policy themes, and they structure their policy development on this basis as a way of appealing to voters to base their electoral choices on these dimensions. For example, Budge and Fairle (1983) demonstrate the "ownership" of policy issues in the United Kingdom: health and education for Labour, and economic policy and national defence for the Conservatives. Similarly, Petrocik (1996) establishes a similar distinction in the United States, with the Democrats being best able to handle the issues of education, welfare, and civil rights, while Republicans are viewed as more competent in the fields of foreign affairs, national defence, and law and order. These "owned" issues are simply a reflection of the policy themes advanced consistently and continually by parties.

The third stage of policy development is the creation and revision of official party policy positions. It normally occurs in the context of national or regional policy conventions or other party infrastructures, where the outcome of the process is the commitment to particular and specific policies, although the exact policy infrastructure and method of determination will obviously vary from one organization to the next. It usually involves some proportion of the party membership and leads to the establishment of relatively more concrete and identifiable policy positions for a party, although the proposals put forward by party members may also be only general statements of interest or calls for action to address particular policy problems. The policy positions put forward at this stage may be short-term, single-issue, or event propositions or may represent longer-term policy positions to be achieved over several governing mandates.

This stage of policy development is the one in which party members are likely to have their greatest impact on the policy choices that governments make through the creation of general party policies. Party members participate in these processes both by advancing specific policies onto a party's policy agenda by submitting specific policy positions to the party in advance of the policy conference or convention, and by assisting in the consideration and adoption of these commitments, usually through some form of membership vote. As a result, party members play policy initiation and legitimization roles for their respective political organizations. Once adopted by the party, these policy positions are then represented to the public as reflecting what the party membership would like to achieve if its members are elected to participate in government formation (Klingemann et al. 1994).

The fourth and final stage of policy development occurs with the creation of election policy commitments and the drafting of election manifestos. While similar to, and sometimes considered synonymous with, the general party policy documents that are established in the third stage of policy development, election manifestos differ in their purpose and method of generation. As with the general policy positions, the election manifesto stage involves the creation of relatively concrete and identifiable policy positions that represent what the party will seek to accomplish from a policy perspective if it is elected to govern. These represent the election policy promises or commitments of the party. However, what differs is that these positions are usually focused on a single electoral government cycle and are used primarily as an electoral marketing device. Their purpose, whether individual or specific commitments or a more comprehensive overall plan for governing, is to convince voters to support the party on the basis of its plans for governing and that those plans coincide with voter interest. As a result, the election manifesto may play down or avoid altogether controversial policy positions established by the broader party membership. Alternatively, it may highlight unaddressed or under-addressed policy issues by the broader party that require a specific position or even contradict established party policy as the result of electoral issue saliency or electoral circumstances. As such, while it is normally anticipated that there would be a high degree of congruence between the contents of general party policy positions and electoral manifestos, there is no guarantee or even expectation that they would be identical in all proposals being advanced.

Election manifestos also differ from general party policy documents in the manner in which they are created. Given the need to be more overtly concerned with improving their electoral standing and the use of the document, and the commitments contained therein, as a marketing device, election manifestos tend to be drafted by a small group of individuals closely associated with the party leader and/or the elected caucus. Historically, the extent of party membership participation in the creation of election manifestos has varied by party and leader, with the possible avenues of involvement including selection of a drafting committee from the broader party membership, approval by the broader party membership, and formal or informal consultations with party members. Depending on party rules, the policy positions set out in manifestos may, and increasingly are, usually not even subject to any form of overall party approval prior to their release and use during an election campaign. Rather, it is anticipated that the policy choices that party leaders include in these documents will conform to or reflect the policy goals and demands of the broader party membership as established at the general party policy positions stage. However, there are usually no strict requirements as to what must be incorporated into an election manifesto, and party leaders tend to be free to consult with whatever policy sources they deem appropriate and relevant in the circumstances.

The tension between the policy demands of the broader party membership and the sources of policy advice received by party leaders is most evident in governing parties where the experiences of governing, additional stakeholder contacts, and the advice of the public service all factor into the choices contained in a party's election manifesto (Flynn 2011). At the same time, all parties have increased the level of professionalization of their party organizations and their reliance upon a small cadre of marketing, polling, and communications specialists associated with the leader to guide their electoral practices, including the drafting of election manifestos. This has, in turn, led to further and increased criticisms of a distancing between party elites and their members, the lack of real policy channelling role for parties to convey membership policy demands into government policy choices, and a diminishment of responsible party government and democracy as a whole. In short, the lack of party member involvement in election manifesto preparation has led to the suggestion that there is no policy input role for the broader party members and organization (Clarke et al. 1996).

Party Policy Input in Canada

Historically, Canadian political parties have provided party members with the opportunity to participate in their policy development by providing policy submissions for acceptance by the broader party membership. This has been a requirement contained in party constitutions in each of the major parties in Canada, along with the requirement that parties hold regular policy conventions for the consideration of these member-led policy proposals. In fact, each of the five major parties that have had some level of representation at the federal level in the last thirty years all provided this opportunity to their membership. Despite this fact, there continues to be some debate over the extent to which party member–led policy proposals are actually carried through into the range of options available for governments to consider in addressing their policy problems. In other words, the question of whether parties and party members actually provide some policy input into the governing policymaking processes remains unanswered. In order to explore this debate, this section examines the policy development of new governing parties in Canada over the thirty years from 1982 to 2012. While it has been suggested that opposition parties have historically had a strong impact on the range and importance of the policy choices considered by governments in Canada (Pétry 1995), this review focuses solely on the policy capacity of governing parties, as they possess the greater potential to influence both the decisions and implementation of government policy choices by virtue of their staffing of the political offices of government. It also only focuses on "new" government parties, the Progressive Conservatives in 1984, the Liberals in 1993, and the Conservatives in 2006, because there is greater potential for party members to exert greater influence on the direction of the party while out of government and there is less impact of external-party influences on governing party policy choices (Flynn 2011). If party members do not have a policy impact on their party organizations at this stage, they are unlikely to do so when a governing party is also receiving policy advice from the public service and the stakeholders that it encounters in government.

The review focuses on the drafting of election campaign manifestos of new governing parties and seeks to determine if there is a connection between the policies proposed or advanced by party members at earlier stages in the policy process with the policy commitments contained in a party's election manifesto. In doing so, it employs a more comprehensive and coordinated approach to party policy development by tracing established party policy positions as approved by the general members to the more specific election manifestos as a first step to consideration of their subsequent implementation by the elected government.

The Progressive Conservatives: 1984

In the year and a half preceding the 1984 election, the Progressive Conservatives were dominated by contestations over the leadership of the party that culminated in the selection of Brian Mulroney as party leader in June 1983. Shortly after taking over, Mulroney pursued policy development that was driven almost exclusively by the elected caucus and did not involve the broader party membership. It was focused on generating a policy agenda for the upcoming election that demonstrated that the Progressive Conservatives were "ready to govern," and it was not an overall general party policy document. Mulroney charged each of his specific policy critics with the responsibility of bringing forward policy recommendations for consideration by the elected caucus and members of the election campaign team at a retreat at Mont Ste Marie, Quebec. Each critic was responsible for developing policy ideas within his or her own individual processes and there was no overall coordination or requirement of consultation or involvement with the party membership. The subsequent retreat, held in the fall of 1983, included all members of the caucus and important members of the party, including key party election campaign officials. The policy recommendations generated by the policy critics were debated and refined during the conference, and key elements of the election policy platform were established. Given the lack of input into policy development, the impact of the broader party membership was restricted to an unarticulated sense among the caucus retreat participants of what was acceptable from the ideological perspective of the broader party membership. The only other main factor that served as a potential constraint on the policy choices of the party leadership were the high budgetary deficit and national debt levels. While these were viewed as a constraint on the range of available policy options, they did not prevent inclusion of a whole range of new spending commitments in the party's election manifesto. Other than the broad ideological constraints, the party membership had limited to no input or influence over the 1984 election manifesto of the Progressive Conservatives.

The Liberals: 1993

In preparation for the 1993 election, the Liberals employed a three-stage policy and election manifesto development. The first stage was a policy conference along the same lines as prior party conferences convened by Mackenzie King in the 1930s and Lester Pearson in the 1960s. It took place in November 1991, and participants, all of whom were invited by Chrétien, included Canadian and international policy experts (non-party members) as well as some influential members of the party. The second stage of policy development was the party's national policy convention in February 1992. As with previous national policy conventions, policy resolutions raised by members of the party were brought forward, debated, and either accepted or rejected by the convention delegates. In accordance with the party's constitution, the policy development committee published the adopted resolutions of the national convention, a total of fifty-three broad "priority resolutions" in all. The third stage occurred in conjunction with the national policy convention and involved Chrétien's appointment of Chaviva Hosek, director of the elected caucus's research bureau, and Paul Martin, Chrétien's leadership rival, as co-chairs of the National Platform Committee. Hosek and Martin undertook an extensive consultation across the country, meeting with party members, the elected caucus, policy experts, interest groups, and interested individuals. This process culminated in the drafting of the party's election manifesto.

As set out in table 13.1, the policy document arising from the 1992 Liberal policy convention campaign contained fifty-three separate policy resolutions and 172 separate policy statements. Eighty of those statements were sufficiently precise to require that a future Liberal government undertake specific policy action if it was elected to government.[1] The subsequent 1993 election manifesto contained 184 policy commitments, of which 42 addressed similar or were consistent with commitments from the official party policy document. Accordingly, 22.8 per cent of the overall Liberal election manifesto consisted of policy proposals that were articulated as the policy demands of the broader membership. This represented the inclusion of 52.5 per cent of the party policy document into the election manifesto. However, when the range of election commitments in the manifesto is also considered from the more narrow definition of a specific policy commitment that required government action, only 64 of the manifesto commitments fell within this definition. As such, the 42 specific commitments were similar to or

Table 13.1 Party-Policy-Specific Commitments' Inclusion in Election Manifesto

	Liberals (1993)	Conservative (2006)
Party policy documents		
Policy resolutions/areas	53	112
Policy statements	172	222
Specific commitments	80	119
Percentage	46.5	53.6
Election Manifesto		
Manifesto statements	184	232
Similar/consistent commitments	42	60
Percentage of manifesto	22.8	25.9
Percentage of party policy	52.5	50.4
Manifesto-specific commitments	64	147
Percentage of manifesto-specific commitments	65.6	40.8

consistent with the commitments arising from party policy documents in which 65.6 per cent of content responsibility originated with the party membership.

The Conservatives: 2006

The Conservative Party of Canada also included a provision in its constitution for party member participation in policy development through consideration of member policy proposals at a national policy convention. Following the aftermath and review of the 2004 election campaign, the Conservatives undertook a policy development that was consistent with this approach. In advance of the national convention, Stephen Harper commissioned each riding association to provide the national office with policy resolutions as voted on by local members. At the same time, policy development meetings were also held with the elected caucus and resulted in the provision of additional policy proposals for consideration. Harper's office vetted and consolidated the policy options and prepared a booklet of proposals for consideration by convention delegates. Following the convention, Harper and one of his assistants drafted the election manifesto, based primarily upon the policies approved at the convention, although departure from the specifics was permissible (Ellis and Woolstencroft 2006).

The 2005 national policy convention produced 112 policy areas and 222 separate policy statements, of which 119 consisted of specific policy commitments for a future Conservative government. Sixty of those commitments, or 50.4 per cent of the overall specific policy commitments of the party membership, were carried forward in a similar or consistent commitment in the election policy manifesto for the 2006 campaign. The Conservatives' election manifesto contained 232 separate commitments, meaning that party members were responsible for 25.9 per cent of the overall manifesto content. Furthermore, the manifesto contained 147 specific policy commitments on the part of a future Conservative government. Sixty of those specific policy commitments came from the party policy document, or 40.8 per cent.

Election Promise Implementation

The potential of party and party membership influence on government policy development is predicated on the underlying assumption that governing parties fulfil their election campaign manifesto commitments. As such, the focus of the policy capacity of parties and party membership shifts from their influence over the content of election manifestos to the implementation of election campaign commitments once the party participates in government. Research on this point has confirmed that governing parties in a range of democracies, including Canada, fulfil election manifesto commitments at fairly significant levels of implementation (for Canada, see Rallings 1987; Pétry and Collette 2009).

For three new governing parties over the last thirty years in Canada, there are mixed successes in implementing election promises. Consideration of a sample of election manifesto commitments reveals that these newly incumbent parties fulfilled their election promises at a lower rate than re-elected governing parties (Flynn 2011). This indicates that experience in governing, greater stakeholder engagement, and public service advice all influence the translation of election promises proposals into government policy choices. However, newly governing parties still fulfilled a sample of their election campaign commitments are a fairly reasonable rate. The 1984 Progressive Conservative government fully implemented their commitments at a rate of 58.3 per cent and took positive action towards honouring their commitments at an overall rate of 83.3 per cent. The 2006 Conservative government also implemented their commitments at a rate of 58.3 per cent and overall took steps to fulfilling their election promises in 64.6 per cent of cases. The 1993 Liberals had the lowest rates of implementation success at 41.7 and positive action towards fulfilling commitments at 50.0 per cent.[2]

Conclusion

Policy capacity includes both the ability to influence the range of options that are presented to governments to address outstanding policy issues, and the eventual choices that are made and implemented. By virtue of the roles that they play in democratic systems of government, political parties are uniquely positioned to affect both sides of the policymaking and capacity equation. Even though there has been much debate and consternation over the participatory nature of institutions in democratic political systems in recent years, including Canada, parties appear to continue to provide an avenue for citizens to provide some influence on government policy choices through their policy channelling functions. In the range of options available for governments to consider, roughly half of the policy statements arising from the national policy conventions of the 1993 Liberal and 2006 Conservative parties required future governments to undertake specific policy action as directed by the party membership. While only one-quarter of the overall content of election campaign manifestos was comparable to party policy statements, the influence of the party members becomes more evident in the consideration of election commitments that specifically required future government action. In the case of the Conservatives in 2006, the party membership was responsible for 40.8 per cent of the specific election commitments to be undertaken by a future Conservative government. The Liberals in 1993 were even better, with 65.6 per cent of their specific election commitments being similar to or comparable with policies derived from and approved by the party membership. Even in circumstances where policy development was driven entirely by party elites, as in the Progressive Conservatives in preparation for the 1984 campaign, the party membership through its underlying ideological belief structure continued to influence the range of policy choices that could be put forward.

Political parties may lack the policy expertise of other policy actors, such as think tanks, interest organizations, and the public service, but their policy capacity is buttressed by the democratic legitimacy that is provided by their open and participatory policy development. Although party members may not have a direct vote on the content of their party's election platforms, their efforts at earlier stages in the process may bear fruit in the policy positions considered for the election manifesto and subsequent consideration for adoption when the party is elected to govern.

The fulfilment of election campaign commitments presents a slightly less optimistic outcome. Research focused on the fulfilment of election campaign promises continues to demonstrate that governing parties implement those commitments at significant levels and at much higher levels than the public tends to expect (Naurin 2002). In Canada, this level of fulfilment has consistently been between two-thirds and three-quarters of election campaign promises (Rallings 1987; Pétry and Collette 2009; Flynn 2011). This means that where party members are able to have their policy demands carried forward into the party's election manifesto, it is likely that they will be implemented into government policy. The downside is that when their party is in opposition and members likely have their greatest impact on election manifesto choices, the implementation of election campaign commitments falls below the average range of promise fulfilment. However, even this negative still demonstrates the policy capacity of political parties on both sides of the policy capacity question. Even in these circumstances, the party that was worst in implementing promises continued to attempt to honour its election commitments half the time. When coupled with the strong level of inclusion of party member policy demands, it demonstrates that parties continue to be an avenue for policy influence. Political parties are fulfilling their policy-channelling role at least partially, by presenting policies influenced and developed by party membership to governments for consideration and are having those policies implemented once in government.

NOTES

1 Specific policy commitments included for consideration in both official party policy and election manifesto documents were defined as any written statement that committed a future government to a specific course of action if the party was elected to govern. Election manifesto commitments were defined as either being similar to or consistent with party

policy if they were worded substantially the same or pursued the same specific policy option as set out in the official party policy document. Election manifesto commitments that did not fall into either the similar or consistent categories were counted as not conforming to party policy.

2 For a greater breakdown of the rates of implementation and action towards implementation as well as the methodology and definitions associated with the same, see Flynn (2011).

14 Policy Dialogue and Engagement between Non-Government Organizations and Government: A Survey of Processes and Instruments of Canadian Policy Workers

BRYAN EVANS AND ADAM WELLSTEAD[1]

Analysts have raised concerns about declining research, evaluation, and analytical capacities within public services (Baskoy, Evans, and Shields 2011; Edwards 2009; Christensen and Laegreid 2001, 2005; Peters 2005; Rhodes 1994). Typically, the decline is attributed to reforms associated with neoliberal restructuring of the state and its concomitant managerial expression in New Public Management (NPM). This observation has given rise to a conceptual shift now commonly characterized as a movement from "government" to "governance" (Rhodes 1996; Stoker 1998; Peters 2000; Treib, Bahr, and Falkner 2007; Tollefson, Zito, and Gale 2012). With respect to policy analysis and advice, this shift has resulted in an environment of new governance arrangements entailing a more distributed policy advisory system where a plurality of actors, particularly non-state actors, engage with government in deliberating policy interventions to address collective problems. In this context, it has been suggested, "a healthy policy research community outside government can [now] play a vital role in enriching public understanding and debate of policy issues" (Anderson 1996, 486). Or is this conceptualization of an expanded policy advisory system, composed of a broad spectrum of state and non-state policy actors, a misreading of what is taking place? The assumption is that there is some equitable distribution of policy capability throughout the system. For many non-governmental organizations, analytical resources, and hence the ability to effectively influence the policy process, may be minimal to non-existent. This limitation may be exacerbated by the movement towards a more evidence-based policymaking process, which places a premium on the possession of analytical skills (Howlett 2009c). Apart from business associations and corporations, however, such capacity in the non-governmental sector is limited (Stritch 2007; Howlett 2009b, 165). Indeed, the redistributed policy advisory system deriving from the shift to a governance paradigm may simply reconstitute old hierarchies of power and influence (Jordan 2007).

Given the near-to-orthodoxy status of the governance perspective and the derivative pluralist frame of multi-actor policy engagement, it is important to build an empirically based insight into how the two worlds of government and non-government policy work compare. This chapter is a first stage in exploring these two worlds. Here, how each conducts the work of policy is examined through data derived through survey research. From this data analysis, we can test how, at least in a Canadian setting, government and non-government policy functions compare and contrast. Of course, the methodology and focus employed in this study could be replicated in any jurisdiction.

While both government and non-government policy actors may compose a specific policy community, their roles in the process – their work – is consequently different. NGO policy work involves "constant advocacy of certain positions and criticism of other stances" by injecting ideas, policy proposals, and expertise into policy advisory system (Stone 2000, 47–8). They do this by employing either or both of two main strategies. First, by pursuing an "insider" strategy where the objective is to "attain influence by working closely with … governments by providing policy solutions and expert advice" and, second, through an "outsider" strategy of campaigning to mobilize public opinion in support of a policy change (Gulbrandsen and Andresen 2004, 56). The onus is upon the NGO policy actors to make their case to government, whose role in turn is to decide on a course of action and on the precise details of what that would or would not include.

The findings presented here suggest that those responsible for policy work within government and non-governmental organizations (NGOs), across four policy communities[2] in the three Canadian provinces (Ontario, British Columbia, and Saskatchewan) surveyed, differ in their capacities, depth of commitment to a specific policy file/field, roles and functions, and perceptions of the policy work that they undertake. The choice to focus on the Canadian provinces is based on two reasons: first, the fact that in Canada, the provinces are responsible for important policy areas, in whole or in part, including the fields surveyed here, and second, the paucity of knowledge of the policy analysis and advisory functions at this level (Howlett and Newman 2010, 125). Based on the results of an online survey of government and NGO policy workers, this largely descriptive comparison allows us to ask if differences between these two groups will affect the shift to new governance arrangements. The results suggests that the ideal, if not the idea, of a new governance terrain may be composed of a wider set of actors, but these actors are by no means equal.

Literature Review

Various definitions of policy capacity have been formulated since interest in the subject emerged in the 1990s. The literature reflects this definitional pluralism, as several schools of thought are discernible. At the base of all such definitional debates is an understanding of policy as "a choice that follows an intellectual effort to determine an effective course of action in a particular context" (Aucoin and Bakvis 2005, 190). However, as this research is concerned with the deliberative process contributing to the framing and, perhaps, the construction of policy options for government decision-makers to choose from, we are concerned with what happens prior to and after the "choice." Ultimately, the substantive contribution and effectiveness of policy actors in the process of engagement is dependent upon the policy capacity inherent in their institutional home. For our purpose, we treat the concept broadly to include policy formulation and political responsiveness to the demands of social forces (Peters 1996, 11; Peters 2008, 2010). And, in the process of policy engagement between state and non-state actors, this more encompassing perspective allows one to think of the role of the public bureaucracy as providing a space for public participation (Peters 2010). Somewhat more narrowly, policy capacity is also understood as "the ability of a government to make intelligent policy choices and muster the resources needed to execute those choices" (Painter and Pierre 2005b, 255). It is in this respect that contributions that encompasses the ability to influence and shape policy decisions resonate with the study of policy engagement. Policy capacity is equally concerned with discussion of alternatives, managing competing demands of diverse stakeholders, and finally making a decision (Goetz and Wollmann 2001, 864).

The new governance arrangements literature suggests that there has been an opening of the policy advice system where a "new range of political practices has emerged between institutional layers of the state and between state institutions and societal organizations" (Hajer and Wagenaar 2003, 1). Both state and non-state policy actors should work in an increasingly collaborative environment, in a process of deliberative policy analysis, to determine the "points of solidarity in the joint realization that they need one another to craft effective political agreements" (3). Indeed, "governance is broader than government, covering non-state actors" (Rhodes 1997, 53). A 2010 New Zealand government study examining the improvement of policy advice noted that such advice is no longer the monopoly of public servants and is increasingly contested by other non-governmental policy actors.

Consequently, public servants must accommodate "the contribution that can be made to analysis and advice by the wider policy community" (Government of New Zealand 2010, 1–2). In short, government is one actor in the policy advice process, which must learn to better engage across policy communities. Such public engagement brings NGO actors into the day-to-day activities of government agencies and departments (Rowe and Frewer 2005, 253). Consequently, there is now an expectation that government policy analysts will engage in greater consultation and dialogue with the public as a core part of their professional role (Wellstead, Stedman, and Lindquist 2009, 37). The emergence of collaborative governance practices involving the direct engagement of government and non-government actors in deliberative policy development (Robertson and Choi 2012, 85) signals a new era in government-stakeholder policy engagement. In such arrangements, the centre of policy work and deliberation is located not within government policy units, but in civil society sites of collaboration (Bradford and Andrew 2010, 5). In this way, collaborative governance redesigns the policy process from an approach that occurs within government institutions to one that is situated outside, at least in part, of the political-bureaucratic structures and where policy is informed by the experience and knowledge of a variety of actors. The policy constructed through this process is not the product of competition and power politics, but rather the result of a consensus-oriented process producing policy outcomes. These partnerships provide a venue to share information and perspectives across sectors. Not only does this positively affect the policy produced, but also more significantly mutual learning increases the capacity of policy actors to collaborate in the solution of collective problems (Booher 2004, 43). And it must be acknowledged that to be effective, collaborative governance processes must openly recognize power disparities between actors within a policy community and strive to mitigate the impact of power imbalances (Purdy 2012).

As such, in order to enhance policy capacity, there needs to be a dispersal of actors within each policy community and where each possesses "unique organizing capacities" (Van Buuren 2009, 213). This differs from more traditional forms of policymaking where decision-making occurs within the "black-box" of government and presents a new interpretation of the policy process, which "is not imprisoned in closed institutions and is not the province of professional politicians" (Newman et al. 2004, 204).

In Canada, there have been several studies of policy capacity within Canada's federal and provincial governments. The studies range from expert panels and reports (Fellegi 1996; Peters 1996; Savoie 2003b), reflections of senior officials (Anderson 1996; Rasmussen 1999; Voyer 2007), and the results of surveys (Howlett 2009b; Bernier and Howlett 2011; Howlett and Joshi-Koop 2011; Wellstead, Stedman, and Howlett 2011; Howlett and Wellstead 2012; Wellstead and Stedman 2012). This recent spate of quantitative research delves into the nitty-gritty details of the "who and how" of front-line policy work. Given the important policy fields for which the Canadian provinces are responsible, further research is required. Howlett (2009b) places the NGO dimension (and this includes business, labour, and civil society organizations) on the research agenda when he asks, "What do policy analysts actually do in contemporary governmental and non-governmental organizations?" And he goes further, urging that students of public policy and management ask if the training and resourcing of policy workers is adequate for the task (163–4). Moreover, taking Howlett's suggestions for additional research further, this work explores how public service policy workers and NGO policy workers engage with one another.

Although these quantitative studies of front-line workers are a noteworthy contribution to understanding the nature of policy work, they are limited to the narrow scope of government-centred decision-making and fail to account for policy work in new governance arrangements. The point is that "policies can no longer be struck in isolation in government" (Lindquist 2009, 9). Contradicting this now axiomatic statement is a body of research (Wellstead and Stedman 2010; Howlett and Wellstead 2012) that has found that government policy workers are notorious for their low levels of interaction outside of their immediate work environment. This chapter is, to our knowledge, the first empirical examination of front-line policy work on "the other side" outside of government and, more importantly, gauges the extent of relationships of these two worlds. As this study is concerned with comparing government and NGO approaches and perspectives towards policy work, some consideration of policy capacity within each sector is undertaken.

The resourcing and availability of policy expertise (Lindquist and Desveaux 2007) within the public service and beyond, the practices and procedures used to apply these resources to address a policy issue, is a basic dimension for investigation (Fellegi 1996, 6). Given that both the political legitimacy and practical efficacy of new governance arrangements is theoretically premised upon a broadly pluralist framework of enabled policy actors, it is necessary to test the veracity of this conceptualization. If policy advisory systems have indeed become "more fluid, pluralized and poly-centric" (Craft and Howlett 2012a, 85), there must be some indication of this new policy development environment in how policy workers, both government and non-government, perform their tasks. And for this pluralized policy advisory system to work optimally, it must be premised on the existence of a "healthy policy-research community outside government" (Anderson 1996, 486). The data analysis here raises serious questions about this assumed policy pluralism and its "health."

Three components of policy capacity relevant to this research are (1) the policy network environment – especially the department's position relative to other players in the policy development process; (2) the human inputs – the number of people involved in policy work, their education, career experience, and skills; and (3) the information inputs – the range and quality of the data available to inform the decision-making process (Edwards 2009, 291–2). Howlett (2009c) has formulated a more focused conceptualization of "policy analytical capacity," which is the "amount of basic research a government can conduct or access, its ability to apply statistical methods, applied research methods, and advanced modelling techniques to this data and employ analytical techniques such as environmental scanning, trends analysis, and forecasting methods in order to gauge broad public opinion and attitudes, as well as those of interest groups and other major policy players, and to anticipate future policy impacts" (162). All of these functions and methods are exercised through the efforts of policy workers. By integrating the insights of Edwards (2009) with Howlett's definition, we construct an additional frame of "how" and through what processes the policy worker applies (or not applies) these skills and techniques. These are the "tools" of the trade, but how are they employed and to what end? What are the processes and structures in which they are applied? How might the processes of policy work affect which tools are used or not used? What knowledge becomes "applied" in the development of policy and what is discarded and why? How do relationships with other actors within the policy community, both governmental and non-governmental actors, contribute to what knowledge is acceptable and not acceptable? Are some actors privileged in the process, and if so, how? These are important questions, the answers to which can assist in unpacking the day-to-day content of the policy process.

Research Questions

Recent Canadian policy capacity surveys, in particular the variables derived from Wellstead and Stedman's (2010) Canadian federal government study, served as the basis for an analysis of this study comparing government policy workers and their NGO counterparts. Three key questions about the nature of government and NGO policy work in a changing governance environment are posed. First, are public service and NGO policy workers different in their key demographic characteristics and work environment? Second how similar or dissimilar are public service and NGO-based policy functions and capacities? More specifically, we compare the size of the respective policy units and the specific policy tasks, both of which are important factors in understanding policy capacity (Wellstead and Stedman 2010). Third, we focus on the whether or not there will be differences in the attitudinal characteristics between the groups. Wellstead and Stedman (2010) found that in many cases attitudes towards the larger policy environment is critical in determining levels of perceived policy capacity. More specifically, we compare what the respondents thought about the role of evidence policymaking, political involvement in the policy process, the influence of outside organizations on policy work, and the importance of networking.

Data and Methods

To probe the above research questions, two survey instruments were designed: (1) a government-based 192 variable (forty-five questions) questionnaire was designed in part from previous capacity surveys by Howlett, and Wellstead (Howlett 2009a; Wellstead, Stedman, and Lindquist 2009); (2) an NGO based 248 variable questionnaire (thirty-eight questions). Questions in both surveys addressed the nature and frequency of the tasks, the extent and frequency of their interactions with other policy actors, and their attitudes towards and views of various aspects of policymaking processes, as well as questions about their educational, previous work, and on-the-job training experiences. Both also contained standard questions about age, gender, and socio-economic status.

The survey instrument was delivered to 2458 provincial policy analysts and 1995 analysts working in the NGO sector in the Canadian provinces of Ontario, Saskatchewan, and British Columbia. Four policy communities were selected for this survey: environment, health, immigration, and labour. The specific provinces and policy sectors dealt with in this study were chosen because they represent heterogeneous cases in terms of politics, history, and economic and demographic scale. With respect to the three provinces, they present cases that include Ontario – Canada's largest province in economic and population terms (13.5 million people and representing 40 per cent of Canadian GDP). Unlike most of Canada's other provinces, Ontario has a competitive three-party political system where, since 1990, all three have governed. British Columbia presents a mid-size province (population of 4.4 million and 12 per cent of national GDP). Provincial elections have been polarized contests between social democrats and a free market coalition that has been housed within various parties. Saskatchewan was chosen as a small province (population of one million and 3 per cent of national GDP). Its economy has been based largely on natural resources and agriculture. Politics have also been highly polarized where the provincial government has alternated between social democrats and a conservative party.

Mailing lists for both surveys were compiled, wherever possible, from publicly available sources such as online telephone directories, using keyword searches for terms such as *policy analyst* appearing in job titles or descriptions. In some cases, additional names were added to lists from hard-copy sources, including government organization manuals. After preliminary interviews with NGO organization representatives, we suspected that respondents would undertake a variety of non-policy-related tasks. As a result, we widened the search to include those who undertook policy-related analysis in their work objectives. Both study populations were small, so a census rather than sample was drawn from each. This method is consistent with other expert-based studies (see, e.g., Laumann and Knoke 1987; Zafonte and Sabatier 1998).

The authors implemented an unsolicited survey in January 2012 using Zoomerang®, an online commercial software service. A total of 1510 returns were collected for a final response rate of 33.99 per cent. With the exception of the NGO labour respondents, the percentage of respondents corresponded closely with population developed by the authors. The data were weighted using the iterative proportional fitting or raking method. The data were analysed using SPSS 20.0. The data generated by the survey provided the basis required to test the hypotheses about tasks, the nature of broad issues, perceived policy capacity, and the attitudes to climate change and policy process, and the nature of the relationship between government policy analysts and those in the environment, health, immigration, and labour NGO communities. The analysis includes a presentation of descriptive analysis, comparison of mean scores between government and NGO responses,[3] and exploratory factor analysis.[4]

Results

Who Are the Respondents (and What Is Their work Environment)?

The health sector was the largest sector of employment for both the NGO and government respondents (38.9 per cent and 39.4 per cent) (table 14.14). Comparatively more government respondents were found in the environmental sector (30.5 per cent). The other sectors, immigration and labour, were equally represented by both groups. Both groups are highly educated groups, with the government respondents holding more professional or graduate degrees (table 14.13). The government respondents tended to be younger. A age difference between the two populations is clearly discernible. The NGO cohort tends to be older, where 52 per cent of respondents were fifty-one years old or older. By comparison, only 37.1 per cent of government respondents were in this age range. Younger government policy analysts tended to be a much larger proportion of the total field of government respondents. Slightly more than 37 per cent were forty or younger. In contrast, slightly more that 20 per cent of the NGO cohort were in this age range. While NGO respondents tend to be older, it may therefore not be too surprising that the survey found this cohort to demonstrate significantly longer attachment to both their present position and organization, in comparison to government policy analysts (table 14.1).

Nearly 43 per cent of the NGO respondents had ten or more years of experience with their organization (table 14.2). Of these, just 14 per cent had twenty or more years in their organization, in contrast to only 6.8 per cent of the government policy analysts. And among the

Table 14.1 Years in Department or Organization***

	Government		NGO	
Years	Number	%	Number	%
Less than 1 year	77	14.7	18	3.0
1–5 years	298	57.0	203	34.0
6–9 years	77	14.7	116	19.4
10–14 years	35	6.7	109	18.3
15–20 years	18	3.4	65	10.9
More than 20 years	18	3.4	86	14.4
Total	523	100.0	597	100.0

*** $p < .001$

long-term veterans, only 3.4 per cent had twenty or more years with their organization. A similar disparity is revealed in future commitment to one's organization (table 14.2). Here, 53.4 per cent of NGO respondents stated that they planned to remain with their current organization for another decade. Government respondents were not interested in long-term organizational commitments – only 16.2 per cent indicated that they intended to remain for ten or more years.

What Do the Respondents Do?

Policy-based NGO respondents did not fall under the generic policy role like their government counterparts. The specific tasks of both groups are highlighted later in the chapter. However, in table 14.3, the general roles of the NGO respondents reveal that they undertake a host of different tasks, most notably management roles such as director (31.8 per cent) or manager (21.9 per cent). Only a minority (15.4 per cent) considered themselves to be policy analysts. A Crombach's alpha = .787 from a reliability test of these roles (with director, coordinator, and manager variables removed) meant that NGO respondents were highly likely to be engaged in all or many of these roles.

We found that NGO policy units were much smaller than those housed in government ministries. In fact, 67.2 per cent of NGO respondents reported that there is no unit dedicated to policy research or advocacy (table 14.4). A further 24.1 per cent reported that while a policy

Table 14.2 Years Anticipated Being in Department or Organization***

	Government		NGO	
Anticipated years	Number	%	Number	%
Less than 1 year	43	9.3	25	4.3
1–5 years	222	42.9	142	24.3
6–9 years	63	12.2	105	17.9
10–14 years	44	8.5	85	14.5
15–20 years	29	5.6	102	17.4
More than 20 years	11	2.1	126	21.5
Don't know	101	19.5	0	0.0
Total	518	100.0	585	100.0

*** $p < .001$

Table 14.3 Roles of NGO Respondents

Role	Number	%
Adviser	106	15.3
Analyst	52	7.5
Communication officer	69	9.9
Coordinator	103	14.8
Director	221	31.8
Liaison officer	32	4.6
Manager	152	21.9
Planner	65	9.4
Policy analyst	107	15.4
Researcher	112	16.1
Strategic analyst	73	10.5
Other	127	18.3

unit did exist, it was composed of ten or fewer staff. These findings contrast significantly with government policy units, with 61.2 per cent who reported the presence of dedicated policy units of up to ten staff and 24.3 per cent who indicated that their policy unit was still larger.

Table 14.4 Size of Policy Work Unit***

	Government		NGO	
Number of people who work in your policy work unit	Number	%	Number	%
0 (there is no dedicated policy unit)	75	14.5	393	67.2
1–5	140	27.0	90	15.4
6–10	177	34.2	51	8.7
11–20	72	13.9	51	8.7
21–30	25	4.8	0	0.0
More than 30	29	5.6	0	0.0
Total	518	100.0	585	100.0

*** $p < .001$

The prevalence of multitasking within NGO policy work is a function of the smaller size of NGOs generally. Consequently, a division of labour within these organizations that allows for a policy role specialization is not possible in many cases. In contrast, governments have the resources that allow for larger policy units staffed with dedicated policy workers. The differential size and policy specialization observed here raises questions about the inferred pluralism of new governance arrangements insofar as they apply to policy engagement between government and non-government policy actors.

The survey data further indicate that government and NGO policy analysts work differently. Table 14.5 lists the mean score and the percentage of those respondents who engage at least weekly in seventeen possible specific policy tasks. In many cases, government respondents are engaged more frequently in all of these tasks For example, 54.4 per cent of the government respondents brief low- or mid-level managers, compared to 4.9 per cent of the NGO policy workers. Similarly, 34.8 per cent of government workers engaged at least weekly in policy research, compared to 16.7 per cent of the NGO respondents.

A factor analysis of the above seventeen items was conducted (table 14.6). There are four distinct loadings with 68.1% of the variance explained: policy work, briefing, consulting, and conducting research.

In table 14.7, the group differences between mean scores from two of the new variables (policy work and briefing) were statistically

Table 14.5 Tasks of Respondents

	Government			Non-government		
	n	Mean (% weekly)	*SD*	*n*	Mean (% weekly)	*SD*
Appraise/assess policy options***	479	3.49 (31.5)	1.34	545	3.09 (17.1)	1.32
Brief Cabinet ministers and ministerial staff***	489	2.16 (6.5)	1.27	543	1.77 (1.3)	.993
Brief senior management***	488	3.38 (23.8)	1.34	536	2.02 (1.9)	1.08
Brief low- or mid-level policy managers***	485	4.11 (54.4)	1.18	534	2.49 (4.9)	1.22
Collect policy-related data or information***	484	3.96 (48.1)	1.27	538	3.22 (23.2)	1.34
Conduct policy-related research***	483	3.54 (34.8)	1.39	516	2.75 (16.7)	1.37
Conduct scientific research	478	1.76 (6.3)	1.19	522	1.75 (7.7)	1.27
Consult with decision-makers***	471	3.60 (27.6)	1.25	522	3.06 (12.6)	1.19
Consult with stakeholders	482	3.33 (24.7)	1.33	536	3.44 (19.6)	1.21
Consult with the public	479	1.98 (4.2)	1.16	536	2.11 (5.6)	1.06
Evaluate policy processes and procedures*	476	2.79 (10.5)	1.27	518	2.59 (7.3)	1.16
Evaluate policy results and outcomes*	478	2.81 (11.2)	1.23	534	2.63 (9.2)	1.17
Identify policy issues	472	3.64 (30.3)	1.20	514	3.21 (18.5)	1.21
Identify policy options	477	3.55 (27.5)	1.22	523	2.94 (12.6)	1.23
Implement or deliver policies or programs**	483	3.01 (26.7)	1.53	522	2.70 (20.5)	1.52
Negotiate with program staff	483	3.10 (24.0)	1.50	521	2.38 (8.4)	1.34
Negotiate with stakeholders on policy matters*	485	2.45 (8.2)	1.30	532	2.33 (5.1)	1.22

* $p < .05$
** $p < .01$
*** $p < .001$

Table 14.6 Factor Analysis of Tasks Undertaken

	Component			
	Policy work	Briefing	Consulting/ administering	Scientific research
Appraise/assess policy options	.687			
Brief Cabinet ministers and ministerial staff		.731		
Brief senior management		.886		
Brief low- or mid-level policy managers		.749		
Conduct scientific research				.926
Consult with stakeholders			.756	
Consult with the public			.645	
Evaluate policy processes and procedures	.754			
Evaluate policy results and outcomes	.789			
Identify policy issues	.817			
Identify policy options	.822			
Implement or deliver policies or programs			.568	
Negotiate with stakeholders on policy matters			.724	

significant, meaning that government respondents undertook more policy work and briefing activities. Again, this corroborates our earlier observation on governments' size and how this translates into capacity for staff to specialize in policy work as opposed to need for multitasking required in NGOs.

The large number of issues across all four policy communities in the three provinces made specific questions impossible. We replicated Wellstead, Stedman, and Howlett's (2011) more generalized issue questions (see table 14.8). There were a number of significant differences between government and NGO respondents across nearly all items. Government respondents spent more time on these critical issue areas. The government respondents indicated (35.2 per cent) that they spent a

Table 14.7 Comparison of Means of Factored Tasks

	Government			NGO		
	n	Mean	*SD*	*n*	Mean	*SD*
Policy work***	442	3.24	1.03	461	2.92	1.01
Brief***	483	3.21	.99	518	2.10	.95
Consult implementation	470	2.78	.99	504	2.75	.87
Conduct scientific research	478	1.76	1.23	522	1.75	1.27

*** $p < .001$
1 = never and 5 = weekly

considerable amount of their time (50 per cent or more) examining issues that required a specialist or technical knowledge and to issues that were difficult for which to identify a single, clear, simple solution (40.2 per cent). In contrast, only 23.1 per cent of the NGO respondents spent more than half of their time examining those issues where it was difficult to identify a single, clear, simple solution (17.9 per cent), followed by issues where the data were not immediately available.

A factor analysis of the fourteen items in table 14.8 was conducted (with a 66.25 per cent of the variance explained) and it produced two distinct loadings (table 14.9): "public" and "complex" issues. For both broad issue areas, the government respondents were more engaged. A comparison of mean scores is found in table 14.10. Again, government policy work is housed in a comparatively resource-rich context, allowing for this observed focused attention.

Respondents were asked how often stakeholders were invited to work with the government on both an informal and formal basis. A comparison of means and the frequency that such interaction occurred often (monthly) revealed distinctly different perceptions of stakeholder involvement with government officials between the two groups (table 14.10). Nearly a third (29.9 per cent) of government respondents indicated that NGO stakeholders worked with them monthly, compared to the 9.3 per cent of NGO respondents who saw themselves meeting informally and infrequently with government officials. The reverse held true for formal encounters between government and NGO officials, with a quarter of the NGO indicating they met with government officials, compared to 14.8 per cent of the government respondents reporting the same sort of formal meetings.

Table 14.8 Types of Issues Dealt With

Issues that ...	Government			NGO		
	n	$\bar{x}$ (> 50% of time)	*SD*	*n*	$\bar{x}$ (> 50% of time)	*SD*
Require public consultation***	463	2.21 (9.3)	1.21	507	1.97 (1.4)	.860
Emerge as the result of political priorities in the Premier's Office or Cabinet***	461	3.17 (20.8)	1.31	498	2.02 (1.6)	.936
Emerge as a result of public pressure on government***	462	2.92 (13.2)	1.20	498	2.44 (4.8)	1.01
Gave a single, clear, relatively simple solution	453	1.96 (1.5)	.907	495	2.04 (2.6)	.906
Require coordination with other levels of government***	455	2.90 (14.7)	1.28	498	2.42 (6.6)	1.17
Require specialist or technical knowledge***	457	3.66 (35.2)	1.25	495	2.79 (13.3)	1.22
Difficult to identify a single, clear, simple solution***	456	3.75 (40.1)	1.28	494	3.14 (23.1)	1.30
Issues for which data are not immediately available***	459	3.48 (25.7)	1.22	499	2.98 (17.0)	1.24
Demand the creation or collection of policy-relevant evidence***	453	3.41 (28.5)	1.31	502	2.99 (17.9)	1.27

*** $p < .001$
1 = 0% of my time and 5 = > 50% of my time

What Are Their Attitudes towards Policymaking?

Table 14.11 lists fifteen variables measuring policy attitudes concerning the effectiveness of policy work. Of them, the comparison of means tests (and the percentage who agreed) revealed statistically significant differences between the government and NGO respondents on ten of these items. For example, when asked if "urgent day-to-day issues seem to take precedence over thinking long term," 43.1 per cent of the

Table 14.9 Factor Analysis of Issues Types

Issues that ...	Component	
	Complex	Public
Require public consultation		.695
Emerge as the result of political priorities in the Premier's Office or Cabinet		.770
Emerge as a result of public pressure on government		.798
Require specialist or technical knowledge	.755	
Difficult to identify a single, clear, simple solution	.851	
Issues for which data are not immediately available	.841	
Demand the creation or collection of policy-relevant evidence	.754	

Table 14.10 Invitation to Work with Government

	Government			NGO		
	n	Mean (% monthly)	*SD*	*n*	Mean (% monthly)	*SD*
How often are stakeholders invited to assist with your (their) work on an informal basis?***	458	3.32 (29.9)	1.498	463	2.21 (9.3)	1.215
How often are stakeholders invited to assist with your (their) work on a formal basis?***	459	2.94 (14.8)	1.344	464	3.13 (25.0)	1.367

*** $p < .001$
1 = Never and 5 = Monthly

government respondents strongly agreed with the statement, compared to 30.4 per cent of their NGO counterparts.

A factor analysis (table 14.12) of the items resulted in five distinct loadings with 68.9 per cent of the variance explained: "evidence" (the importance of evidence-based policy work), "political" (the role of political influence in policy work), "network" (the importance of networking), and influence-outside (the influence of organizations outside of the formal policy process). These five new items reveal a multifaceted

Table 14.11 General Governance Attitudes

	Government			NGO		
	n	Mean (% strongly agree)	*SD*	*n*	Mean (% strongly agree)	*SD*
Urgent day-to-day issues seem to take precedence over thinking "long term"***	436	4.17 (43.1)	.93	450	3.79 (30.4)	1.07
I am increasingly consulting with the public as I do my policy-related work**	435	2.52 (3.7)	1.11	441	2.74 (5.2)	1.04
Policy directions seem to increasingly be on what is most politically acceptable*	434	3.80 (26.3)	.94	442	3.64 (22.2)	1.04
There seems to be less governmental capacity to analyse policy options than there used to be***	430	3.42 (15.3)	1.01	436	3.69 (23.2)	.96
My policy-related work increasingly involves networks of people across other regions, or levels of government, or even outside of government	429	3.55 (22.6)	1.16	434	3.70 (25.3)	1.12
Policy problems increasingly require strong technical expertise	427	3.58 (14.1)	.92	436	3.59 (14.9)	.92
Much of the policy capacity is outside the formal structure of government***	425	2.84 (6.1)	1.03	428	3.51 (13.6)	.88
Those who have more authority in decision-making usually have less specialized technical expertise*	432	3.92 (31.7)	.94	427	3.80 (23.4)	.91
An important role of government is to foster involvement in the policy process by other non-governmental organizations/stakeholders	428	3.70 (18.2)	.88	440	4.31 (50.7)	.85
Interest groups seem to have a greater influence in policymaking than they used to**	427	3.43 (13.1)	.90	437	3.22 (13.3)	1.08
Well-organized data, research, and analysis originating from government department are used in policymaking***	430	3.42 (15.1)	1.06	429	2.74 (3.0)	1.01
Formal government institutions are becoming less relevant to policymaking**	423	2.89 (4.3)	.93	423	3.08 (5.7)	.89
Decisions about government programs and operations are increasingly made by those outside of government**	426	2.71 (3.1)	.91	432	2.89 (7.2)	1.02
Evidence is increasingly being asked for in government policy development and evaluation***	432	3.79 (26.2)	.95	436	3.51 (20.9)	1.09

* $p < .05$
** $p < .01$
*** $p < .001$
1 = strongly disagree and 5 = strongly agree

set of common attitudes between the two groups that influence policy work (table 14.6).

The mean scores from the summed variables in table 14.12 illustrate that the government-based respondents considered evidence-based policy work and political influence on policy work to be more important than their NGO counterparts did. However, the NGO policy workers surveyed placed more importance on networking and the role of outside organizations on policymaking. A comparison of mean scores of these can be found in table 14.16.

Discussion

In this chapter, three major questions about the nature of government and NGO policy workers in three Canadian provinces across five significant fields were posed. The first question focused on whether or not there were demographic and work environment differences between the two groups. In other words, who were the respondents? The government-based respondents had a higher level of education, thus partially supporting, but were younger than their NGO counterparts. Government respondents were more likely to leave their organization within five years, is consistent with the literature on job mobility in large bureaucracies (Page and Jenkins 2005).

The second major question asked whether or not there are differences in the tasks and working environments of these two groups. Not surprising is the greater institutional support that government policy workers have in the policy unit. When it came to the actual work that the respondents did, those working for government departments were more engaged in what the public management literature called "policy work." This may be explained in part by the more encompassing roles that NGO policy actors play. We suspect that NGO-based policy work is done "from the side of the desk." With large supporting policy units and more time to engage in policy work, government respondents will be more engaged in specific and complex policy tasks than NGO respondents were also supported. The perceived level of engagement between NGO and government officials had mixed results. NGO respondents saw themselves less engaged in an informal sense, but more involved in formal arrangements with government officials. We can further deduce that NGO respondents may see their participation as an afterthought than real players in decision-making. The types of issues addressed by the respondents different from the factor analysis of issue

Table 14.12 Factor Analysis of General Governance Attitudes

	Component				
	Evidence	Political	Network	Influence	Outside
Urgent day-to-day issues seem to take precedence over thinking "long term"		.855			
I am increasingly consulting with the public as I do my policy-related work			.857		
Policy directions seem to increasingly be on what is most politically acceptable		.787			
My policy-related work increasingly involves networks of people across other regions, or levels of government, or even outside of government			.750		
Much of the policy capacity is outside the formal structure of government					.668
An important role of government is to foster involvement in the policy process by other non-governmental organizations/stakeholders					.823
Interest groups seem to have a greater influence in policy-making than they used to				.792	
Well-organized data, research, and analysis originating from government department are used in policymaking	.768				
Decisions about government programs and operations are increasingly made by those outside of government				.727	
Evidence is increasingly being asked for in government policy development and evaluation	.818				

areas, we found that the government respondents dealt with issues emerging from the public either directly or from their political masters. They also dealt with more complex issues. This, we suspect, on the basis of Wellstead, Stedman, and Lindquist (2009), is a function of policy units.

The last question attempted to gauge what the study's respondents thought of policymaking in general. This raises concern about the role and legitimacy of evidence-based policy work in new governance arrangements. In addition to working more regularly on issues that stem from public concern, government respondents were more likely to agree that their work has become more politicized and is under greater scrutiny from outside influences. Therefore the greater importance placed on networking by NGO respondents was expected.

Implications and Conclusion

This comparative analysis reveals that the worlds of Canadian provincial government and NGO policy analysts are rather different in structures, understanding, and perhaps, and speculatively, policy knowledge and expertise. Further data analysis will explore this in more depth. However, at this stage we can say a few things about how these policy work worlds are constructed.

One of the most significant findings distinguishing the two groups is the depth of long-term commitment found among NGO policy analysts to their organization and substantive policy field. This seems to imply much greater conviction and commitment to the "cause" among this cohort, as compared to their public service counterparts. Perhaps the shift to a more corporate or enterprise-wide career track model in the public services, as opposed to growing deep roots in a specific field, has created a much more mobile policy professional. And the clearly larger and more steeply hierarchical career ladders of public service require such mobility if one is to enter senior management.

The other major difference, though not a surprising one, is organizational size and scale. NGOs, for the most part, simply do not have the capacity to create dedicated policy units, and this policy work is thus only one aspect of work in this sector. Multitasking is the order of the day. In contrast, the public services tended to have sizeable policy units dedicated to a singular policy function.

What policy analysts in each sector do is also telling. The primary function of government respondents was briefing mid-level managers.

Table 14.13 Sectors in Which Respondents Are Employed

Policy Community/ Field	NGO			Government		
	Number	Respondent %	Population %	Number	Respondent %	Population %
Environment	102	16.5	20.5	167	30.5	27.5
Health	241	38.9	34.3	216	39.4	39.5
Immigration	66	10.6	14.8	54	9.9	11.7
Labour	104	16.8	30.3	69	12.6	15.2
Other	107	17.3	0	42	7.7	6.0
Total	620	100.0		548	100.0	

Table 14.14 Background of Respondents

	Government		Non-government	
	Number	%	Number	%
Gender				
Male	205	41.4	214	44.1
Female	290	58.6	274	55.9
Age***				
30 or younger	54	10.8	23	4.7
31–40	131	26.3	80	16.4
41–50	129	25.9	131	26.8
51–60	148	29.7	171	35.0
Over 60	37	7.4	83	17.0
Education***				
High school graduate	11	2.2	24	4.9
College or technical institute diploma	39	7.7	72	14.6
University degree	148	29.2	146	29.6
Graduate or professional degree	308	60.9	252	51.0

*** $p < .001$

Table 14.15 Comparison of Means of Factored Issues

	Government			NGO		
	n	Mean	*SD*	*n*	Mean	*SD*
Public issues***	458	2.77	.995	481	2.71	.684
Complex issues***	434	3.12	.753	470	2.14	.811

*** $p < .001$
1 = 0% of my time and 5 = > 50% of my time

Table 14.16 Summed Governance Attitudinal Variables

	Government			NGO		
	n	Mean	*SD*	*n*	Mean	*SD*
Evidence***	429	3.61	.8454	424	3.13	.8369
Political***	433	3.99	.7831	441	3.72	.8538
Network**	428	3.04	.9292	430	3.22	.8608
Influence	420	3.08	.7321	426	3.06	.8136
Outside***	422	3.28	.7088	421	3.91	.6751

** $p < .01$
*** $p < .001$

In contrast, the primary function of NGO staff was consulting with their stakeholders. Obviously the first indicates a priority of internal policy work cohesion, while the second appears to express a more outward-looking orientation. No doubt this is the need for NGOs to engage their funders, members, and communities. The service delivery and advocacy roles identified in this survey would support this conclusion, at least in part. And the types of issues each world deals with tend to be starkly different. This reflects the different structural and political realities of each sector. But this may well speak to the need for more formal and institutionalized spaces to allow better dialogue between both sides of each policy community to better deliberate with one another, if that is a genuine objective. While contemporary governance arrangements appear to speak to shifts in the patterns of interaction found in policy advisory systems (Craft and Howlett 2012a, 86), the image of a pluralist, polycentric model of governance is far from realized in the process of policy engagement in the three Canadian provinces surveyed here.

NOTES

1 The authors wish to gratefully acknowledge the Social Sciences and Humanities Research Council of Canada for generously funding this research project as well as the contributions of our research assistants, Alex Howlett, Christopher Redmond, and Alvin Ying.
2 Approximately 4,000 NGOs were invited to respond to the survey. A list of organizations contacted will be provided upon request.
3 Inter-sector differences were tested using comparison of means (independent-samples) *t*-tests.
4 Factor analysis is a statistical procedure used to uncover relationships among many variables. This allows numerous inter-correlated variables to be condensed into fewer dimensions, called factors. The internal consistency of the factored variables was estimated using reliability analysis and Cronbach's α (alpha) statistic.

PART 4

Improving Canadian Policy Work

15 Targeted Supply-Side Policy Capacity Dynamics: High-Calibre Policy Worker Recruitment in Canada

JONATHAN CRAFT AND SIOBHAN HARTY

Introduction

Recruitment and retention continue to be strong components of the Canadian federal public-sector management-reform agenda (Privy Council Office 2006; Lindquist and Paquet 2000; Tellier 1990). Demographic, fiscal, and social imperatives, along with securing sufficient levels of public sector policy capacity[1] continue to be driving forces behind high-profile initiatives such as PS 2000 (1989–93), La Relève (1997–8), Public Service Renewal (2006–11), and the Blueprint 2020 (2013). In response to different internal and external drivers of change, several clerks of the Privy Council[2] have focused on public service renewal to ensure there is requisite policy capacity within the federal public service. Reform efforts have been operationalized through far-ranging plans, strategies, and initiatives to address perceived capacity shortages and other human resources and organizational needs[3] (Aucoin and Bakvis 2005; Bakvis 2000; Lindquist and Desveaux 2007; Peters 1996). Despite such efforts, empirical evidence suggests shortages and uneven policy capacity within the federal government (Howlett and Wellstead 2012; Wellstead, Stedman, and Lindquist 2009; Wellstead, Stedman, and Howlett 2011; Wellstead and Stedman 2010). However, there has been no study of the policy workers recruited expressly to mitigate such shortages. Through a case study of the government of Canada's Recruitment of Policy Leaders (RPL) program, this chapter provides new insight and evidence on the effectiveness of a targeted supply-side policy analytical capacity measure.

It proceeds in four parts, beginning with a concise review of the salient literature on policy capacity. This is bounded by a focus on targeted supply-side recruitment dimensions with other conceptual, organizational, and supply-and-demand considerations addressed by others in this volume. The second section contextualizes the development and evolution of RPL as a targeted recruitment initiative through a brief review of previous and contemporary government of Canada renewal campaigns. In the third section, RPL's utility and effectiveness are evaluated on the basis of three hypotheses. The hypotheses are tested against new and existing data provided by the RPL program leadership and the Public Service Commission of Canada (PSC). We conclude by summarizing our main findings, highlighting in what ways the RPL program has met the federal public service's policy capacity needs, and suggesting some additional gaps it could fill. RPL's effectiveness as a targeted supply-side recruitment instrument was confirmed. The program attracts and places high-calibre policy workers in mid-level to senior policy roles. Recruits were found to contribute to fostering policy analytical capacity (PAC) on several of the dimensions identified in the literature and serve as a unique measure to mitigate potential "mid-level" PAC supply shortages.

Elite Policy Worker Recruitment and Policy Analytical Capacity Supply-Side Dynamics

As detailed in the introduction to this volume and emphasized in ensuing chapters, policy work requires "policy capacity." Approaches and metrics have differed considerably in how that concept has been operationalized, with some focusing on "organizational capacity" (Tiernan 2011), others on intergovernmental policy capacity (Inwood, Johns, and O'Reilly 2011), and still others on the micro-level supply of "policy analytic" skills and abilities of policy analysts (Howlett 2009a). Despite theoretical and methodological diversity, a shared "discourse of declining policy capacity" has emerged. Canadian and international evidence points to a troubling erosion of public sector policy capacity (Tiernan and Wanna 2006; Painter and Pierre 2005c; Howlett and Wellstead 2012). Recruitment programs such as RPL, the only one of its kind in Canada, are crucial for meeting the challenges of policy-capacity deficiencies through expedited recruitment of high-calibre policy workers.

Contemporary Canadian analysis has added to the empirical focus of capacity studies through a focus on the narrower "policy analytical capacity" of government. That is, its ability to produce valuable, policy-relevant research and analysis on topics of its choosing (Howlett 2009a;

Tiernan 2011). As per table 15.1, the constitutive dimensions of PAC can be grouped into three broad categories: organizational structure/culture, research supply, and research demand (Howlett and Oliphant 2010; Fellegi 1996). These components of PAC are often conceived of in "production function" model terms, whereby the quality of policy advice provided depends on a matching of the "supply" and "demand" for policy analysis. Effective policy organizations are those that have the capacity to anticipate likely policy demands.

The first category groups together organizational and cultural factors required for high levels of PAC. These are often arrayed by the organization's openness to receiving policy advice, its risk tolerance and ability to foster innovative policy thinking, and the organizational capacity to perform policy research and analysis (Riddell 1998; Fellegi 1996).

Demand-side factors have also figured prominently in conceptual and empirical studies of PAC. The "discourse on policy-capacity decline" is in part a manifestation of widespread agreement that many demand-side dynamics have shifted. For one, Canadian political decision-makers are argued to have become less deferential to public service policy analysis, seeking greater political control over policy development (Savoie 2003a; Prince 2007). While this contention is not shared universally, there is widespread evidence that decision-makers can now draw from greater diversity of non-public-service supply (Dobuzinskis, Howlett, and Laycock 2007; Howlett 2013; Atkinson et al. 2013). In addition, the emergence of "wicked" problems and ongoing public sector reforms have led some to call into question the ability of the public service to address complex and boundary spanning policy challenges in a context where vertical authorities continue to prevail (Savoie 2003). Further, as Fellegi (1996) and Anderson (1996), among others have noted, public sector mangers themselves impact demand considerations depending on their propensities to encourage the generation of robust policy inputs from their staffs.

Finally there is a supply-side component. A requisite level of personnel with the appropriate analytic skill levels and training are fundamental to PAC (Riddell 2007). The ontology of policy analytical capacity constitutes several dimensions that refer to various skills and knowledge forms. From a PAC supply side, these involve the educational background of policy workers and their formal training. That is, their ability to do applied research, modelling policy analysis/evaluation, statistical methods, and trends and analysis and/or forecasting as in relation to the future state of the economy or of public opinion (Howlett

Table 15.1 Policy Analytical Capacity Components

PAC category	PAC factor
Organizational culture and structure	Organizational culture of openness and risk tolerance
	Promotion of innovative thinking in organization
Research demand	Market for research produced
	Rigorous research (withstands professional challenge)
Analytical supply	Educational background of employees of organization
	Organizational analytical resource integration ability
	Availability of quality data

Source: Craft and Howlett (2013b).

2009a; Wellstead, Stedman, and Howlett 2011). Here too studies have identified public sector managers as important, suggesting that they too must possess skills and qualifications akin to but beyond those of policy analysts (Peters 1996). Many of the above are related to another supply side factor, the organization's ability to combine the use of different styles or techniques of analysis (Fellegi 1996, 14–15). A final supply-side PAC determinant is the quality and quantity of the data produced by an agency. That is, that timely and appropriate data on any given subject under consideration are essential to enhancing the quality of the policy analysis that can be provided.

Addressing "Supply Side" Policy Analytic Capacity Dynamics through Targeted Recruitment: Recruitment of Policy Leaders Program

Many of the issues that motivated deputy ministers to launch the Recruitment of Policy Leaders program are the same as those who drove the Public Service Renewal agenda launched by the former clerk of the Privy Council, Kevin Lynch, and continued until 2011 by Clerk Wayne Wouters. When Lynch launched PSR, he framed the issue in the context of demographic change in Canada: "The Public Service is in a process of renewal as its workforce ages and new public servants join the ranks. For this reason, more than ever before, now is an ideal time to improve our approaches to the recruitment, development and management of our people" (Privy Council Office 2006, 4). Compared to earlier attempts at renewal, the urgency of the initiative he launched, according to Lynch, was due to the immediate demographic pressures associated with the aging of the public service (see table 15.2).

In November 2006, the importance of renewal was driven home by the appointment of an Advisory Committee on the Public Service that was mandated to advise the prime minister and the clerk of the Privy Council on a range of policy, program, and regulatory issues to promote public service renewal. The committee has so far delivered several annual reports to the prime minister that provide timely advice on key management issues such as recruitment, human resource governance and accountability, performance management, policy capacity, innovation and risk, the employment model, and technology.

The first report of the Prime Minister's Advisory Committee was upfront about the very real challenge of branding the public service in order to attract recruits, contending that "there is a need for a strong and positive Public Service 'brand' that will support the marketing of the Public Service as an attractive employment option for talented Canadians" (Canada 2007, 8). According to the management literature, today's knowledge workers will change jobs more frequently than the baby boom generation and will be less motivated by the promise of "jobs for life." The idea that a pension plan will be a big enough "pull" for newer policy workers is not strongly supported by research evidence on their effort-reward calculus in other public sector fields (Kowske, Rasch, and Wiley 2010; Lavoie-Tremblay et al. 2010; Barford and Hester 2011; Sparks 2012).

The context then, for launching the Recruitment of Policy Leaders initiative in 2000 remains relevant. It was introduced as a pilot program run out of the Privy Council Office[4] to address head-on the challenge of renewing the public service's policy capacity in the context of an aging population, the transition to a knowledge economy, and the global employment opportunities for Canadians with advanced degrees. The auditor general of Canada, in her 2000 Report to Parliament, had noted, "In light of the increased competition for university graduates, the public sector need[s] to be a more aggressive recruiter of graduates" (Canada 2000, 21–5).

The RPL program emerged against the backdrop of increasing concerns among policymakers about Canada's ability to attract and retain

Table 15.2 Distribution of Federal Public Service (FPS) Employees by Age: Select Years, 1983–2012

Age category	Age	1983	1988	1993	1998	2003	2012
< 25	Under 17	351	45	12	4	31	9
	17–18	916	248	77	106	160	121
	19–20	4,373	1,618	1,209	1,054	1,165	1,389
	21–2	8,610	3,722	3,402	2,212	3,396	3,273
	23–4	12,235	7,414	5,686	2,903	5,302	4,979
25–34	25–6	14,779	10,837	8,253	4,188	7,336	7,650
	27–8	16,586	13,483	10,915	5,590	8,443	9,867
	29–30	17,305	15,344	13,131	6,865	8,652	11,091
	31–2	17,783	16,929	14,968	8,689	9,415	12,552
	33–4	17,139	18,102	16,491	10,836	10,053	13,343
35–44	35–6	16,746	18,630	17,928	12,513	10,771	14,235
	37–8	12,488	18,463	19,039	14,467	12,935	14,113
	39–40	11,669	18,082	19,530	15,674	14,910	14,328
	41–2	10,552	15,457	19,453	16,652	16,287	14,943
	43–4	9,478	12,233	18,428	17,168	17,607	14,854
45–54	45–6	9,188	11,605	18,071	17,212	18,032	16,019
	47–8	9,113	9,998	13,036	16,696	18,327	18,339
	49–50	9,218	9,572	12,033	15,522	18,187	18,758
	51–2	9,468	8,963	10,330	11,020	17,268	19,241
	53–4	8,741	8,303	8,492	7,832	15,407	18,686
55–64	55–6	8,197	7,524	6,778	6,168	11,589	14,867
	57–8	8,251	6,568	5,317	4,260	6,751	12,204
	59–60	7,354	5,265	4,026	2,684	4,743	8,874
	61–2	5,992	3,765	2,665	1,538	2,694	5,837
	63–4	3,700	2,964	1,678	1,077	1,580	4,069
65+	65–6	375	924	800	534	737	2,100
	67–8	119	266	390	301	406	1,057
	69+	156	207	428	366	553	1,294
Total		250,882	246,531	252,566	204,131	242,737	278,092

Source: Treasury Board Secretariat (2012).

Note: Includes all employment tenures and active employees only (i.e., employees on leave without pay are excluded). The information provided is based on 31 March data. Historical numbers were revised to reflect the entire FPS population.

highly skilled knowledge workers. The pilot project, known initially as "Recruitment of Outstanding Canadians," targeted Canadian graduate students at top-ranked foreign universities (Oxford, Cambridge, Harvard, etc.) and, using high-profile recruitment teams composed of deputy minister "champions," interviewed potential candidates for a career in the public service. Candidates had an initial interview at their university and, if they met broad-based merit criteria, were placed in a pre-screened inventory. The second stage of the recruitment initiative consisted in a series of interviews in Ottawa with deputy ministers or assistant deputy ministers, organized by past recruits. If successful, candidates were typically appointed to senior-level positions as policy analysts. This was the first time since the 1960s that the federal government had actively recruited Canadian graduate students with international scholarships, such as Rhodes and Commonwealth Scholars.

Between fiscal years (FY) 2000–1 and 2003–4, seventy-five candidates were placed in a range of federal departments and agencies. In 2004, after the initial success of the pilot in recruiting and retaining highly qualified Canadians, a committee of deputy ministers approved a proposal for the development of a formal targeted recruitment plan that would be extended to Canadians based at Canadian universities (Public Service Commission of Canada 2008, appendix A, 1). Administration of the program was moved to the Public Service Commission,[5] although deputies continued to serve as champions, and past recruits continued to play a central role as volunteers who screened candidates and served as "sherpas" through the interview process. The formalization of the program was meant to embed the program within the Public Service Commission's "merit principle" for hiring, while giving it the profile and stability it needed to meet its objectives. The RPL strategy was, however, officially positioned as a tool by which the government could address the supply-side considerations of policy capacity erosion as well as a tangible example of "renewal" or capacity building. Indeed, the PSC's "Record of Decision" on the matter states that an intent of the RPL was "to attract high caliber individuals to policy-oriented Federal Public Service middle to senior-level positions," as "there is an insufficient number of employees of this caliber within the Public Service to satisfy requirements"[6] (8).

Approximately 1000–1500 Canadians apply annually through an online system. RPL alumni working in the federal government screen the applications using criteria developed jointly with the Public Service Commission.[7] Typically, 200–300 candidates are invited annually to a structured interview that is conducted by a senior official – deputy minister or assistant deputy minister – and a past recruit. The Public Service Commission, through consultation with appropriate stakeholders, develops the interview questions. Depending on the interview results, 50–60 candidates can expect to be invited to Ottawa for interviews with either deputy ministers or assistant deputy ministers. Of these, approximately 20–30 candidates are placed annually via a "partially assessed pool" established by the Public Service Commission (see table 15.3).[8]

On the basis of the literature on policy analytical capacity and the explicit intention of the RPL program as a targeted recruitment strategy to increase the supply of PAC, some hypotheses can be set out. First, it can be hypothesized that the program results in "immediate" PAC supply-side gains, as its recruits come "ready made" with advanced degrees and previous policy-relevant employment experience (H1). Second, RPL's targeted nature and program flexibility result in supply-side PAC efficiency gains (H2). That is, because of the unique nature of the program's recruitment design, RPL will result in quicker PAC supply gains as the program features shorter placement timeframes than traditional general recruitment mechanisms. Third, RPL offers a unique temporal supply-side PAC advantage in that its recruits will provide a supply-side benefit of increasing "mid to senior" level PAC (H3). Together these hypotheses allow for testing on the overall PAC supply gains that RPL delivers, its benefits as a targeted recruitment mechanism, and its ability to quickly address the stated public services PAC shortages.

Data and Analysis

Three data sets were used to test these hypotheses. The first was developed as part of the Public Service Commission's 2008 evaluation of the RPL program (Public Service Commission, 2008). The data were gathered from an online survey that targeted twelve populations involved in the RPL program.[9] In total, 2014 surveys were sent out and 461 responses were received for a response rate of 23 per cent. For the purposes of this research, the results for the following four populations are used: unsuccessful applicants – no interview; unsuccessful applicants – failed interview; successful applicants – accepted offer, still in the federal public service; and non-RPL policy analysts. The second data set, developed in 2008–9, focuses on the career trajectories of RPL candidates in placement and was collected by RPL candidates in placement

Table 15.3 Recruitment of Policy Leaders by Campaigns (2005–6 to 2013–14)

Fiscal year	Number of campaigns	Number of applicants	Number of qualified candidates	Number of appointments
2005–6	2	2084	95	66
2006–7	1	1005	51	29
2007–8	1	996	60	32
2008–9	1	1485	48*	26
2009–10	1	1715	58	19
2010–11	1	–	44	30
2011–12	1	1401	43	18
2012–13	1	1200	31	7
2013–14	1	–	28	7

Source: Compiled from Public Service Commission of Canada, annual reports.

using a survey. In total, 187 surveys were sent out and 88 responses were received for a response rate of 47 per cent. The survey asked respondents to provide the tenure in months of the different positions held in the public service, the rank, and the department or agency. The third data set is an RPL-based survey of its own recruits conducted in 2012. The survey was distributed to just over 200 RPL recruits with 115 usable responses, for a response rate of approximately 50 per cent. While the 2012 survey included several questions similar to those in the 2008 survey, it was not a direct replication.

> H1: RPL serves as a means to increase policy capacity through targeted supply-side recruitment of high-calibre policy workers.

The 2008 data collected as part of the RPL program review reveal that successful RPL candidates currently in placement were more likely than unsuccessful candidates to indicate that they would have either "probably not" or "definitely not" applied to the public service if RPL had not existed (49 per cent). This group can be compared to successful applicants who were offered a job and turned it down. They were the least likely group to apply to the public service if RPL had not existed (60 per cent). It is possible that these candidates were also trying out their different career options but were, in the end, not very committed to the public service. By contrast, unsuccessful applicants were less likely to indicate that they would not have applied to the public service if RPL had not existed (13 per cent and 27 per cent, depending on the category). On a basic level, H1 is confirmed, given that RPL contributes to PAC supply-side gains as it incentivizes high-calibre recruits to join the ranks of the public service.

The 2008 review of RPL also included explicit survey questions to gauge the impact of the program recruits on policy-capacity supply. RPL was found to have a positive contribution on enhancing the public service's policy capacity. The 2008 program review noted that 46 per cent of human resources managers and directors, hiring managers, departmental liaisons, deputy ministers and other senior officials, as well as non-RPL policy analysts agreed that the RPL recruits have made a positive contribution to policy development and analysis within their policy group or branch. In more general terms, the RPL's ability to attract and successfully recruit high-calibre employees was identified as the greatest strength of the program. As the report succinctly concludes, "The most notable testimony to the success of the RPL Program is that its clients, i.e., senior government managers and policy groups within the federal departments and agencies, believe that the RPL Program is a very successful mechanism for recruiting highly-qualified policy specialists. The Program attracts highly-qualified individuals, and many clients of the program see the program as an efficient mechanism for recruiting mid-to-senior level talent" (Public Service Commission 2008, 40).

On a micro-level, a subsequent 2012 survey conducted by RPL of its recruits provides new data that confirm two important PAC determinants. The first is the high educational attainment of RPL candidates. As per table 15.4, the majority of RPL respondents have a master's degree, while nearly one-third hold a doctorate.

As per table 15.5, the most recent survey also demonstrates that applicants are being hired primarily into policy-related positions. Given the nature of the recruitment program, this is not surprising, but it confirms also that their initial placements are at mid-to-senior policy levels.[10] These findings demonstrate RPL's success in attracting and placing candidates in mid-level policy positions. This is important not only for the immediate PAC supply-side gains this produces, but also, as will be explored below, has temporal implications for the longer-term PAC supply benefits it confers.

Table 15.4 Educational Attainment of RPL Recruits, 2012

	Number	% of total
Master's	55	47.8
Law degree	7	6.1
Doctorate	36	31.3
Post-doctorate	17	14.8
Total	115	100.0

Source: Survey of RPL conducted by the Program Leadership Team (2012).

Table 15.5 Initial Placement of RPL Candidates, 2012 Survey Findings

Group and level	Number	% of total
EC 04	5	4.3
EC 05	39	33.9
EC 06	28	24.3
EC 07	2	1.7
ES 04	15	13.0
ES05	5	4.3
ES 06	3	2.6
PM 05	3	2.6
PM 06	4	3.5
LA 02	1	0.9
CO 01	1	0.9
CO 02	1	0.9
Missing	8	7.0
Total	115	100.0

Source: RPL leadership team internal survey (2012).

Available statistics for the years 2005–9 detailed in table 15.6 point to similar long-term trends, confirming that during that period the majority of successful recruits were placed in policy positions at the

Table 15.6 Initial Placement by Group and Level, 2005–2009

Group and level	2005	2006	2007	2008	2009
AS-03	–	–	1		–
AS-06	1	–	–		–
BAA	–	–	1	1	–
BI-03	–	1	–	–	–
BI-04	–	–	–	–	1
CO-02	2	–	1	–	–
CS-03	1	–	–	–	–
EC-04	–	–	–	–	–
EC-05	–	–	3	10	12
EC-06	–	–	2	8	7
EC-07	–	–	1	1	1
ES-04	29	13	8	–	–
ES-05	24	9	9	–	–
ES-06	2	5	4	–	–
ES-07	2	–	–	–	–
EN-ENG-05	1	–	1	–	–
LA-01	2	–	2	–	1
LA-02	1	1	–	–	–
PC-03	1	3	–	–	–
PM-04	1	1	–	–	–
PM-05	2	1	–	2	–
PM-06	1	–	–	–	–
SE-RES-02	–	1	–	–	–

Source: RPL leadership team internal statistics.

mid-level. Changes to the employment classifications over that period precludes literal comparisons but suggests similar findings.

H2: RPL's targeted nature and program flexibility result in supply-side PAC efficiency gains.

A second key purported benefit of RPL for PAC supply is the benefits it confers through the program's flexible recruitment process. As detailed above, RPL's recruitment campaigns are unique and differ markedly from the traditional general recruitment processes of the government of Canada. Interviews conducted for the 2008 assessment of RPL reported that respondents (applicants and senior executives) characterized the program's nimble nature as a clear strength in that it facilitates quick "manoeuvring" by the government of Canada (Public Service Commission 2008, 39).

Evaluating and comparing the placement period for each campaign or against other benchmarks can be a challenge. There are no clear comparative processes or programs, given RPL's multi-department, external, targeted recruitment design. The 2008 review of the RPL program found that RPL was indeed a faster recruitment process, thus producing temporal supply-side PAC benefits. The review noted that until 2008, the time required for RPL staffing averaged 37.2 weeks, as compared to 2006 statistics for similar large hiring staffing processes found to take, on average, 38.5 weeks (Public Service Commission 2008, 40). The 2012 survey of RPL policy workers returned results identical to their 2008 levels. Respondents (successful candidates from various campaigns) indicated that it took, on average, 37.2 weeks for them to receive their formal letter of offer from the government of Canada. The temporal benefit recorded in 2008 had, however, disappeared by 2011, with RPL processes now significantly longer than general recruitment. The staffing time for public advertised staff collective indeterminate advertised appointments was 21.8 weeks in 2011 (Public Service Commission 2012, 30). One contributing factor may be the flexibility of the recruitment processes. As noted in the 2008 report, successful RPL candidates are initially placed in the partially assessed pool with candidates working in conjunction with the PSC to determine the timing of their entry into government. Often, candidates could be completing an advanced degree, a work assignment, or a family transition back to Canada from an international location. Thus, there is the potential for "candidate-induced delay" that is simply not a factor in the traditional recruitment and staffing processes. Further, a reduced number of vacancies at the mid to senior policy levels tied to overarching expenditure management and budgetary austerity may be another contributing factor. This is reflected in the lower rate of appointment in 2011–12, when there was a 40 per cent decrease, compared to appointments made in 2010–11.

H3: RPL provides unique temporal supply-side PAC benefits as recruits advance to senior levels.

When asked about their aspirations, successful RPL applicants in the federal public service were in complete agreement (71 per cent) that they would like to occupy a more senior level position. By comparison, only 53 per cent of non-RPL analysts completely agreed with this statement. Taking into account the percentages of candidates who "completely" and "mostly" agreed with the statement, the results for the two groups were very similar: 89 per cent for RPL candidates and 87 per cent for non-RPL analysts. Table 15.7 presents data on the number of promotional and lateral/downward moves per fiscal year made by RPL candidates in placements and all other indeterminate (permanent) staff. Most RPL candidates are placed in the "scientific and professional" classification group in the National Capital Region (Ottawa and environs); those RPL candidates in other classification groups (lawyers or doctors) are omitted from the table. A control group of all other indeterminate staff in the scientific and professional group in the National Capital Region is used. Looking at the totals for the years presented, the data show that the average percentage of promotions and lateral moves is quite similar across the two groups: when RPL candidates decided to make a move, it was more likely to be promotional (54 per cent) than lateral (46 per cent). Non-RPL candidates made a promotional move in 52 per cent of cases and a lateral one in 48 per cent of cases. Looking more closely at given fiscal years, there is clearly variance across the two groups.

For fiscal years 2003–4, 2004–5, and 2005–6, RPL recruits in placement were more likely to make a promotional move than non-RPL policy analysts. However, this wasn't the case for more recent recruits (2006–7, 2007–8). Table 15.7 presents further data on the career trajectory of RPL recruits in placement that captures whether they took a ladder (promotional opportunity) or a bridge (lateral move) in the same or a different organization. The data are by cohort and represent the nature of the move from their first to their second placement only. As the data show, when RPL recruits in placements decided to make their first move, it was more likely a promotional (55 per cent) than a lateral (45 per cent) one. But whatever move they decided to make, it was more likely to be within the same organization, as opposed to moving to a new organization. In 65 per cent of the cases, a climb up the ladder to their second placement was in the same organization. Similarly, as per table 15.8, in 60 per cent of cases, when they stepped onto a bridge, it was within the same organization.

Table 15.7 Ladders or Bridges: RPL and Non-RPL Scientific and Professional Group, National Capital Region, 2003–4 to 2008–9

Year	Recruitment of Policy Leaders candidates				All other indeterminate staff			
	Promotions		Lateral and downward movements		Promotions		Lateral and downward movements	
	Number	%	Number	%	Number	%	Number	%
2001–2	1	50	1	50	–	–	–	–
2002–3	4	67	2	33	–	–	–	–
2003–4	5	63	3	37	1835	53	1630	47
2004–5	13	65	7	35	1723	50	1708	50
2005–6	9	60	6	40	1854	49	1915	51
2006–7	12	41	17	59	2013	49	2132	51
2007–8	1	33	2	66	2848	55	2305	45
2008–9	–	–	–	–	3057	55	2525	45
Total	45	54	38	46	13300	52	12215	48

Sources: RPL Survey (2008); Public Service Commission of Canada, annual reports.

There is thus strong evidence to support Hypothesis 3: RPL recruits add to temporal PAC as they seek out and often succeed in promotions to senior levels. That these policy workers make vertical progression often within the same department supports an unexpected but added dimension of PAC. That is, recruits who advance are more likely to climb a ladder and remain in the *same* department, contributing to the institutionalization of PAC within organizations. This is a potentially interesting finding, given the high degree of mobility or "churn" among senior officials, particularly deputy ministers (Bourgault and Dunn 2013).

The 2012 RPL survey found that a bare majority of respondents (51 per cent) had worked in only one department. While additional data are required to confirm the prevalence and durability of such a pattern, this temporal dimension of RPL PAC supply-side gains draws further attention to the importance of their initial placements. If the majority of placed RPL candidates remain in the same department but their self-selection bias results in an uneven pattern of their distribution, PAC gains are likely to be unevenly distributed at both mid to senior levels.

Table 15.8 Ladders or Bridges: Career Pathways of RPL Recruits in Placement (from First to Second Placement) (%)

Career path	2001–2	2002–3	2003–4	2004–5	2005–6	2006–7	2007–8	Total
Ladder	83	50	57	62	64	86	100	55
In same organization	60	75	100	50	67	0	100	65
In different organization	40	25	0	50	33	100	0	35
Bridge	17	50	43	38	36	14	0	45
In same organization	100	75	67	60	80	83	0	60
In different organization	0	25	33	40	20	17	0	40

Source: RPL Survey (2008).

The Public Service Commission has also reported on the top departmental users of RPL (although these data are not available for every year). In 2008–9, four federal departments made the greatest use of the RPL program: Foreign Affairs and International Trade Canada, Heritage Canada, the Canadian International Development Agency, and Environment Canada. In 2009–10, the top five users of the RPL program were Environment Canada, the Canadian International Development Agency, Industry Canada, Agriculture and Agri-Food Canada, and Canadian Heritage. In 2010–11 (the latest year for which the Public Service Commission has provided these data), the top four users of the RPL program were Environment Canada, Human Resources and Skills Development Canada, Industry Canada, and the Public Health Agency of Canada. A review of the 2012 survey data reveals a dramatically uneven pattern of placements, with the vast majority of respondents identifying three departments – Foreign Affairs, Environment Canada, and Human Resources and Skills Development Canada – as their first placements as per table 15.9.

Should such a pattern hold over time, the results could suggest a continued uneven pattern of PAC gains at both mid and senior levels. However, some departments, including central agencies, have their own recruitment programs. As well, programs such as the Accelerated Economic Training Program, which recruit high-quality postgraduates

Table 15.9 Location of RPL Candidate Placements

Department	Number	% of total
AANDC	3	2.6
Agriculture	3	2.6
CBSA	1	0.9
CSPS	1	0.9
Heritage	8	7.0
CIDA	7	6.1
CRTC	2	1.7
CIC	9	7.8
Environment	13	11.3
Finance	3	2.6
DFO	3	2.6
DFAIT	19	16.5
Health	5	4.3
HRSDC	9	7.8
Industry	4	3.5
Infrastructure Canada	3	2.6
Justice	2	1.7
Library of Parliament	1	0.9
NRCan	5	4.3
PCO	1	0.9
PHAC	5	4.3
Public Safety	6	5.2
Transport Canada	1	0.9
Treasury Board	1	0.9
Total	115	100.0

Source: 2012 RPL leadership team internal survey.

from Canadian universities, are well established within the federal government and might be the program of choice in many departments and agencies. More research would be required to determine the effects for PAC of having an unequal distribution of RPL recruits across federal institutions. A final point of the distribution of PAC supply brought into the public service through RPL relates to its geographic distribution. A review of available PSC data suggests that all recruits have initially been placed in the National Capital Region. This is likely the product of the greater amount of mid- to senior-level policy work that is conducted in the NCR, but compounds the uneven or "lumpy" distribution of policy capacity within government (Howlett and Wellstead 2012; Voyer 2007). The issue of supply-and-demand congruence of RPL policy recruits was noted in the 2008 review of the program. The report recommended that "the RPL Program should include a planning capacity function, which would produce a rolling multi-year forecast of the number of policy analysts across the federal government. This would help the RPL Program to identify the number of policy analysts that need to be recruited during each recruitment campaign. This would address a criticism held by some stakeholders that the current RPL Program is supply, rather than demand driven" (Public Service Commission 2008, 4). Given the more general pattern of findings that has emerged from careful and large-scale empirical analysis of Canadian policy workers, RPL as currently designed and operated is unable to address non-NCR PAC supply shortages, despite the prevalence of acute regional deficiencies (Wellstead, Stedman, and Lindquist 2009). However, changes to a demand-driven RPL model may negatively affect the unique supply-side nature of the program design.

Conclusion

The erosion of policy capacity in the federal public service has received considerable attention. Yet little analysis has been undertaken of the measures the government of Canada has implemented to address PAC shortages. RPL, as an explicit mechanism designed to recruit high-calibre policy workers is, as a targeted supply-side measure, successful in meeting its own program objectives and unique in its ability to address PAC shortages. It is unique in that it places recruits in mid-to-senior policy positions, fostering immediate PAC supply gains and facilitating potential long-term PAC gains at senior levels through faster promotion of policy workers. The data reveal that RPL recruits in placement are more likely to take ladders in the same organization than bridges across organizations. This suggests potential additional temporal or long-term PAC gains from policy workers remaining in departments and fostering "institutional memory."

Some limits regarding the program's ability to meet supply-side policy analytical capacity dynamics were also clear. First, a lack of established annual recruitment targets and reliance on the availability of mid- to senior-level employment vacancies make RPL particularly susceptible to public service expenditure management. This seems to have been the case in the most recent expenditure management period of 2008–14, which saw dramatic reductions in RPL appointments. Second, the data reveal a pattern of placement and geographic distribution resulting in uneven patterns of PAC supply gains. Unsurprisingly, RPL's program design results in placements almost exclusively in the National Capital Region. This focuses any PAC capacity gains in Ottawa, further contributing to a "lumpy" distribution of Canadian PAC supply (Howlett and Wellstead 2012; Voyer 2007). A subsidiary finding, based on 2012 survey results, is that certain departments are overrepresented in the placement of candidates. Additional data are required to determine if this is representative of the entire RPL population and a long-term trend. If so, it suggests that the discretion provided to successful candidates in self-selecting preferred departments of employment may incentivize applications, but may also produce in uneven distribution of PAC supply-side gains.

Greater in-depth survey work of RPL recruits and others hired to mitigate supply-side PAC shortages is required. A growing body of empirical evidence has been collected to analyse the policy work of federal and provincial public service workers in Canada, but have yet to be replicated among the RPL community. This next step is essential for the comparison of analytical techniques and policy work practices of such recruits against the broader public service population.

NOTES

1 Several competing definitions of policy capacity have been advanced (see Christensen and Gazley 2008; Parsons 2004; Riddell 2008). From the Canadian context, Fellegi (1996) conceptualized policy capacity as "a loose concept which covers the whole gamut of issues associated with the government's arrangements to review, formulate and implement policies within its jurisdiction. It obviously includes the nature and quality of the resources available for these purposes – whether in the public service or beyond – and the practices and procedures by which these resources are

mobilized and used." Others, however, are more concerned with the ability of the state to respond to change, the intellectual and organizational resources of the state (Cummings and Nørgaard 2004), the management of knowledge and organizational learning (Parsons 2004), or effective policy formulation (Goetz and Wollmann 2001). Regardless of their specific orientations, observers generally agree that policy capacity is important and a significant determinant and indicator of a high-performing government (see, for example, Aucoin and Bakvis 2005; O'Connor, Roos, and Vickers-Willis 2007; Painter and Pierre 2005c; Weber and Khademian 2008).

2 The clerk of the Privy Council is the head of the Canadian federal public service, deputy minister to the prime minister, and secretary to the Cabinet. The clerk is a non-partisan public servant.

3 Many of the recent renewal agendas have focused on a range of human resource needs in the government as well as the legislation, policies, and systems to recruit, manage, and retain these resources effectively, such as pride and recognition, values and ethics, compensation, technology in the workplace, etc.

4 The Privy Council Office is the prime minister's department. It serves an advisory function and manages the Cabinet system. It is staffed by non-partisan public servants.

5 The Public Service Commission of Canada (PSC) is an independent agency responsible for safeguarding the values of a professional Public Service: competence, non-partisanship, and representativeness.

6 Public Service of Canada, Record of Decision 04-12-MPA-158; 2004 (includes Briefing Note).

7 Selection criteria include master's degree (or higher) or a professional degree; a major scholarship (university-level, national or international); policy-relevant experience acquired through education or work; and extracurricular leadership development.

8 A partially assessed pool is a list of candidates who have been assessed for some merit criteria, but who require further assessment (e.g., for official languages proficiency or security clearance) prior to being eligible for appointment. This allows tailoring to specific requirements in order to ensure the right fit.

9 These are: Population 1: unsuccessful applicants, no first interview; Population 2: unsuccessful applicants (interviewed); Population 3: successful applicants (no offer/withdrew); Population 4: successful applicants (accepted offer, still in federal public service); Population 5: successful applicants (accepted offer, no longer in federal public service);

Population 6: educational institution representatives; Population 7: employers/potential employers (HR managers/directors); Population 8: employers/potential employers (directors/hiring managers); Population 9: non-RPL policy analysts; Population 10: sherpas; Population 11: departmental liaisons; and Population 12: stewardship and advisory stakeholders (deputy ministers, assistant deputy ministers).

10 The Economics and Social Science Services Group (EC) is an employment classification that, as Treasury Board Secretariat defines it, "comprises positions that are primarily involved in the conduct of surveys, studies and projects in the social sciences; the identification, description and organization of archival, library, museum and gallery materials; the editing of legislation or the provision of advice on legal problems in specific fields; and the application of a comprehensive knowledge of economics, sociology or statistics to the conduct of economic, socio-economic and sociological research, studies, forecasts and surveys; the research, analysis and evaluation of the economic or sociological effects of departmental or interdepartmental projects, programs and policies; the development, application, analysis and evaluation of statistical and survey methods and systems; and the development, analysis and interpretation of qualitative and quantitative information and socio-economic policies and recommendations" (Treasury Board Secretariat N.d.). The scale for this group is from EC-1 to EC-8.

16 (Re)Scaling Policy Capacity between Government and the Voluntary Sector in Canada

KARINE LEVASSEUR

Introduction

The academic study of public policy, which Thomas Dye famously defines as "whatever governments choose to do or not do," is gaining momentum in Canada, despite its relatively young age (Howlett 2008, 2). Much of this study, not surprisingly, has centred on how governments have formulated, implemented, and evaluated policy solutions, given the privileged status of government representatives and institutions in the policy process (Lemieux 2000; Paquet 2009). Over the years, however, scholars and practitioners have called into question the capacity of governments in Canada to fulfil this policy function (see Canada 1996a; Peters 1996, 38; Savoie 2003, 1–2).

At a time when the policy capacity of governments in Canada may be declining, the introduction of new actors to the public policy process is also thought to occur. The literature contends there is a shift in governing, from a model that was led largely by "government" to one that is collaboratively led by a variety of "partners" such as government, charities, non-profit organizations, private businesses, and so forth (Osborne 2006; Rhodes 1996; Salamon 2002). Assessing the policy capacity of these new partners becomes an important implication under this form of collaborative governance.

Despite this resulting implication, much of the literature has focused on the policy capacity of government in Canada with comparatively little attention paid to the policy capacity of non-government actors, particularly voluntary sector organizations. Furthermore, much of the literature in this area tends to be somewhat aggregated and compartmentalized, to mean the literature either examines policy capacity in government *or* in the voluntary sector, with few opportunities to assess how these differentiated capacities intersect at various levels.

This chapter seeks to understand policy capacity in both government and the voluntary sector. It begins with a review of the policy capacity literature in both government and the voluntary sector. The chapter then provides an assessment of the literature and develops a framework to understand policy capacity in light of collaborative forms of governing. Beyond just incorporating non-governmental actors into the assessment of policy capacity, the proposed framework also situates policy capacity within a multi-scalar approach to highlight the importance of disaggregating the analysis of policy capacity. In short, this chapter contends that much can be learned from the study of policy capacity at a micro-level – or programmatic level – to include voluntary organizations and corresponding divisions/branches within government departments, and assess what this means for policy development in Canada.

Literature Review

Policy Capacity in Government

With disagreement in the literature about what constitutes policy capacity, conceptualizing this key term is no easy task. Bakvis (2000, 73) suggests that policy capacity includes the "intellectual dimension of governance that is the capacity of the system to think through the challenges it faces." Baskoy, Evans, and Shields (2011, 219) echo this conceptualization by carefully breaking down and analysing the term *policy capacity* into its basic components – *policy* and *capacity*. They conclude that "policy and capacity have one thing in common – that is, intellectual effort in governing." Painter and Pierre (2005c, 2–3) similarly define policy capacity as "the ability to marshal the necessary resources to make intelligent collective choices about and set strategic directions for the allocation of scarce resources to public ends." Despite the common thread running through these definitions related to the application of intelligence to public problems, policy capacity remains an imprecise concept. Some authors imply a broader meaning of policy capacity to include the various stages of the policy cycle, as evidenced by the work of Peters (1996, 11): "The idea of policy capacity of government is difficult to conceptualize. Does it include the implementation … or should it be concerned only with formulating clever and potentially effective policies? Also, does it include the political capacity of the system to respond to changing demands from interest groups and the mass public, or does it assume that government should be more autonomous ... In the broadest sense a concept of policy capacity would include all the above factors."

Others, still, seek to delineate or narrow the application of policy capacity to varying degrees. Painter and Pierre's (2005c, 2–3) conceptualization differentiates between three types of capacity: state, policy, and administrative. Administrative capacity involves the inputs (e.g., staffing levels) that generate the outputs of government activity, whereas state capacity involves the ability of the state to generate support or buy-in for policy decisions. Howlett's (2009a) framework limits the meaning of policy capacity, which he terms as "policy analytical capacity," to emphasize the research and analytical functions associated with the policy process. Williams (2012) takes Howlett's concept of "policy analytical capacity" and further pushes our thinking. For Williams, understanding policy capacity necessitates an understanding of the analytical capacity and the broader governing structures. Governance arrangements can include the institutional playing field upon which analytical capacity is deployed. So it may be entirely possible to have high levels of policy analytical capacity, but if the institutional design – federalism, for example – prohibits learning or the dissemination of policy ideas, then the overall policy capacity is low. Rayner (2012, 77) suggests that when governance arrangements allow for smooth coordination among a variety of actors, this may nurture policy analytical capacity by allowing actors to draw on the strengths of other actors. Conversely, when the governance arrangements are poorly coordinated, this may lead to missed opportunities to identify problems or key information.

Varying and overlapping reasons are cited within the literature to explain the possible decline in policy capacity in Canada. Some scholars cite the influence of New Public Management (NPM), with its emphasis on repositioning public servants away from the provision of policy advice towards the administration of policy decisions (Rasmussen 1999, 332; see also Peters 1996). Beyond this separation of policy and administration, however, Bakvis (2000, 71) contends that NPM's ideological underpinning for a smaller and leaner government may also contribute to a decline in policy capacity: "[NPM] practices have emphasized expenditure reduction and the streamlining of operations ... Essentially, most governments ... [in the 1990s] have lacked the financial wherewithal to launch activist, interventionist type policies. By implication, much of the infrastructure supporting activist government activities has atrophied, or at least this is what one would expect."

By association, fiscal constraints, notably Program Review, and globalization are also thought to have contributed to a loss in policy capacity (Rasmussen 1999; Peters 1996). Some scholars conclude there has been a decline in policy capacity in recent years. One such scholar is Peters (1996, 38), who suggests, "There is evidence that the capacity of government to make and implement policy has been diminishing over the past several years." However, Baskoy, Evans, and Shields (2011, 218) are quick to warn there is debate within the literature on whether policy capacity is on the decline. Their survey of deputy and assistant/associate deputy ministers across federal, provincial, and territorial jurisdictions reveals there is consensus that policy capacity has changed in recent years. A greater share of respondents report a decline in policy capacity, but this decline may be jurisdiction-specific, with federal and territorial officials reporting an improvement in their policy capacity, but not their provincial counterparts (224). Bakvis (2000, 84) also aptly illustrates this disagreement through his own work on the impact of Program Review on federal policy capacity. On the one hand, he suggests that the Department of Environment, which sustained a 25 per cent staff reduction under Program Review, experienced a significant decline in policy capacity. On the other hand, Transport Canada, which was also sizeably reduced under Program Review, particularly in its operations, reverted to focusing largely on policy and increased its share of policy capacity. Given his examination of policy capacity before and after Program Review, Bakvis (2000, 98) concludes that policy capacity is not determined solely by the "loss of resources, but of the way those resources were deployed or not deployed."

Given these concerns, public policy is gaining popularity both domestically and abroad, including the concept of policy capacity. On the domestic front, Pal (2010, 24) suggests there was a feeling coming out of the 1990s – a period of significant fiscal restraint in Canada – that merely "minding the store" under NPM practices was insufficient in light of the increasingly complex policy challenges to which government needed to respond. Painter and Pierre (2005c, 10) similarly contend, "In a dynamic external environment, possession of a strong policy capacity by the state is crucial to appropriate and swift responses." Wellstead and Stedman (2010, 906) summarize the need to rebuild policy capacity within government in three simple words: "averting policy failure," with logic following that the better the policy capacity, the better the analysis, advice, and cost-savings (Andersen 1996, 428). While more research into the policy capacity of government is needed – particularly how to build and deploy capacity, given the less than rosy financial position that governments in Canada find themselves today – this chapter contends that research is also needed into the policy capacity of new governance partners, notably the voluntary sector.[1]

Policy Capacity in the Voluntary Sector

The economic, social, and policy importance of the voluntary sector in Canada cannot be underestimated. It comprises approximately 165,000 non-profit organizations, of which roughly half are charities registered with Canada Revenue Agency (Canada, 2010).[2] It contributes 8.5 per cent of total GDP in Canada and employs over two million full-time equivalent workers (Hall et al. 2005, 7–9). In scope, this sector includes an array of organizations in arts, sports/recreation, environment, human rights, education (including universities), health (including hospitals), and social services, by way of example. Despite this diversity, voluntary sector organizations are generally thought to represent identities, provide opportunities for citizen engagement, deliver programs and services, and bring different perspectives to public policy development (Phillips 2000; Warren 2001).

The literature defines capacity in the voluntary sector rather broadly as the total resources – human, financial, skills/knowledge, technological, and other – needed to work towards and accomplish the goals of the organization (Panel on Accountability and Governance in the Voluntary Sector 1999; see also Carter 2011, 433–4). More specifically, policy capacity within this sector is defined broadly as the "ability to collaboratively generate and apply knowledge, networks, contacts and processes to ensure sound policy development in both the sector and the government, in a way that benefits the sector and the public" (Federal Government of Canada/Voluntary Sector Joint Initiative 1999, 33). Phillips (2007, 505) similarly contends that policy capacity includes "providing policy analysis and advice, participating effectively, and exerting influence in policy development." In short, to participate effectively in the public policy process, voluntary organizations require sufficient structural, intellectual, human, and funding resources.

The literature outlines several discernible issues and trends that have emerged in Canada that call into question the policy capacity of this sector. The first trend relates to the funding regime. In recent years, there has been a withdrawal of funding from various levels of government, coupled with an increasingly competitive fundraising environment in recessionary times that may translate into fewer resources available for policy work (Mulholland 2010; see also Canadian Council for International Cooperation 2006, 2–4). The *amount* of funding is not the sole area of concern for policy capacity. Rather, changes in the *type* of funding further exacerbate these resource constraints. The literature documents an important shift away from core funding to short-term project funding (Scott 2003). Core funding supports the overall operation and effectively provides discretion to the voluntary organization on how to use the funding to supports its goals and activities, including policy development. Comparatively, project funding, which usually involves a contract between government and a voluntary organization, generally provides funding only to support the delivery of specified deliverables. This shift in funding undermines the capacity of these organizations in two ways. First, this type of short-term funding makes it difficult for voluntary organizations to build the requisite infrastructure to strategize for the long term, which is essential for engagement in policy (Hall et al. 2003, 72). Second, contract funding requires resources to be deployed to support service delivery and rarely, if ever, policy work (Phillips 2007, 507; Levasseur 2014).

The second trend relates to the rise of evidence-based policy. Phillips (2007, 502) suggests this emerging trend is not merely a return to the rational model of policy decision-making, but may actually have more to do with pragmatism. She notes that increasingly "politics tends to be more pragmatically oriented rather than ideologically driven" (502). The resulting implication for voluntary organizations is the need to generate rigorous research with thorough analysis that produces vertically and horizontally consistent policy options. This emphasis on producing evidence comes at a potential cost, though. Laforest and Orsini (2005) caution that while this emphasis on evidence promotes greater standardization and professionalism among voluntary organizations, it also limits their creativity to produce and support other forms of policy involvement, namely advocacy and the representation of identity. They further warn that a reliance on evidence causes further divisions within the sector, whereby those voluntary organizations that produce acceptable evidence are afforded greater access to the state: "This recent trend establishes norms for policy dialogue that will facilitate the policy-making process and ultimately plays a significant role in shaping the terms of access, and in conferring legitimacy and credibility to the participants, for they outline the appropriate behavior and rules of engagement that guide the exchange. Grounding policy in an evidence base fulfills the federal government's obsession with accountability and results-based management" (484).

Further exacerbating this is the downloading of government services to voluntary organizations. Indeed, Laforest's (2001) analysis of the impacts of government downloading of services to the voluntary sector reveals that governments have also downloaded some of their policy functions beyond just research and analysis. She contends that voluntary organizations are no longer just advocating, but are now actively involved in "provid[ing] policy advice, research, [consultation, and mediation of policy]" (8). Given these trends towards evidence-based policy and downloading of policy functions, voluntary organizations are expected to enhance and expand the way they participate in policy development. This makes the study of policy capacity in the voluntary sector even more pressing.

The last issue is the regulation of non-partisan policy involvement by registered charities.[3] Charities in Canada must devote essentially all of their resources to charitable activities such that their advocacy[4] activities are "ancillary and incidental" (Income Tax Act, s. 149.1 (6.2)). The distinction between a "charitable activity" and an "advocacy activity" is important to note here. Charitable activities that involve education (e.g., educating Canadians about their human rights) or responding to government's request for information are not subject to this limitation. However, advocacy activities that attempt to persuade opinions or influence policy decisions are restricted. Even though charities are permitted a degree of advocacy,[5] charities may shy away from this role altogether. Some charities may prefer to concentrate on service delivery with no interest in advocacy, but other charities may not engage in advocacy because of this limitation. Working within what's dubbed the "advocacy chill" within the literature, they may be concerned that involvement in advocacy may trigger a review by Canada Revenue Agency, with the possibility of sanctions or deregistration of charitable status. Given the benefits that flow from having charitable status – including financial and legitimacy benefits (Levasseur 2008) – policy participation, and thus investments in policy capacity may be eroded in light of these concerns (Phillips 2007; Canadian Council for International Cooperation 2006, 2–4; Mulholland 2010, 141).

The advocacy debate is intensifying in light of the proposed Northern Gateway pipeline to connect Alberta's oilsands to the BC coast to support the export of crude. Concerns have been raised that the federal government targeted environmental charities that oppose the pipeline in light of the comments made by Prime Minister Stephen Harper that charities in receipt of foreign money are undermining the pipeline review (Paris 2012; McCarthy and Chase 2012; Mann 2012; Proussalidis 2012). The 2012 federal budget committed additional resources to the Canada Revenue Agency to tighten the monitoring of advocacy activities. This enhancement of oversight may have less to do with good governance and more to do with political motivation to temper opposition to the pipeline. As Orsini (2012) notes, "Perhaps more pernicious than this cynical, politically motivated attempt to punish 'radical' environmentalists, is that this policy change has the potential to ripple across the already fragile non-profit sector ... Stephen Harper's majority government has issued a stern warning to charities to quit doing advocacy, and behave more like charities, in the most paternalistic sense of that term."

These issues and trends would logically lead to the assumption that policy capacity is limited in the voluntary sector, but is it? Assessing the policy capacity of the voluntary sector is challenging, because the sector is inherently diverse in size, scope, and mandate. While concern has been raised about the weak policy capacity possessed by these actors, larger organizations at the provincial and national level are thought to possess more policy capacity than smaller, grass-roots organizations (Mulholland 2010, 141). However, there are notable differences, depending on the sub-sector involved. One survey concludes that some sub-sectors report greater difficulty in participating in the policy process, including universities and colleges (64 per cent), health (62 per cent), environment (56 per cent), and social services (54 per cent) (Canada, Statistics Canada 2004, 47). In the area of health, survey results reveal that health-based voluntary organizations have limited human resources capacity to engage in policy development (Voice in Health Policy 2003).

The primary concern here is that voluntary organizations may not have resources such as assigned staff to engage in policy development. Having assigned staff to policy development, coupled with an ability to generate research, are critical factors for policy success, according to Berry and Arons (2003). Phillips (2007) raises another equally plausible concern. Even when staff members are assigned this important function, few may actually have the requisite training and skill set in policy development:

> Policy staff tend to have come through the voluntary sector, moving from program delivery and administration to policy work, rather than coming to the sector with experience from government or the private sector. Unlike industry and business associations, government relations in voluntary organizations are not the next step for early retiring senior public servants or political refugees from ministerial offices following lost elections. This means that those responsible for government relations in the voluntary sector may have strong abilities to establish strong networks within the sector ... but are less likely to know the people or processes of government well. (507)

Overall, the literature emphasizes concern about the capacity of voluntary organizations to participate in the policy process. How these levels of policy capacity match with government policy capacity becomes the driving question for this chapter.

Locating the Intersection of Policy Capacity in Canada

From this literature review, two observations can be made. First, much of the literature on policy capacity has been firmly rooted within a government perspective, either at the federal level in Canada (see Bakvis 2000; Townsend and Kunimoto 2009; Wellstead and Stedman 2010; Voyer 2007), within a single sub-national jurisdiction (see Rasmussen 1999; Singleton 2001a), across sub-national jurisdictions (Howlett 2009b), or across national and sub-national jurisdictions (Baskoy, Evans, and Shields 2011). Other examinations look at a specific element of policy capacity, such as intergovernmental policy capacity (Inwood, Johns, and O'Reilly 2011) or how recruitment practices can improve policy capacity within government (Lindquist and Desveaux 2007). Comparatively, there is a dearth of attention given to the policy capacity of the voluntary sector in Canada. While there may be disagreement within the literature related to whether policy capacity is declining in government, what research has been done on the voluntary sector suggests there are genuine concerns about weak policy capacity. That said, however, some pockets of the voluntary sector, namely larger and provincially/nationally based organizations, may possess more policy capacity. Further academic study of the policy capacity of voluntary sector organizations in Canada would be a welcome addition to the literature.

Besides an overshadowing of the policy capacity in the voluntary sector, the literature is compartmentalized, meaning policy capacity is generally examined *either* through a government *or* a voluntary sector lens. Few studies actively research how policy capacity in government *and* the voluntary sector unfolds or what this means for policy development. This is despite claims of movement towards more collaborative models of governance. The relationship between Canada's voluntary sector and the state is becoming increasingly important, because of the changing nature of collaborative governance, where the state works with a variety of "new" partners to develop and implement public policy (Stoker 1998; Osborne 2006; Salamon 2002; Rhodes 1996). Under this model, we would expect to see partners, and their associated policy capacity, working together on policy matters.

Second, while the literature suggests there is limited and possibly declining policy capacity in the voluntary sector and government respectively, the results are sometimes too aggregated to discern the precise impact this has on policy development. The report by the Office of the Auditor General in Manitoba nicely illustrates this point. In its review of policy capacity across the government of Manitoba, broad trends and recommendations are drawn, but none specific to a particular department or division within each department. For example, the report concludes that 60 per cent of senior managers identify a need for improved analytical skills and subject matter expertise (Singleton 2001b, 7), but which departments are in need of these improved skill sets? Do some divisions/branches enjoy higher levels of policy capacity than other divisions/branches in the same department? Given that some policy issues are highly technical or specialized, which may suggest that much of the policy work begins and ends in a specified division or branch of a division sometimes with little policy contribution from the broader department or central government, analysis at such a macro scale may obscure our understanding of the impact that policy capacity has on policy development.

In light of these observations, this chapter argues that an understanding of policy capacity requires an analysis of the capacity of partners – notably government and voluntary sector for the purposes of this chapter – across various spaces. In this sense, we need to conceptualize policy capacity in a multi-scalar approach. Derived from the geography literature, *scale* can be defined as the location where action occurs (Mahon, Andrew, and Johnston 2007). Much of the policy literature has privileged the nation state in analysis, but Mahon, Andrew, and Johnston (41) contend that policy creation and contestation occurs at a variety of places and spaces from the local to the global: "Policy analysis, like much of the social science theory on which it draws, has assumed the centrality of the nation-state. Thus, the main focus has been on national policies, though the reality of federalism has often forced students of Canadian policy to include federal-provincial bargaining and some analysis of policy development at the provincial scale ... [N]ational-state centrism ... made good sense for much of the twentieth century, but as the century drew to a close, the adequacy of such a uni-scalar analysis came increasingly under question."

The argument put forward by Mahon, Andrew, and Johnston is that policy studies must be conducted at various levels. This argument can be extended to the study of policy capacity. Rather than relying on scale as a geographically constructed approach, this chapter borrows inspiration from Laforest's (2011, 21) metaphorical use of scale to understand policy capacity. In her examination of how the federal state relates to the voluntary sector in Canada, she emphasizes how scale shapes mobilization efforts and relationships at the broadest level, which encompasses the relationships between entire sectors, to the microscopic level, which emphasizes organizational dynamics. By adopting her approach for this study, the framework presented here situates policy capacity as occurring *between* government and voluntary organizations *across* multiple scales. As outlined in figure 16.1, policy capacity at the micro level consists of organizational structures between a government department, which includes divisions/branches within a single department, and corresponding voluntary organizations. At the meso level, policy capacity encompasses the policy capacity of actors within a specified policy field, while at the macro level focuses analysis at the broader scale between entire sectors notably governments and the voluntary sector.

Applying a multi-scalar approach to the study of policy capacity has already begun. Craft and Howlett (2012b) outline a multi-scalar approach that explores the linkages, duplication, and gaps in policy capacity between the micro, meso, and macro levels in the area of climate change. While studying policy capacity at the meso and macro levels is important for the identification of broad trends in the evolution of policy capacity over time, emphasis is placed on the micro level in this chapter. With this focus, this chapter attempts to understand how differentiated policy capacities between voluntary organizations *and* corresponding government departments – particularly their divisions/branches – intersect. Research by Howlett and Oliphant (2010) also starts to reflect this approach. Their study operationalizes the concept

Figure 16.1 Scaling Policy Capacity

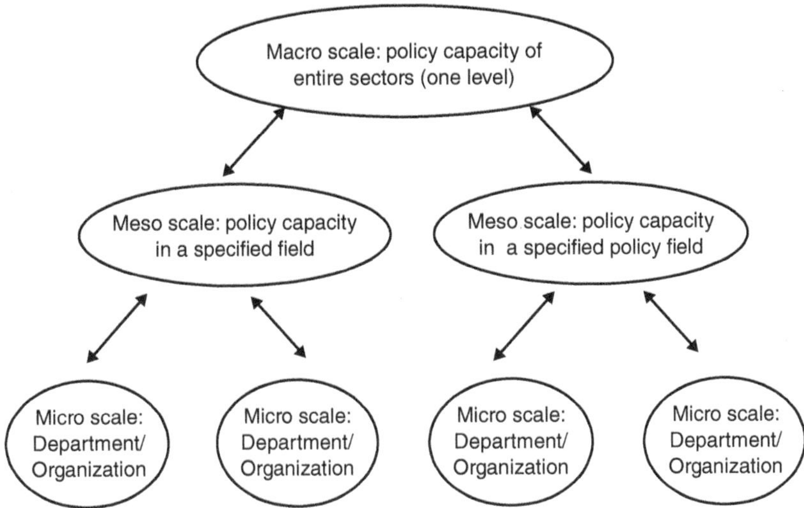

Source: Laforest (2011, 22).

of policy capacity[6] in the area of climate change and relies on seven indicators to measure the capacity of three environmental actors beyond just government – Environment Canada and the BC Ministry of Environment – and a voluntary organization – the David Suzuki Foundation. They conclude (30) that Environment Canada and the foundation have "satisfactory" capacity in four of the seven identified areas, whereas the BC Ministry of Environment has a "satisfactory" level in all seven areas. The contribution made by their research rests with its incorporation of a voluntary sector organization into its analysis of policy capacity.

Conclusion

Understanding the dynamics of policy capacity within each organization involved in policy work is a critical first step in understanding and enhancing policy effectiveness, and the framework advanced here attempts to provide insight into what these differentiated policy capacities mean for policy development.

To be sure, this line of inquiry is particularly challenging, because isolating the impact of policy capacity on policy outcomes, particularly when policy recommendations may not be adopted for a variety of reasons (e.g., ideology). Even so, there is merit in assessing the differentiated policy capacities of these actors at a programmatic level on the ability to identify problems, conduct analysis, disseminate knowledge, nurture networks, build policy support/influence and develop recommendations even if a policy is not adopted.

The emphasis here is not placed on whether a policy was adopted or even deemed a "success or failure," since there is considerable subjectivity involved in such assessments. Rather, the framework presented in this chapter hopes to demonstrate how differentiated policy capacities have an impact on the process for developing policy, and as a result, several important questions are raised: Is there a substitution effect when the policy capacity of the corresponding government department is limited such that voluntary organizations can exert more influence? Or is there the potential for governments to be captured by non-government actors because departments may be unable to fully "assess the merits of externally generated advice, develop and evaluate policy options" (Boston 1994, 8; see also Bakvis 2000, 73)? Or is the ability of voluntary organizations to exert influence on the public policy process actually strengthened when policy capacity within the corresponding government department is well developed? If policy capacity is limited in both the key department and voluntary organizations, is there a stalemate in the development of policy? Is there even a correlation? Is policy capacity conceptualized in government and the voluntary sector in dissimilar ways, or can we merely export conceptualizations of policy capacity developed for government to voluntary organizations?

To answer these questions, and to develop a typology for understanding the intersection of differentiated policy capacity on policy development, future research must begin with the conceptualization and operationalization of policy capacity. This is needed to support the measurement of the policy capacity in key voluntary organizations and corresponding government departments, particularly at a divisional and branch level. Ideally, four cases studies would be identified and explored, with each case study outlining the implications for policy development resulting from varying levels of policy capacity. One case study would involve low levels of policy capacity in the key voluntary organizations and corresponding government department, while another case study would involve high levels of policy capacity in both partners. The remaining two case studies would include low levels of policy capacity in the corresponding government department, coupled with high levels of capacity in voluntary organizations, and vice-versa.

In summary, the argument put forward in this chapter is simple: understanding how policy development occurs or does not occur requires future research into the differentiated policy capacities of government and voluntary sector organizations at the programmatic level. The value added by this proposed framework is its ability to consider the capacity of different actors, beyond just government, that feed into the policy process. It also disaggregates the scale to provide a better understanding of how various levels of policy capacity among partners influence the development of public policy.

NOTES

1 While more research into the policy capacity for all governance partners (i.e., private sector, unions) is needed, this chapter limits its focus to government and the voluntary sector as a starting point to develop a framework for analysis.
2 Only registered charities are permitted to issue income tax receipts for donations that can then be used for tax credits or deductions.
3 A full treatment of this issue is not possible here, but see Bridge 2002; IMPACS 2002; Webb 2000 for additional details.
4 Advocacy is defined as "the act of speaking or of disseminating information intended to influence individual behaviour or opinion, corporate conduct, or public policy and law" (Federal Government of Canada/Voluntary Sector Joint Initiative 1999, 50) and involves mobilization and the promotion of a particular policy option (Carter 2011, 432).
5 The Canada Revenue Agency quantifies advocacy based on the expenditure of resources and developed a sliding scale approach based on the size of the charity. Small charities with budgets less than $50,000 may spend up to 20 per cent of their resources on advocacy or up to $10,000. Large charities with budgets more than $200,000 may spend a maximum of 10 per cent of their resources to such activities. Medium-size charities may spend 12 or 15 per cent, depending on their overall budgets.
6 Howlett and Oliphant employ the term "policy analytical capacity" defined earlier in this chapter.

17 Towards Policy Analysis 2.0: Platforms for Knowledge Sharing and Collaboration among Policy Analysts

JUSTIN LONGO

The empirical research for this chapter is based on semi-structured interviews with members of corporate policy units in the government of British Columbia (BC), and a broader survey of government of BC policy analysts. This mixed-methods research investigated how the application of Web 2.0 tools to the policy analysis environment in the BC government is perceived by practising policy analysts there. Despite enthusiasm for the prospects for policy analysis 2.0 in the wider academic and commercial environment, and anecdotal reports of technologically progressive policy networks in BC and elsewhere, there was little support for the use of Web 2.0 tools in support of policy analysis; in fact, respondents refrained from sharing knowledge using internal Web 2.0 approaches in order to avoid contributing to their colleagues' information overload. Frequent, unprompted references to the importance of e-mail and cloud file-sharing indicate at least a preliminary movement towards a technology-supported approach to policy formulation. However, it was the open architecture of policy analysis 2.0 at which respondents balked, concerned that such tools would overwhelm the focused approach to policy analysis they were familiar with, and raised concerns about their responsibilities within the system of ministerial accountability.

Introduction

In 2010, the BC government issued a technology and organizational transformation strategy – Citizens @ the Centre: BC Government 2.0 (British Columbia 2010) – with one objective being the use of new technologies to transform the operations of government and encourage collaboration and knowledge sharing across organizational and system silos. In presenting this strategy and tying it to the emerging concept of Government 2.0, the document explicitly acknowledged the implications of the social Internet – Web 2.0 – for the future of public administration. In 2012, the annual report from Canada's Clerk of the Privy Council (Wouters 2012) commissioned a new committee of deputy ministers to look into the use of social media in support of policy development. This committee builds on development over the past several years to improve collaboration and knowledge sharing in the government of Canada using Web 2.0 tools.

In these two recent examples, public sector leaders in Canada are not alone in emphasizing the importance of the social web for the future of governance. In the United States, the Obama administration has focused on openness and transparency in applying Web 2.0 approaches to policy development and civic engagement (United States 2009), and in the United Kingdom, Prime Minister David Cameron publicly released a letter to Cabinet ministers on transparency and open data, focused on improving government transparency and accountability, reforming public services, fostering innovation, empowering citizens, and driving economic activity (United Kingdom 2011). Gov 2.0 represents an important concept that has emerged in recent years in both the practice of public sector governance and as a technological and cultural phenomenon in its own right (Gøtze and Pedersen 2009). Built upon the architecture of the social web, Gov 2.0 is defined here as instances where Web 2.0 approaches and technologies are applied to public administration functions, public policy development, and governance processes. The use of Web 2.0 technologies and methods by government and in governance settings is an issue of growing interest, and is a research area with multiple facets (O'Reilly 2010; Osimo 2008).

There is a great deal of enthusiasm for the many applications of Gov 2.0 – and it has emerged from a range of sources: from political actors using social networking services to connect with their constituencies (Wyld 2007) and supplanting polling with "social listening," to the coalition of bureaucratic, political, and non-government actors who are promoting "open data" as a mechanism to improve civic engagement and policy outcomes (Guerin 2014). Part of the support for Gov 2.0 reflects its potential as a knowledge management tool applied to the policy formulation process within public sector organizations (Karacapilidis, Loukis, and Dimopoulos 2005). Popular books such as *Wikinomics* (Tapscott and Williams 2006) and *Enterprise 2.0* (McAfee

2006) hold out the promise that Gov 2.0 can fundamentally improve collaborative work environments, and governments are beginning to experiment with Gov 2.0 in part as a way of improving policy analysis capacity and improving the policy formulation process (Cook 2008; Noveck 2009) and considering the implications for public policy analysts (Edwards and Hoefer 2010; McNutt 2008). As a shorthand label, the use of Web 2.0 collaboration technologies used to facilitate internal organizational knowledge-sharing and collaboration in support of policy analysis and formulation is labelled here as "policy analysis 2.0."

In an era of increasingly complex governance challenges, horizontal policy formulation is promoted as a key response (6 et al. 2002). Policy analysis has been dramatically influenced over the past half century by the impacts of changing information and communication technologies (Beer 1974; Simon et al. 1986; 6 2004). But the field – and our society – is now on the cusp of transformative change in the context of new information and communications technologies (ICTs), especially increasing Web 2.0 deployment (Benkler 2006; Shirky 2008) and Web 3.0 capacity (Cohen 2006; Till et al. 2014). The twenty-first-century digital economy will continue to see an explosion in the scale of observations, records, data, information, knowledge, and opinions that must be taken into account in the development of public policy and governance decisions (Dobell, Longo, and Walsh 2011; Nowotny, Scott, and Gibbons 2001; Pereira and Funtowicz 2006). For the policy analysis function to continue to assert its relevance in this environment, the impact of these technological developments at least requires attention and better understanding.

In the context of policy complexity requiring horizontal policy analysis, the focus of this chapter is on internal-to-government policy formulation and how the adoption of Web 2.0 tools is affecting this environment, especially internal knowledge sharing and collaboration among public service knowledge workers. While policy analysis 2.0 is built on a technology infrastructure, the policy analysis system is a human network made up of individual policy analysts and the networks they form with their colleagues, clients, and stakeholders. The question this chapter explores is whether the application of Web 2.0 enterprise social-collaboration technologies represents an effective approach to promoting knowledge sharing and collaboration in the internal-to-government policy analysis environment, to the end of promoting horizontal policy analysis and generating effective responses to complex policy challenges. The empirical research for this chapter is based on semi-structured interviews with members of corporate policy units in the government of British Columbia, and a broader survey of government of BC policy analysts. This mixed-methods research investigated how the application of Web 2.0 tools to the policy analysis environment in the BC government is perceived by practising policy analysts there, and what prospects there are for their wider application.

Policy Complexity and the Web 2.0 Solution

Policymaking is hard enough as it is (Pressman and Wildavsky 1973), but when policy challenges range from hard to complicated to complex, strategies for dealing with those challenges must also adapt (Dror 1986). While the lament about policy complexity is not new (see, e.g., Kidneigh 1954), what is new is our understanding of how complex problems differ from the hard work of governing. While not all policy issues are complex, the modern public policy environment seems increasingly marked by complexity (Geyer and Rihani 2010; Huxham, Vangen, and Eden 2000). Complex public policy challenges exhibit conditions such as partial order (Kim 2012) and profound uncertainty (Dryzek 1983). They often emerge rapidly in ways that challenge our mental models and predictive capacity (Howlett and Ramesh 1995). Complex policy environments can be thermodynamically open and nonlinear (Homer-Dixon 2010), have whole-system implications (Kendall 2000), and have probabilistic rather than deterministic outcomes that are subject to interpretation (Fischer 2003). And a key feature of complex policy environments is their multi-stakeholder nature.

When confronted with a complex policy situation, an appropriate response from the policy analysis system is required (Morçöl 2012), such as agility (Doz and Kosonen 2008; Hämäläinen, Kosonen, and Doz 2012), openness (Bertot, Jaeger, and Grimes 2010), acceptance of mistakes and failure (Parsons 2006; Potts 2009), learning (Rose 1993), adaptation (Gunderson, Holling, and Light 1995), and collaboration and knowledge sharing across many different actors with a diversity of expertise and perspectives.

One specific approach to dealing with complexity in a public policy context is horizontality, the act of working across the ministries and divisions of a government in order to harness the organization's capacity and resources and direct them towards an appropriate response to the complex problem (Parsons 2004). The concept of horizontality is also captured under a range of related terms including horizontal governance, holistic governance, joined-up government, cross-cutting policy issues management, coherent and cohesive policy responses, co-ordination and integration between government agencies, and collaboration across and between governments (6 et al. 2002).

A range of methods for achieving a more coherent policy stance through well-coordinated, whole-of-governmental responses has been promoted, e.g., through a top-down orchestrated understanding of the complexity of government, led by collegial senior executives orchestrating strategic collaborations (e.g., Canada 1996a); as a situation requiring a fundamental reconceptualization of the structure and incentives of government (e.g., March and Olson 1983); or through an "open method of coordination" (e.g., Radaelli 2008). All of these perspectives share an approach to coordinated action that responds to situations of fragmented governance, with emphasis placed at different levels in the organization or governance system. However, whether the increasing complexity of policy problems, the opportunities afforded by new technologies, and the continued pressures on governments to "do more with less" lead to a renewed emphasis on horizontality remains to be seen (Lindquist 2012).

The mechanism for addressing the horizontality challenge that is the focus here is the promotion of greater organization-wide collaboration, knowledge sharing, and active knowledge seeking among a network of knowledge workers (Galbraith 1973; Weber and Khademian 2008). Efforts by organizations to improve knowledge transfer and collaboration among workers and organizational units have been found to contribute to improved organizational performance in a range of private sector settings (Argote and Ingram 2000; Darr, Argote, and Epple 1995; Stewart 2002). And in recent years, some evidence that this is also true in the public sector has started to emerge (Binz-Scharf, Lazer, and Mergel 2012; Willem and Buelens 2007; Yang and Maxwell 2011).

But how is this enhanced knowledge sharing and collaboration accomplished in practice? Other than exhorting civil servants to collaborate more with their colleagues (perhaps using recognition [Wasko and Faraj 2005], incentives [Bartol and Srivastava 2002] or through reference to reciprocity [Ko, Kirsch, and King 2005], trust [Kankanhalli, Tan, and Wei 2005], or shared norms [Bock et al., 2005]), one mechanism that has received increasing attention of late is to build collaboration and knowledge sharing into the workflow and communication channels of workers through the use of Web 2.0–based enterprise social collaboration tools. Such tools allow knowledge workers within organizations to connect with each other over a social networking platform and, building on those connections, share knowledge and collaborate to greater effect than if they were to work in isolation. By augmenting the organizational social network with a technology-based social networking platform, the knowledge worker is better positioned to access more of the knowledge resources embodied in an organization. Enterprise collaboration tools also propose to help solve the problem that has come to plague many organizations by moving communications and document sharing into a shared collaborative space. Examples of the use of enterprise collaboration systems in government continue to grow, including leading work among government agencies in Canada and the United States (Akerley, Cowan, and Belanger 2008).

Web 2.0 denotes a second-generation Internet built on web technology but focused on user control, simple user-publishing of web content, social media communication, participation, and peer-to-peer collaboration. Web 2.0, or the "participative web," is driven by the use of platforms that become embedded in people's lives: as of 2012, some 60 per cent of American adults use social networking sites like Facebook or Twitter (Rainie et al. 2012). Under a Web 2.0 model, the distinction between consumers of information and producers of content is blurred; the technology used in the one-to-many broadcasting of the early web now supports many-to-many interactions. Web 2.0 technologies – such as blogs and microblogs, reader commentary, wikis, social networking services, content sharing, collaboration, and tagging – continue to grow in popularity and function.

"Gov 2.0" – the application of Web 2.0 tools and approaches to public-sector governance – has been studied in recent years as a subdomain of the e-government literature. Governments have generally developed Gov 2.0 programs in support of external communication strategies (Wyld 2007) and as a platform for citizen engagement (Chadwick 2009). However, Gov 2.0 can also broaden policy development through specialized collaboration and knowledge-sharing tools. These tools are web-based applications and platforms designed for corporate use (as opposed to open access social tools like Facebook and Twitter) that facilitate collaboration without relying on formal workflows or hierarchical structures. The tool might be a wiki (a document that any user can change or add to), a blog (a statement, paragraph, or longer document that any authorized user can comment on), or a related forum and platform. These workspaces can be used to pose questions, connect to knowledge sources, initiate discussions, or co-create and collaborate on documents (Fyfe and Crookall 2010). The key is that users can easily start conversations across their entire network, and other users within the organization can join that conversation, whether they are known to the originator or not, without the need for corporate approval or technical web support (McAfee 2006).

While potentially transformative, enterprise collaboration systems built on a Web 2.0 framework represent a continuation from previous knowledge-management systems, which were found to have limited effect on corporate performance (Grudin 1988). However, in the context of the policy analysis system, these tools can have a potentially profound impact. Collaboration systems build on social networks, and embodying principles of openness across the organization can "flatten" traditional hierarchies by providing a platform for bringing all knowledge workers at all levels in an organization into a collaborative space. But in the modern government organization, in the age of the "street level bureaucrat" (Lipsky 1971), it is hard to imagine a public servant who is not a "knowledge worker." Building on that premise, under an enterprise collaboration system, every workplace interaction, every meeting with a stakeholder group, every transaction with a citizen, every experience in a worker's past, and every new bit of information collected adds to the knowledge resources of the organization.

For anyone who doubts that open collaboration systems can solve knowledge and workflow coordination problems, we need look no further than successes such as Wikipedia or a growing number of open source software products (Benkler 2006; Shirky 2008). The challenge for the policy analysis system will be in developing a comparable collaboration infrastructure that can efficiently evaluate policy contributions from outside the traditional policy network systems. Whereas in the past, knowledge-management systems sought to capture those information collection moments and organize them in a knowledge repository that other knowledge workers could draw on, enterprise collaboration systems are built on the understanding that knowledge resides in people, not machines (Hinds and Bailey 2003). And if the system can be engineered so that someone who can benefit from some knowledge resource can be connected to someone in the organization who has that knowledge, a profound transformation of the organization can occur. In the realm of complex policy problems requiring horizontal solutions, organizations can ill afford to waste the knowledge that exists untapped throughout their organizations.

Where social networks cannot facilitate pan-organizational knowledge sharing, and where information and communications technologies (ICTs) reinforce organizational boundaries rather than transcend them, the use of Web 2.0–based enterprise social collaboration tools has emerged as a prospective mechanism for facilitating cross-organizational knowledge sharing and collaboration. When applied to government policy formulation settings, "policy analysis 2.0" builds on earlier experience using computer-supported cooperative work systems to facilitate collaboration among policy workers, but does so using the open architecture of Web 2.0 platforms. As such, policy analysis 2.0 potentially represents a significant realignment of the traditional policy analysis approach.

Looking for Policy Analysis 2.0 in Practice

This research was conducted with public servants working in the government of British Columbia. With an annual budget of $44 billion, the government directly employed approximately 31,700 public servants in sixteen ministries and public agencies in 2011/12 (British Columbia 2012). In 2010, the deputy minister issued to the premier a "transformation and technology strategy" for the BC Public Service entitled Citizens @ the Centre: B.C. Government 2.0 (British Columbia 2010). This report envisaged the use of new technologies to transform the operations of government, addressing management across organizational and system silos, and introducing new methods for citizen engagement and the incorporation of citizen inputs into government decision-making. Building on three principles (empowering citizens; improving citizens' access to services; and encouraging collaboration in the public service), Citizens @ the Centre was a strategy to deal with the rapidly changing governance and technology environment. It proposed three shifts in the public service's operating philosophy: citizen participation, service innovation, and business innovation. It is towards this third shift – a focus on the changing corporate environment, and the transformation of internal business practices specifically as they relate to the policy formulation process – that this research was oriented.

Research participants included public servants connected directly to the policy analysis system in the BC government, using a web-based questionnaire sent to practising "policy analysts" (n = 129; rr = 52 per cent) and semi-structured interviews with members of corporate policy units (n = 14).[1] The web questionnaire included questions in demographic and career characteristics; respondent views on the policy process; organizational social network / sociometric survey; views on the impacts and importance of technology use in the policy process; and building on Ajzen's (1991) theory of planned behaviour (TPB), measures of attitudes, subjective norms, and perceived behavioural control regarding knowledge sharing and collaboration practices in the policy process. Behavioural intention was measured with eight scenarios interspersed throughout the survey – four each related to knowledge sharing and collaboration – set in the context of government policy formulation, with all scenarios asking for a "Yes" or "No" response to a direct action question related to the scenario (Francis et al. 2004).

Forced hierarchical regression analysis was used to determine relationships between behavioural intent (the dependent variable) and the independent variables. The forced model was assessed by entering the effect of age and gender first, followed by attitudes and subjective norms (the two theory components relevant to the TPB precursor – the theory of reasoned action [Fishbein and Ajzen 2010]), with perceived behavioural control then added for the TPB model, followed finally by respondent career stability variables (organizational disruptions, lateral career movements, and career advancement).

For the semi-structured interviews with practising policy analysts as members of separate corporate policy units, interviews were transcribed verbatim and, taking a deductive approach based on an a priori list of codes (Miles and Huberman 1994), were analysed with the assistance of a computerized qualitative data analysis software program (NVivo 9). The interviews were supplemented by demographic and career profile data collected from respondents through a brief web-based questionnaire.

Technology and the Policy Analysis System

What role and impact does new technology have in the quest to remake the government as a knowledge organization? How can policy analysts share more knowledge without becoming responsible for adding to their colleagues' information overload (Edmunds and Morris 2000; Eppler and Mengis 2004)? Is knowledge sharing simply a new term for a computerized knowledge-management system (KMS) or an electronic knowledge repository (EKR), in which we store information within an organization using better search functions and linked data sets (Dawes, Cresswell, and Pardo 2009)? Or is it something different, implying a person-centred system where tacit knowledge (i.e., practical knowledge and intuition, as opposed to explicit knowledge that is easily codified, stored, and transmitted to others) is self-organized and shared among knowledge workers (Ackerman, Pipek, and Wulf 2003)? This section provides a contextual understanding of the policy formulation process and an assessment of the potential impact of new Gov 2.0 approaches and technologies on the policy formulation environment.

The role that emerging ICTs might play in policy formulation, and in supporting knowledge sharing and collaboration as the foundation of horizontal policy solutions, was explored largely through semi-structured interviews with policy analysts. Despite the enthusiasm for Gov 2.0 approaches to policy analysis in the wider literature (see above), little evidence of such a transformation was revealed in the interview data. The interview protocol addressed the subject of technology in support of workplace collaboration and knowledge sharing, principally by asking respondents for their reaction to a hypothetical scenario: their deputy minister had made a decision that the ministry was suffering from too many e-mails, and that she was determined to replace the internal e-mail system with a "Facebook-like" platform. The concept for this question was not entirely fictitious, but was derived from recent moves in a small number of firms to do just that: replacing the reliance on internal e-mail systems with an alternative communication platform. In early 2011, the CEO of the leading European IT firm Atos Origin declared the use of e-mail for intra-firm communication to be "unsustainable," and announced plans to phase in a ban on internal e-mails over a three-year period. While e-mail would still be used for external communication, internal e-mail would be replaced by collaboration and social media tools (Thompson 2011). While e-mail filtering (both manual and automated) are necessary advances, one prediction is that by 2016, social networking services will replace e-mail as the principal method of interpersonal communications for 20 per cent of business users (Nairn 2011).

In the scenario presented to respondents, this platform was described as a secure internal network limited to British Columbia government employees, each identified by a true-identity profile (real names and likenesses), where communications could happen in a number of different, integrated streams: on their "wall" would be the open conversations that anyone in the organization could see and anyone could contribute to; instant messaging would allow for minor interactions and include a presence indicator; normal messaging – which would essentially be e-mail, but integrated into the overall corporate communications platform – would be accommodated; and cloud file-sharing would allow for document sharing and collaboration. While e-mail would still be available for communication with external parties, public servants were expected to use the new platform principally for internal communication. In addition to their reaction to this scenario, respondents' references to the impact of technology on the policy formulation process emerged in the context of their comments on other aspects of the interview guide.

There was some enthusiasm for new technology platforms as a potential enabler of organization-wide collaboration, with open knowledge platforms seen as one tool to help manage repeated requests for information from throughout the organization. Three respondents from the same ministry independently noted that they frequently receive similar internal requests for information that could be short-circuited if the requester had access to a prior response they had written. However, e-mail was consistently mentioned as an indispensable technology for policy analysis, as a communication and information-sharing tool that increased consistency, improved accuracy, and ultimately made policy people more productive. As one respondent noted, "A great deal of the policy record now happens through e-mail … To be able to coordinate all of the people that need to have input into that in the formulation of what potentially is new policy or a new mandate, e-mail is just a brilliant tool to be able to connect simultaneously with that many people."

While one respondent criticized the use of e-mail as a way for some bureaucrats to avoid talking to colleagues directly (see, e.g., Valentine, Staats, and Edmondson 2012), e-mail was generally seen as having the benefit of largely displacing the use of the telephone as the primary internal communication tool. The concept of a "ban on e-mail" imposed by the deputy minister was anathema to some respondents: when considering the implications of the "Facebook-like platform" preceded by a corporate decision to "ban internal e-mails," one respondent felt this would be not only difficult to implement but also counter-productive, both in constraining people from accomplishing their work and in how the adaptive workarounds that would be attempted (e.g., increased numbers of phone calls and meetings) would diminish the electronic record that is accumulated through e-mails.

When considering the implications of a fully collaborative technology system (e.g., the "Facebook-like platform" raised in the interview question), some respondents were cautious that such a tool be adopted only when there was a clear case for doing so, and even then would need to overcome organizational and cultural barriers to adoption and general concerns about productivity and security. Some respondents were more sceptical still, questioning how new Web 2.0 technologies represented an improvement over existing systems, as noted by a respondent: "In terms of policy, I don't know if it would be useful because most of the policy analysis that we do requires revealed documents, talking to people, searches on the Internet, and I don't know to what extent Web 2.0 gets you there ... in terms of use of the technology, I find it difficult to think how Twitter and Facebook are going to supplant e-mail and SharePoint and phone calls because you need a robust mechanism to go back and forth and have extensive and detailed communications."

One principal reason for advocating slow adoption of technological change was the belief, articulated directly by several respondents, that there would be significant resistance by the bureaucracy to fundamental changes in the supporting technology. This resistance was characterized as fear of the new technology by some colleagues, a preference for existing systems and technologies, the lack of a demonstrated case for more elaborate methods (particularly in small office settings), the movement by some public servants in the Freedom of Information era to "not writing anything down," and a lack of support from the executive during "a time and a culture of demotivation or lack of trust." One example pointing to the challenge of adopting new technologies in the context of a large organization was, "If executive isn't on board, if they are insisting that stuff gets e-mailed to them when you are trying to get everybody to start going to a particular [SharePoint] location to get the most recent, up-to-date copy, then you'll find that ... multiple versions of a document can float around in e-mails and on drives."

As for a "Facebook-like platform," respondents noted that the open nature of that platform would have the unintended consequence of constraining the "frank and fearless" types of conversations that are necessary for resolving an issue while fully exposing the range of implications and perspectives. Perhaps surprisingly, given the myth of the millennial generation and their affinity for Web 2.0 (Ng, Schweitzer, and Lyons 2010), two respondents – both millennials – were highly sceptical of the push for using social media as a means for increased knowledge sharing and collaboration in government. Both indicated that that scepticism was linked to general trends of declining trust and disengagement among public servants, and cynicism that organizational enthusiasm for Web 2.0 was anything more than the newest management fad. While these respondents spoke in favour of collaboration among public servants, they both noted that the new technology could inhibit the goal of robust interaction.

What Constrains Collaboration and Knowledge Sharing?

The focus of this section is on examining the factors that influence knowledge sharing and collaboration among policy analysts in the British Columbia public service. Specifically, the research question explored here asks how the theory of planned behaviour (TPB) (Ajzen 1991) helps to understand the intention of respondents to collaborate and share knowledge with other policy analyst colleagues throughout government. The TPB is a widely cited social psychology model where behavioural intention is predicted by three explanatory variables: attitude towards the behaviour; subjective norms (i.e., the respondent's perception of the expectations of other members of the organization whom the respondent cares about); and perceived behavioural control (a person's perception of the ease or difficulty of performing the behaviour).

Building on the TPB and research studies testing the applicability of the TPB to public-sector knowledge-sharing (Kankanhalli, Tan, and Wei 2005; Willem and Buelens 2007; Zhang, Cresswell, and Thompson 2005), this section reports on a test of whether the attitudes and perceived behavioural control of policy analysts, and their beliefs about organizational norms, predict their behavioural intentions in organization-wide knowledge sharing and collaboration.

Hierarchical regression modelling was used to test the hypothesis that "policy analysts who score higher on measures of attitudes, subjective norms and perceived behavioural control regarding knowledge sharing and collaboration will have greater behavioural intention to share knowledge and collaborate with colleagues throughout the organization." In the causal model, intention to share knowledge and collaborate was assessed against the variables that are theorized to lead to intention, along with personal variables (age and gender) entered first and career variables entered last.

Knowledge sharing and collaboration is important for organizational performance. Individuals' attitudes towards knowledge sharing and collaboration, their subjective evaluation of what people important to them believe about those actions, and their perception about how much they can act on their intentions, predict their behaviour, according to the theory of planned behaviour. Attitudes generally reflect what respondents believe and what their experience tells them about the behaviour, norms reflect what respondents hear from colleagues and superiors, and perceived behavioural control, in this context, measures whether respondents feel they have the authority, facility, or capacity to act upon their beliefs and to undertake what they are encouraged to do.

Underlying the research hypothesis being tested was the idea that, if policy analysts score higher on measures of their attitudes, subjective norms, and perceived behavioural control with respect to knowledge sharing and collaboration, the TPB model predicts that they will be more likely to have greater behavioural intention to share knowledge and collaborate with colleagues throughout the organization. The results of the hierarchical regression analysis do not support this hypothesis, as the addition of perceived behavioural control in step 3 – which completes the test of the TPB model – added nothing to the model over and above step 2, and the model was not statistically significant. However, in step 2, with the entry of the independent variables attitudes and norms – which represents in effect a test of the theory of reasoned action (Ajzen and Fishbein 2005; Fishbein and Ajzen 1975) – the model was significant and explained 11 per cent of the variance in behavioural intention. From a theoretical standpoint, these results suggest that the theory of reasoned action, the precursor to the TPB that does not include perceived behavioural control, was more parsimonious than the TPB in explaining policy analyst behaviour. The conclusion is that what policy analysts believe to be true – how knowledge sharing and collaboration contribute to effective policy analysis – and what they believe they are encouraged to do by those around them in the organization whose opinion they value, help to explain whether they will be likely to intend to share knowledge and collaborate with colleagues. This result has important implications for public sector managers and leaders seeking to increase the likelihood that policy analysts will share knowledge and collaborate with their colleagues. Where policy analysts can be encouraged to share knowledge and collaborate, their subjective norms should reflect such encouragement. Less directly, the internalization of such encouragement should have an impact on policy analysts' attitudes.

While perceived behavioural control was not an explanatory variable of statistical significance in the hierarchical regression model, its weakness was revealed in the mean scores and one-way ANOVA analysis, and in individual Pearson correlations. In practical terms, this weakness allows us to infer what the relationship might be between perceived behavioural control and the intention to share knowledge and collaborate. One possible interpretation is that policy analysts may not feel they have the authority or ability to act in a way that their attitudes and norms would predict. Ability to access and make efficient use of in-house knowledge resources, confidence in being able to connect with colleagues to jointly solve problems, and organizational support to reach out across government appear to be lacking in the results from the mean scores. These results seem to confirm other findings in the literature on barriers to knowledge sharing in governmental organizations (e.g., Landsbergen and Wolken 2001). These barriers arise from concerns over privacy and confidentiality, statutory authority, public scrutiny risk avoidance, intra- and inter-organizational mistrust, inexperience, lack of awareness of collaboration opportunities, and lack of resources (Andersen and Dawes 1991). While data interoperability challenges – stemming from incompatible technologies and an absence of data standards – are often the focus of intra- and inter-organizational information sharing, barriers to knowledge sharing and collaboration may be as much (if not more) a function of the organizational setting (Lord and Ranft 2000) and interpersonal factors (Dawes, Cresswell, and Pardo 2009; Riege 2005).

From the semi-structured interviews, respondents revealed clear positive attitudes towards knowledge sharing and collaboration, and with respect to subjective norms their assessment of their environment is that generally there is a rhetoric of collaboration and knowledge sharing that permeates the government. But perhaps surprisingly, subjective norms appeared to be influential in limited circumstances (in collaboration for staff members, and knowledge seeking for women). That subjective norms were not more widely influential suggests that neither direct nor implied messaging from one's superiors and colleagues provides policy analysts with a clear signal and encouragement to engage in collaboration and knowledge sharing. What seemed clearer, however, was that perceived behavioural control did not appear in itself to be related to behaviour. Perceived behavioural control can be as challenging to measure as behaviour, raising the question as to whether policy analysts who claimed to have behavioural control have actual behavioural control. The respondents appeared open to opportunities for collaboration and knowledge sharing but may be faced with some dilemmas: if they are responsible to their minister and the performance of their unit, how can that be balanced with the risk and benefit-sharing implicit in collaborative arrangements; and do they have the authority and freedom to "work outside of the box," to suggest collaborative solutions to colleagues in other ministries, other governments, or even outside of government (Kernaghan 2000)? Again, collaboration was supported in principle but appears difficult to identify in practice when those efforts would have to cross ministry lines or reach beyond the walls of government.

Concluding Thoughts

Computer technology and policy analysis shared an intertwined history, both marked by a democratizing trend of user-orientation and accessibility. As technology develops, and organizations and governance expectations change, there is potential for a reconfiguration of policy analysis. Enterprise social collaboration can flatten the organizational hierarchy and expand the notion of who in the organization might contribute to policy analysis.

In governments marked by high rates of turnover, Web 2.0 tools that support intra-organizational knowledge sharing and collaboration have the added benefit of levelling the social capital playing field by making it easier for policy analysts to find knowledge sources and potential collaborators with whom they may not have prior contact (Wellman 2001). In settings with low social capital – perhaps due to low levels of trust, or high rates of turnover (Putnam 1993) – being able to locate knowledge sources among colleagues outside of one's social network may be enhanced in an environment supported by a Web 2.0 infrastructure (Donath and Boyd 2004). A small number of respondents indicated that Web 2.0 technology could circumvent the absence of a sharing ethic or strong organizational social network in that the technology could allow knowledge to be accessed from someone the knowledge seeker does not consider part of his or her social network without requiring inter-personal contact. In some respects, references to the use of the government directory and shared drives indicate that this already happens. But we should remember that tacit knowledge is held and transferred between people, not computers (Snowden 2002; Stacey 2002), thus technology is only part of the solution (Kogut and Zander 1992). So while new technology can help to facilitate a knowledge organization, an organizational culture of sharing and collaboration – where the incentives to share knowledge align with the rhetoric that promotes it – are crucial to becoming a knowledge organization (Connelly et al. 2012). Overlaying a technology solution to support knowledge sharing in the absence of attending to the people-part of the solution will likely run into barriers (Grudin 1988). Alternatively, concerns about confidentiality and information control / accountability in the public sector were at the root of most opposition to "Facebook-like platforms" from the interview respondents (Connelly et al. 2012).

The policy analysis system is built on ideas such as having more knowledge is better than less (Quade 1975); working together is beneficial for dealing with complexity (Kenis and Schneider 1991); and the analyst's stature as a policy team player is enhanced by contributing policy knowledge where it is useful (Lin 2007). And while the rhetoric of modern government often speaks of innovation (Lewis, Alexander, and Considine 2009), we often speak of bureaucrats being risk averse with a lack of tolerance for mistakes, with colleagues, superiors, and the audit functions of government bearing much of the blame (Dobell 1999). As well, a number of policy-related barriers to sharing among government agencies have been recently documented by Landsbergen and Wolken (2001), including privacy concerns, ambiguity about statutory authority, openness to public scrutiny, lack of inter-organizational trust, lack of experience, lack of awareness of opportunities to share, lack of resources, outmoded procurement methods, incompatible technologies, and lack of data standards. The respondents' attitudes (and to some extent their beliefs about organizational norms) align with this complex setting. In seeking to understand the lack of completeness in the model, the disconnect between those attitudes and perceived norms, on the one hand, and perceived behavioural control on the other, our attention is drawn to the question of whether individual policy analysts have actual behavioural control. That is, do they truly have the authority to collaborate, do they have the capacity to seek knowledge, and do they have the legal latitude to share knowledge with their colleagues across government?

Analysis of the policy-formulation environment in government reveals that the rhetoric of the knowledge organization is in conflict with the reality facing the individual policy analyst – a reality mired in role ambiguity, mixed incentives, limited institutional capacity, and a risk-averse organizational culture. While there may be some scope for reinvigorating the knowledge organization through new knowledge sharing and collaboration technologies, freeing the organization from the bounds that limit knowledge sharing and collaboration by individual actors will require a fundamental reconceptualization of the practice of policy analysis and the culture of the policy formulation environment.

Hypothesizing that horizontal policy-formulation approaches offer some positive responses to the challenges of complex policy settings, the focus on knowledge sharing and collaboration among practising policy analysts served to frame and guide the research. Building on the theory of planned behaviour, the foregoing details how the attitudes, subjective norms, and perceived behavioural control of policy analysts influence their intentions and behaviour with respect to organization-wide knowledge sharing and collaboration. Additional factors – such as how policy analysts conceptualize their profession and their role in the policy formulation process, how computerized knowledge-management systems and collaboration technologies are affecting the policy environment, and how the organizational social network contributes to the work of policy analysts – were also explored in order to develop more fully the profile of the contemporary policy analyst.

The overall objective of this mixed methods study has been to explore the policy analysis environment in contemporary practice, to consider its current character, and begin to map its possible future development. Primary tools were semi-structured interviews with policy analysts as members of corporate policy units in the government of British Columbia, and an online survey of public servants connected directly to the policy analysis system in that government. A number of specific questions were used to guide that exploration: What are the characteristics of the contemporary policy analyst, and what do practising policy analysts themselves think of their profession and their role in the policy process? How does the organizational social network figure into the modern governance environment? How has technology affected the work of the policy analyst, and what might the future hold for the computer-supported policy analyst? And if knowledge sharing and collaboration hold the key to horizontal policy formulation and the unlocking of solutions to complex policy challenges, what are the chances that the knowledge organization can flourish out of the contemporary policy environment?

Lastly, the theory of planned behaviour predicts that the intention to act will be formed, and actual behaviour will follow, to the extent that individuals' attitudes towards knowledge sharing and collaboration, their subjective evaluation of what people important to them believe about those actions, and their perception about the degree to which they are able to act on their intentions are aligned. Attitudes generally reflect what respondents believe and what their experience tells them about the behaviour; norms reflect what respondents hear from colleagues and superiors; and perceived behavioural control, in this context, measures whether respondents feel they have the authority, facility, or capacity to act upon their beliefs and to undertake what they are encouraged to do. The results show that attitudes and norms were important predictors of behavioural intention in knowledge sharing and collaboration. However, perceived behavioural control – the ability to access in-house knowledge resources, confidence in being able to connect with colleagues to jointly solve problems, and genuine organizational support to reach out across government – appears to be lacking. The interpretation is that policy analysts may not feel they have the authority or ability to act on their beliefs or in a way that they think their colleagues and superiors would support. There may also be the negative incentives that actually encourage knowledge hoarding and hiding in order to protect one's position. This result seems related directly to the issues of culture, trust, and incentives noted above. Government leaders can reiterate in blog posts and tweets that the success of the knowledge organization hinges on the individual innovations of public servants to find collaboration opportunities, and share knowledge with their colleagues throughout government. But if the actual culture of the organization – not just its climate, which is more easily influenced through messaging, but its culture – does not change to reinforce that messaging, if the behaviour of government leaders fails to build a truly horizontal organization as the basis for building trusting relationships among public servants, if the incentives – real and perceived – that truly inspire the emergence of a knowledge organization are not in place, knowledge workers inside the organization will continue to react in rational ways. They may believe it's the right thing to do; they may hear it's the right thing to do; but when it comes to actual knowledge sharing and collaboration, they may decide that policy analysis 2.0 might just have to wait.

This work, I will argue, should instead be seen as part of an effort to renew the policy analysis function, to give it new purpose and capacity, and to endow policy analysis with both the mission and the tools to make it more relevant in the post-positivist age of complexity, uncertainty, contestation, and constraint. Whether through concepts such as ubiquitous evergreen policy analysis (where all public servants take on the role of "policy analyst" and none are anointed with that title, and where "policy analysis" is an additional output of the work of the public servant and not an isolated activity in its own right), the bringing together of policy-relevant insights from all corners of a geographically diverse federal government (Wellstead and Stedman 2010), big data analytics (for disentangling signals from noise, and promoting analysis over intuition [Silver 2012] and countering the rise of "decision-based evidence-making" [Tingling and Brydon 2010]), moving towards open governance (through new forms of data analysis, public ideation platforms or new mechanisms for citizen engagement [Dobell, Longo, and Walsh 2011]) or engendering the knowledge organization (as was the focus here). "Towards Policy Analysis 2.0" was not simply meant to focus on the application of Web 2.0 technologies and work modes to the traditional function of policy analysis, but also implies a new version of that function, a new articulation of policy analysis, grounded in the past and enhanced – certainly – by new technologies and new modes of social and workplace interaction, but also drawing energy and inspiration from new political realities, new economic consequences, and new social expectations. While there is much for the practising policy analyst to despair over, I am hopeful for continued movement towards policy analysis 2.0.

NOTE

1 The full web questionnaire and interview protocol are available online (see Longo 2013).

PART 5

Conclusion

18 Policy Work System Dynamics: Implications for Practice, Pedagogy, and Scholarship

ADAM WELLSTEAD, JONATHAN CRAFT, AND MICHAEL HOWLETT

Introduction: From Black Boxes to Translucent Mechanisms in Canadian Policy Work

There is a long history of matching excellence in policy work to policy capacity in Canada. A key contention of the federal government's path-breaking 1996 deputy minister's task force report *Strengthening Our Policy Capacity,* for example, was that "public servants will have to re-think how they conceive and develop policy proposals" and that policy capacity issues would figure prominently in this re-conceptualization (Canada 1996b).

Whether and the extent to which this has been achieved has been an ongoing empirical question until the publication of the chapters in this volume. It was not clear whether or not there had been a "reorientation" of policy work and if whatever work was being done was adequate to deal with a rapidly changing, complex, government environment (Canada 1996b).

Two important aspects of recent development have been pointed to in the most recent literature on policy work and policy advice: politicization and externalization (Veselý 2013; Craft and Howlett 2013a). These dual dynamics of public service advisory practices related to the ratio of internal and external sources policy advice, and its sources were noted by Halligan (1995) and continue today (Craft and Wilder 2016).

Halligan's (1995) analysis, however, was largely anecdotal and followed others in portraying the actual work of providing policy advice and formulation as "a black box" (148). In the literature that followed his path-breaking work, scholars began to describe the features of policy work within the black box, rendering it translucent, if not completely transparent (Rasmussen 1999; Anderson 1996; Savoie 2003; Page and Jenkins 2005). As sketched out in chapter 2, the nature of policy advisory activities themselves has also been well examined, with scholars contending that older "speaking truth to power" models of policy advice (Wildavsky 1979) have given way in many policymaking circumstances to more fluid, pluralized, and polycentric advice-giving realities that have been characterized as "sharing truth with many actors of influence" or "weaving" policy knowledge (Maley 2011; Prince 2007; Parsons 2004). Scholars now include activities such as policy advice, political advice, and non-traditional work (stakeholder engagement) in both governments and NGOs in their assessments of policy work and by doing so, a "translucent box" has now emerged in which we can begin to discern answers in detail about how it works" (Bunge 1963, 1997).

The chapters in this volume contribute to this project and in so doing have greatly extended our notion of policy work well beyond the emphases of traditional "technical" policy analysis – often limited to formal modes of policy appraisal such as the use and application of techniques such as regulatory impact or cost-benefit analysis, which animated earlier studies. Successive surveys of Canadian policy workers detailed in the chapters in the book, for example, have found that, like their international counterparts, many public sector analysts are less technical experts than "process generalists" with very little training in formal policy analysis techniques such as cost-benefit analysis or risk assessment, who rarely deal with policy matters in the substantive areas in which they may have been trained (Feldman 1989; Page and Jenkins 2005). Distinct sets of job duties are also chronicled relating to formulation, consultation, implementation, financial analysis, evaluation, data management, communications, environmental assessment, and the use of legal skills and work. Differences in governmental vs non-governmental patterns of interaction are also detailed in the findings of these survey chapters.

In addition to better understanding what constitutes policy work (e.g., traditional policy analysis, technical analysis, consulting and advising, coordinating), the chapters in the book also show that the contexts that make up a *policy work system* need to be analysed. That is, which particular configuration of actors and policy work is better than another, and how can we tell?

The nature of "optimality" in such systems, and what constitutes the capacity of such systems to generate superior results are other issues that the chapters help address. The data presented here show how the policy work system involves not only consideration of changes in governance practices leading to shifts in the provenance of advice, but also to its content. Departures from the orthodox, largely internal, rational-technical, "speaking truth" type of policy advising towards more diffuse and fragmented "sharing of influence" approach reflect changes in the contemporary policy work environment and practices where there has been an erosion of whatever policy advisory hegemony the professional public service once exercised. In a more porous, fluid, and diversified contemporary policy work landscape, the types of policy work practices that are required have changed, and the chapters both detail these changes and describe and assess their implications for policy work and policy workers for the first time at various levels of government and in the non-governmental sector.

Revisiting Policy Capacity

Each of the chapters presents a snapshot of a specific aspect of policy work, highlighting the changing environment of policy advice systems in which policy work takes place. Individually, each represents a significant contribution to the growing Canadian literature on the subject and outlines key mechanisms at work in the policy process in Canada.

This conceptual and empirical work, however, brings concerns about a second issue to the forefront, which is the availability of adequate "policy capacity" in both governmental and non-governmental organizations to attain high-quality results from their efforts. Empirical research has been undertaken, by or on behalf of government agencies for some time now, attempting to measure observable objective indicators to measure policy capacity (Singleton 2001b; Ontario Executive Research Group 1999; Hicks and Watson 2007). Inputs such as the number of policy staff, their education levels, available resources, and ongoing training are detailed in the chapters here. However, the survey-based chapters show many other factors involved in policy work are also related to policy capacity.

An important determinant of overall policy capacity, for example, is policy and politically based attitudes held by rank-and-file policy workers, but other contributions in this volume also suggest that policy capacity is found at different levels and units of analysis. Table 18.1 reflects a broader understanding of policy capacity that includes all of the individual, organizational, and system-wide factors raised in the

Table 18.1 Policy Capacity Framework

Skills resources	Analytical	Managerial	Political
Individual	Individual analytical capacity – Knowledge, skills, and expertise in policy analysis and evaluation	Individual managerial capacity – Managerial expertise in planning, organizing, budgeting, contracting, staffing, directing, and controlling	Individual political capacity – Knowledge about policy process and stakeholders' positions and interests – Skills in communication, negotiation, and consensus building
Organization (state and non-state actors)	Organizational analytical capacity – Availability of and (or) accessibility to policy professionals with adequate individual analytical capacity – Practices and organizational machinery (both hardware and software) for collecting and analysing data – Organizational culture embracing evidence-based policymaking	Organizational managerial capacity – Organizational commitment to policy effectiveness – Ability to mobilize resources to design, implement, and evaluate policies – Level of coordination of the internal process – Performance management and administrative accountability	Organizational political capacity – Agency's standing in the policy process – Processes for stakeholder engagement – Level of access to key policymakers
Policy system or subsystem (sectoral, regional, national)	System-wide analytical capacity – The extent and quality of system-wide data; access to the data – Availability and use of policy advisory services – Institutional requirements and standards for policy analysis and evaluation – Policy learning capability	System-wide managerial capacity – Intergovernmental and inter-agency coordination – Effectiveness of policy network and policy community – Clarity in the roles and responsibilities of different actors in the policy process	System-wide political capacity – Political accountability for policies – Public trust in government – Level of participation of non-state actors in policy process – Role of the presence of policy entrepreneur(s)

chapters here. These suggest any considerations of improving or optimizing policy work must take into consideration multiple factors within the analytical, management, and political contexts in which that work takes place. Thus there is no "silver bullet" or sole factor that determines organizational capacity but rather an "ecosystem" of factors that must be carefully nurtured and managed if high-quality analysis is to be attained.

Naturally, many of the chapters in this volume focus on individual policy workers, and thus the measures of capacity tend to focus on the quality and quantity of skills and/or knowledge needed for analysis and policy work in each respective context. Chapter 7 (O'Reilly, Inwood, and Johns) and chapter 16 (Levasseur) address these systematic concerns; for example, looking at aspects such as intergovernmental and organizational capacity and their effects on policy work.

As the chapters in this volume attest, however, policy work and the capacity to undertake it look considerably different when the boundaries of investigation are expanded to include a broader set of actors and activities. The survey and interview data analysed in this volume not only speak to differences and complexity in the types of work policy actors undertake in different sectors, but also how they vary by level of government and type of governmental or non-governmental organization.

Scholarly, Pedagogical, and Practitioner Implications

For those who teach the art and craft of policy in any of Canada's seventeen schools of public administration and policy or in in-house public service training and instruction institutions, a few additional conclusions are warranted.

Broadly, this volume's findings are similar to those reported in comparable international studies, in that policy work in contemporary government involves a more diverse set of practices and activities than previously portrayed (Colebatch 2006a; Colebatch, Hoppe, and Noordegraaf 2010; Van Nispen and Scholten 2014; Blum and Schubert 2013).

This suggests that policy workers, to some degree, confront similar challenges in the practice of policy work and engage in similar types of policy work. This is directly pertinent to pedagogy in that it raises questions as to what is prized in instruction and what foundational policy work skills are required in today's policy landscape.

From a Canadian perspective, Clark, Eisen, and Pal's (n.d.) "Atlas of Public Policy and Management: An Online Database of Pedagogy and Advice" provides the most comprehensive current attempt to review and measure the distribution of instruction by subject matter in Canadian university policy and public administration programs. The authors suggest Canadian policy curricula are based on four main thematic areas: tools and skills, management functions, institutions and context, and policy sectors. Table 18.2 presents the averages for these categories based on the subsidiary dimensions outlined by the authors.

The atlas shows that within these four categories, on average, Canadian policy schools continue to dedicate the lion's share of their instruction to traditional policy work tasks and methods such as economic analysis, quantitative methods, public financial management, evaluation and performance measurement, compared to training in such as areas as leadership, communications, and professional practice. However, the high standard deviation scores in all of the categories reveal a considerable variation of instructional emphasis. Similarly, while programs provide substantial instruction on the context of policy work and the institutions within which it occurs, the emphasis is placed on ethics and accountability and clear understandings of democratic institutions and policy process. In addition, it suggests there are pedagogical opportunities to provide instruction that can facilitate students' ability to use "soft" policy skills. Further, the evidence, particularly from the surveys conducted, confirms a shift towards policy process generalists rather than subject matter experts.

Chapters in this volume dealing with provincial and sub-national governments suggest this composition is even more acute in the provinces and territories, where analysts have little formal training in formal policy analytical techniques and work mainly in small units deeply embedded in provincial and territorial ministries in the provincial or territorial capitals. They lack substantive knowledge of the areas in which they work and tend to bring process-related knowledge to the table. They also tend to work on a relatively small number of issue areas, often on a "firefighting" basis, like their federal counterparts in the regions. While there may be basic commonalities in the analytical practices and behaviour of analysts at all three levels of government, as Howlett and Wellstead's discussion (chapter 6) has pointed out, they are different, and these differences reflect the institutional characteristics of government at each level, especially the smaller size and

Table 18.2 Curriculum Design by Thematic Areas

	Average (%)	Standard deviation
Tools and skills	46.96	14.48
Strategy and structure	10.79	5.76
Economic analysis	6.68	4.51
Quantitative methods and management sciences	12.09	6.83
Leadership, communication, professional practice	17.39	13.88
Institutions and context	26.79	14.35
Democratic institutions and policy process	13.71	7.32
Ethics and accountability	2.22	3.21
Socio-economic, political, and global contexts	10.86	11.25
Management functions	12.56	10.94
Public financial management	4.05	4.44
Evaluation and performance measurement	2.32	3.58
Other management functions	6.21	6.87
Policy sectors	13.68	10.19
Fiscal, monetary, and tax policy	3.10	3.63
International development	1.68	2.36
Health	1.36	1.74
Other policy sectors	7.55	5.60
Total	100	

Source: Calculated from Clark, Eisen, and Pal (2014).

operating characteristics of provincial and territorial governments and their different task assignments and analytical needs.

However, other measures reveal similarities in the impact of changing governance contexts such as trends towards increased consultation and participation overtaking more traditional technical policy evaluations. Sub-national-level analysts, however, have more interactions with societal policy actors and experience more direct control by senior management than analysts employed by central governments. O'Reilly, Inwood, and Johns make an important contribution in this area in chapter 7, showing these federal and provincial differences have implications for intergovernmental policy capacity and the types of policy challenges that face governments in addressing multi-level policy work.

Taken together, these findings support the existence of distinct policy work styles at different levels of government that are a product of the prevailing governance arrangements, institutional and contextual settings within which policy work is undertaken (Howlett and Lindquist 2004; Dobuzinskis, Howlett, and Laycock 2007), and these differences should inform study and training in this country in a way they currently do not.

Table 18.1 is also interesting from the perspective of how policy managers report their own policy work. The data presented by Howlett reveal that policy managers perform tasks similar to those of non-managers but are themselves a group that requires careful analysis. Intra-group distinctions and variance suggest, pedagogically, that programs that cater to executive training may wish to offer specialized courses that can speak to the "politics" of policy work at the management level. That is, courses that can prepare managers for how the incentive structure of players in the policy process is aligned with their respective behaviour patterns and how the interaction of how these players affects policy outcomes, are needed if policy work is to be relevant to practitioners (Wu et al. 2010). Further, despite engaging in similar forms of policy work to that of non-managers, managers enjoy some advantages over non-managers in their access to key decision-makers and their ability to deal with longer-term issues, underscoring the significant role played by managers in policy formulation and design. Those who teach management cohorts or those expected to become managers should emphasize the full spectrum of policy work skills required, such as negotiation and stakeholder management, in addition to more traditional analytical techniques and skills.

Differences in the capacity and types of policy work undertaken in policy sectors have long been acknowledged (Peters 1996; Halligan 1995; Prince 1983). Pedagogically, this diversity is also reflected in Clark and Pal's 2011 analysis, which shows significant variance among the policy sectors that receive different treatment in program offerings. This in part reflects differences in available expertise within these programs as well as curriculum differences attributable to different jurisdictional standards and expectations.

The evidence in this volume, however, makes clear that sectoral differences extend beyond government to broader sectors of society. That is, among the policy-capacity challenges that policy workers face is that policy work practices within the public and non-governmental sectors differ markedly. Here too survey findings confirm a trend towards more generalist professional public service policy workers. While public sector challenges relate to the changing contexts of public sector policy work and budgetary issues affecting the range of skills available and the capacity required to have and exercise them, the non-governmental policy sector struggles with low PAC and inability to staff policy work–related positions.

As Evans and Wellstead (chapter 14) and Levasseur (chapter 16) conclude, this is attributable in large part to differences in organizational size and scale. NGOs, for the most part, simply do not have the capacity to create dedicated policy units, and this policy work is thus only one aspect of work in this sector. As Levasseur notes, there are differences across non-governmental sectors, with some organizations capable of engaging in policy work and process participation while others are not. This indicates that the "lumpy" or uneven distribution of capacity across government departments and agencies extends to the non-governmental sectors as well. With large supporting policy units and more time to engage in policy work, government workers can be expected to be more engaged in specific and complex policy tasks than NGO respondents. Again, differences in the practices and capabilities of these two major groups of policy workers should be better reflected in pedagogy than it now in Canada schools and policy training institutions.

Future Research Directions

Finally, while the results of these chapters are important for pedagogy and practitioners, the work contained in this volume also has a sizeable impact outside of Canada. Many of the same methods and survey questions have been employed in studies of policy workers undertaken in countries like in Australia (Head et al. 2014; Carson and Wellstead 2014) and the Czech Republic (Veselý 2013), among others, providing an important comparative dimension to this study and to the study of policy work in general.

This volume advances scholarship on policy work, but certainly has not exhausted the research agenda. The chapters suggest additional research is needed to better study sectoral policy work dynamics, for example, including changes in capacities and practices over time. There is also a clear need to better study work practices of particular sets of policy workers such as professionals and scientific workers as well as "street-level" workers. While this volume contributes to this end, additional research is needed to examine policy workers at the middle to senior management levels, as well as those in a broader range of non-governmental organizations beyond interest associations such as lobbyists, think tanks, and advocacy groups, and additional study of the partisan-political sphere of advisory activities is also highly recommended.

There are also important lines of inquiry that future scholarship should explore that fell outside the empirical mandate of this volume. Notions of policy work, policy capacity, and advisory arrangements need to be framed from critical, feminist, and interpretivist scholarly perspectives, much as was done in Klenk's chapter 12, where the social construction of knowledge was found to be problematic when examining aspects of evidence-based policy practices. But the empirical survey and interview research provided in this book provide improved depictions of how complex policy work has become and thus help augment the case study and fact-base of researchers interested in these questions while providing important insights for practitioners and teachers in this field.

References

6, Perri. 2004. *E-Governance: Styles of Political Judgement in the Information Age Polity*. London: Palgrave Macmillan.

6, Perri, Diana Leat, Kimberly Seltzer, and Gerry Stoker. 2002. *Towards Holistic Governance: The New Reform Agenda*. Basingstoke, UK: Palgrave.

Abelson, Donald E. 2002. *Do Think Tanks Matter? Assessing the Impact of Public Policy Institutes*. Montreal and Kingston: McGill-Queen's University Press.

– 2007. "Any Ideas? Think Tanks and Policy Analysis in Canada." In *Policy Analysis in Canada: The State of the Art*, ed. L. Dobuzinskis, M. Howlett, and D. Laycock, 298–310. Toronto: University of Toronto Press.

Aberbach, J.D., and B.A. Rockman. 1989. "On the Rise, Transformation, and Decline of analysis in the US Government." *Governance: An International Journal of Policy, Administration and Institutions* 2 (3): 293–314. http://dx.doi.org/10.1111/j.1468-0491.1989.tb00094.x.

Ackerman, M.S., V. Pipek, and V. Wulf. 2003. *Sharing Expertise beyond Knowledge Management*. Cambridge, MA: MIT Press.

Adams, D. 2004. "Usable Knowledge in Public Policy." *Australian Journal of Public Administration* 63 (1): 29–42. http://dx.doi.org/10.1111/j.1467-8500.2004.00357.x.

Ajzen, I. 1991. "The Theory of Planned Behavior." *Organizational Behavior and Human Decision Processes* 50 (2): 179–211. http://dx.doi.org/10.1016/0749-5978(91)90020-T.

Ajzen, Icek, and Martin Fishbein. 2005. "The Influence of Attitudes on Behavior." In *The Handbook of Attitudes*, ed. D. Albarracín, B.T. Johnson, and M.P. Zanna, 173–221. Mahwah, NJ: Erlbaum.

Akerley, Marj, Peter Cowan, and Anna Belanger. 2008. "Collaborative Revolution." Canadian Government Executive, 8 October, http://canadiangovernmentexecutive.ca/collaborative-revolution/.

Albert, M.A., A. Fretheim, and D. Maiga. 2007. "Factors Influencing the Utilization of Research Findings by Health Policy-Makers in a Developing Country: The Selection of Mali's Essential Medicines." *Health Research Policy and Systems* 5 (2): 1–8.

Amara, N., M. Ouimet, and R. Landry. 2004. "New Evidence on Instrumental, Conceptual, and Symbolic Utilization of University Research in Government Agencies." *Science Communication* 26 (1): 75–106. http://dx.doi.org/10.1177/1075547004267491.

Andersen, David F., and Sharon S. Dawes. 1991. *Government Information: A Primer and Casebook*. Englewood Cliffs, NJ: Prentice-Hall.

Anderson, G. 1996. "The New Focus on the Policy Capacity of the Federal Government." *Canadian Public Administration* 39 (4): 469–88. http://dx.doi.org/10.1111/j.1754-7121.1996.tb00146.x.

Andersen, J.A. 2010. "Public versus Private Managers: How Public and Private Managers Differ in Leadership Behavior." *Public Administration Review* 70 (1): 131–41. http://dx.doi.org/10.1111/j.1540-6210.2009.02117.x.

Argote, Linda, and Paul Ingram. 2000. "Knowledge Transfer: A Basis for Competitive Advantage in Firms." *Organizational Behavior and Human Decision Processes* 82 (1): 150–69. http://dx.doi.org/10.1006/obhd.2000.2893.

Atkinson, M., D. Beland, G.P. Marchildon, K. McNutt, P. Phillips, and K. Rasmussen. 2013. *Governance and Public Policy in Canada: A View from the Provinces*. Toronto: University of Toronto Press.

Aucoin, P. 1986. "Organizational Change in the Machinery of Canadian Government: From Rational Management to Brokerage Politics." *Canadian Journal of Political Science / Revue canadienne de science politique* 19 (1): 3–28. http://dx.doi.org/10.1017/S0008423900057954.

– 2010. "Canada." In *Partisan Appointees and Public Servants: An International Analysis*, ed. C. Eichbaum and R. Shaw, 64–93. Boston, MA: Edward Elgar Publishing. http://dx.doi.org/10.4337/9781849803298.00008.

– 2012. "New Political Governance in Westminster Systems: Impartial Public Administration and Management Performance at Risk." *Governance: An International Journal of Policy, Administration and Institutions* 25 (2): 177–99. http://dx.doi.org/10.1111/j.1468-0491.2012.01569.x.

Aucoin, P., and H. Bakvis. 2005. "Public Service Reform and Policy Capacity." In *Challenges to State Policy Capacity: Global Trends and Comparative Perspectives*, ed. M. Painter and J. Pierre, 185–204. New York: Palgrave Macmillan.

Australian National Audit Office (ANAO). 2001. *Developing Policy Advice, Auditor-General Audit Report No. 21 2001–2002 Performance Audit*. Canberra: ANAO.

Axworthy, T. 1988. "Of Secretaries to Princes." *Canadian Public Administration* 31 (2): 247–64. http://dx.doi.org/10.1111/j.1754-7121.1988.tb01316.x.
Bache, I., and M. Flinders. 2004. *Multi-Level Governance*. New York: Oxford University Press. http://dx.doi.org/10.1093/0199259259.001.0001.
Baehr, P.R. 1981. "Futures Studies and Policy Analysis in the Political Process: The Netherlands Scientific Council for Government Policy." In *Policy Analysis and Policy Innovation: Patterns, Problems and Potentials*, ed. P.R. Baehr and B. Wittrock, 93–118. Beverly Hills, CA: Sage Publications.
Bakvis, H. 1997. "Advising the Executive: Think Tanks, Consultants, Political Staff and Kitchen Cabinets." In *The Hollow Crown: Countervailing Trends in Core Executives*, ed. P. Weller, H. Bakvis, and R.A.W. Rhodes, 84–125. Basingstoke, UK: Macmillan. http://dx.doi.org/10.1007/978-1-349-25870-3_5.
– 2000. "Rebuilding Policy Capacity in the Era of the Fiscal Dividend: A Report from Canada." *Governance: An International Journal of Policy, Administration and Institutions* 13 (1): 71–103. http://dx.doi.org/10.1111/0952-1895.00124.
Banfield, E.C. 1977. "Policy Science as Metaphysical Madness." In *Statesmanship and Bureaucracy*, ed. A. Robert & Goldwin, 1–35. Washington, DC: American Enterprise Institute for Public Policy.
Barabási, A.L., and R. Albert. 1999. "Emergence of Scaling in Random Networks." *Science* 286 (5439): 509–12.
Barford, I., and P.T. Hester. 2011. "Analysis of Generation Y Workforce Motivation Using Multiattribute Utility Theory." *Defense Acquisition Research Journal* 18 (1): 63–80.
Bartlett, D. 2011. "The Neglect of the Political: An Alternative Evidence-Based Practice for I-O Psychology." *Industrial and Organizational Psychology: Perspectives on Science and Practice* 4 (1): 27–31. http://dx.doi.org/10.1111/j.1754-9434.2010.01289.x.
Bartol, K., and A. Srivastava. 2002. "Encouraging Knowledge Sharing: The Role of Organizational Reward Systems." *Journal of Leadership & Organizational Studies* 9 (1): 64–76. http://dx.doi.org/10.1177/107179190200900105.
Baskoy, Tuna, Bryan Evans, and John Shields. 2011. "Assessing Policy Capacity in Canada's Public Services: Perspectives of Deputy and Assistant Deputy Ministers." *Canadian Public Administration* 54 (2): 217–34. http://dx.doi.org/10.1111/j.1754-7121.2011.00171.x.
Baughman, W.A., D.W. Dorsey, and D. Zarefsky. 2011. "Putting Evidence in Its Place: A Means Not an End." *Industrial and Organizational Psychology: Perspectives on Science and Practice* 4 (1): 62–4. http://dx.doi.org/10.1111/j.1754-9434.2010.01297.x.
Beer, Stafford. 1974. *Designing Freedom*. Toronto: CBC Learning Systems.

Behm, A., L. Bennington, and J. Cummane. 2000. "A Value-Creating Model for Effective Policy Services." *Journal of Management Development* 19 (3): 162–78. http://dx.doi.org/10.1108/02621710010318756.

Bekke, H.A.G.M., and F.M. van der Meer. 2000. *Civil Service Systems in Western Europe*. Cheltenham, UK: Edward Elgar.

Belkhodja, O., N. Amara, R. Landry, and M. Ouimet. 2007. "The Extent and Organizational Determinants of Research Utilization in Canadian Health Services Organizations." *Science Communication* 28 (3): 377–417. http://dx.doi.org/10.1177/1075547006298486.

Benkler, Yochai. 2006. *The Wealth of Networks: How Social Production Transforms Markets and Freedom*. New Haven, CT: Yale University Press.

Bennett, S., and M. McPhail. 1992. "Policy Process Perceptions of Senior Canadian Federal Civil Servants: A View of the State and Its Environment." *Canadian Public Administration* 35 (3): 299–316. http://dx.doi.org/10.1111/j.1754-7121.1992.tb00696.x.

Benoit, L. 2006. "Ministerial Staff: The Life and Times of Parliament's Statutory Orphans." Commission of Inquiry into the Sponsorship Program and Advertising Activities, Restoring Accountability. Ottawa: Public Works and Government Services Canada.

Bernier, L., and M. Howlett. 2009. *La capacité d'analyse des politiques au gouvernement du Québec: Résultats du sondage auprès des fonctionnaires québécois*. Report to the Institute of Public Administration of Canada, Quebec City Branch.

– 2011. "La capacité d'analyse des politiques au gouvernement du Québec : Resultats du sondage auprès de fonctionnaires québécois." *Canadian Public Administration* 54 (1): 143–52. http://dx.doi.org/10.1111/j.1754-7121.2011.00168.x.

Berry, J., and D. Arons. 2005. *A Voice for Non-profits*. Washington, DC: Brookings Institution Press.

Bertot, John C., Paul T. Jaeger, and Justin M. Grimes. 2010. "Using ICTs to Create a Culture of Transparency: E-government and Social Media as Openness and Anti-Corruption Tools for Societies." *Government Information Quarterly* 27 (3): 264–71. http://dx.doi.org/10.1016/j.giq.2010.03.001.

Bevir, M., and R.A.W. Rhodes. 2001. "Decentering Tradition: Interpreting British Government." *Administration & Society* 33 (2): 107–32. http://dx.doi.org/10.1177/00953990122019703.

Bevir, M., R.A.W. Rhodes, and P. Weller. 2003. "Traditions of Governance: Interpreting the Changing Role of the Public Sector." *Public Administration* 81 (1): 1–17. http://dx.doi.org/10.1111/1467-9299.00334.

Beyer, J.M., and H.M. Trice. 1982. "The Utilization Process: A Conceptual Framework and Synthesis of Empirical Findings." *Administrative Science Quarterly* 27 (4): 591–622. http://dx.doi.org/10.2307/2392533.

Bilodeau, Nancy, Claude Laurin, and Aidan Vining. 2007. "Choice of Organizational Form Makes a Real Difference: The Impact of Corporatization on Government Agencies in Canada." *Journal of Public Administration: Research and Theory* 17 (1): 119–47. http://dx.doi.org/10.1093/jopart/mul014.

Binz-Scharf, Maria Christina, David Lazer, and Ines Mergel. 2008. "Searching for Answers: Networks of Practice among Public Administrators." Harvard Kennedy School Faculty Research Workshop Papers RWP08-046.

– 2012. "Searching for Answers: Networks of Practice among Public Administrators." *American Review of Public Administration* 42 (2): 202–25. http://dx.doi.org/10.1177/0275074011398956.

Black, N. 2001. "Evidence-Based Policy: Proceed with Care." *BMJ (Clinical Research Ed.)* 323 (7307): 275–9. http://dx.doi.org/10.1136/bmj.323.7307.275.

Blondel, Jean, and Maurizio Cotta, eds. 1996. *Party Government: An Inquiry into the Relationship between Government and Supporting Parties in Liberal Democracies*. New York: St Martin's.

Bloomfield, Brian P., and Ardha Best. 1992. "Management Consultants: Systems Development, Power and the Translation of Problems." *Sociological Review* 40 (3): 533–60. http://dx.doi.org/10.1111/j.1467-954X.1992.tb00401.x.

Bloomfield, Brian P., and Ardha Danieli. 1995. "The Role of Management Consultants in the Development of Information Technology: The Indissoluble Nature of Socio-political and Technical Skills." *Journal of Management Studies* 32 (1): 23–46. http://dx.doi.org/10.1111/j.1467-6486.1995.tb00644.x.

Blum, Sonja, and Klaus Schubert, eds. 2013. *Policy Analysis in Germany*. Bristol, UK: Policy. http://dx.doi.org/10.1332/policypress/9781447306252.001.0001.

Boardman, C., B. Bozeman, and B. Ponomariov. 2010. "Private Sector Imprinting: An Examination of the Impacts of Private Sector Job Experience on Public Manager's Work Attitudes." *Public Administration Review* 70 (1): 50–9. http://dx.doi.org/10.1111/j.1540-6210.2009.02110.x.

Bock, Gee-Woo, Robert W. Zmud, Young-Gul Kim, and Jae-Nam Lee. 2005. "Behavioral Intention Formation in Knowledge Sharing: Examining the Roles of Extrinsic Motivators, Social-Psychological Forces, and Organizational Climate." In "Information Technologies and Knowledge Management," special issue of *MIS Quarterly* 29, no. 1 (2005): 87–111.

Bogenschneider, K., and T.J. Corbett. 2010. *Evidence-Based Policy-Making*. New York: Routledge.

Booher, David E. 2004. "Collaborative Governance Practices and Democracy." *National Civic Review* 93 (4): 32–46. http://dx.doi.org/10.1002/ncr.69.

Boston, J. 1994. "Purchasing Policy Advice: The Limits of Contracting Out." *Governance: An International Journal of Policy, Administration and Institutions* 7 (1): 1–30. http://dx.doi.org/10.1111/j.1468-0491.1994.tb00167.x.

Boston, J., J. Martin, J. Pallot, and P. Walsh. 1996. *Public Management: The New Zealand Model*. Auckland: Oxford University Press.

Bourgault, J. 2002. "The Role of the Deputy Ministers in Canadian Government." In *The Handbook of Canadian Public Administration*, ed. Christopher Dunn, 430–49. Toronto: Oxford University Press.

Bourgault, J., and C. Dunn, eds. 2013. *Deputy Ministers in Canada: Comparative and Jurisdictional Perspectives*. Toronto: IPAC/University of Toronto Press.

Bozeman, B., and L.V. Blankenship. 1979. "Science Information and Governmental Decision-Making: The Case of the National Science Foundation." *Public Administration Review* 39 (1): 53–7. http://dx.doi.org/10.2307/3110379.

Bradford, Neil, and Caroline Andrew. 2010. *Local Immigration Partnership Councils: A Promising Canadian Innovation*. Report prepared for Citizenship and Immigration Canada.

Bridge, Richard. 2002. "The Law Governing Advocacy by Charitable Organizations: The Case for Change." *The Philanthropist* 17 (2): 2–33.

Briner, R.B., D. Denyer, and D.M. Rousseau. 2009. "Evidence-Based Management: Concept Clean-up Time?" *Academy of Management Perspectives* 23 (4): 19–32.

Brinkerhoff, D.W. 2010. "Developing Capacity in Fragile States." *Public Administration and Development* 30 (1): 66–78. http://dx.doi.org/10.1002/pad.545.

Brinkerhoff, D.W., and B.L. Crosby. 2002. *Managing Policy Reform: Concepts and Tools for Decision-Makers in Developing and Transitional Countries*. Bloomfield, CT: Kumarian.

Brinkerhoff, D.W., and P.J. Morgan. 2010. "Capacity and Capacity Development: Coping with Complexity." *Public Administration and Development* 30 (1): 2–10. http://dx.doi.org/10.1002/pad.559.

Brint, Steven. September 1990. "Rethinking the Policy Influence of Experts: From General Characterizations to Analysis of Variation." *Sociological Forum* 5 (3): 361–85.

British Columbia. 2010. *Citizens @ the Centre: B.C. Government 2.0; A Transformation and Technology Strategy for the British Columbia Public Service*. Victoria, BC: Government of the Province of British Columbia. http://www.gov.bc.ca/citz/citizens_engagement/gov20.pdf.

– 2012. *Estimates: Fiscal Year Ending March 31, 2013*. Victoria, BC: Ministry of Finance. http://www.bcbudget.gov.bc.ca/2012/estimates/2012_Estimates.pdf.

Bryman, A. 2004. "Interviewing in Qualitative Research." *Social Research Methods* 2:318–44.

Bryce, James. 1921. *Modern Democracies*. New York: Macmillan.

Budge, Ian, and D.J. Fairle. 1983. *Explaining and Predicting Elections: Issue Effects and Party Strategies in Twenty-Three Democracies*. London: Allen & Unwin.

Budge, Ian, David Robertson, and Derek Hearl, eds. 1987. *Ideology, Strategy and Party Change: Spatial Analysis of Postwar Election Programmes in 19 Democracies*. Cambridge, MA: Cambridge University Press. http://dx.doi.org/10.1017/CBO9780511558771.

Bunge, M. 1963. "A General Black Box Theory." *Philosophy of Science* 30 (4): 346–58. http://dx.doi.org/10.1086/287954.

– 1997. "Mechanism and Explanation." *Philosophy of the Social Sciences* 27 (4): 410–65. http://dx.doi.org/10.1177/004839319702700402.

Burns, J.P., and B. Bowornwathana. 2001. *Civil Service Systems in Asia*. Cheltenham, UK: Edward Elgar.

Bushnell, Peter. 1991. "Policy Advice: Planning for Performance." *Public Sector* 14 (1): 14–16.

Butcher, John, Benoit Freyens, and John Wanna. 2009. *Policy in Action: The Challenge of Service Delivery*. Sydney: University of New South Wales Press.

Campbell, C. 1988. Review of *The Political Roles of Senior Government Officials in Advanced Democracies. British Journal of Political Science* 18 (2): 243–72. http://dx.doi.org/10.1017/S0007123400005081.

Campbell, C., and G.J. Szablowski. 1979. *The Superbureaucrats: Structure and Behaviour in Central Agencies*. Toronto: Macmillan of Canada.

Canada. 1996a. *Managing Horizontal Policy Issues: Report of the Task Force on Managing Horizontal Policy Issues*. Ottawa: Privy Council Office.

– 1996b. *Strengthening Our Policy Capacity* – Report of the Task Force on Strengthening the Policy Capacity of the Federal Government. Ottawa.

– 2000. *Report of the Auditor General of Canada: Chapter 21 – Post-Secondary Recruitment Program of the Federal Public Service*. http://www.oag-bvg.gc.ca/internet/English/parl_oag_200012_21_e_11208.html.

– 2007. *Fourteenth Annual Report to the Prime Minister on the Public Service of Canada*.

– 2010. *Fourth Report to the Prime Minister: A Relevant and Connected Public Service*. http://www.pco-bcp.gc.ca/index.asp?lang=eng&Page=information&Sub=publications&Doc=ar-ra/17-2010/4th-4eme/index-eng.htm. Accessed 15 February 2010.

– 2015. *Twenty-Second Annual Report to the Prime Minister on the Public Service of Canada*. http://www.clerk.gc.ca/local_grfx/docs/22rpt/22rpt-eng.pdf.

Canada. Statistics Canada. 2004. *Cornerstones of Community: Highlights from the National Survey of Non-profit and Voluntary Organizations*. Ottawa: Statistics Canada.

Canadian Council for International Co-operation. 2006. *Building Knowledge and Capacity for Policy Influence: Reflections and Resources*. Ottawa: CCIC.

Canadian Public Service Commission. 2008. *Public Service Staffing Advertisements and Notifications*. Ottawa: Canadian Public Service Commission.

Carroll, Barbara Wake, Gerald Bierling, and Michael Rosenblatt. 2000. "Movers and Stayers: Mobility Patterns among Senior Public Servants in Canadian Provinces." *Canadian Public Administration* 42 (3): 198–217.

Carson, D., and A. Wellstead. 2014. "Government with a Cast of Dozens: Policy Capacity Risks and Policy Work in the Northern Territory." *Australian Journal of Public Administration* 72 (2): 162–75,

Carter, Susan. 2011. "Public Policy and the Nonprofit Sector." *Philanthropist* 23 (4): 427–35.

Carty, R. Kenneth. 1991. *Canadian Parties in the Constituencies: Royal Commission on Electoral Reform and Party Financing Research Studies*, vol. 23. Toronto: Dundurn.

– 2006. *The Shifting Place of Political Parties in Canadian Public Life*. Montreal: Institute for Research on Public Policy.

Cassell, C. 2011. "Evidence-Based I-O Psychology: What Do We Lose on the Way?" *Industrial and Organizational Psychology: Perspectives on Science and Practice* 4 (1): 23–6. http://dx.doi.org/10.1111/j.1754-9434.2010.01288.x.

Chadwick, A. 2009. "Web 2.0: New Challenges for the Study of E-Democracy in an Era of Informational Exuberance." *I/S: A Journal of Law and Policy for the Information Society* 5 (1): 9–41.

Christensen, R., and B. Gazley. 2008. "Capacity for Public Administration: Analysis of Meaning and Measurement." *Public Administration and Development* 28 (4): 265–79. http://dx.doi.org/10.1002/pad.500.

Christensen, T., and P. Laegreid. 2001. *New Public Management: The Transformation of Ideas and Practice*. Aldershot, UK: Ashgate.

– 2005. "Autonomization and Policy Capacity: The Dilemmas and Challenges Facing Political Executives." In *Challenges to State Policy Capacity: Global Trends and Comparative Perspectives*, ed. M. Painter and J. Pierre, 137–63. New York: Palgrave Macmillan.

Christian, William, and Colin Campbell. 1996. *Parties, Leaders and Ideologies in Canada*. Toronto: McGraw-Hill Ryerson.

Clark, Alistair. 2004. "The Continued Relevance of Local Parties in Representative Democracies." *Politics* 24 (1): 35–45. http://dx.doi.org/10.1111/j.1467-9256.2004.00203.x.

Clark, Ian D., Ben Eisen, and Leslie A. Pal., eds. N.d. "The Atlas of Public Policy and Management: An Online Database of Pedagogy and Advice." http://portal.publicpolicy.utoronto.ca.

– 2014."What Are the Core Components of Master's-Level Public Management Education and How Is Learning within Them Assessed?" Paper presented at the 3rd Annual CAPPA Research Conference, Kingston, ON, May 21–2.

Clark, Timothy. 1995. *Managing Consultants: Consultancy as the Management of Impressions*. Maidenhead, UK: Open University Press.

Clark, Timothy, and Robin Fincham. 2002. *Critical Consulting: New Perspectives on the Management Advice Industry*. Oxford: Blackwell Business.

Clark, Timothy, and Graeme Salaman. 1996. "Telling Tales: Management Consultancy as the Art of Story Telling." In *Metaphor and Organizations*, ed. David Grant and Clifford Oswick, 166–83. New York: Sage Publications.

Clarke, Harold D., Lawrence LeDuc, Jane Jenson, and Jon H. Pammett. 1996. *Absent Mandate: Canadian Electoral Politics in an Age of Restructuring*. 3rd ed. Vancouver: Gage Publishing.

Clarke, Harold D., and Marianne C. Stewart. 1998. "The Decline of Parties in the Minds of Citizens." *Annual Review of Political Science* 1 (1): 357–78. http://dx.doi.org/10.1146/annurev.polisci.1.1.357.

Cohen, Daniel. 2006. "From Babel to Knowledge: Data Mining Large Digital Collections." *D-Lib Magazine* 12 (3). http://dx.doi.org/10.1045/march2006-cohen.

Cohn, D. 2007. "Academics and Public Policy: Informing Policy Analysis and Policy-making." In *Policy Analysis in Canada: The State of the Art*, ed. L. Dobuzinskis, M. Howlett, and D. Laycock, 574–97. Toronto: University of Toronto Press.

Colebatch, H.K. 2005. "Policy Analysis, Policy Practice and Political Science." *Australian Journal of Public Administration* 64 (3): 14–23. http://dx.doi.org/10.1111/j.1467-8500.2005.00448.x.

– , ed. 2006a. *Beyond the Policy Cycle: The Policy Process in Australia*. Sydney: Allen & Unwin.

– 2006b. "What Work Makes Policy?" *Policy Sciences* 39 (4): 309–21. http://dx.doi.org/10.1007/s11077-006-9025-4.

– , ed. 2006c. *The Work of Policy: An International Survey*. New York: Rowman and Littlefield.

Colebatch, Hal K., Robert Hoppe, and Mirko Noordegraaf, eds. 2011. *Working for Policy*. Amsterdam: Amsterdam University Press. http://dx.doi.org/10.5117/9789089642530.

Colebatch, H.K., and B.A. Radin. 2006. "Mapping the Work of Policy." In *The Work of Policy: An International survey*, ed. H.K. Colebatch, 217–26. New York: Rowman and Littlefield.

Condit, C.M., J. Lynch, and E. Winderman. 2012. "Recent Rhetorical Studies in Public Understanding of Science, Multiple Purposes and Strengths." *Public Understanding of Science (Bristol, England)* 21 (4): 386–400. http://dx.doi.org/10.1177/0963662512437330.

Connelly, C.E., D. Zweig, J. Webster, and J.P. Trougakos. 2012. "Knowledge Hiding in Organizations." *Journal of Organizational Behavior* 33 (1): 64–88. http://dx.doi.org/10.1002/job.737.

Cook, Niall. 2008. *Enterprise 2.0: How Social Software Will Change the Future of Work*. London: Ashgate.

Corcoran, Jan, and Fiona McLean. 1998. "The Selection of Management Consultants: How Are Governments Dealing with This Difficult Decision? An Exploratory Study." *International Journal of Public Sector Management* 11 (1): 37–54. http://dx.doi.org/10.1108/09513559810199889.

Cote, A., K. Baird, and I. Green. 2007. *A Vital National Institution: What a Cross-Section of Canadians Think about the Prospects for Canada's Public Service in the 21st Century*. Ottawa: Public Policy Forum.

Craft, Jonathan. 2013. "Appointed Political Staffs and the Diversification of Policy Advisory Sources: Theory and Evidence from Canada." *Policy and Society* 32 (3): 211–23. http://dx.doi.org/10.1016/j.polsoc.2013.07.003.

– 2015a. "Conceptualizing the Policy Work of Partisan Advisers." *Policy Sciences Journal* 48 (2): 135–58. http://dx.doi.org/10.1007/s11077-015-9212-2.

– 2015b. "Revisiting the Gospel: Appointed Political Staffs and Core Executive Policy Coordination." *International Journal of Public Administration* 38 (1): 56–65. http://dx.doi.org/10.1080/01900692.2014.928316.

– 2016. *Backrooms and Beyond: Partisan Advisers and the Politics of Policy Work in Canada*. Toronto: University of Toronto Press.

Craft, Jonathan, and Michael Howlett. 2012a. "Policy Formulation, Governance Shifts and Policy Influence: Location and Content in Policy Advisory Systems." *Journal of Public Policy* 32 (2): 79–98. http://dx.doi.org/10.1017/S0143814X12000049.

– 2012b. "Subsystems Structuring, Shifting Mandates and Policy Capacity: Assessing Canada's Ability to Adapt to Climate Change." *Canadian Political Science Review* 6 (1): 3–14.

– 2013a. "The Dual Dynamics of Policy Advisory Systems: The Impact of Externalization and Politicization on Policy Advice." *Policy and Society* 32 (3): 187–97. http://dx.doi.org/10.1016/j.polsoc.2013.07.001.

– 2013b. "Policy Capacity and the Ability to Adapt to Climate Change: Canadian and U.S. Case Studies." *Review of Policy Research* 30 (1): 1–18. http://dx.doi.org/10.1111/ropr.12000.

Craft, Jonathan, and Matt Wilder. 2016. "Catching a Second Wave: Context and Compatibility in Advisory System Dynamics." *Policy Studies Journal: The Journal of the Policy Studies Organization*, DOI: 10.1111/psj.12133.

Craig, David. 2006. *Plundering the Public Sector.* Edinburgh: Robinson Publishing.

Cross, W. 2004. *Political Parties.* Vancouver: UBC Press.

– 2007. "Policy Study and Development in Canada's Political Parties." In *Policy Analysis in Canada: The State of the Art*, ed. L. Dobuzinskis, M. Howlett, and D. Laycock, 233–42. Toronto. University of Toronto Press.

Cross, William, and Lisa Young. 2002. "Policy Attitudes of Party Members in Canada: Evidence of Ideological Politics." *Canadian Journal of Political Science* 35 (4): 859–80. http://dx.doi.org/10.1017/S0008423902778475.

– 2006. *Are Canadian Political Parties Empty Vessels? Membership, Engagement and Policy Capacity*. Montreal: Institute for Research on Public Policy.

Cummings, S., and O. Nørgaard. 2004. "Conceptualising State Capacity: Comparing Kazakhstan and Kyrgyzstan." *Political Studies* 52 (4): 685–708. http://dx.doi.org/10.1111/j.1467-9248.2004.00503.x.

Czarniawska-Joerges, Barbara. 1989. "Merchants of Meaning: Management Consulting in the Swedish Public Sector." In *Organizational Symbolism*, ed. Barry A. Turner, 139–50. Berlin: Walter De Gruyter.

Czarniawska, Barbara, and Carmelo Mazza. 2003. "Consulting as a Liminal Space." *Human Relations* 56 (3): 267–90. http://dx.doi.org/10.1177/0018726703056003612.

Dalton, Russell, and Manfred Kuechler, eds. 1990. *Challenging the Political Order: New Social and Political Movements in Western Democracies*. New York: Oxford University Press.

Dalton, Russell, and Martin Wattenberg. 2000. "Unthinkable Democracy: Political Change in Advanced Industrial Democracies." In *Parties with Partisans: Political Change in Advanced Industrial Democracies*, ed. Russell Dalton and Martin Wattenberg, 2–18. New York: Oxford University Press.

D'Aquino, T. 1974. "The Prime Minister's Office: Catalyst or Cabal? Aspects of the Development of the Office in Canada and Some Thoughts about Its Future." *Canadian Public Administration* 17 (1): 55–79. http://dx.doi.org/10.1111/j.1754-7121.1974.tb01655.x.

Darr, Eric D., Linda Argote, and Dennis Epple. 1995. "The Acquisition, Transfer, and Depreciation of Knowledge in Service Organizations:

Productivity in Franchises." *Management Science* 41 (11): 1750–62. http://dx.doi.org/10.1287/mnsc.41.11.1750.

Davies, Anne. 2001. *Accountability: A Public Law Analysis of Government by Contract*. Oxford: Oxford University Press. http://dx.doi.org/10.1093/acprof:oso/9780198299486.001.0001.

– 2008. *The Public Law of Government Contracts*. Oxford: Oxford University Press. http://dx.doi.org/10.1093/acprof:oso/9780199287390.001.0001.

Davis, Glyn. 2000. "Conclusion: Policy Capacity and the Future of Governance." In *The Future of Governance*, ed. Glyn Davis and Michael Keating, 230–42. St Leonards, AUS: Allen Unwin.

Dawes, Sharon S., Anthony M. Cresswell, and Theresa A. Pardo. 2009. "From 'Need to Know' to 'Need to Share': Tangled Problems, Information Boundaries, and the Building of Public Sector Knowledge Networks." *Public Administration Review* 69 (3): 392–402. http://dx.doi.org/10.1111/j.1540-6210.2009.01987_2.x.

Dent, Helen. 2002. "Consultants and the Public Service." *Australian Journal of Public Administration* 61 (1): 108–13. http://dx.doi.org/10.1111/1467-8500.00265.

Di Francesco, M. 1999. "Measuring Performance in Policy Advice Output: Australian Developments." *International Journal of Public Sector Management* 12 (5): 420–31. http://dx.doi.org/10.1108/09513559910300181.

– 2000. "An Evaluation Crucible: Evaluating Policy Advice in Australian Central Agencies." *Australian Journal of Public Administration* 59 (1): 36–48. http://dx.doi.org/10.1111/1467-8500.00138.

Dluhy, Milan. 1981. "Policy Advice-Givers: Advocates? Technicians? Or Pragmatists?" In *New Strategic Perspectives on Social Policy*, ed. John E. Tropman, Milan Dluhy, and Roger M. Lind, 201–16. New York: Pergamon.

Dobell, A.R., Justin Longo, and Jodie Walsh. 2011. *Techniques, Tools and Toys in the 21st Century: Web-Enabled Platforms for Citizen Science and Civic Engagement in Integrated Coastal and Marine Spatial Planning*. Sienna: Aquatic Ecosystem Health and Management Society.

Dobell, Rodney. 1999. "Evaluation and Entitlements: Hartle's Search for Rationality in Government." In *Rationality in Public Policy: Retrospect and Prospect – A Tribute to Douglas G. Hartle*, ed. Richard M. Bird, Michael J. Trebilcock, and Thomas A. Wilson, 79–108. Canadian Tax Paper No. 104. Toronto: Canadian Tax Foundation.

Dobuzinskis, Laurent, Michael Howlett, and David Laycock. 2007. *Policy Analysis in Canada*. Toronto: University of Toronto Press.

Doern, G.B. 1971. "The Development of Policy Organization in the Executive Arena. In *The Structures of Policy-Making in Canada*, ed. G.B. Doern and P. Aucoin, 38–78. Toronto: Macmillan of Canada.

Donath, J., and D. Boyd. 2004. "Public Displays of Connection." *BT Technology Journal* 22 (4): 71–82. http://dx.doi.org/10.1023/B:BTTJ.0000047585.06264.cc.

Downs, Anthony. 1957. *An Economic Theory of Democracy*. New York: Harper & Row Publishers.

Doz, Yves, and Mikko Kosonen. 2008. *Fast Strategy: How Strategic Agility Will Help You Stay Ahead of the Game*. Philadelphia: Wharton School Publishing.

Dror, Yehezkel. 1967. "Policy Analysts: A New Professional Role in Government Service." *Public Administration Review* 27 (3): 197–203. http://dx.doi.org/10.2307/973282.

– 1986. *Policymaking under Adversity*. New Brunswick, NJ: Transaction Books.

Druckman, Alan. 2000. "The Social Scientist as Consultant." *American Behavioral Scientist* 43 (10): 1565–77. http://dx.doi.org/10.1177/00027640021957917.

Dryzek, John S. 1983. "Don't Toss Coins in Garbage Cans: A Prologue to Policy Design." *Journal of Public Policy* 3 (4): 345–67. http://dx.doi.org/10.1017/S0143814X00007510.

Dunn, W. 2004. *Public Policy Analysis: An Introduction*. Upper Saddle River, NJ: Pearson/Prentice Hall.

Dupré, J. Stephan. 1985. "Reflections on the Workability of Executive Federalism." In *Intergovernmental Relations: Research Study Volume 63 for the Royal Commission on the Economic Union and Development Prospects for Canada*, ed. Richard Simeon, 1–32. Toronto: University of Toronto Press.

Durning, D., and W. Osuna. 1994. "Policy Analysts' Roles and Value Orientations: An Empirical Investigation Using Q Methodology." *Journal of Policy Analysis and Management* 13 (4): 629–57. http://dx.doi.org/10.2307/3325491.

Edmunds, Angela, and Anne Morris. 2000. "The Problem of Information Overload in Business Organisations: A Review of the Literature." *International Journal of Information Management* 20 (1): 17–28. http://dx.doi.org/10.1016/S0268-4012(99)00051-1.

Edwards, Heather R., and Richard Hoefer. 2010. "Are Social Work Advocacy Groups Using Web 2.0 Effectively?" *Journal of Policy Practice* 9 (3–4): 220–39. http://dx.doi.org/10.1080/15588742.2010.489037.

Edwards, Linda. 2009. "Testing the Discourse of Declining Policy Capacity: Rail Policy and the Department of Transport." *Australian Journal of Public Administration* 68 (3): 288–302. http://dx.doi.org/10.1111/j.1467-8500.2009.00640.x.

Eichbaum, C., and R. Shaw. 2007. "Ministerial Advisers and the Politics of Policy-making: Bureaucratic Permanence and Popular Control." *Australian Journal of Public Administration* 66 (4): 453–67. http://dx.doi.org/10.1111/j.1467-8500.2007.00556.x.

– , eds. 2010. *Partisan Appointees and Public Servants: An International Analysis of the Role of the Political Adviser*. Northhampton, MA: Edward Elgar. http://dx.doi.org/10.4337/9781849803298.

Ellis, Faron, and Peter Woolstencroft. 2006. "A Change of Government, Not a Change of Country: Conservatives in the 2006 Federal Election." In *The Canadian Federal Election of 2006*, ed. Jon H. Pammett and Christopher Dornan, 58–92. Toronto: Dundurn.

Elmore, Richard E. 1991. "Teaching, Learning and Education for the Public Service." *Journal of Policy Analysis and Management* 10 (2): 167–80. http://dx.doi.org/10.2307/3325170.

Enserink, B., J.F.M. Koppenjan, and I.S. Mayer. 2013. "A Policy Sciences View on Policy Analysis." In *Public Policy Analysis: New Developments*, ed. W.A.H. Thissen and W.E. Walker, 11–40. New York: Springer. http://dx.doi.org/10.1007/978-1-4614-4602-6_2.

Eppler, Martin J., and Jeanne Mengis. 2004. "The Concept of Information Overload: A Review of Literature from Organization Science, Accounting, Marketing, MIS, and Related Disciplines." *Information Society* 20 (5): 325–44. http://dx.doi.org/10.1080/01972240490507974.

Erdős, P., and A. Rényi. 1959. "On Random Graphs I." *Publicationes Mathematicae* 6:290–7.

Ernst, Berit, and Alfred Kieser. 2002. "In Search of Explanations for the Consulting Explosion." In *The Expansion of Management Knowledge: Carriers, Flows, and Sources*, ed. Kerstin Sahlin-Andersson and Lars Engwall, 47–72. Stanford: Business Books.

Esselment, Anna, Jennifer Lees-Marshment, and Alex Marland. 2014. "The Nature of Political Advising to Prime Ministers in Australia, Canada, New Zealand and the UK." *Commonwealth & Comparative Politics* 52 (3): 358–75.

Evans, Bryan, Tuna Baskoy, and John Shields. 2011. "Assessing Policy Capacity in Canada's Public Services: Perspectives of Deputy and Assistant Deputy Ministers." *Canadian Public Administration* 54 (2): 110–24.

Evans, Bryan, Janet Lum, and John Shields. 2007. "Profiling of the Public Service Elite: A Demographic and Career Trajectory Survey of Deputy and Assistant Deputy Ministers in Canada." *Canadian Public Administration* 50 (4): 609–34. http://dx.doi.org/10.1111/j.1754-7121.2007.tb02209.x.

Evetts, Julia. 2003a. "The Construction of Professionalism in New and Existing Occupational Contexts: Promoting and Facilitating Occupational Change." *International Journal of Sociology and Social Policy* 23 (4/5): 22–35. http://dx.doi.org/10.1108/01443330310790499.

– 2003b. "The Sociological Analysis of Professionalism: Occupational Change in the Modern World." *International Sociology* 18 (2): 395–415. http://dx.doi.org/10.1177/0268580903018002005.

Farrell, David M., and Paul Webb. 2000. "Political Parties as Campaign Organizations." In *Parties with Partisans: Political Change in Advanced Industrial Democracies*, ed. Russell Dalton and Martin Wattenberg, 102–28. New York: Oxford University Press.

FEACO. 2002. *Survey of the European Management Consultancy Market*. Brussels: FEACO.

Federal Government of Canada / Voluntary Sector Joint Initiative. 1999. *Working Together: Report of the Joint Tables*. Ottawa: Queen's Printer.

Feldman, M. 1989. *Order without Design: Information Production and Policy Making*. Palo Alto, CA: Stanford University Press.

Fellegi, I. 1996. *Strengthening Our Policy Capacity*. Ottawa: Ontario Deputy Ministers Task Forces.

Fischer, Frank. 2003. *Reframing Public Policy: Discursive Politics and Deliberative Practices*. New York: Oxford University Press. http://dx.doi.org/10.1093/019924264X.001.0001.

Fishbein, M., and I. Ajzen. 1975. *Belief, Attitude, Intention, and Behavior: An Introduction to Theory and Research*. Reading, MA: Addison-Wesley.

– 2010. *Predicting and Changing Behavior: The Reasoned Action Approach*. New York: Psychology.

Fleischer, J. 2009. "Power Resources of Parliamentary Executives: Policy Advice in the UK and Germany." *West European Politics* 32 (1): 196–214.

Flemming, J. 1997. "Le rôle de l'adjoint exécutif d'un ministre fédéral." *Optimum: La Revue de gestion du secteur public* 27 (2): 70–6.

Flynn, Greg. 2011. "Rethinking Policy Capacity in Canada: The Role of Parties and Election Platforms in Government Policy-making." *Canadian Public Administration* 54 (2): 235–53. http://dx.doi.org/10.1111/j.1754-7121.2011.00172.x.

Flyvbjerg, B. 2006. "Five Misunderstandings about Case-Study Research." *Qualitative Inquiry* 12 (2): 219–45. http://dx.doi.org/10.1177/1077800405284363.

Forester, John. 1983. "What Analysts Do." In *Values, Ethics and the Practice of Policy Analysis*, ed. William N. Dunn, 47–62. Lexington, KY: Lexington Books.

Fox, Charles J. 1990. "Implementation Research: Why and How to Transcend Positivist Methodology." In *Implementation and the Policy Process: Opening Up the Black Box*, ed. D.J. Palumbo and D.J. Calisto, 199–212. New York: Greenwood.

Francis, Jillian J., Martin P. Eccles, Marie Johnston, Anne Walker, Jeremy Grimshaw, Robbie Foy, Eileen F.S. Kaner, Liz Smith, and Debbie Bonetti. 2004. *Constructing Questionnaires Based on the Theory of Planned Behaviour: A Manual for Health Services Researchers.* Newcastle: University of Newcastle, Centre for Health Services Research.

French, R.D., and R. Van Loon. 1984. *How Ottawa Decides: Planning and Industrial Policy Making 1968–1984.* 2nd ed. Toronto: James Lorimer.

Fyfe, Toby, and Paul Crookall. 2010. *Social Media and Public Sector Policy Dilemmas.* Toronto: Institute of Public Administration of Canada.

Gagliardi, A.R., N. Fraser, F.C. Wright, L. Lemieux-Charles, and D. Davis. 2008. "Fostering Knowledge Exchange between Researchers and Decision-makers: Exploring the Effectiveness of a Mixed-Methods Approach." *Health Policy (Amsterdam)* 86 (1): 53–63. http://dx.doi.org/10.1016/j.healthpol.2007.09.002.

Gains, F., and G. Stoker. 2011. "Special Advisors and the Transmission of Ideas from the Policy Primeval Soup." *Policy and Politics* 39 (4): 485–98. http://dx.doi.org/10.1332/030557310X550169.

Galbraith, J.R. 1973. *Designing Complex Organizations.* Reading, MA: Addison-Wesley.

Garson, G.D. 1986. "From Policy Science to Policy Analysis: A Quarter Century of Progress." In *Policy Analysis: Perspectives, Concepts, and Methods,* ed. W.N. Dunn, 3–22. Greenwich, CT: JAI.

Garsten, Christina. 1999. "Betwixt and Between: Temporary Employees as Liminal Subjects in Flexible Organizations." *Organization Studies* 20 (4): 601–17. http://dx.doi.org/10.1177/0170840699204004.

Geva-May, I., and A. Maslove. 2006. "Canadian Public Policy Analysis and Public Policy Programs: A Comparative Perspective." *Journal of Public Affairs Education* 12 (4): 413–38.

– 2007. "In between Trends: Developments of Public Policy Analysis and Policy Analysis Instruction in Canada, the United States and the European Union." In *Policy Analysis in Canada: The State of the Art,* ed. L. Dobuzinskis, M. Howlett, and D. Laycock, 186–216. Toronto: University of Toronto Press.

Geyer, Robert, and Samir Rihani. 2010. *Complexity and Public Policy: A New Approach to Twenty-First Century Politics, Policy and Society.* New York: Routledge.

Gigerenzer, G., and W. Gaissmaier. 2011. "Heuristic Decision Making." *Annual Review of Psychology* 62 (1): 451–82. http://dx.doi.org/10.1146/annurev-psych-120709-145346.

Gill, Judith I., and Laura Saunders. 1992. "Toward a Definition of Policy Analysis." *New Directions for Institutional Research* 76:5–13.

Goetz, K.H., and H. Wollmann. 2001. "Governmentalizing Central Executives in Post-Communist Europe: A Four-Country Comparison." *Journal of European Public Policy* 8 (6): 864–87. http://dx.doi.org/10.1080/13501760110098260.

Goldenberg, E. 2006. *The Way It Works: Inside Ottawa*. Toronto: McClelland & Stewart.

Gøtze, J., and C.B. Pedersen, eds. 2009. *State of the eUnion: Government 2.0 and Onwards*. Copenhagen: AuthorHouse.

Government of New Zealand. State Services Commission. 2010. *Improving the Quality and Value of Policy Advice: Findings of the Committee to Review of Expenditure on Policy Advice*. Wellington.

Gow, James I., and Sharon L. Sutherland. 2004. "Comparison of Canadian Masters Programs in Public Administration, Public Management and Public Policy." *Canadian Public Administration* 47 (3): 379–405.

Granovetter, M. 1983. "The Strength of Weak Ties: A Network Theory Revisited." *Sociological Theory* 1:201–33. http://dx.doi.org/10.2307/202051.

– 2003. "Ignorance, Knowledge, and Outcomes in a Small World." *Science* 301 (5634): 773–4. http://dx.doi.org/10.1126/science.1088508.

Gravetter, Frederick J., and Lori-Ann B. Forzano. 2010. *Research Methods for the Behavioral Sciences*. 4th ed. Florence, KY: Wadsworth Publishing.

Greenhalgh, T., and J. Russell. 2006. "Reframing Evidence Synthesis as Rhetorical Action in the Policy Making Drama." *Healthcare Policy* 1 (2): 34–42.

Gregory, R., and Z. Lonti. 2008. "Chasing Shadows? Performance Measurement of Policy Advice in New Zealand Government Departments." *Public Administration* 86 (3): 837–56. http://dx.doi.org/10.1111/j.1467-9299.2008.00737.x.

Griggs, S., and D. Howarth. 2011. "Policy Expertise and Critical Evaluation." In *Social Science and Policy Challenges*, ed. G. Papanagnou, 113–42. Fontenoy, France: UNESCO.

Grossback, Lawrence J., David A.M. Peterson, and James A. Stimson. 2005. "Comparing Competing Theories on the Causes of Mandate Perceptions." *American Journal of Political Science* 49 (2): 406–19. http://dx.doi.org/10.1111/j.0092-5853.2005.00131.x.

Grudin, Jonathan. 1988. "Why CSCW Applications Fail: Problems in the Design and Evaluation of Organizational Interfaces." *Proceedings of the 1988 ACM Conference on Computer-Supported Cooperative Work*, 85–93. http://dx.doi.org/10.1145/62266.62273.

Guerin, Joel. 2014. *Open Data Now*. New York: McGraw-Hill.

Gulbrandsen, Lars, and Steinar Andresen. 2004. "NGO Influence in the Implementation of the Kyoto Protocol: Compliance, Flexibility Mechanisms and Sinks." *Global Environmental Politics* 4 (4): 54–75. http://dx.doi.org/10.1162/glep.2004.4.4.54.

Gunderson, L.H., C.S. Holling, and S.S. Light, eds. 1995. *Barriers and Bridges to the Renewal of Ecosystems and Institutions*. New York: Columbia University Press.

Guttman, Daniel, and Barry Willner. 1976. *The Shadow Government: The Government's Multi-Billion-Dollar Giveaway of its Decision-Making Powers to Private Management Consultants, "Experts," and Think Tanks*. 1st ed. New York: Pantheon Books.

Hailu, G., P. Boxall, and B. McFarlane. 2005. "The Influence of Place Attachment on Recreation Demand." *Journal of Economic Psychology* 26 (4): 581–98. http://dx.doi.org/10.1016/j.joep.2004.11.003.

Hajer, Maarten, and Hendrik Wagenaar, eds. 2003. *Deliberative Policy Analysis: Understanding Governance in the Network Society*. Cambridge: Cambridge University Press. http://dx.doi.org/10.1017/CBO9780511490934.

Hall, Michael, Alison Andrukow, Cathy Barr, Kathy Brock, Margaret de Wit, Louis Jolin Don Embuldeniya, David Lasby, Benoît Lévesque, Eli Malinsky, Susan Stowe, et al. 2003. *A Capacity to Serve: A Qualitative Study of the Challenges Facing Canada's Nonprofit and Voluntary Organizations*. Toronto: Canadian Centre for Philanthropy.

Hall, Michael, C. Barr, M. Easwaramoorthy, S. Sokolowski, and L. Salamon. 2005. *The Canadian Nonprofit and Voluntary Sector in Comparative Perspective*. Toronto: Imagine Canada.

Halligan, J. 1995. "Policy Advice and the Public Service." In *Governance in a Changing Environment*, ed. B. Guy Peters and D.T. Montreal, 138–72. Montreal and Kingston: McGill-Queen's University Press.

Hämäläinen, Timo, Mikko Kosonen, and Yves L. Doz. 2012. "Strategic Agility in Public Management." INSEAD Working Paper No. 2012/30/ST. http://dx.doi.org/10.2139/ssrn.2020436.

Havelock, R.G. 1975. "Research on the Utilization of Knowledge." In *Information for Action: From Knowledge to Wisdom*, ed. M. Kochen, 87–107. New York: Academic.

Hawke, G.R. 1993. *Improving Policy Advice*. Wellington, NZ: Institute of Policy Studies.

Head, B.W. 2008. "Three Lenses of Evidence-Based Policy." *Australian Journal of Public Administration* 67 (1): 1–11. http://dx.doi.org/10.1111/j.1467-8500.2007.00564.x.

Head, Brian, Michele Ferguson, Adrian Cherney, and Paul Boreham. 2014. "Are Policy-makers Interested in Social Research? Exploring the Sources and Uses of Valued Information among Public Servants in Australia." *Policy and Society* 33 (2): 89–101. http://dx.doi.org/10.1016/j.polsoc.2014.04.004.

Heclo, H., and A. Wildavsky. 1974. *Private Government of Public Money*. Berkeley: University of California Press.

Hicklin, A., and E. Godwin. 2009. "Agents of Change: The Role of Policy Managers in Public Policy." *Policy Studies Journal: The Journal of the Policy Studies Organization* 37 (1): 13–20. http://dx.doi.org/10.1111/j.1541-0072.2008.00292.x.

Hicks, R., and P. Watson. 2007. *Policy Capacity: Strengthening the Public Service's Support to Elected Officials*. Edmonton: Government of Alberta.

Hinds, Pamela J., and Diane Bailey. 2003. "Out of Sight, Out of Sync: Understanding Conflict in Distributed Teams." *Organization Science* 14 (6): 615–32. http://dx.doi.org/10.1287/orsc.14.6.615.24872.

Hilbe, J.M., 2007. "The Co-evolution of Statistics and Hz. Real Data Analysis." In *Real Data Analysis*, ed. Shlomo Sawilowsky, 3–20. Charlotte, NC: Information Age Publishing.

Hird, J.A. 2005a. "Policy Analysis for What? The Effectiveness of Nonpartisan Policy Research Organizations." *Policy Studies Journal: The Journal of the Policy Studies Organization* 33 (1): 83–105. http://dx.doi.org/10.1111/j.1541-0072.2005.00093.x.

– 2005b. *Power, Knowledge and Politics: Policy Analysis in the States*. Washington, DC: Georgetown University Press.

Hodgkinson, G.P. 2012. "The Politics of Evidence-Based Decision-Making." In *Oxford Handbook of Evidence-Based Management*, ed. D.M. Rousseau, 404–19. Oxford: Oxford University Press.

Hodgkinson, G.P., and D.M. Rousseau. 2009. "Bridging the Rigour-Relevance Gap in Management Research: It's Already Happening!" *Journal of Management Studies* 46 (3): 534–46. http://dx.doi.org/10.1111/j.1467-6486.2009.00832.x.

Hodgkinson, G.P., and K. Starkey. 2011. "Not Simple Returning to the Same Answer Over and Over Again: Reframing Relevance." *British Journal of Management* 22 (3): 355–69. http://dx.doi.org/10.1111/j.1467-8551.2011.00757.x.

Hollander, M.J., and M.J. Prince. 1993. "Analytical Units in Federal and Provincial Governments: Origins, Functions and Suggestions for effectiveness." *Canadian Public Administration* 36 (2): 190–224. http://dx.doi.org/10.1111/j.1754-7121.1993.tb00723.x.

Homer-Dixon, Thomas. 2010. *Complexity Science and Public Policy*. New Directions Series. Toronto: Institute of Public Administration of Canada.

Honadle, B. 1981. "A Capacity Building Framework: A Search for Concept and Purpose." *Public Administration Review* 41 (5): 575–80.

Hooghe, L., and G. Marks. 2001. "Types of Multi-level Governance." *European Integration Online Papers* 5 (11).

– 2003. "Unraveling the Central State, but How? Types of Multi-level Governance." *American Political Science Review* 97 (2): 233–43.

Hoppe, R. 1999. "Policy Analysis, Science, and Politics: From 'Speaking Truth to Power' to 'Making Sense Together.'" *Science & Public Policy* 26 (3): 201–10.

Hoppe, R., and M. Jeliazkova. 2006. "How Policy Workers Define Their Job: A Netherlands Case Study." In *The Work of Policy: An International Survey*, ed. H.K. Colebatch, 35–60. New York: Rowman and Littlefield.

House of Commons Committee of Public Accounts. 2007. *Central Government's Use of Consultants.* Thirty-First Report of Session 2006–7. London: House of Commons.

– 2010. *Central Government's Use of Consultants and Interims*. London: Stationery Office.

House of Commons Committee on Health. 2009. *The Use of Management Consultants by the NHS and the Department of Health*. Fifth Report of Session 2008–9. London: House of Commons.

Howard, Michael. 1996. "A Growth Industry? Use of Consultants Reported by Commonwealth Departments 1974–1994." *Canberra Bulletin of Public Administration* 80 (September): 62–74.

Howlett, M. 1999. "Federalism and Public Policy." In *Canadian Politics*, 3rd ed., ed. J. Bickerton and A. Gagnon, 523–39. Peterborough, ON: Broadview.

– 2008. "Enhanced Policy Analytical Capacity as a Prerequisite for Effective Evidence-Based Policy Making: Theory, Concepts and Lessons from the Canadian Case." Paper presented to the International Research Symposium on Public Management XII, Brisbane, Australia.

– 2009a. "Policy Advice in Multi-level Governance Systems: Sub-National Policy Analysts and Analysis." *International Review of Public Administration* 13 (3): 1–16.

– 2009b. "Policy Analytical Capacity and Evidence-Based Policy-making: Lessons from Canada." *Canadian Public Administration* 52 (2): 153–75. http://dx.doi.org/10.1111/j.1754-7121.2009.00070_1.x.

– 2009c. "A Profile of B.C. Provincial Policy Analysts: Troubleshooters or Planners?" *Canadian Political Science Review* 3 (3): 55–68.

– 2011. "Public Managers as the Missing Variable in Policy Studies: An Empirical Investigation Using Canadian Data." *Review of Policy Research* 28 (3): 247–63. http://dx.doi.org/10.1111/j.1541-1338.2011.00494.x.

– 2013. *Canadian Public Policy: Selected Studies in Process and Style*. Toronto: University of Toronto Press.

Howlett, M., and S. Joshi-Koop. 2011. "Transnational Learning, Policy Analytical Capacity, and Environmental Policy Convergence: Survey Results from Canada." *Global Environmental Change* 21 (1): 85–92. http://dx.doi.org/10.1016/j.gloenvcha.2010.10.002.

Howlett, M., and E. Lindquist. 2004. "Policy Analysis and Governance: Analytical and Policy Styles in Canada." *Journal of Comparative Policy Analysis: Research and Practice* 6 (3): 225–49. http://dx.doi.org/10.1080/1387698042000305194.

– 2007. "Beyond Formal Policy Analysis: Governance Context and Analytical Styles in Canada." In *Policy Analysis in Canada: The State of the Art*, ed. L. Dobuzinskis, M. Howlett, and D. Laycock, 266–98. Toronto: University of Toronto Press.

Howlett, M., and Joshua Newman. 2010. "Policy Analysis and Policy Work in Federal Systems: Policy Advice and Its Contribution to Evidence-Based Policy-making in Multi-level Governance Systems." *Policy and Society* 29 (2): 123–36. http://dx.doi.org/10.1016/j.polsoc.2010.03.004.

Howlett, M., and S. Oliphant. 2010. "Environment Research Organizations and Climate Change Policy Analytical Capacity: An Assessment of the Canadian Case." *Canadian Political Science Review* 4 (2–3): 18–35.

Howlett, Michael, and M. Ramesh. 1995. *Studying Public Policy: Policy Cycles and Policy Subsystems*. Toronto: Oxford University Press.

Howlett, Michael, M. Ramesh, and A. Perl. 2009. *Studying Public Policy: Policy Cycles and Policy Subsystems*. 3rd ed. Toronto: Oxford University Press.

Howlett, M., and A. Wellstead. 2012. "Professional Policy Work in Federal States: Institutional Autonomy and Canadian Policy Analysis." *Canadian Public Administration* 55 (1): 53–68. http://dx.doi.org/10.1111/j.1754-7121.2012.00205.x.

Hunn, D.K. 1994. "Measuring Performance in Policy Advice: A New Zealand Perspective." In *Performance Measurement in Government: Issues and Illustrations*, ed. OECD, 25–37. Paris: OECD.

Huxham, Chris, Siv Vangen, and C. Eden. 2000. "The Challenge of Collaborative Governance." *Public Management Review* 2 (2): 337–58.

Inglehart, Ronald. 1997. *Modernization and Postmodernization: Cultural, Economic and Political Change in 43 Societies*. Princeton, NJ: Princeton University Press.

Innvaer, S., G. Vist, M. Trommald, and A. Oxman. 2002. "Health Policy-makers' Perceptions of Their Use of Evidence: A Systematic Review." *Journal of Health*

Services Research & Policy 7 (4): 239–44. http://dx.doi.org/10.1258/135581902320432778.

Institute for Media Policy and Civil Society (IMPACS), in association with the Canadian Centre for Philanthropy. 2002. *Let Charities Speak: Report of the Charities and Advocacy Dialogue.* Vancouver: IMPACS–CCP.

Inwood, Gregory J., Carolyn M. Johns, and Patricia L. O'Reilly. 2011. *Intergovernmental Policy Capacity in Canada: Inside the Worlds of Finance, Environment, Trade and Health Policy*. Montreal and Kingston: McGill-Queen's University Press.

Jaensch, Dean. 1994. *Power Politics: Australia's Party System*. 3rd ed. Sydney: Allen & Unwin.

Jann, W. 1991. "From Policy Analysis to Political Management? An Outside Look at Public Policy Training in the United States." In *Social Sciences and Modern States: National Experiences and Theoretical Crossroads*, ed. P. Wagner, B. Wittrock, and H. Wollman, 110–30. Cambridge: Cambridge University Press. http://dx.doi.org/10.1017/CBO9780511983993.004.

Jarrett, M.C. 1998. "Consultancy in the Public Sector." In *Management Consultancy: A Handbook of Best Practices*, ed. P. Sadler, 369–83. London: Kogan.

Jeffrey, B. 2010. *Divided Loyalties: The Liberal Party of Canada, 1984–2008.* Toronto: University of Toronto Press.

Jenkins-Smith, H. 1982. "Professional Roles of Policy Analysts." *Journal of Policy Analysis and Management* 2 (11): 88–100.

Johns, Carolyn M., Patricia L. O'Reilly, and Gregory J. Inwood. 2007. "Formal and Informal Dimensions of Intergovernmental Administrative Relations in Canada." *Canadian Public Administration* 50 (1): 21–41. http://dx.doi.org/10.1111/j.1754-7121.2007.tb02001.x.

Jones, P.R., and J.G. Cullis. 1993. "Public Choice and Public Policy: The Vulnerability of Economic Advice to the Interpretation of Politicians." *Public Choice* 75 (1): 63–77. http://dx.doi.org/10.1007/BF01053881.

Jordan, Grant. 2007. "Policy without Learning: Double Devolution and Abuse of the Deliberative Idea." *Public Policy and Administration* 22 (1): 48–73. http://dx.doi.org/10.1177/0952076707071504.

Kankanhalli, A., B.C.Y. Tan, and K.-K. Wei. 2005. "Understanding Seeking from Electronic Knowledge Repositories: An Empirical Study." *Journal of the American Society for Information Science* 56 (11): 1156–66. http://dx.doi.org/10.1002/asi.20219.

Karacapilidis, N., E. Loukis, and S. Dimopoulos. 2005. "Computer-Supported G2G Collaboration for Public Policy and Decision Making." *Journal of Enterprise Information Management* 18 (5): 602–24. http://dx.doi.org/10.1108/17410390510624034.

Katz, Richard. 1987. "Party Government and Its Alternatives." In *Party Governments: European and American Experiences*, ed. Richard Katz, 1–26. Berlin: De Gruyter.

Keller, G. 2004. *Statistics for Management and Economics*. Florence, KY: South-Western College Publications.

Kelloway, E.K. 1995. *Using LISREL for Structural Equation Modeling: A Researcher's Guide*. Thousand Oaks, CA: Sage Publications.

Kendall, Jeremy. 2000. "The Mainstreaming of the Third Sector into Public Policy in England in the Late 1990s: Whys and Wherefores." *Policy & Politics* 4 (1): 541–62.

Kenis, P., and V. Schneider. 1991. "Policy Networks and Policy Analysis: Scrutinizing a New Analytical Toolbox." In *Policy Networks: Empirical Evidence and Theoretical Considerations*, ed. B. Marin and R. Mayntz, 25–59. Boulder, CO: Westview.

Kernaghan, Ken. 2000. "The Post-Bureaucratic Organization and Public Service Values." *International Review of Administrative Sciences* 66 (1): 91–104. http://dx.doi.org/10.1177/0020852300661008.

Kernaghan, K., and D. Siegel. 1995. *Public Administration in Canada*. 3rd ed. Scarborough, ON: Nelson Canada.

Kidneigh, J.C. 1954. "Simplification in Administration: A Point of View." *Social Service Review* 28 (2): 137–45. http://dx.doi.org/10.1086/639606.

Kim, Hak-Soo. 2012. "Climate Change, Science and Community." *Public Understanding of Science (Bristol, England)* 21 (3): 268–85. http://dx.doi.org/10.1177/0963662511421711.

King, Anthony. 1969. "Political Parties in Western Democracies: Some Skeptical Reflections." *Polity* 2 (2): 111–41.

King, S. 2003. *Regulating the Behavior of Ministers, Special Advisors and Civil Servants*. London: Constitution Unit, School of Public Policy, University College London.

Kipping, Matthias, and Lars Engwall, eds. 2003. *Management Consulting: Emergence and Dynamics of a Knowledge Industry*. New York: Oxford University Press.

Klenk, N.L., and G.M. Hickey. 2011. "Government Science in Forestry: Characteristics and Policy Utilization." *Forest Policy and Economics* 13 (1): 37–45. http://dx.doi.org/10.1016/j.forpol.2010.08.005.

Klijn, E. 2008. "Complexity Theory and Public Administration: What's New?" *Public Management Review* 10 (3): 299–317.

Kline, Elliot H., and C. Gregory Buntz. 1979. "On the Effective Use of Public Sector Expertise: Or Why the Use of Outside Consultants Often Leads to the Waste of In-House Skills." *Public Administration Review* 39 (3): 226–9. http://dx.doi.org/10.2307/975943.

Klingemann, Hans-Deiter, Richard I. Hofferbert, Ian Budge, and Hans Keman. 1994. *Parties Policies and Democracy*. Boulder, CO: Westview.

Ko, D.-G., L.J. Kirsch, and W.R. King. 2005. "Antecedents of Knowledge Transfer from Consultants to Clients in Enterprise System Implementations." *Management Information Systems Quarterly* 29 (1): 59–85.

Kogut, Bruce, and Udo Zander. 1992. "Knowledge of the Firm, Combinative Capabilities, and the Replication of Technology." *Organization Science* 3 (3): 383–97. http://dx.doi.org/10.1287/orsc.3.3.383.

Koliba, C., and R. Gajda. 2009. "'Communities of Practice' as an Analytical Construct: Implications for Theory and Practice." *International Journal of Public Administration* 32 (2): 97–135. http://dx.doi.org/10.1080/01900690802385192.

Kothari, A., S. Birch, and C. Charles. 2005. "'Interaction' and Research Utilisation in Health Policies and Programs: Does It Work?" *Health Policy (Amsterdam)* 71 (1): 117–25. http://dx.doi.org/10.1016/j.healthpol.2004.03.010.

Kothari, A., L. MacLean, and N. Edwards. 2009. "Increasing Capacity for Knowledge Translation: Understanding How Some Researchers Engage Policy Makers." *Evidence & Policy* 5 (1): 33–51. http://dx.doi.org/10.1332/174426409X395402.

Kowske, Brenda, Rena Rasch, and John Wiley. 2010. "Millennials' (Lack of) Attitude Problem: An Empirical Examination of Generational Effects on Work Attitudes." *Journal of Business and Psychology* 25 (2): 265–79. http://dx.doi.org/10.1007/s10869-010-9171-8.

Laforest, Rachel. 2001. "Governance and the Voluntary Sector: Rethinking the Contours of Advocacy." Paper presented at the Annual Meeting of the Canadian Political Science Association, Toronto.

– 2011. *Voluntary Sector Organizations and the State*. Vancouver: UBC Press.

Laforest, Rachel, and Michael Orsini. 2005. "Evidence-Based Engagement in the Voluntary Sector: Lessons from Canada." *Social Policy and Administration* 39 (5): 481–97. http://dx.doi.org/10.1111/j.1467-9515.2005.00451.x.

Lahusen, Christian. 2002. "Commercial Consultancies in the European Union: The Shape and Structure of Professional Interest Intermediation." *Journal of European Public Policy* 9 (5): 695–714. http://dx.doi.org/10.1080/13501760210162311.

Lalonde, M. 1971. "The Changing Role of the Prime Minister's Office." *Canadian Public Administration* 14 (4): 509–37. http://dx.doi.org/10.1111/j.1754-7121.1971.tb00296.x.

Landry, R., N. Amara, and M. Lamari. 2001. "Utilization of Social Science Research Knowledge in Canada." *Research Policy* 30 (2): 333–49. http://dx.doi.org/10.1016/S0048-7333(00)00081-0.

Landry, R., M. Lamari, and N. Amara. 2003. "The Extent and Determinants of the Utilization of University Research in Government Agencies." *Public Administration Review* 63 (2): 192–205. http://dx.doi.org/10.1111/1540-6210.00279.

Landsbergen, David, Jr, and George Wolken Jr. 2001. "Realizing the Promise: Government Information Systems and the Fourth Generation of Information Technology." *Public Administration Review* 61 (2): 206–20. http://dx.doi.org/10.1111/0033-3352.00023.

Lapsley, I., and R. Oldfield. 2001. "Transforming the Public Sector: Management Consultants as Agents of Change." *European Accounting Review* 10 (3): 523–43. http://dx.doi.org/10.1080/713764628.

Larsen, J.K. 1980. "Knowledge Utilization: What Is It? Knowledge, Creation, Diffusion." *Utilization* 14 (3): 267–90.

Larson, P. 1999. "The Canadian Experience." In *Redefining Management Roles: Improving the Functional Relationship between Ministers and Permanent Secretaries*, ed. S. Agere, 55–74. Toronto: University of Toronto Press/ Commonwealth Association for Public Administration and Management.

Laumann, Edward O., and David Knoke. 1987. *The Organizational State: Social Choice in National Policy Domains.* Madison, WI: University of Wisconsin Press.

Lavis, J.N., H. Davies, A. Oxman, J.-L. Denis, K. Golden-Biddle, and E. Ferlie. 2005. "Towards Systematic Reviews That Inform Health Care Management and Policy-Making." *Journal of Health Services Research & Policy* 10 (S1): S35–S48. http://dx.doi.org/10.1258/1355819054308549.

Lavoie-Tremblay, Melanie, Maxime Paquet, Marie-Anick Duchesne, Anelise Santo, Ana Gavrancic, François Courcy, and Serge Gagnon. 2010. "Retaining Nurses and Other Hospital Workers: An Intergenerational Perspective of the Work Climate." *Journal of Nursing Scholarship* 42 (4): 414–22. http://dx.doi.org/10.1111/j.1547-5069.2010.01370.x.

Lawson, Mary, and Peter Merkl, eds. 1988. *When Parties Fail: Emerging Alternative Organizations*. Princeton, NJ: Princeton University Press. http://dx.doi.org/10.1515/9781400859498.

Learmonth, M., and N. Harding. 2006. "Evidence-Based Management: The Very Idea." *Public Administration* 84 (2): 245–66. http://dx.doi.org/10.1111/j.1467-9299.2006.00001.x.

Learmonth, M., A. Lockett, and K. Dowd. 2012. "Promoting Scholarship That Matters: The Uselessness of Useful Research and the Usefulness of Useless Research." *British Journal of Management* 23:35–44.

Lee, W.M. 1971. "The Executive Function: A Ministerial Assistant's View." *Quarterly of Canadian Studies* 1 (1): 141–4.

Lemieux, V. 2000. "Government Roles in Governance Processes." In *Modernizing Governance: A Preliminary Exploration*. Texts prepared by Jane Jenson/Martin Papillon, Paul G. Thomas, Vincent Lemieux, and Peter Aucoin, 117–46. Ottawa: Canadian Centre for Management and Development.

Lenoski, G. 1977. "Ministerial Staffs and Leadership Politics." In *Apex of Power*, ed. T.A. Hockin, 2nd ed., 165–75. Scarborough, ON: Canada: Prentice Hall.

Levasseur, Karine. 2008. "Charitable Status in Canada: A Governance and Historical Institutional Lens on Charitable Registration." PhD diss., Carleton University.

– 2014. "Unearthing the Hidden Gems of Registered Charities and Their Participation in the 2011 Manitoba Election." In *Disengaged? Fixed Date, Democracy, and Understanding the 2011 Manitoba Election*, ed. Andrea Rounce and Jared Wesley, 268–96. Regina: University of Regina Press.

Lewis, J., D. Alexander, and M. Considine. 2009. *Networks, Innovation and Public Policy: Politicians, Bureaucrats and the Pathways to Change inside Government*. New York: Palgrave Macmillan.

Light, Paul C. 2006. "The New True Size of Government." School Research Brief no. 2. New York: NYU Wagner.

Lin, H.F. 2007. "Effects of Extrinsic and Intrinsic Motivation on Employee Knowledge Sharing Intentions." *Journal of Information Science* 33 (2): 135–49.

Lindblom, C.E. 1958a. "Policy Analysis." *American Economic Review* 48 (3): 298–312.

– 1958b. "Tinbergen on Policy-making." *Journal of Political Economy* 66 (6): 531–8. http://dx.doi.org/10.1086/258104.

– 1980. *The Policy-making Process*. 2nd ed. New Jersey: Prentice-Hall.

Lindblom, C.E., and D.K. Cohen. 1979. *Usable Knowledge: Social Science and Social Problem Solving*. New Haven, CT: Yale University Press.

Lindquist, E. 1998. "A Quarter Century of Canadian Think Tanks: Evolving Institutions, Conditions and Strategies." In *Think Tanks across Nations: A Comparative Approach*, ed. D. Stone, A. Denham, and M. Garnett, 127–44. Manchester: Manchester University Press.

– 2009. *There's More to Policy Than Alignment*. CPRN Research Report.

– 2012. "Horizontal Management in Canada Ten Years Later." *Optimum Online* 42 (3). http://optimumonline.ca/frontpage.phtml.

Lindquist, E., and J. Desveaux. 2007. "Policy Analysis and Bureaucratic Capacity: Context, Competences, and Strategies." In *Policy Analysis in*

Canada: The State of the Art, ed. L. Dobuzinskis, M. Howlett, and D. Laycock, 116–42. Toronto: IPAC-University of Toronto Press.

Lindquist, E., and G. Paquet. 2000. "Government Restructuring and the Federal Public Service: The Search for a New Cosmology." In *Government Restructuring and Career Public Service in Canada*, ed. E. Lindquist, 71–111. Toronto: Institute of Public Administration of Canada.

Lippitt, Ronald. 1975. *Consulting Process in Action: Examining the Dynamics of the Client–Consultant Working Relationship*. New York: Development Publications.

Lipsky, M. 1971. "Street-Level Bureaucracy and the Analysis of Urban Reform." *Urban Affairs Review* 6 (4): 391–409. http://dx.doi.org/10.1177/107808747100600401.

– 1980. *Street-Level Bureaucracy: Dilemmas of the Individual in Public Services*. New York: Russell Sage Foundation.

Liu, Xinsheng, Eric Lindquist, Arnold Vedlitz, and Kenneth Vincent. 2010. "Understanding Local Policymaking: Policy Elites' Perceptions of Local Agenda Setting and Alternative Policy Selection." *Policy Studies Journal: The Journal of the Policy Studies Organization* 38 (1): 69–91. http://dx.doi.org/10.1111/j.1541-0072.2009.00345.x.

Longo, Justin. 2013. "Towards Policy Analysis 2.0." PhD diss., University of Victoria.

Lord, M.D., and A.L. Ranft. 2000. "Organizational Learning about New International Markets: Exploring the Internal Transfer of Local Market Knowledge." *Journal of International Business Studies* 31 (4): 573–89. http://dx.doi.org/10.1057/palgrave.jibs.8490923.

Macdonald, David. 2011. *The Shadow Public Service: The Swelling Ranks of Federal Government Outsourced Workers*. Ottawa: Canadian Centre for Policy Alternatives.

Macintyre, Alasdair. 1977. "Utilitarianism and Cost-Benefit Analysis: An Essay on the Relevance of Moral Philosophy to Bureaucratic Theory." In *Values in the Electric Power Industry*, ed. Kenneth Sayre, 217–37. Paris: Philosophical Institute of the University of Notre Dame.

MacRae, D. 1991. "Policy Analysis and Knowledge Use." *Knowledge and Policy* 4 (3): 27–40. http://dx.doi.org/10.1007/BF02693086.

MacRae, D., and D. Whittington. 1997. *Expert Advice for Policy Choice: Analysis and Discourse*. Washington, DC: Georgetown University Press.

MacRae, Duncan Jr, and James A. Wilde. 1985. *Policy Analysis for Public Decisions*. Lanham, MD: University Press of America.

Mahon, R.C. Andrew, and R. Johnston. 2007. "Policy Analysis in an Era of Globalization: Capturing Spatial Dimensions and Scalar Strategies." In

Critical Policy Studies, ed. M. Orsini and M. Smith, 41–64. Vancouver: UBC Press.

Mair, Peter. 1994. "Party Organizations: From Civil Society to the State." In *How Parties Organize: Change and Adaptation in Party Organizations in Western Democracies*, ed. Richard S. Katz and Peter Mair, 1–22. London: Sage Publications. http://dx.doi.org/10.4135/9781446250570.n1.

Majone, Giandomenico. 1997. "From the Positive to the Regulatory State: Causes and Consequences of Changes in the Mode of Governance." *Journal of Public Policy* 17 (2): 139–67. http://dx.doi.org/10.1017/S0143814X00003524.

Maley, M. 2000. "Conceptualising Advisers' Policy Work: The Distinctive Policy Roles of Ministerial Advisers in the Keating Government, 1991–96." *Australian Journal of Political Science* 35 (3): 449–70. http://dx.doi.org/10.1080/713649346.

– 2011. "Strategic Links in a Cut-throat World: Rethinking the Role and Relationships of Australian Ministerial Staff." *Public Administration* 89 (4): 1469–88. http://dx.doi.org/10.1111/j.1467-9299.2011.01928.x.

Mallory, J.R. 1967. "The Minister's Office Staff: An Unreformed Part of the Public Service." *Canadian Journal of Public Administration* 10 (1): 25–34. http://dx.doi.org/10.1111/j.1754-7121.1967.tb00962.x.

Malloy, J.M. 1989. "Policy Analysts, Public Policy and Regime Structure in Latin America." *Governance: An International Journal of Policy, Administration and Institutions* 2 (3): 315–38. http://dx.doi.org/10.1111/j.1468-0491.1989.tb00095.x.

Mann, Bill. 2012. "Pipeline Opponents Could Lose Tax-Exempt Status." *MarketWatch*, 12 January.

March, James G., and Johan P. Olson. 1983. "Organizing Political Life: What Administrative Reorganization Tells Us about Government." *American Political Science Review* 77 (2): 281–96.

Marsden, P.V., and K.E. Campbell. 1984. "Measuring Tie Strength." *Social Forces* 63 (2): 482–501. http://dx.doi.org/10.1093/sf/63.2.482.

Marsh, Michael. 2005. "Parties in Society." In *Politics in the Republic of Ireland*, 4th ed., ed. John Coakley and Michael Gallagher, 168–97. New York: Routledge.

Martin, J.F. 1998. *Reorienting a Nation: Consultants and Australian Public Policy*. Aldershot, UK: Ashgate.

May, P.J., and I. Geva-May. 2005. "Policy Maps and Political Feasibility." In *Thinking like a Policy Analyst: Policy Analysis as a Clinical Profession*, ed. I. Geva-May, 127–51. London: Palgrave Macmillan.

Mayer, I., P. Bots, and E. van Daalen. 2004. "Perspectives on Policy Analysis: A Framework for Understanding and Design." *International Journal of Technology Policy and Management* 4 (1): 169–91.

Mays, N., C. Pope, and J. Popay. 2005. "Systematically Reviewing Qualitative and Quantitative Evidence to Inform Management and Policy-making in the Health Field." *Journal of Health Services Research & Policy* 10 (S1): S6–S20. http://dx.doi.org/10.1258/1355819054308576.

McAfee, Andrew P. 2006. "Enterprise 2.0: The Dawn of Emergent Collaboration." *MIT Sloan Management Review* 47 (3): 21–8.

McArthur, D. 2007. "Policy Analysis in Provincial Governments in Canada: From PPBS to Network Management." In *Policy Analysis in Canada: The State of the Art*, ed. L. Dobuzinskis, M. Howlett, and D. Laycock, 132–45. Toronto: University of Toronto Press.

McCarthy, Shawn, and Steven Chase. 2012. "Foes of Northern Gateway Pipeline Fear Revocation of Charitable Status." *Globe and Mail*, 10 January.

McGann, J.G., and E.C. Johnson. 2005. *Comparative Think Tanks, Politics and Public Policy*. Cheltenham, UK: Edward Elgar.

McGivern, Chris. 1983. "Some Facets of the Relationship between Consultants and Clients in Organizations." *Journal of Management Studies* 20 (3): 367–86. http://dx.doi.org/10.1111/j.1467-6486.1983.tb00213.x.

McKeown, Tui, and Margaret Lindorff. 2011. "Temporary Staff, Contractors, and Volunteers: The Hidden Workforce in Victorian Local Government." *Australian Journal of Public Administration* 70 (2): 185–201. http://dx.doi.org/10.1111/j.1467-8500.2011.00722.x.

McNutt, John G. 2008. "Web 2.0 Tools for Policy Research and Advocacy." *Journal of Policy Practice* 7 (1): 81–5. http://dx.doi.org/10.1080/15588740801909994.

McPherson, M., L. Smith-Lovin, and J.M. Cook. 2001. "Birds of a Feather: Homophily in Social Networks." *Annual Review of Sociology* 27 (1): 415–44. http://dx.doi.org/10.1146/annurev.soc.27.1.415.

Meier, K.J. 2009. "Policy Theory, Policy Theory Everywhere: Ravings of a Deranged Policy Scholar." *Policy Studies Journal: The Journal of the Policy Studies Organization* 37 (1): 5–11. http://dx.doi.org/10.1111/j.1541-0072.2008.00291.x.

Meltsner, A.J. 1975. "Bureaucratic Policy Analysts." *Policy Analysis* 1 (1): 115–31.

– 1976. *Policy Analysts in the Bureaucracy*. Berkeley, CA: University of California Press.

– 1990. *Rules for Rulers: The Politics of Advice*. Philadelphia, PA: Temple University Press.

Meredith, Harry, and Joe Martin. 1970. "Management Consultants in the Public Sector." *Canadian Public Administration/Administration publique du Canada* 13 (4): 383–95.

Meyers, K., and S. Vorsanger. 2003. "Street-Level Bureaucracy and the Implementation of Public Policy." In *Handbook of Public Administration*, ed. G. Peters and J. Pierre, 245–56. London: Sage. http://dx.doi.org/10.4135/9781848608214.n20.

Miles, M.B., and A.M. Huberman. 1994. *Qualitative Data Analysis*. 2nd ed. Thousand Oaks, CA: Sage.

Mintrom, M. 2003. *People Skills for Policy Analysts*. Washington, DC: Georgetown University Press.

– 2007. "The Policy Analysis Movement." In *Policy Analysis in Canada: The State of the Art*, ed. L. Dobuzinskis, M. Howlett, and D. Laycock, 71–84. Toronto: University of Toronto Press.

Mitchell, V.-W. 1994. "Problems and Risks in the Purchasing of Consultancy Services." *Service Industries Journal* 14 (3): 315–39. http://dx.doi.org/10.1080/02642069400000036.

Mitton, C., C.E. Adair, E. McKenzie, S.B. Patten, and B.W. Perry. 2007. "Knowledge Transfer and Exchange: Review and Synthesis of the Literature." *Milbank Quarterly* 85 (4): 729–68. http://dx.doi.org/10.1111/j.1468-0009.2007.00506.x.

Morçöl, Göktuğ. 2012. *A Complexity Theory for Public Policy*. New York: Routledge.

Morçöl, Göktuğ, and Nadezda P. Ivanova. 2010. "Methods Taught in Public Policy Programs: Are Quantitative Methods Still Prevalent?" *Journal of Public Affairs Education* 16 (2): 255–77.

Morrell, K. 2008. "The Narrative of 'Evidence-Based' Management: A Polemic." *Journal of Management Studies* 45 (3): 613–35. http://dx.doi.org/10.1111/j.1467-6486.2007.00755.x.

Mulgan, Richard. 2000. "The 'Mandate': A Response to Goot." *Australian Journal of Political Science* 35 (2): 317–22. http://dx.doi.org/10.1080/713649333.

Mulholland, Elizabeth. 2010. "New Ways to Keep Up Our End of the Policy Conversation." *Philanthropist* 23 (2): 140–5.

Müller, W.C. 2000. "Political Parties in Parliamentary Democracies: Making Delegation and Accountability Work." *European Journal of Political Research* 37 (3): 309–33. http://dx.doi.org/10.1111/1475-6765.00515.

Munro, G.D. 2010. "The Scientific Impotence Excuse: Discounting Belief-Threatening Scientific Abstracts." *Journal of Applied Social Psychology* 40 (3): 579–600. http://dx.doi.org/10.1111/j.1559-1816.2010.00588.x.

Murray, C. 2007. "The Media." In *Policy Analysis in Canada: The State of the Art*, ed. L. Dobuzinskis, M. Howlett, and D. Laycock, 286–97. Toronto: University of Toronto Press.

Mushkin, Selma J. 1977. "Policy Analysis in State and Community." *Public Administration Review* 37 (3): 245–53. http://dx.doi.org/10.2307/974817.

Nairn, Geoff. 2011. "The Trouble with Office Email." *Financial Times*, 17 February.

National Audit Office. 2001. *Purchasing Professional Services*. London: National Audit Office.

– 2006. *Central Government's Use of Consultants: Methodology*. London: National Audit Office.

– 2010. *Central Government's Use of Consultants and Interims*. London: National Audit Office.

Naurin, Elin. 2002. "The Pledge Paradox: Why Do People Think That Parties Break Their Promises." Paper presented at the ECPR Joint Session, 22–7 March, Turin.

Nelson, R.H. 1989. "The Office of Policy Analysis in the Department of the Interior." *Journal of Policy Analysis and Management* 8 (3): 395–410. http://dx.doi.org/10.2307/3324931.

Nesbitt-Larking, Paul. 2002. "Canadian Political Culture: The Problem of Americanization." In *Crosscurrents: Contemporary Political Issues*, 4th ed., ed. Mark Charlton and Paul Barker, 4–22. Toronto: Thomson Nelson.

Newman, Janet, Marian Barnes, Helen Sullivan, and Andrew Knops. 2004. "Public Participation and Collaborative Governance." *Journal of Social Policy* 33 (2): 203–23. http://dx.doi.org/10.1017/S0047279403007499.

New Zealand, State Services Commission. 1991. *Review of the Purchase of Policy Advice from Government Departments*. Wellington: State Services Commission.

Ng, Eddy S.W., Linda Schweitzer, and Sean T. Lyons. 2010. "New Generation, Great Expectations: A Field Study of the Millennial Generation." *Journal of Business and Psychology* 25 (2): 281–92. http://dx.doi.org/10.1007/s10869-010-9159-4.

Nicholson, J. 1996. "Measures for Monitoring Policy Advice." In *Evaluating Policy Advice: Learning from Commonwealth Experience*, ed. J. Uhr and K. Mackay, 26–40. Canberra: Federalism Research Centre ANU.

– 1997. "Monitoring the Efficiency, Quality, and Effectiveness of Policy Advice to Government." In *Monitoring Performance in the Public Sector: Future Directions from International Experience*, ed. John Maybe and Eduardo Zapico-Goni, 237–52. New Brunswick, NJ: Transaction Publishers.

Nilsson, M., A. Jordan, J. Turnpenny, J. Hertin, B. Nykvist, and D. Russel. 2008. "The Use and Non-Use of Policy Appraisal Tools in Public Policy Making:

An Analysis of Three European Countries and the European Union." *Policy Sciences* 41 (4): 335–55. http://dx.doi.org/10.1007/s11077-008-9071-1.

Noordegraaf, M. 2000. "Professional Sense-Makers: Managerial Competencies Amidst Ambiguities." *International Journal of Public Sector Management* 13 (4): 319–32. http://dx.doi.org/10.1108/09513550010350292.

– 2010. "Academic Accounts of Policy Experience." In *Working for Policy*, ed. H. Colebatch, R. Hoppe, and M. Noordegraaf, 45–67. Amsterdam: University of Amsterdam Press.

Noveck, Beth S. 2009. *Wiki Government: How Technology Can Make Government Better, Democracy Stronger, and Citizens More Powerful*. Washington, DC: Brookings Institution Press.

Nowotny, Helga, Peter Scott, and Michael Gibbons. 2001. *Re-thinking Science: Knowledge and the Public in an Age of Uncertainty*. Cambridge: Polity.

Nutley, S.M., I. Walter, and H.T. Davies. 2007. *Using Evidence: How Research Can Inform Public Services*. Bristol, UK: Policy.

O'Connor, A., G. Roos, and T. Vickers-Willis. 2007. "Evaluating an Australian Public Policy Organization's Innovation Capacity." *European Journal of Innovation Management* 10 (4): 532–58. http://dx.doi.org/10.1108/14601060710828817.

O'Connor, L.J. 1991. "Chief of Staff." *Policy Options* 12 (3): 23–6.

Office of the Auditor General of British Columbia. 2001. *Management Consulting Engagements in Government*. Victoria.

Oh, C.H. 1997. "Explaining the Impact of Policy Information on Policy-making." *Knowledge and Policy* 10 (3): 25–55. http://dx.doi.org/10.1007/BF02912505.

Oliphant, S., and M. Howlett. 2010. "Assessing Policy Analytical Capacity: Insights from a Study of the Canadian Environmental Policy Advice System." *Journal of Comparative Policy Analysis* 12 (4): 439–41. http://dx.doi.org/10.1080/13876988.2010.495510.

Oliver, Kathryn, Simon Innvaer, Theo Lorenc, Jenny Woodman, and James Thomas. 2014. "A Systematic Review of Barriers to and Facilitators of the Use of Evidence by Policymakers." *BMC Health Services Research* 14 (1): 2.

Ontario Executive Resources Group. 1999. *Investing in Policy: Report on Other Jurisdictions and Organizations*. Toronto: Ontario Ministry of the Environment.

O'Reilly, Tim. 2010. "Government as a Platform." In *Open Government: Collaboration, Transparency and Participation in Practice*, ed. Daniel Lathrop and Laurel Ruma, 11–40. Sebastopol, CA: O'Reilly Media.

Orsini, Michael. 2012. "Why the Federal Government Picked a Fight with Charities." *Ottawa Citizen*, 2 April.

Orton, L., F. Lloyd-Williams, D. Taylor-Robinson, M. O'Flaherty, and S. Capewell. 2011. "The Use of Research Evidence in Public Health Decision

Making Processes: Systematic Review." *PLoS One* 6 (7): e21704. http://dx.doi.org/10.1371/journal.pone.0021704.

Osbaldeston, G. 1987. "The Public Servant and Politics." *Policy Options* 8 (1): 3–7.

Osborne, S. 2006. "The New Public Governance?" *Public Management Review* 8 (3): 377–87. http://dx.doi.org/10.1080/14719030600853022.

O'Shea, James, and Charles Madigan. 1998. *Dangerous Company: Management Consultants and the Businesses They Save and Ruin*. New York: Penguin Books.

Osimo, David. 2008. *Web 2.0 in Government: Why and How?* Luxembourg: Office for Official Publications of the European Communities.

Ouimet, M., P.-O. Bédard, J. Turgeon, J.N. Lavis, F. Gélineau, F. Gagnon, and C. Dallaire. 2010. "Correlates of Consulting Research Evidence among Policy Analysts in Ministries: A Cross-Sectional Survey." *Evidence & Policy* 6 (4): 433–60. http://dx.doi.org/10.1332/174426410X535846.

Ouimet, M., R. Landry, S. Ziam, and P.-O. Bédard. 2009. "The Absorption of Research Knowledge by Public Civil Servants." *Evidence & Policy* 5 (4): 331–50. http://dx.doi.org/10.1332/174426409X478734.

Page, E., and B. Jenkins. 2005. *Policy Bureaucracy: Government with a Cast of Thousands*. London: Oxford University Press. http://dx.doi.org/10.1093/acprof:oso/9780199280414.001.0001.

Page, Edward C. 2010. "Bureaucrats and Expertise: Elucidating a Problematic Relationship in Three Tableaux and Six Jurisdictions." *Sociologie du Travail* 52 (2): 255–73. http://dx.doi.org/10.1016/j.soctra.2010.03.021.

Painter, M., and J. Pierre. 2005a. *Challenges to State Policy Capacity: Global Trends and Comparative Perspectives*. London: Palgrave Macmillan.

– 2005b. "Conclusions: Challenges to Policy Capacity." In *Challenges to State Policy Capacity: Global Trends and Comparative Perspectives*, ed. M. Painter and J. Pierre, 255–61. London: Palgrave Macmillan.

– 2005c. "Unpacking Policy Capacity: Issues and Themes." In *Challenges to State Policy Capacity: Global Trends and Comparative Perspectives*, ed. Martin Painter and Jon Pierre, 1–18. New York: Palgrave Macmillan.

Pal, L. 2001. *Beyond Policy Analysis: Public Issue Management in Turbulent Times*. 2nd ed. Toronto: Nelson.

– 2010. *Beyond Policy Analysis*. 4th ed. Toronto: Thomson Nelson.

Panebianco, Angelo. 1988. *Political Parties: Organization and Power*. Trans. Marc Silver. Cambridge: Cambridge University Press.

Panel on Accountability and Governance in the Voluntary Sector. 1999. *Building on Strength: Improving Governance and Accountability in Canada's Voluntary Sector*. Ottawa: PAGVS.

Paquet, Gilles. 2009. *Scheming Virtuously: The Road to Collaborative Governance*. Ottawa: Invenire Books.

Paris, Max. 2012. "Attack on 'Radicals' Sign of Tougher Federal Strategy: Government Expected to Get More Aggressive in Defending Major Economic Projects." CBC News, 11 January.

Parsons, W. 2004. "Not Just Steering but Weaving: Relevant Knowledge and the Craft of Building Policy Capacity and Coherence." *Australian Journal of Public Administration* 63 (1): 43–57. http://dx.doi.org/10.1111/j.1467-8500.2004.00358.x.

Parsons, Wayne. 2006. "Innovation in the Public Sector: Spare Tyres and Fourth Plinths." *Innovation Journal* 11 (2). http://www.innovation.cc/.

Pattenaude, Richard L. 1979. "Introduction to Symposium on Consultants in the Public Sector." *Public Administration Review* 39 (3): 203–5.

Patton, C.V., and D.S. Sawicki. 1993. *Basic Methods of Policy Analysis and Planning*. Englewood Cliffs, NJ: Prentice Hall.

Peled, A. 2002. "Why Style Matters: A Comparison of Two Administrative Reform Initiatives in the Israeli Public Sector, 1989–1998." *Journal of Public Administration: Research and Theory* 12 (2): 217–40. http://dx.doi.org/10.1093/oxfordjournals.jpart.a003530.

Pereira, Guimarães, and Silvio Funtowicz. 2006. "Knowledge Representation and Mediation for Transdisciplinary Frameworks to Inform Debates, Dialogues and Deliberation." *International Journal of Transdisciplinary Research* 1 (1): 34–50.

Perl, Anthony, and Donald J. White. 2002. "The Changing Role of Consultants in Canadian Policy Analysis." *Policy and Society* 21 (1): 49–73. http://dx.doi.org/10.1016/S1449-4035(02)70003-9.

Perry, J. 1997. "Antecedents of Public Service Motivation." *Journal of Public Administration: Research and Theory* 2:181–97.

Peters, B.G. 1996. "The Policy Capacity of Government." Canadian Centre for Management Development, Research Paper No. 18.

– 2000. *The Future of Governing*. 2nd ed. Lawrence: University of Kansas Press.

– 2005. "Policy Instruments and Policy Capacity." In *Challenges to State Policy Capacity: Global Trends and Comparative Perspectives*, ed. M. Painter and J. Pierre, 73–91. New York: Palgrave Macmillan.

– 2008. "Meta Governance and Public Management." In *New Public Governance*, ed. S. Osborne, 36–51. Cheltenham, UK: Edward Elgar.

– 2010. "Bureaucracy and Democracy." *Public Organization Review* 10 (3): 209–22. http://dx.doi.org/10.1007/s11115-010-0133-4.

Petrocik, J.R. 1996. "Issue Ownership in Presidential Elections, with a 1980 Case Study." *American Journal of Political Science* 40 (3): 825–50. http://dx.doi.org/10.2307/2111797.

Pétry, François. 1995. "The Party Agenda Model: Election Programmes and Government Spending in Canada." *Canadian Journal of Political Science* 28 (1): 51–84.

Pétry, François, and Benoit Collette. 2009. "Measuring How Political Parties Keep Their Promises: A Positive Perspective from Political Science." In *Do They Walk like They Talk: Speech and Action in Policy Processes*, ed. Louis M. Imbeau, 39–52. New York: Springer. http://dx.doi.org/10.1007/978-0-387-89672-4_5.

Phillips, Susan D. 2000. *Redefining Government Relationships with the Voluntary Sector: On Great Expectations and Sense and Sensibility*. Ottawa: Voluntary Sector Roundtable.

– 2007. "Policy Analysis and the Voluntary Sector: Evolving Policy Styles." In *Policy Analysis in Canada: The State of the Art*, ed. L. Dobuzinskis, M. Howlett, and D. Laycock, 272–84. Toronto: University of Toronto Press.

Piattoni, Simona. 2009. "Multi-level Governance: A Historical and Conceptual Analysis." *Journal of European Integration* 31 (2): 163–80. http://dx.doi.org/10.1080/07036330802642755.

Plassé, M. 1994. *Ministerial Chiefs of Staff in the Federal Government in 1990: Profiles, Recruitment, Duties, and Relations with Senior Public Servants*. Ottawa: Canadian Centre for Management Development.

Policy Excellence Initiative. 2007. *Policy Excellence and the Nova Scotia Public Service*. Halifax: Policy Advisory Council and Treasury and Policy Board.

Pollard, W.E. 1987. "Decision Making and the Use of Evaluation Research." *American Behavioral Scientist* 30 (6): 661–76. http://dx.doi.org/10.1177/000276487030006009.

Potts, Jason. 2009. "The Innovation Deficit in Public Services: The Curious Problem of Too Much Efficiency and Not Enough Waste and Failure." *Policy & Practice* 11 (1): 34–43.

Prasser, S. 2006. *Providing Advice to Government*. Papers on Parliament. Canberra: Senate of Australia.

Preskill, H., and S. Boyle. 2008. "A Multidisciplinary Model of Evaluation Capacity Building." *American Journal of Evaluation* 29 (4): 443–59. http://dx.doi.org/10.1177/1098214008324182.

Pressman, Jeffrey L., and Aaron Wildavsky. 1973. *Implementation: How Great Expectations in Washington Are Dashed in Oakland; Or, Why It's Amazing That Federal Programs Work at All, This Being a Saga of the Economic Development Administration as Told by Two Sympathetic Observers Who Seek to Build Morals on a Foundation*. Berkeley: University of California Press.

Prince, M.J. 1979. "Policy Advisory Groups in Government Departments." In *Public Policy in Canada: Organization, Process, Management*, ed. G.B. Doern and P. Aucoin, 275–300. Toronto: Gage.

– 1983. *Policy Advice and Organizational Survival*. Aldershot, UK: Gower.

– 2007. "Soft Craft, Hard Choices, Altered Context: Reflections on 25 Years of Policy Advice in Canada." In *Policy Analysis in Canada: The State of the Art*, ed. L. Dobuzinskis, M. Howlett, and D. Laycock, 95–106. Toronto: University of Toronto Press.

Prince, M., and Chenier, J. 1980. The Rise and Fall of Policy Planning and Research Units. *Canadian Public Administration* 23 (4): 519–41.

Privy Council Office. 2006. *Thirteenth Annual Report to the Prime Minister on the Public Service of Canada*. Ottawa: PCO.

– 2011. *Accountable Government: A Guide for Ministers and Ministers of State*. Ottawa: PCO.

Project on Government Oversight. 2011. *Bad Business: Billions of Taxpayer Dollars Wasted on Hiring Contractors*. Washington, DC: Project on Government Oversight.

Proussalidis, Bill Daniel. 2012. "Charities Should Be Allowed to Be Politically Active: Ecojustice Canada." *Winnipeg Sun*, 11 January.

Public Service Commission of Canada. 2008. *Evaluation of the Recruitment of Policy Leaders Program*. http://www.psc-cfp.gc.ca/abt-aps/inev-evin/2008/rpl-rlp-eval-eng.htm.

– 2010. *Use of Temporary Help Services in Public Service Organizations*. Ottawa: Public Service Commission.

– *Annual Report*. Various years.

Punnett, R.M. 1977. *The Prime Minister in Canadian Government and Politics*. Toronto: Macmillan of Canada.

Purdy, Jill M. 2012. "A Framework for Assessing Power in Collaborative Governance Processes." *Public Administration Review* 72 (3): 409–17. http://dx.doi.org/10.1111/j.1540-6210.2011.02525.x.

Putnam, H. 2002. *The Collapse of the Fact/Value Dichotomy and Other Essays*. Cambridge, MA: Harvard University Press.

Putnam, Robert D. 1993. *Making Democracy Work: Civic Traditions in Modern Italy*. Princeton, NJ: Princeton University Press.

Quade, E.S. 1975. *Analysis for Public Decisions*. New York: Elsevier.

Radaelli, Claudio M. 1995. "The Role of Knowledge in the Policy Process." *Journal of European Public Policy* 2 (2): 159–83. http://dx.doi.org/10.1080/13501769508406981.

– 2008. "Europeanization, Policy Learning, and New Modes of Governance." *Journal of Comparative Policy Analysis* 10 (3): 239–94. http://dx.doi.org/10.1080/13876980802231008.

Radcliffe, Sarah. 2010. "Non-Rational Aspects of the Competition State: The Case of Policy Consultancy in Australia." *Policy Studies* 31 (1): 117–28. http://dx.doi.org/10.1080/01442870903387363.

Radin, B.A. 1992. "Policy Analysis in the Office of the Assistant Secretary for Planning and Evaluation in the HEW/HHS: Institutionalization and the Second Generation." In *Organizations for Policy Analysis: Helping Government Think*, ed. C.H. Weiss, 144–60. London: Sage Publications.

– 1997. "Presidential Address: The Evolution of the Policy Analysis Field: From Conversation to Conversations." *Journal of Policy Analysis and Management* 16 (2): 204–18.

– 2000. *Beyond Machiavelli: Policy Analysis Comes of Age*. Washington, DC: Georgetown University Press.

– 2006. *Challenging the Performance Movement: Accountability, Complexity and Democratic Values*. Washington, DC: Georgetown University Press.

– 2013. *Beyond Machiavelli: Policy Analysis Comes of Age*. 2nd ed. Washington, DC: Georgetown University Press.

Rainie, Lee, Aaron Smith, Kay Lehman Schlozman, Henry Brady, and Sidney Verba. 2012. "Social Media and Political Engagement." Pew Research Center. Internet & American Life Project. http://www.pewinternet.org/Reports/2012/Political-engagement/Summary-of-Findings.aspx.

Rallings, Colin. 1987. "The Influence of Election Programmes: Britain and Canada 1945–1979." In *Ideology, Strategy and Party Change: Spatial Analysis of Postwar Election Programmes in 19 Democracies*, ed. Ian Budge, David Robertson, and Derek Hearl, 1–14. Cambridge: Cambridge University Press.

Rasmussen, K. 1999. "Policy Capacity in Saskatchewan: Strengthening the Equilibrium." *Canadian Public Administration* 42 (3): 331–48. http://dx.doi.org/10.1111/j.1754-7121.1999.tb01554.x.

Rayner, Jeremy. 2012. "Shifting Mandates and Climate Change Policy Capacity: The Forestry Case." *Canadian Political Science Review* 6 (1): 75–85.

Rehfuss, John. 1979. "Managing the Consultantship Process." *Public Administration Review* 39 (3): 211–14. http://dx.doi.org/10.2307/975939.

Rein, M., and S.W. White. 1977. "Can Research Help Policy?" *Public Interest* 49:119–36.

Rhodes, R.A.W. 1994. "The Hollowing Out of the State: The Changing Nature of the Public Service in Britain." *Political Quarterly* 65 (2): 138–51. http://dx.doi.org/10.1111/j.1467-923X.1994.tb00441.x.

– 1996. "The New Governance: Governing without Government." *Political Studies* 44 (4): 652–67. http://dx.doi.org/10.1111/j.1467-9248.1996.tb01747.x.

– 1997. "Shackling the Leader? Coherence, Capacity and the Hollow Crown." In *The Hollow Crown? Counterveiling Trends in Core Executives*, ed. Patrick Weller, Herman Bakvis, and R.A.W. Rhodes, 198–223. London: Macmillan.

Rhodes, R.A.W., P. 't Hart, and M. Noordegraaf, eds. 2007. *Observing Government Elites: Up Close and Personal*. London: Palgrave Macmillan. http://dx.doi.org/10.1057/9780230592360.

Riccucci, N. 2005. "Street Level Bureaucrats and Intra State Variation in the Implementation of Temporary Assistance for Needy Families Policies." *Journal of Public Administration Research and Theory* 15 (1): 89–111.

Rich, R.F. 1997. "Measuring Knowledge Utilization: Processes and Outcomes." *Knowledge and Policy* 10 (3): 11–24. http://dx.doi.org/10.1007/BF02912504.

Rich, R.F., and C.H. Oh. 2000. "Rationality and Use of Information in Policy Decisions: A Search for Alternatives." *Science Communication* 22 (2): 173–211. http://dx.doi.org/10.1177/1075547000022002004.

Riddell, N. 1998. *Policy Research Capacity in the Federal Government*. Ottawa: Policy Research Initiative.

– 2007. *Policy Research Capacity in the Federal Government*. Ottawa: Policy Research Initiative.

Riege, Andreas. 2005. "Three-Dozen Knowledge-Sharing Barriers Managers Must Consider." *Journal of Knowledge Management* 9 (3): 18–35. http://dx.doi.org/10.1108/13673270510602746.

Rieper, Olaf, and Jacques Toulemonde. 1997. *Politics and Practices of Intergovernmental Evaluation*. New Brunswick, NJ: Transaction Publishers.

Robertson, Peter J., and Taehyon Choi. 2012. "Deliberation, Consensus, and Stakeholder Satisfaction." *Public Management Review* 14 (1): 83–103. http://dx.doi.org/10.1080/14719037.2011.589619.

Rochet, C. 2004. "Rethinking the Management of Information in the Strategic Monitoring of Public Policies by Agencies." *Industrial Management & Data Systems* 104 (3): 201–8. http://dx.doi.org/10.1108/02635570410525753.

Rose, Richard. 1984. *Do Parties Make a Difference*. 2nd ed. Chatham, NJ: Chatham House Publishers. http://dx.doi.org/10.1007/978-1-349-17350-1.

– 1993. *Lesson Drawing in Public Policy: A Guide to Learning across Time and Space*. Cambridge: Cambridge University Press.

Rosenblum, Robert, and Daniel McGillis. 1979. "Observations on the Role of Consultants in the Public Sector." *Public Administration Review* 39 (3): 219–26. http://dx.doi.org/10.2307/975942.

Rowe, Gene, and Lynn J. Frewer. 2005. "A Typology of Public Engagement Mechanisms." *Science, Technology & Human Values* 30 (2): 251–90. http://dx.doi.org/10.1177/0162243904271724.

RPL Survey. 2008. Internal Survey of Recruitment of Policy Leaders Program Recruits. Personal communication with one of the authors.

Sabatier, P. 1978. "The Acquisition and Utilization of Technical Information by Administrative Agencies." *Administrative Science Quarterly* 23 (3): 396–417. http://dx.doi.org/10.2307/2392417.

Saint-Martin, Denis. 1998a. "Management Consultants, the State, and the Politics of Administrative Reform in Britain and Canada." *Administration & Society* 30 (5): 533–68. http://dx.doi.org/10.1177/0095399798305003.
- 1998b. "The New Managerialism and the Policy Influence of Consultants in Government: An Historical-Institutionalist Analysis of Britain, Canada and France." *Governance: An International Journal of Policy, Administration and Institutions* 11 (3): 319–56. http://dx.doi.org/10.1111/0952-1895.00074.
- 2004. *Building the New Managerialist State: Consultants and the Politics of Public Sector Reform in Britain, Canada and France*. Oxford: Oxford University Press. http://dx.doi.org/10.1093/acprof:oso/9780199269068.001.0001.
- 2005a. "Management Consultancy." In *Oxford Handbook of Public Management*, ed. Ewan Ferlie, Lawrence Lynn, and Christopher Pollitt, 671–94. Oxford: Oxford University Press.
- 2005b. "The Politics of Management Consulting in Public Sector Reform." In *Handbook of Public Management*, ed. Christopher Pollitt and Lawrence Lynn, 84–106. Oxford: Oxford University Press.
- 2006. "Le consulting et l'État: une analyse comparée de l'offre et de la demande." *Revue française d'administration publique* 120 (4): 743–56.

Salamon, Lester M. 2002. "The New Governance and the Tools of Public Action: An Introduction." In *The Tools of Government: A Guide to the New Governance*, ed. Lester M. Salamon, 1–47. Oxford: Oxford University Press.

Sartori, Giovanni. 1962. *Democratic Theory*. Detroit: Wayne State University Press.

Savoie, D.J. 1983. "The Ministers Staff: The Need for Reform." *Canadian Public Administration* 26 (4): 509–24. http://dx.doi.org/10.1111/j.1754-7121.1983.tb01042.x.
- 1999. *Governing from the Centre: The Concentration of Power in Canadian Politics*. Toronto: University of Toronto Press.
- 2003a. *Breaking the Bargain: Public Servants, Ministers, and Parliament*. Toronto: IPAC/University of Toronto Press.
- 2003b. *Strengthening the Policy Capacity of Government*. Report to the Panel on the Role of Government, Research Paper Series, Vol. 1, 239–90.
- 2004. *Thatcher, Reagan, Mulroney: In Search of a New Bureaucracy*. Toronto: University of Toronto Press.

Schumpeter, Joseph A. 1942. *Capitalism, Socialism and Democracy*. New York: Harper & Brothers.

Scott, Katherine. 2003. *Funding Matters: The Impact of Canada's New Funding Regime on Nonprofit and Voluntary Sector Organizations*. Ottawa: Canadian Council on Social Development.

Segsworth, Robert V., and Dale H. Poel. 1997. "Two Cases of Intergovernmental Evaluation in Canada: 'Parallel Play' and Cooperation without Policy

Consequences." In *Politics and Practices of Intergovernmental Evaluation*, ed. Olaf Rieper and Jacques Toulemonde, 75–98. New Brunswick, NJ: Transaction Publishers.

Sharp, M. 1995. *Which Reminds Me: A Memoir*. Toronto: University of Toronto Press.

Shirky, Clay. 2008. *Here Comes Everybody: The Power of Organizing without Organizations*. New York: Penguin.

Shulock, N. 1999. "The Paradox of Policy Analysis: If It Is Not Used, Why Do We Produce So Much of It?" *Journal of Policy Analysis and Management* 18 (2): 226–44. http://dx.doi.org/10.1002/(SICI)1520-6688(199921)18:2<226::AID-PAM2>3.0.CO;2-J.

Silver, N. 2012. *The Signal and the Noise: The Art and Science of Prediction*. London: Allen Lane.

Simon, H.A., G.B. Dantzig, R. Hogarth, C.R. Piott, H. Raiffa, T.C. Schelling, K.A. Shepsle, R. Thaier, A. Tversky, and S. Winter. 1986. "Decision Making and Problem Solving." In *Research Briefings 1986: Report of the Research Briefing Panel on Decision Making and Problem Solving*, 11–31. Washington, DC: National Academy.

Simpson, J. 2001. *The Friendly Dictatorship*. Toronto: McClelland & Stewart.

Singleton, Jon. 2001a. *Report on a Review of the Policy Development Capacity within Government Departments*. Winnipeg: Office of the Auditor General.

– 2001b. *A Review of the Policy Capacity between Departments*. Winnipeg: Office of the Auditor General.

Smith, Bruce L.R. 1977. "The Non-Governmental Policy Analysis Organization." *Public Administration Review* 37 (3): 253–8. http://dx.doi.org/10.2307/974818.

Smith, S. 2003. "Street-Level Bureaucracy and Public Policy." In *Handbook of Public Administration*, ed. G. Peters and J. Pierre, 354–65. London: Sage. http://dx.doi.org/10.4135/9781848608214.n29.

Snowden, Dave. 2002. "Complex Acts of Knowing: Paradox and Descriptive Self-Awareness." *Journal of Knowledge Management* 6 (2): 100–11. http://dx.doi.org/10.1108/13673270210424639.

South Australia. 1993. *Use of External Consultants by Government Departments*. Seventh Report of the Economic and Finance Committee. Adelaide: Parliament of South Australia.

Sparks, Amy M. 2012. "Psychological Empowerment and Job Satisfaction between Baby Boomer and Generation X Nurses." *Journal of Nursing Management* 20 (4): 451–60. http://dx.doi.org/10.1111/j.1365-2834.2011.01282.x.

Speers, K. 2007. "The Invisible Public Service: Consultants and Public Policy in Canada." In *Policy Analysis in Canada: The State of the Art*, ed. L. Dobuzinskis, M. Howlett, and D. Laycock, 220–31. Toronto: University of Toronto Press.

Stacey, R.D. 2002. "The Impossibility of Managing Knowledge." Lecture at the Royal Society of Arts, 27 February, *RSA Journal*, 149 (5501): 49–51, http://www.jstor.org/stable/41380374.

State Services Commission. 1999. *Essential Ingredients: Improving the Quality of Policy Advice.* Wellington: New Zealand State Services Commission.

– 2001. *Review of the Purchase of Policy Advice from Government Departments.* Wellington: New Zealand State Services Commission.

Stewart, Thomas A. 2002. *The Wealth of Knowledge: Intellectual Capital and the Twenty-First Century Organization*. London: Nicholas Brealey.

Stoker, G. 1998. "Governance as Theory: Five Propositions." *International Social Science Journal* 50 (155): 17–28. http://dx.doi.org/10.1111/1468-2451.00106.

Stone, D. 2000. "Non-governmental Policy Transfer: The Strategies of Independent Policy Institutes." *Governance: An International Journal of Policy, Administration and Institutions* 13 (1): 45–70. http://dx.doi.org/10.1111/0952-1895.00123.

Stone, D., and A. Denham, eds. 2004. *Think Tank Traditions: Policy Research and the Politics of Ideas*. Manchester: Manchester University Press.

Stritch, A. 2007. "Business Associations and Policy Analysis in Canada." In *Policy Analysis in Canada: The State of the Art*, ed. L. Dobuzinskis, M. Howlett, and D. Laycock, 242–59. Toronto: University of Toronto Press.

Sturdy, Andrew. 1997. "The Consultancy Process; An Insecure Business?" *Journal of Management Studies* 34 (3): 389–413. http://dx.doi.org/10.1111/1467-6486.00056.

Tapscott, Don, and Anthony D. Williams. 2006. *Wikinomics: How Mass Collaboration Changes Everything*. New York: Portfolio.

Tellier, P. 1968. "Pour une réforme des cabinets de ministres fédéraux." *Canadian Public Administration* 11 (4): 414–27. http://dx.doi.org/10.1111/j.1754-7121.1968.tb00601.x.

– 1990. "Public Service 2000: The Renewal of the Public Service." *Canadian Public Administration* 33 (2): 123–32. http://dx.doi.org/10.1111/j.1754-7121.1990.tb01390.x.

Thissen, W.A.H., and P.G.J. Twaalfhoven. 2001. "Toward a Conceptual Structure for Evaluating Policy Analytic Activities." *European Journal of Operational Research* 129 (3): 627–49. http://dx.doi.org/10.1016/S0377-2217(99)00470-1.

Thomas, P.G. 2008. "Political-Administrative Interface in Canada's Public Sector." *Optimum Online* 38 (2). http://optimumonline.ca/frontpage.phtml.
– 2010. "Who Is Getting the Message? Communications at the Centre of Government. In *Public Policy Issues and the Oliphant Commission: Independent Research Studies*, ed. C. Forcese, 77–133. Ottawa: Minister of Public Works and Government Services Canada.
Thompson, Derek. 2011. "The Case for Banning Email at Work." *Atlantic Monthly*, 1 December. http://www.theatlantic.com/business/archive/2011/12/the-case-for-banning-email-at-work/249252/.
Thompson, P.R., and M.R. Yessian. 1992. "Policy Analysis in the Office of Inspector General, U.S. Department of Health and Human Services." In *Organizations for Policy Analysis: Helping Government Think*, ed. C.H. Weiss, 161–77. London: Sage Publications.
Thorburn, Hugh G. 2007. "Interest Groups, Social Movements, and the Canadian Parliamentary System." In *Canadian Parties in Transition*, 3rd ed., ed. Alain-G. Gagnon and A. Brian Tanguay, 385–410. Peterborough, ON: Broadview.
Tiernan, Anne. 2011. "Advising Australian Federal Governments: Assessing the Evolving Capacity and Role of the Australian Public Service." *Australian Journal of Public Administration* 70 (4): 335–46. http://dx.doi.org/10.1111/j.1467-8500.2011.00742.x.
Tiernan, A., and J. Wanna. 2006. "Competence, Capacity, Capability: Towards Conceptual Clarity in the Discourse of Declining Policy Skills." Paper presented at the Govnet International Conference, Australian National University, Canberra.
Till, B., A.R. Dobell, J. Longo, and P. Driessen. 2014. "Self-Organizing Maps for Latent Semantic Analysis of Blogospheric Free-Form Text in Support of Public Policy Analysis." *Wiley Interdisciplinary Reviews: Data Mining and Knowledge Discovery* 4 (1): 71–86.
Tingling, P.M., and M.J. Brydon. 2010. "Is Decision-Based Evidence Making Necessarily Bad?" *MIT Sloan Management Review* 51 (4): 71–6.
Tisdall, Patricia. 1982. *Agents of Change: The Development and Practice of Management Consultancy*. London: Heinemann.
Todorova, G., and B. Durisin. 2007. "Absorptive Capacity: Valuing a Reconceptualization." *Academy of Management Review* 32 (3): 774–86. http://dx.doi.org/10.5465/AMR.2007.25275513.
Tollefson, C., A. Zito, and F. Gale. 2012. "Symposium Overview: Conceptualizing New Governance Arrangements." *Public Administration* 90 (1): 3–18. http://dx.doi.org/10.1111/j.1467-9299.2011.02003.x.

Townsend, T., and B. Kunimoto. 2009. *Capacity, Collaboration and Culture: The Future of the Policy Research Function in the Government of Canada*. Ottawa: Policy Research Initiative.

Treasury Board Secretariat. N.d. *Economics and Social Science Services (EC) Group: Job Evaluation Standard*. http://www.tbs-sct.gc.ca/cla/snd/ec-eng.asp#_Toc159814558.

– 2007. "Economics and Social Science Services (EC) Group: Job Evaluation Standard." http://www.tbs-sct.gc.ca/cla/snd/ec-eng.asp#_Toc159814558.

– 2011. "Policies for Minister's Offices." Her Majesty the Queen in Right of Canada, represented by the President of the Treasury Board.

Treasury Board Secretariat of Canada. 1996. *Regional Participation in the Policy Process*. Ottawa: Treasury Board Secretariat of Canada.

– 2012. "Demographic Snapshop of the Federal Public Service, 2012." http://www.tbs-sct.gc.ca/res/stats/demo12-eng.asp.

Treib, O., H. Bahr, and G. Falkner. 2007. "Modes of Governance: Towards a Conceptual Clarification." *Journal of European Public Policy* 14 (1): 1–20. http://dx.doi.org/10.1080/13501760601071406.

Tribe, Laurence H. 1972. "Policy Science: Analysis or Ideology?" *Philosophy & Public Affairs* 2 (1): 66–110.

Uhr, John, and Keith Mackay, eds. 1996. *Evaluating Policy Advice: Learning from Commonwealth Experience*. Canberra: Federalism Research Centre, Australian National University.

United Kingdom. 2011. "Letter to Cabinet Ministers on Transparency and Open Data," 7 July. https://www.gov.uk/government/news/letter-to-cabinet-ministers-on-transparency-and-open-data.

United States. 2009. "Transparency and Open Government." White House. https://www.whitehouse.gov/the_press_office/TransparencyandOpenGovernment.

Valentine, Melissa A., Bradley R. Staats, and Amy C. Edmondson. 2012. "The Rich Get Richer: Enabling Conditions for Knowledge Use in Organizational Work Teams." HBS Working Paper Number: 13-001. Social Science Research Network. http://dx.doi.org/10.2139/ssrn.2101693.

Van Buuren, Arwin. 2009. "Knowledge for Governance, Governance of Knowledge: Inclusive Knowledge Management in Collaborative Governance Processes." *International Public Management Journal* 12 (2): 208–35. http://dx.doi.org/10.1080/10967490902868523.

Van Helden, G. Jan, Harrie Aardema, Henk J. ter Bogt, and Tom L.C.M. Groot. 2010. "Knowledge Creation for Practice in Public Sector Management Accounting by Consultants and Academics: Preliminary Findings and

Directions for Future Research." *Management Accounting Research* 21 (2): 83–94. http://dx.doi.org/10.1016/j.mar.2010.02.008.

van Houten, Donald R., and Paul Goldman. 1981. "Contract Consulting's Hidden Agenda: The Quest for Legitimacy in Government." *Pacific Sociological Review* 24 (4): 461–93. http://dx.doi.org/10.2307/1388778.

Van Nispen, Frans, and Peter Scholten, eds. 2014. *Policy Analysis in the Netherlands*. Bristol: Policy. http://dx.doi.org/10.1332/policypress/9781447313335.001.0001.

Verheijen, T. 1999. *Civil Service Systems in Central and Eastern Europe*. Cheltenham, UK: Edward Elgar.

Verschuere, B. 2009. "The Role of Public Agencies in the Policy Making Process." *Public Policy and Administration* 24 (1): 23–46. http://dx.doi.org/10.1177/0952076708097907.

Veselý, A. 2013. "Externalization of Policy Advice: Theory, Methodology and Evidence." *Policy and Society* 32 (3): 199–209. http://dx.doi.org/10.1016/j.polsoc.2013.07.002.

Vincent-Jones, Peter. 2006. *The New Public Contracting: Regulation, Responsiveness, Relationality*. New York: Oxford University Press.

Voice in Health Policy. 2003. "VOICE in Health Policy: Policy Capacity of Voluntary Organizations Working in Health."

Voyer, J. 2007. "Policy Analysis in the Federal Government: Building the Forward-Looking Policy Research Capacity." In *Policy Analysis in Canada: The State of the Art*, ed. L. Dobuzinskis, M. Howlett, and D. Laycock, 123–31. Toronto: University of Toronto Press.

Wagner, P., and H. Wollman. 1986. "Social Scientists in Policy Research and Consulting: Some Cross-National Comparisons." *International Social Science Journal* 110:601–17.

Waller, M. 1992. "Evaluating Policy Advice." *Australian Journal of Public Administration* 51 (4): 440–6. http://dx.doi.org/10.1111/j.1467-8500.1992.tb01092.x.

– 1996. "Framework for Policy Evaluation." In *Evaluating Policy Advice: Learning from Commonwealth Experience*, ed. John Uhr and Keith Mackay, 9–20. Canberra: Federalism Research Centre–ANU.

Warren, Mark E. 2001. *Democracy and Association*. Princeton, NJ: Princeton University Press.

Wasko, M.M., and S. Faraj. 2005. "Why Should I Share? Examining Social Capital and Knowledge Contribution in Electronic Networks of Practice." *Management Information Systems Quarterly* 29 (1): 35–57.

Webber, D.J. 1986. "Analyzing Political Feasibility: Political Scientists' Unique Contribution to Policy Analysis." *Policy Studies Journal: The Journal of the*

Policy Studies Organization 14 (4): 545–53. http://dx.doi.org/10.1111/j.1541-0072.1986.tb00360.x.
– 1992. "The Distribution and Use of Policy Knowledge in the Policy Process." In *Advances in Policy Studies Since 1950*, ed. W.N. Dunn and R.M. Kelly, 383–418. New Brunswick, NJ: Transaction Publishers.
Weber, Edward P., and Anne M. Khademian. 2008. "Wicked Problems, Knowledge Challenges, and Collaborative Capacity Builders in Network Settings." *Public Administration Review* 68 (2): 334–49.
Weible, C.M. 2008. "Expert-Based Information and Policy Subsystems: A Review and Synthesis." *Policy Studies Journal: The Journal of the Policy Studies Organization* 36 (4): 615–35. http://dx.doi.org/10.1111/j.1541-0072.2008.00287.x.
Weimer, D.L., and A.R. Vining. 1999. *Policy Analysis: Concepts and Practice*. Upper Saddle River, NJ: Prentice Hall.
– 2004. *Policy Analysis: Concepts and Practice*. Upper Saddle River, NJ: Prentice Hall.
Weiss, C.H. 1977. "Research for Policy's Sake: The Enlightenment Function of Social Science Research." *Policy Analysis* 3 (4): 531–45.
– 1979a. "The Many Meanings of Research Utilization." *Public Administration Review* 39 (5): 426–31. http://dx.doi.org/10.2307/3109916.
Weiss, L. 1979b. *The Myth of the Powerless State*. Ithaca, NY: Cornell University Press.
– 1980. "Knowledge Creep and Decision Accretion." *Science Communication* 1 (3): 381–404. http://dx.doi.org/10.1177/107554708000100303.
– 1986. "The Circuitry of Enlightenment: Diffusion of Social Science Research to Policymakers." *Knowledge: Creation, Diffusion, Utilization* 8 (2): 274–81.
– 1991. "Policy Research: Data, Ideas or Arguments?" In *Social Sciences and Modern States: National Experiences and Theoretical Crossroads*, ed. P. Wagner, B. Wittrock, and H. Wollman, 307–32. Cambridge: Cambridge University Press. http://dx.doi.org/10.1017/CBO9780511983993.014.
– , ed. 1992. *Organizations for Policy Analysis: Helping Government Think*. London: Sage Publications.
Weiss, C.H., and M.J. Bucuvalas. 1980. *Social Science Research and Decision-Making*. New York: Columbia University Press.
Weller, P., and B. Stevens. 1998. "Evaluating Policy Advice: The Australian Experience." *Public Administration* 76 (3): 579–89. http://dx.doi.org/10.1111/1467-9299.00118.
Wellman, B. 2001. "Computer Networks as Social Networks." *Science* 293 (5537): 2031–4, http://dx.doi.org/10.1126/science.1065547.
Wells, P. 2006. *Right Side Up: The Fall of Paul Martin and the Rise of Stephen Harper's New Conservatism*. Toronto: McClelland & Stewart.

Wellstead, A., and R. Stedman. 2010. "Policy Capacity and Incapacity in Canada's Federal Government: The Intersection of Policy Analysis and Street-Level Bureaucracy." *Public Management Review* 12 (6): 893–910. http://dx.doi.org/10.1080/14719037.2010.488863.

– 2012. *The Role of Climate Change Policy Work in Canada. Canadian Political Science Review* 6 (1): 117–24.

Wellstead, A.M., R.C. Stedman, and M. Howlett. 2011. "Policy Analytical Capacity in Changing Governance Contexts: A Structural Equation Model (SEM) Study of Contemporary Canadian Policy Work." *Public Policy and Administration* 26 (3): 353–73. http://dx.doi.org/10.1177/0952076710381933.

Wellstead, A., R. Stedman, S. Joshi, and E. Lindquist. 2007. *Beyond the National Capital Region: Federal Regional Policy Capacity.* Report prepared for the Treasury Board Secretariat of Canada.

Wellstead, A.M., R.C. Stedman, and E.A. Lindquist. 2009. "The Nature of Regional Policy Work in Canada's Federal Public Service." *Canadian Political Science Review* 3 (1): 1–23.

White, G. 2005. *Cabinets and First Ministers*. Vancouver: UBC Press.

Wildavsky, A. 1969. "Rescuing Policy Analysis from PPBS." *Public Administration Review* 29 (2): 189–202. http://dx.doi.org/10.2307/973700.

– 1979. *Speaking Truth to Power: The Art and Craft of Policy Analysis*. Boston: Little-Brown. http://dx.doi.org/10.1007/978-1-349-04955-4.

Wilding, R.W.L. 1976. "The Use of Management Consultants in Government Departments." *Management Services in Government* 31 (2): 60–70.

Willem, Annick, and Marc Buelens. 2007. "Knowledge Sharing in Public Sector Organizations: The Effect of Organizational Characteristics on Interdepartmental Knowledge Sharing." *Journal of Public Administration: Research and Theory* 17 (4): 581–606. http://dx.doi.org/10.1093/jopart/mul021.

Williams, A. 2010. "Is Evidence-Based Policy-Making Really Possible? Reflections for Policymakers and Academics on Making Use of Research in the Work of Policy." In *Working for Policy*, ed. H. Colebatch, R. Hoppe, and M. Noordegraaf, 195–209. Amsterdam: Amsterdam University Press.

Williams, B. 1980. "The Para-Political Bureaucracy in Ottawa." In *Parliament, Policy and Representation*, ed. Harold D. Clark, Colin Campbell, F.Q. Quo, and Arthur Goddard, 215–29. Toronto: Methuen.

Williams, R. 2012. "Operationalizing 'Policy Capacity': A Case Study of Climate Change Adaptation in Canadian Finance Agencies." *Canadian Political Science Review* 6 (1): 65–74.

Willmott, H. 2012. "Reframing Relevance as 'Social Usefulness': A Comment on Hodgkinson and Starkey's 'Not Simply Returning to the Same Answer Over and Over Again.'" *British Journal of Management* 23 (4): 598–604. http://dx.doi.org/10.1111/j.1467-8551.2012.00839.x.

Wilson, R. Paul. 2015. "A Profile of Ministerial Policy Staff in the Government of Canada." *Canadian Journal of Political Science* 48 (2): 455–71.

– 2016. "Trust But Verify: Ministerial Policy Advisors and Public Servants in the Government of Canada." *Canadian Public Administration* 59 (3).

Wolinetz, Steven B. 2007. "Cycles and Brokerage: Canadian Parties as Mobilizers of Interest." In *Canadian Parties in Transition*, 3rd ed., ed. Alain-G. Gagnon and A. Brian Tanguay, 179–96. Peterborough, ON: Broadview.

Wollmann, H. 1989. "Policy Analysis in West Germany's Federal Government: A Case of Unfinished Governmental and Administrative Modernization?" *Governance: An International Journal of Policy, Administration and Institutions* 2 (3): 233–66. http://dx.doi.org/10.1111/j.1468-0491.1989.tb00092.x.

Workman, Samuel, Bryan D. Jones, and Ashley E. Jochim. 2009. "Information Processing and Policy Dynamics." *Policy Studies Journal: The Journal of the Policy Studies Organization* 37 (1): 75–92. http://dx.doi.org/10.1111/j.1541-0072.2008.00296.x.

Wouters, Wayne G. 2012. *Nineteenth Annual Report to the Prime Minister on the Public Service of Canada.*

Wu, X., M. Ramesh, M. Howlett, and S. Fritzen. 2010. *The Public Policy Primer: Managing Public Policy*. London: Routledge.

Wyld, David C. 2007. *The Blogging Revolution: Government in the Age of Web 2.0.* Washington, DC: IBM Center for the Business of Government.

Yang, Tung-Mou, and Terrence A. Maxwell. 2011. "Information-Sharing in Public Organizations: A Literature Review of Interpersonal, Intra-Organizational and Inter-Organizational Success Dactors." *Government Information Quarterly* 28 (2): 164–75. http://dx.doi.org/10.1016/j.giq.2010.06.008.

Yanow, D. 1996. *How Does a Policy Mean?* Washington, DC: Georgetown University Press.

Zafonte, Matthew, and Paul Sabatier. 1998. "Shared Beliefs and Imposed Interdependencies as Determinants of Ally Networks in Overlapping Subsystems." *Journal of Theoretical Politics* 10 (4): 473–505. http://dx.doi.org/10.1177/0951692898010004005.

Zhang, Jing, A.M. Cresswell, and F. Thompson. 2005. "Participants' Expectations and the Success of Knowledge Networking in the Public Sector." In *Digital Government: Strategies and Implementation from Developing and Developed Countries*, ed. W. Huang, K. Siau, and K.K. Wei, 260–81. Hershey, PA: Ideal Group.

Zussman, D. 2003. "Evidence-Based Policy Making: Some Observations of Recent Canadian Experience." *Social Policy Journal of New Zealand* 20:64–71.

– 2009. *Political Advisors*. Paris: OECD.

Permission Credits

Some chapters in this volume are based on previously published articles. Where this is the case, details of the original publications are below with grateful acknowledgment of the permission to reprint.

Chapter 2: Michael Howlett and Adam Wellstead, "Policy Analysts in the Bureaucracy Revisited: The Nature of Professional Policy Work in Contemporary Government," *Politics & Policy* 39, no. 4 (2011): 613–33. doi:10.1111/j.1747-1346.2011.00306.x.

Chapter 3: Adam Wellstead and Richard Stedman, "Policy Capacity and Incapacity in Canada's Federal Government: The Intersection of Policy Analysis and Street-Level Bureaucracy," *Public Management Review* 12, no. 6 (2010): 893–910. doi:10.1080/14719037.2010.488863.

Chapter 4: Michael Howlett and Joshua Newman, "Policy Analysis and Policy Work in Federal Systems: Policy Advice and Its Contribution to Evidence-Based Policy-Making in Multi-Level Governance Systems," *Policy and Society* 29, no. 1 (2010): 123–36. doi:10.1016/j.polsoc.2010.03.004.

Chapter 5: Luc Bernier and Michael Howlett, "The Policy Analytical Capacity of the Government of Quebec: Results from a Survey of Officials," *Canadian Political Science Review* 6, no. 2 (2012): 117–30.

Chapter 6: Michael Howlett and Adam Wellstead, "Professional Policy Work in Federal States: Institutional Autonomy and Canadian Policy Analysis," *Canadian Public Administration* 55, no. 1 (2012): 53–68.

Chapter 8: Michael Howlett, "Public Managers as the Missing Variable in Policy Studies: An Empirical Investigation Using Canadian Data," *Review of Policy Research* 28, no. 3 (2011): 247–63. doi:10.1111/j.1541-1338.2011.00494.x.

Chapter 10: Michael Howlett and Andrea Migone, "Policy Advice through the Market: The Role of External Consultants in Contemporary Policy Advisory Systems," *Policy & Society* 32, no. 3 (2013): 241–54.

Chapter 14: Bryan Mitchell Evans and Adam Wellstead, "Policy Dialogue and Engagement between Non-Governmental Organizations and Government: A Survey of Processes and Instruments of Canadian Policy Workers," *Central European Journal of Public Policy* 7, no. 1 (2013): 60–87.

Contributors

Pierre-Olivier Bédard – School of Government and International Affairs, Durham University, Durham, Ireland

Luc Bernier – École nationale d'administration publique, Quebec City, Quebec

Jonathan Craft – Department of Political Science and School of Public Policy and Governance, University of Toronto, Toronto, Ontario

Bryan Evans – Department of Politics and Public Administration, Ryerson University, Toronto, Ontario

Greg Flynn – Department of Political Science, McMaster University, Hamilton, Ontario

Siobhan Harty – Privy Council Office, Government of Canada, Ottawa, Ontario

Michael Howlett – Department of Political Science, Simon Fraser University, Burnaby, British Columbia, and Lee Kuan Yew School of Public Policy, National University of Singapore, Singapore

Gregory J. Inwood – Department of Politics and Public Administration, Ryerson University, Toronto, Ontario

Carolyn M. Johns – Department of Politics and Public Administration, Ryerson University, Toronto, Ontario

Nicole Klenk – Department of Physical & Environmental Sciences, University of Toronto, Scarborough, Ontario

Grégory Léon – Département de science politique et Centre de recherche du CHUQ, Université Laval, Quebec City, Quebec

Karine Levasseur – Department of Political Studies, University of Manitoba, Winnipeg, Manitoba

Evert Lindquist – School of Public Administration, University of Victoria, Victoria, British Columbia

Justin Longo – Johnson-Shoyama Graduate School of Public Policy, University of Regina, Regina, Saskatchewan

Andrea Migone – Institute of Public Administration of Canada, Toronto, Ontario

Joshua Newman – Social and Policy Studies, Flinders University of South Australia, Adelaide, Australia

Patricia L. O'Reilly – Department of Politics and Public Administration, Ryerson University, Toronto, Ontario

Mathieu Ouimet – Département de science politique et Centre de recherche du CHUQ, Université Laval, Quebec City, Quebec

Richard Stedman – Department of Natural Resources, Cornell University, Ithaca, New York, United States

Adam Wellstead – Department of Social Sciences, Michigan Technological University, Houghton, Michigan, United States

www.ingramcontent.com/pod-product-compliance
Lightning Source LLC
LaVergne TN
LVHW090147080826
844660LV00013B/698/J

* 9 7 8 1 4 4 2 6 4 7 3 7 4 *